P9-BYR-382

State and Local Government

00/01

Tenth Edition

EDITOR

Bruce Stinebrickner
DePauw University

Bruce Stinebrickner is a professor of political science at DePauw University in Greencastle, Indiana. After receiving his Ph.D. from Yale University in 1974, he taught American politics at Lehman College of the City University of New York and at the University of Queensland in Brisbane, Australia, before joining the Department of Political Science at DePauw in 1987. He chaired his departments at Queensland and DePauw for a total of 11 years. In addition to his decade of overseas teaching at Queensland, he has taught and lectured about American politics in Argentina and Germany.

Professor Stinebrickner's research interests focus on public policy, particularly at the level of American state and local government. He is currently researching several issues relating to child custody, including adoption, foster care, and child neglect and abuse. He has served as editor for 10 editions of *Annual Editions: State and Local Government*, and has also edited Dushkin/McGraw-Hill's *Annual Editions* on American government and on American public policy.

Dushkin/McGraw-Hill
Sluice Dock, Guilford, Connecticut 06437

Visit us on the Internet
http://www.dushkin.com/annualeditions/

Credits

1. Earyl Commentaries
Unit photo—Library of Congress.
2. Intergovernmental Relations
Unit photo—WHO photo by Kalisher. 30—Bru Associates illustration.
3. Linkages between Citizens and Governments
Unit photo—SYGMA photo by A. Tannenbaum.
4. Government Institutions and Officeholders
Unit photo—State of Connecticut, Dept. of Economic Development/Dominick J. Ruggiero.
5. Cities and Suburbs, Counties and Towns
Unit photo—United Nations photo by Milton Grant.
6. Finances and Economic Development
Unit photo—Las Vegas News Bureau.
7. Service Delivery and Policy Issues
Unit photo—Dushkin/McGraw-Hill photo.

Copyright

Cataloging in Publication Data
Main entry under title: Annual Editions: State and local government. 2000/2001.
    1. Local government—United States—Periodicals. 2. State governments—United States—Periodicals. I. Stinebrickner, Bruce. II. Title: State and local government.
ISBN 0-07-235523-9   87-643275   ISSN 1093-7021   352'.000973'05

Tenth Edition

Cover image © 1999 PhotoDisc, Inc.

Printed in the United States of America 4 5 6 7 8 9 0 QSR 0 9 8 7 6 5 4 3 2 1 Printed on Recycled Paper

In publishing ANNUAL EDITIONS we recognize the enormous role played by the magazines, newspapers, and journals of the public press in providing current, first-rate educational information in a broad spectrum of interest areas. Many of these articles are appropriate for students, researchers, and professionals seeking accurate, current material to help bridge the gap between principles and theories and the real world. These articles, however, become more useful for study when those of lasting value are carefully collected, organized, indexed, and reproduced in a low-cost format, which provides easy and permanent access when the material is needed. That is the role played by ANNUAL EDITIONS.

New to ANNUAL EDITIONS is the inclusion of related World Wide Web sites. These sites have been selected by our editorial staff to represent some of the best resources found on the World Wide Web today. Through our carefully developed topic guide, we have linked these Web resources to the articles covered in this ANNUAL EDITIONS reader. We think that you will find this volume useful, and we hope that you will take a moment to visit us on the Web at *http://www.dushkin.com* to tell us what you think.

This book is the tenth edition of an anthology on state and local government. Beginning in 1984 with the first edition, the book has been designed for use in college courses on state and local government and in state and local government segments of courses on American government. The educational goal is to provide a collection of up-to-date articles that are informative and interesting to students exploring the area.

The 50 state governments and approximately 83,000 local governments in the United States have a great deal in common. They also exhibit remarkable diversity. Inevitably the contents of the book as a whole reflect this theme of commonality *and* diversity. Some of the selections treat individual states or localities in considerable detail. Other articles focus on particular aspects of more than one state or local government. Still other articles explicitly compare and contrast regions, states, or localities. Taken together, the selections provide an overview of similarities and differences among state and local governments in the United States.

Keeping the idea of similarities and dissimilarities in mind can help students who are beginning their study of state and local governments. In many state and local government courses, a home state or region is given special attention. In such courses, the theme of commonality and diversity can serve to highlight what is and is not typical about that home state or region.

When Republican Newt Gingrich became Speaker of the House of Representatives in 1995, he and his fellow Republican members of Congress said that they would shift significant government responsibilities from the national government in Washington to the 50 states. Both the unfunded mandates act of 1995 and the welfare reform act of 1996, two prominent bills signed into law by President Clinton, were aimed at making the states more important and more autonomous actors in the American federal system. Taking their turn in this process of devolution, some state governments shifted certain responsibilities to their local governments. Selections in Unit 2 of this book focus on intergovernmental relations and provide a mixed assessment of how much shifting of power and responsibility has actually occurred. More generally, every selection in this book can be read against this background of increasing attention to the most appropriate division of powers and responsibilities among national, state, and local governments. The book is divided into seven units. Unit 1 is devoted to several eighteenth- and nineteenth-century commentaries on American federalism and state and local governments. As already noted, Unit 2 treats relations among national, state, and local governments. Unit 3 covers elections, political parties, interest groups, referenda, and related matters, and pays considerable

attention to unusual features of state and local "linkages." Unit 4 turns to government institutions. Metropolitan areas, in which cities, suburbs, and county governments coexist, provide the subject matter for unit 5, while unit 6 is devoted to revenues, expenditures, and economic development. Unit 7 concludes the book with an examination of service delivery and policy issues facing state and local governments.

The book generally groups articles treating particular aspects of the governing processes of state or local government in the same units or sections. For example, unit 4 covers government institutions at both state and local levels, with sections treating state and local legislatures, executives, and courts, respectively. Unit 5, which mainly considers metropolitan areas, is an exception to this rule in that it focuses primarily on issues involving local governments.

Deciding what articles to use in this revised edition of *Annual Editions: State and Local Government* was not an easy task. I tried to assess articles according to significance and relevance of subject matter, readability for students, and usefulness for stimulating students' interest in state and local government. Potential selections were evaluated not only as they stood alone, but also as complements to other likely selections. I want to thank the Advisory Board members who provided detailed critiques of the ninth edition of *Annual Editions: State and Local Government* as well as suggestions for improvements for this tenth edition. I would also like to thank Taren and Aden Stinebrickner-Kauffman for the capable research assistance that they provided.

The next edition of this book will bring another opportunity to make changes. State and local government is a particularly diverse field of study, and numerous newspapers and regional magazines across the country carry articles that might be suitable for use. I earnestly solicit reactions to this book as well as suggestions of articles for use in the next edition. In other words, readers are cordially invited to become advisers and collaborators in future editions by completing and mailing the postpaid article rating form at the end of this book.

Bruce Stinebrickner

Bruce Stinebrickner
Editor

Contents

UNIT 1

Early Commentaries

Three selections provide historical perspectives on federalism and on state and local governments in the United States.

UNIT 2

Intergovernmental Relations

Four selections discuss relations among national, state, and local governments in the three-tier system of government in the United States.

The concepts in bold italics are developed in the article. For further expansion please refer to the Topic Guide and the Index.

UNIT 3

Linkages between Citizens and Governments

Nine articles explore various mechanisms that are supposed to help make state and local governments responsive to citizens: elections, political parties, lobbying, media, referenda, initiatives, and so forth.

The concepts in bold italics are developed in the article. For further expansion please refer to the Topic Guide and the Index.

UNIT 4

Government Institutions and Officeholders

Thirteen selections treat the
functioning of legislatures,
executives, and courts.

UNIT 5

Cities and Suburbs, Counties and Towns

Seven selections comment on issues, problems, and opportunities facing governments of metropolitan areas.

The concepts in bold italics are developed in the article. For further expansion please refer to the Topic Guide and the Index.

UNIT 6

Finances and Economic Development

Seven articles examine revenue-
raising methods that state and local
governments use, as well as
challenges and problems of
development that state and
local governments face.

UNIT 7

Service Delivery and Policy Issues

Eleven selections treat the means that state and local governments use in delivering services to the public.

The concepts in bold italics are developed in the article. For further expansion please refer to the Topic Guide and the Index.

x

B. POLICY ISSUES

The concepts in bold italics are developed in the article. For further expansion please refer to the Topic Guide and the Index.

This topic guide suggests how the selections and World Wide Web sites found in the next section of this book relate to topics of traditional concern to state and local government students and professionals. It is useful for locating interrelated articles and Web sites for reading and research. The guide is arranged alphabetically according to topic.

The relevant Web sites, which are numbered and annotated on pages 4 and 5, are easily identified by the Web icon (☺) under the topic articles. By linking the articles and the Web sites by topic, this ANNUAL EDITIONS reader becomes a powerful learning and research tool.

TOPIC AREA	TREATED IN	TOPIC AREA	TREATED IN
Cities	30. Can Cities Escape Political Isolation? 31. How to Save Our Shrinking Cities 32. Suburban Myth 33. Who Pays for Sprawl? ☺ *1, 2, 3, 20, 21, 23, 24, 25, 26, 28*	**Federalism**	1. The Federalist, No. 17 2. The Federalist, No. 45 3. Nature of the American State 4. Judicial Federalism 5. Devil in Devolution 6. Powerless Pipsqueaks and the Myth of Local Control ☺ *1, 2, 3, 4, 5*
Counties	36. Are New England's Counties as Expendable as They Seem? ☺ *1, 2, 3, 20, 22, 24, 26, 28*	**Fire Departments**	54. Rescuing the Fire Department
Courts	4. Judicial Federalism 27. Justice by Numbers 28. Bench Press 29. When the Verdict Is Just a Fantasy ☺ *8, 9*	**Gender Issues**	18. Women in the Legislature: Numbers Inch Up Nationwide 19. Women as Leaders: Vive la Difference ☺ *15, 17*
Criminal Justice System	27. Justice by Numbers 51. Answer to Drunk Driving: Lower the Blood Alcohol Limit? 52. Comeback of the Cops ☺ *29, 31, 32*	**Governors**	22. Gulf of Government 23. It Pays to Know Where the Bodies Are Buried 24. Roaring Forward 25. Conservative Governors and the Joy of Spending ☺ *19*
Devolution	5. Devil in Devolution 6. Powerless Pipsqueaks and the Myth of Local Control ☺ *7, 8, 11, 13*	**Housing**	35. Fair Share in Suburbia ☺ *24*
Economic Development	41. Romancing the Smokestack 42. New Urban Gamble 43. Terrible Ten: Corporate Candy Store Deals of 1998 ☺ *25, 26, 27, 28*	**Interest Groups**	11. Who's Got Clout? Interest Group Power in the States 28. Bench Press ☺ *1, 10, 11, 13, 14*
Elections and Electoral Systems	8. Reform Gets Rolling: Campaign Finance of the Grass Roots 10. My Life as a School Board Candidate: Lessons Learned in Local Politics ☺ *6, 14, 15, 17, 18, 19*	**Land Use**	32. Suburban Myth 33. Who Pays for Sprawl? 35. Fair Share in Suburbia ☺ *20, 21, 22, 23, 24*
		Lotteries	38. It's Not a Miracle, It's a Mirage 39. Game of Mystery Bucks 42. New Urban Gamble ☺ *27*
Family Issues	50. I'll Stand Bayou 53. Making the Case for Graduated Driver Licensing	**Mayors**	26. Nobody in Charge ☺ *20, 23*

◉ AE: State and Local Government

The following World Wide Web sites have been carefully researched and selected to support the articles found in this reader. If you are interested in learning more about specific topics found in this book, these Web sites are a good place to start. The sites are cross-referenced by number and appear in the topic guide on the previous two pages. Also, you can link to these Web sites through our DUSHKIN ONLINE support site at *http://www.dushkin.com/online/.*

The following sites were available at the time of publication. Visit our Web site—we update DUSHKIN ONLINE regularly to reflect any changes.

General Sites

1. Alliance for Redesigning Government
http://www.alliance.napawash.org/alliance/index.html
This site allows the visitor to hypothetically reinvent federal, state, and local government by using basic concepts, actual cases, available resources, and contacts with practitioners.

2. Government on Line
http://www.gol.org
An information service that links state and local government to the information technology industry, this site provides summary information about successful programs.

3. State and Local Government on the Net
http://www.yahoo.com
Click on Regional, then U.S. States to search individual states for elected officials, state government jobs, and state groups, and for other links to local government sites.

Early Commentaries

4. Anti-Federalist Papers
http://www.constitution.org/afp/afp.htm
The Anti-Federalist Papers offered on this home page of the Constitution Society have been collated by Morton Borden in response to growing concern that noncompliance with the U.S. Constitution and state constitutions is creating a crisis of legitimacy threatening to freedom and civil rights.

5. The Federalist Papers Online
http://www.mcs.net/~knautzr/fed/fedpaper.html
This site contains the full text of all 85 essays as well as the Declaration of Independence and the Constitution, complete with the Bill of Rights and all the Amendments.

Intergovernmental Relations

6. Congress
http://congress.org
User-friendly, this site is a very effective starting point for Web users in search of Capitol Hill current political information. The site allows access to a complete and reliable directory of information about the members of the U.S. House of Representatives and Senate, and it includes a congressional directory, House and Senate committee assignments, as well as the ability to communicate with specific members.

7. Council of State Governments
http://www.csg.org
This important resource is dedicated to promoting state solutions regionally and nationally. From it you can access the federalism plan of states' leaders, court victories in federalism, other proposals, and other Web resources.

8. National Center for State Courts
http://ncsc.dni.us
Click here to find the latest news about the courts, information about state courts, and the best court-related Web sites.

9. Supreme Court/Legal Information Institute (LII)
http://supct.law.cornell.edu/supct/index.html
Open this site for current and historical information about the Supreme Court. The LII archive contains many opinions issued since May 1990 as well as a collection of nearly 600 of the most historical decisions of the Court.

Linkages between Citizens and Governments

10. Council for Ethics in Legislative Advocacy
http://www.lobbyistdirectory.com/indxcela.htm
CELA advocates a nationally uniform standard of ethics in the lobbying industry. From this site visit Ethics in the News and the National Lobbyist Directory home page.

11. Direct Democracy Center
http://www.primenet.com/~conduit/
In response to voter apathy, this organization has organized a site on the Web for free and open discussion of direct democracy as an alternative to our present form of government.

12. PEJ Local TV News Project
http://www.journalism.org/LocalTV.htm
The Project for Excellence in Journalism has created this news project in order to clarify the definition of quality in local television news. Explore this site to find out how the project will work and its goals, and to contribute your own thoughts.

13. U.S. Federalism Web Site
http://www.min.net/~kala/fed/edemoc.htm
This site concerns federalism and electronic democracy and contains many links to direct democracy and other citizen-power sites.

Government Institutions and Officeholders

14. Americans Back in Charge Foundation
http://www.abic.org
Everything you need to know about the term limits movement both nationally and at the state level is available at this site, including a study of the effects of term limits on members of the California legislature.

15. Center for the American Woman in Politics
http://www-rci.rutgers.edu/~cawp/cawpfs.html
At this site of CAWP you can find full-text fact sheets on everything from women in elective office to statewide elective executive women. It includes a gender gap fact sheet and facts on sex differences in voter turnout.

16. Council on Licensure, Enforcement and Regulation
http://www.clearhq.org
CLEAR is an association of individuals, groups, and agencies that is a forum for improving the quality and understanding of regulation in order to enhance public protection.

17. EMILY's List of Women in State Legislatures
http://www.emilyslist.org/news/st_legis/ak.htm

This state-by-state list of women in state legislatures also contains a search feature and What's New.

18. National Conference of State Legislatures
http://www.ncsl.org/index.htm
This rich mine contains Legislative Policy Issues, Internet Links, About State Legislatures, State-Federal Relations, and more.

19. NGA Online
http://www.nga.org
The National Governor's Association and the NGA Center for Best Practices are joined at this excellent site. Navigate through The Organization, The Governors, News and Information, Key State Issues, and a Site Index. What's New and Noteworthy appear on the first page.

Cities and Suburbs, Counties and Towns

20. ICMA: International City/County Management Association
http://www.icma.org/information/othersites/
The list of Web sites offered here by ICMA include: Communications, Economic Development, Housing Resources, Human Resources, Public Safety, Public Works, and Technology.

21. Innovation Groups
http://www.ig.org
IG is a network of top cities and local government leaders that provides support to pioneer new approaches to managing cities. The group provides networking, research, and training opportunities to local governments.

22. National Association of Counties
http://www.naco.org/links/counties.cfm
The National Association of Counties offers this entry into county government sites state by state.

23. National League of Cities
http://www.nlc.org
The NLC Web site leads to Legislative Priorities, Local Government Access, Policy Process, News and Events, Other Resources, and a search capability, all useful aids to people in municipal government.

Finances and Economic Development

24. Assessor.com
http://www.assessor.com
This is a primary site for understanding the property tax and what it means to householders. There are useful links to local assessment sites in every state, independent resources, and professional and educational organizations, including the Lincoln Institute of Land & Policy.

25. Council for Urban Economic Development (CUED)
http://www.cued.org
This organization for public sector economic development links urban site selectors, economic development practitioners, and researchers to useful information about industrial parks, tax rates, local leadership, climate, and other pertinent information for local economies.

26. Economic Development Administration
http://www.doc.gov/eda
This Department of Commerce site links to current fact sheets, the year 2000, regulations and notices, contacts and resources, all helpful to understanding state and local economic development issues.

27. Good Things Lotteries Do
http://www.gtech.com/good.htm
Here is the site that sets out the good things lotteries do for the government: 35 percent of lottery proceeds helps finance education, health, and public works projects.

28. National Association of Development Organizations (NADO)
http://www.nado.org/links/index.html
Called "the economic development community's tool box on the World Wide Web," this site leads to every national, state, and local government resource, to a host of independent agencies, and to other community development resources, including grant-giving foundations, rural development groups, and public interest groups.

Service Delivery and Policy Issues

29. American Bar Association Juvenile Justice Center
http://www.abanet.org/crimjust/juvjus/links.html
From this site it is easy to access information about juvenile justice and other youth-related information. Crime statistics, advocacy tips, and legal resources are available here.

30. American Public Transit Association
http://www.apta.com
This site has information about every aspect of transportation and excellent links to federal and state agencies and organizations that deal with transportation issues, including links to all state departments of transportation.

31. CECP Juvenile Justice Links
http://www.air-dc.org/cecp/links/jj.html
At this site fact sheets and articles on juvenile justice issues such as violent juvenile offenders, delinquency programs, and youth-oriented anti-crime programs are available along with links to many juvenile justice organizations.

32. COPS Home Page
http://www.usdoj.gov/cops/index.html
This home page of the Office of Community Oriented Policing Services is dedicated to helping communities fight crime by putting 100,000 additional officers on America's streets and by promoting community policing strategies nationwide. Their Web presence leads to Success Stories and Links.

33. National Highway Traffic Safety Administration
http://www.nhtsa.dot.gov/people/outreach/stateleg/bac.htm
This section of the State Legislative Fact Sheet contains information on blood alcohol concentrations (BAC) and driving a motor vehicle. It contains Key Facts, Why 0.08?, Point/Counterpoint, Impact on the Criminal Justice System, and a map of States with BAC Per Se Laws.

34. U.S. Charter Schools
http://www.uscharterschools.org
All you might need to know about charter schools is available at this page, including Starting & Running a Charter School, Resource Directory and Links, State Information & Contacts, Charter School Profiles, and Search for Information.

We highly recommend that you review our Web site for expanded information and our other product lines. We are continually updating and adding links to our Web site in order to offer you the most usable and useful information that will support and expand the value of your Annual Editions. You can reach us at: http://www.dushkin.com/annualeditions/.

www.dushkin.com/online/

Unit Selections

1. **The Federalist, No. 17,** Alexander Hamilton
2. **The Federalist, No. 45,** James Madison
3. **Nature of the American State,** James Bryce

Key Points to Consider

❖ How does the picture of local governments provided by Bryce compare with American local governments today?

❖ Do you think that the observations of Hamilton, Madison, and Bryce are out of date by now? Why or why not?

❖ Students of politics frequently refer to the "historic" writings of Plato, Aristotle, Machiavelli, Hobbes, Locke, Rousseau, and others. Selections in this section are examples of early or historic writings on American politics. Why do you think that those who study politics so often look to the classics, even centuries after they were first written?

❖ Do you find the arguments and logic of Federalist No. 17 and No. 45 persuasive? Can you detect any flaws or mistakes?

❖ Which author do you find most interesting and helpful—Alexander Hamilton, James Madison, or James Bryce? Why?

DUSHKIN ONLINE **Links**   **www.dushkin.com/online/**

These sites are annotated on pages 4 and 5.

The American political system includes three levels of government—national, state, and local. Although not unique among nations today, this arrangement was unusual in the late eighteenth century when the United States became independent. Early commentaries on the American political system paid considerable attention to each of the levels of government as well as to relations among the three levels. These writings suggest the important role that state and local governments have always played in the United States.

Debate about the desirability of the proposed new Constitution of 1787—the Constitution that remains in force to this day—often focused on the relationship between the national government and the states. Some people thought that the states were going to be too strong in the proposed new union, and others argued that the national government would be. Three prominent supporters of the new Constitution—Alexander Hamilton, James Madison, and John Jay—wrote a series of articles in 1787–1788 explaining and defending it. Many of these articles, which came to be known as *The Federalist Papers*, treated the federal relationship between the national government and the states. So did many of the writings of other early observers. This shows the importance that was attached to the new federal relationship right from the start.

Local government was also the subject of considerable attention in early commentaries on the American political system. Alexis de Tocqueville, a French nobleman visiting the United States early in the nineteenth century, recorded his observations in a book entitled *Democracy in America* (1835). Tocqueville remarked on the extraordinary vitality of American local government institutions, comparing what he saw in the United States with European institutions at the time. Today American local government still plays a prominent role in the overall governing process, probably more so than in any other nation in the world.

Later in the nineteenth century, a second foreign observer, James Bryce, published another historic commentary on the United States, *The American Commonwealth* (1888). Bryce, an Englishman, discussed American federalism and American state and local governments. He described the similarities and differences among local government structures in different regions of the country, the nature of the states, and the lamentable performance of city governments. Like Tocqueville, Bryce was able to identify and analyze distinctive elements of the American system of government and make a lasting contribution to the study of the American political system.

Selections in this first section of the book come from *The Federalist Papers* and Bryce's *American Commonwealth*. These historic observations on American federalism and state and local governments provide a baseline against which to assess the picture of contemporary state and local government that emerges in the rest of the book.

Early Commentaries

THE FEDERALIST NO. 17
(HAMILTON)

To the People of the State of New York:

AN OBJECTION, of a nature different from that which has been stated and answered, in my last address, may perhaps be likewise urged against the principle of legislation for the individual citizens of America. It may be said that it would tend to render the government of the Union too powerful, and to enable it to absorb those residuary authorities, which it might be judged proper to leave with the States for local purposes. Allowing the utmost latitude to the love of power which any reasonable man can require, I confess I am at a loss to discover what temptation the persons intrusted with the administration of the general government could ever feel to divest the States of the authorities of that description. The regulation of the mere domestic police of a State appears to me to hold out slender allurements to ambition. Commerce, finance, negotiation, and war seem to comprehend all the objects which have charms for minds governed by that passion; and all the powers necessary to those objects ought, in the first instance, to be lodged in the national depository. The administration of private justice between the citizens of the same State, the supervision of agriculture and of other concerns of a similar nature, all those things, in short, which are proper to be provided for by local legislation, can never be desirable cares of a general jurisdiction. It is therefore improbable that there should exist a disposition in the federal councils to usurp the powers with which they are connected; because the attempt to exercise those powers would be as troublesome as it would be nugatory; and the possession of them, for that reason, would contribute nothing to the dignity, to the importance, or to the splendor of the national government.

But let it be admitted, for argument's sake, that mere wantonness and lust of domination would be sufficient to beget that disposition; still it may be safely affirmed, that the sense of the constituent body of the national representatives, or, in other words, the people of the several States, would control the indulgence of so extravagant an appetite. It will always be far more easy for the State governments to encroach upon the national authorities, than for the national government to encroach upon the State authorities. The proof of this proposition turns upon the greater degree of influence which the State governments, if they administer their affairs with uprightness and prudence, will generally possess over the people; a circumstance which at the same time teaches us that there is an inherent and intrinsic weakness in all federal constitutions; and that too much pains cannot be taken in their organization, to give them all the force which is compatible with the principles of liberty.

The superiority of influence in favor of the particular governments would result partly from the diffusive construction of the national government, but chiefly from the nature of the objects to which the attention of the State administrations would be directed.

It is a known fact in human nature, that its affections are commonly weak in proportion to the distance or diffusiveness of the object. Upon the same principle that a man is more attached to his family than to his neighborhood, to his neighborhood than to the community at large, the people of each State would be apt to feel a stronger bias towards their local governments than towards the government of the Union; unless the force of that principle should be destroyed by a much better administration of the latter.

This strong propensity of the human heart would find powerful auxiliaries in the objects of State regulation.

The variety of more minute interests, which will necessarily fall under the superintendence of the local administrations, and which will form so many rivulets of influence, running through every part of the society, cannot

From *The Federalist Papers*, Alexander Hamilton, 1787.

be particularized, without involving a detail too tedious and uninteresting to compensate for the instruction it might afford.

There is one transcendent advantage belonging to the province of the State governments, which alone suffices to place the matter in a clear and satisfactory light,—I mean the ordinary administration of criminal and civil justice. This, of all others, is the most powerful, most universal, and most attractive source of popular obedience and attachment. It is that which, being the immediate and visible guardian of life and property, having its benefits and its terrors in constant activity before the public eye, regulating all those personal interests and familiar concerns in which the sensibility of individuals is more immediately awake, contributes, more than any other circumstance, to impressing upon the minds of the people, affection, esteem, and reverence towards the government. This great cement of society, which will diffuse itself almost wholly through the channels of the particular governments, independent of all other causes of influence, would insure them so decided an empire over their respective citizens as to render them at all times a complete counterpoise, and, not unfrequently, dangerous rivals to the power of the Union.

The operations of the national government, on the other hand, falling less immediately under the observation of the mass of the citizens, the benefits derived from it will chiefly be perceived and attended to by speculative men. Relating to more general interests, they will be less apt to come home to the feelings of the people; and, in proportion, less likely to inspire an habitual sense of obligation, and an active sentiment of attachment.

The reasoning on this head has been abundantly exemplified by the experience of all federal constitutions with which we are acquainted, and of all others which have borne the least analogy to them.

Though the ancient feudal systems were not, strictly speaking, confederacies, yet they partook of the nature of that species of association. There was a common head, chieftain, or sovereign, whose authority extended over the whole nation; and a number of subordinate vassals, or feudatories, who had large portions of land allotted to them, and numerous trains of *inferior* vassals or retainers, who occupied and cultivated that land upon the tenure of fealty or obedience to the persons of whom they held it. Each principal vassal was a kind of sovereign within his particular demesnes. The consequences of this situation were a continual opposition to authority of the sovereign, and frequent wars between the great barons or chief feudatories themselves. The power of the head of the nation was commonly too weak, either to preserve the public peace, or to protect the people against the oppressions of their immediate lords. This

period of European affairs is emphatically styled by historians, the times of feudal anarchy.

When the sovereign happened to be a man of vigorous and warlike temper and of superior abilities, he would acquire a personal weight and influence, which answered, for the time, the purposes of a more regular authority. But in general, the power of the barons triumphed over that of the prince; and in many instances his dominion was entirely thrown off, and the great fiefs were erected into independent principalities of States. In those instances in which the monarch finally prevailed over his vassals, his success was chiefly owing to the tyranny of those vassals over their dependents. The barons, or nobles, equally the enemies of the sovereign and the oppressors of the common people, were dreaded and detested by both; till mutual danger and mutual interest effected a union between them fatal to the power of the aristocracy. Had the nobles, by a conduct of clemency and justice, preserved the fidelity and devotion of their retainers and followers, the contests between them and the prince must almost always have ended in their favor, and in the abridgment or subversion of the royal authority.

This is not an assertion founded merely in speculation or conjecture. Among other illustrations of its truth which might be cited, Scotland will furnish a cogent example. The spirit of clanship which was, at an early day, introduced into that kingdom, uniting the nobles and their dependents by ties equivalent to those of kindred, rendered the aristocracy a constant overmatch for the power of the monarch, till the incorporation with England subdued its fierce and ungovernable spirit, and reduced it within those rules of subordination which a more rational and more energetic system of civil polity had previously established in the latter kingdom.

The separate governments in a confederacy may aptly be compared with the feudal baronies; with this advantage in their favor, that from the reasons already explained, they will generally possess the confidence and good-will of the people, and with so important a support, will be able effectually to oppose all encroachments of the national government. It will be well if they are not able to counteract its legitimate and necessary authority. The points of similitude consist in the rivalship of power, applicable to both, and in the CONCENTRATION of large portions of the strength of the community into particular DEPOSITS, in one case at the disposal of individuals, in the other case at the disposal of political bodies.

A concise review of the events that have attended confederate governments will further illustrate this important doctrine; an inattention to which has been the great source of our political mistakes, and has given our jealousy a direction to the wrong side. This review shall form the subject of some ensuing papers.

PUBLIUS

THE FEDERALIST
NO. 45
(MADISON)

To the People of the State of New York:

HAVING shown that no one of the powers transferred to the federal government is unnecessary or improper, the next question to be considered is, whether the whole mass of them will be dangerous to the portion of authority left in the several States.

The adversaries to the plan of the convention, instead of considering in the first place what degree of power was absolutely necessary for the purposes of the federal government, have exhausted themselves in a secondary inquiry into the possible consequences of the proposed degree of power to the governments of the particular States. But if the Union, as has been shown, be essential to the security of the people of America against foreign danger; if it be essential to their security against contentions and wars among the different States; if it be essential to guard them against those violent and oppressive factions which embitter the blessings of liberty, and against those military establishments which must gradually poison its very fountain; if, in a word, the Union be essential to the happiness of the people of America, is it not preposterous, to urge as an objection to a government, without which the objects of the Union cannot be attained, that such a government may derogate from the importance of the governments of the individual States? Was, then, the American Revolution effected, was the American Confederacy formed, was the precious blood of thousands spilt, and the hard-earned substance of millions lavished, not that the people of America should enjoy peace, liberty, and safety, but that the government of the individual States, that particular municipal establishments, might enjoy a certain extent of power, and be arrayed with certain dignities and attributes of sovereignty? We have heard of the impious doctrine in the Old World, that the people were made for kings, not kings for the people. Is the same doctrine to be revived in the New, in another shape—that the solid happiness of the people is to be sacrificed to the views of political institutions of a different form? It is too early for politicians to presume on our forgetting that the public good, the real welfare of the great body of the people, is the supreme object to be pursued; and that no form of government whatever has any other value than as it may be fitted for the attainment of this object. Were the plan of the convention adverse to the public happiness, my voice would be, Reject the plan. Were the Union itself inconsistent with the public happiness, it would be, Abolish the Union. In like manner, as far as the sovereignty of the States cannot be reconciled to the happiness of the people, the voice of every good citizen must be, Let the former be sacrificed to the latter. How far the sacrifice is necessary, has been shown. How far the unsacrificed residue will be endangered, is the question before us.

Several important considerations have been touched in the course of these papers, which discountenance the supposition that the operation of the federal government will by degrees prove fatal to the State governments. The more I revolve the subject, the more fully I am persuaded that the balance is much more likely to be disturbed by the preponderacy of the last than of the first scale.

We have seen, in all the examples of ancient and modern confederacies, the strongest tendency continually betraying itself in the members, to despoil the general government of its authorities, with a very ineffectual capacity in the latter to defend itself against the encroachments. Although, in most of these examples, the system has been so dissimilar from that under consideration as greatly to weaken any inference concerning the latter from the fate of the former, yet, as the States will retain, under the proposed Constitution, a very extensive portion of active sovereignty, the inference ought not to be wholly disregarded. In the Achæan league it is probable that the federal head had a degree and species of power, which gave it a considerable likeness to the government framed by the convention. The Lycian Confederacy, as far as its principles and form and transmitted, must have borne a still greater analogy to it. Yet history does not inform us that either of them ever degenerated, or tended to degenerate, into one consolidated government. On the contrary, we know that the ruin of one of them proceeded from the incapacity of the federal authority to prevent the dissensions, and finally the disunion, of the subordinate authorities. These cases are the more worthy of our attention, as the external causes by which the component parts were pressed together were much more numerous and powerful than in our case; and consequently less powerful ligaments within would be sufficient to bind the members to the head, and to each other.

In the feudal system, we have seen a similar propensity exemplified. Notwithstanding the want of proper sympathy in every instance between the local sovereigns and the people, and the sympathy in some instances between the general sovereign and the latter, it usually happened that the local sovereigns prevailed in the rivalship for encroachments. Had no external dangers enforced internal harmony and subordination, and particularly, had the local sovereigns possessed the affections of the people, the great kingdoms in Europe would at this time consist of as many independent princes as there were formerly feudatory barons.

The State governments will have the advantage of the Federal government, whether we compare them in respect to the immediate dependence of the one on the other; to the weight of personal influence which each side will possess; to the powers respectively vested in them; to the predilection and probable support of the people; to the disposition and faculty of resisting and frustrating the measures of each other.

The State governments may be regarded as constituent and essential parts of the federal government; whilst the latter is nowise essential to the operation or organization of the former. Without the intervention of the State legislatures, the President of the United States cannot be elected at all. They must in all cases have a great share in his appointment, and will, perhaps, in most cases, of themselves determine it. The Senate will be elected absolutely and exclusively by the State legislatures. Even the House of Representatives, though drawn immediately from the people, will be chosen very much under the influence of that class of men, whose influence over the people obtains for themselves an election into the State legislatures. Thus, each of the principal branches of the federal government will owe its existence more or less to the favor of the State governments, and must consequently feel a dependence, which is much more likely to beget a disposition too obsequious than too overbearing towards them. On the other side, the component parts of the State governments will in no instance be in-

debted for their appointment to the direct agency of the federal government, and very little, if at all, to the local influence of its members.

The number of individuals employed under the Constitution of the United States will be much smaller than the number employed under the particular States. There will consequently be less of personal influence on the side of the former than of the latter. The members of the legislative, executive, and judiciary departments of thirteen and more States, the justices of peace, officers of militia, ministerial officers of justice, with all the country, corporation, and town officers, for three millions and more of people, intermixed, and having particular acquaintance with every class and circle of people, must exceed, beyond all proportion, both in number and influence, those of every description who will be employed in the administration of the federal system. Compare the members of the three great departments of the thirteen States, excluding from the judiciary department the justices of peace, with the members of the corresponding departments of the single government of the Union; compare the militia officers of three millions of people with the military and marine officers of any establishment which is within the compass of probability, or, I may add, of possibility, and in this view alone, we may pronounce the advantage of the States to be decisive. If the federal government is to have collectors of revenue, the State governments will have theirs also. And as those of the former will be principally on the sea-coast, and not very numerous, whilst those of the latter will be spread over the face of the country, and will be very numerous, the advantage in this view also lies on the same side. It is true, that the Confederacy is to possess, and may exercise, the power of collecting internal as well as external taxes throughout the States; but it is probable that this power will not be resorted to, except for supplemental purposes of revenue; that an option will then be given to the States to supply their quotas by previous collections of their own; and that the eventual collection, under the immediate authority of the Union, will generally be made by the officers, and according to the rules, appointed by the several States. Indeed it is extremely probable, that in other instances, particularly in the organization of the judicial power, the officers of the States will be clothed with the correspondent authority of the Union. Should it happen, however, that separate collectors of internal revenue should be appointed under the federal government, the influence of the whole number would not bear a comparison with that of the multitude of State officers in the opposite scale. Within every district to which a federal collector would be allotted, there would not be less than thirty or forty, or even more, officers of different descriptions, and many of them persons of character and weight, whose influence would lie on the side of the State.

The powers delegated by the proposed Constitution to the federal government are few and defined. Those which are to remain in the State governments are numerous and indefinite. The former will be exercised principally on external objects, as war, peace, negotiation, and foreign commerce; with which last the power of taxation will, for the most part, be connected. The powers reserved to the several States will extend to all the objects which, in the ordinary course of affairs, concern the lives, liberties, and properties of the people, and the internal order, improvement, and prosperity of the State.

The operations of the federal government will be most extensive and important in times of war and danger; those of the State governments in times of peace and security. As the former periods will probably bear a small proportion to the latter, the State governments will here enjoy another advantage over the federal government. The more adequate, indeed, the federal powers may be rendered to the national defence, the less frequent will be those scenes of danger which might favor their ascendancy over the governments of the particular States.

If the new Constitution be examined with accuracy and candor, it will be found that the change which it proposes consists much less in the addition of NEW POWERS to the Union, than in the invigoration of its ORIGINAL POWERS. The regulation of commerce, it is true, is a new power; but that seems to be an addition which few oppose, and from which no apprehensions are entertained.

The powers relating to war and peace, armies and fleets, treaties and finance, with the other more considerable powers, are all vested in the existing Congress by the articles of Confederation. The proposed change does not enlarge these powers; it only substitutes a more effectual mode of administering them. The change relating to taxation may be regarded as the most important; and yet the present Congress have as complete authority to REQUIRE of the States indefinite supplies of money for the common defense and general welfare, as the future Congress will have to require them of individual citizens; and the latter will be no more bound than the States themselves have been, to pay the quotas respectively taxed on them. Had the States complied punctually with the articles of Confederation, or could their compliance have been enforced by as peaceable means as may be used with success towards single persons, our past experience is very far from countenancing an opinion, that the State governments would have lost their constitutional powers, and have gradually undergone an entire consolidation. To maintain that such an event would have ensued, would be to say at once, that the existence of the State governments is incompatible with any system whatever that accomplishes the essential purposes of the Union.

PUBLIUS

Nature of the American State

James Bryce

. . . As the dissimilarity of population and of external conditions seems to make for a diversity of constitutional and political arrangements between the States, so also does the large measure of legal independence which each of them enjoys under the Federal Constitution. No State can, as a commonwealth, politically deal with or act upon any other State. No diplomatic relations can exist nor treaties be made between States, no coercion can be exercised by one upon another. And although the government of the Union can act on a State, it rarely does act, and then only in certain strictly limited directions, which do not touch the inner political life of the commonwealth.

Let us pass on to consider the circumstances which work for uniformity among the States, and work more powerfully as time goes on.

He who looks at a map of the Union will be struck by the fact that so many of the boundary lines of the States are straight lines. Those lines tell the same tale as the geometrical plans of cities like St. Petersburg or Washington, where every street runs at the same angle to every other. The States are not natural growths. Their boundaries are for the most part not natural boundaries fixed by mountain ranges, nor even historical boundaries due to a series of events, but purely artificial boundaries, determined by an authority which carved the national territory into strips of convenient size, as a building company lays out its suburban lots. Of the States subsequent to the original thirteen, California is the only one with a genuine natural boundary, finding it in the chain of the Sierra Nevada on the east and the Pacific ocean on the west. No one of these later States can be regarded as a naturally developed political organism. They are trees planted by the forester, not self-sown with the help of the seed-scattering wind. This absence of physical lines of demarcation has tended and must tend to prevent the growth of local distinctions. Nature herself seems to have designed the Mississippi basin, as she has designed the unbroken levels of Russia, to be the dwelling-place of one people.

Each State makes its own Constitution; that is, the people agree on their form of government for themselves, with no interference from the other States or from the Union. This form is subject to one condition only: it must be republican.[1] But in each State the people who make the constitution have lately come from other States, where they have lived under and worked constitutions which are to their eyes the natural and almost necessary model for their new State to follow; and in the absence of an inventive spirit among the citizens, it was the obvious course for the newer States to copy the organizations of the older States, especially as these agreed with certain familiar features of the Federal Constitution. Hence the outlines, and even the phrases of the elder constitutions reappear in those of the more recently formed States. The precedents set by Virginia, for instance, had much influence on Tennessee, Alabama, Mississippi, and Florida, when they were engaged in making or amending their constitutions during the early part of this century.

Nowhere is population in such constant movement as in America. In some of the newer States only one-fourth or one-fifth of the inhabitants are natives of the United States. Many of the townsfolk, not a few even of the farmers, have been till lately citizens of some other State, and will, perhaps, soon move on farther west. These Western States are like a chain of lakes

From *The American Commonwealth*, James Bryce, 1888.

through which there flows a stream which mingles the waters of the higher with those of the lower. In such a constant flux of population local peculiarities are not readily developed, or if they have grown up when the district was still isolated, they disappear as the country becomes filled. Each State takes from its neighbours and gives to its neighbours, so that the process of assimilation is always going on over the whole wide area.

Still more important is the influence of railway communication, of newspapers, of the telegraph. A Greek city like Samos or Mitylene, holding her own island, preserved a distinctive character in spite of commercial intercourse and the sway of Athens. A Swiss canton like Uri or Appenzell, entrenched behind its mountain ramparts, remains, even now under the strengthened central government of the Swiss nation, unlike its neighbours of the lower country. But an American State traversed by great trunk lines of railway, and depending on the markets of the Atlantic cities and of Europe for the sale of its grain, cattle, bacon, and minerals, is attached by a hundred always tightening ties to other States, and touched by their weal or woe as nearly as by what befalls within its own limits. The leading newspapers are read over a vast area. The inhabitants of each State know every morning the events of yesterday over the whole Union.

Finally the political parties are the same in all the States. The tenets (if any) of each party are the same everywhere, their methods the same, their leaders the same, although of course a prominent man enjoys especial influence in his own State. Hence, State politics are largely swayed by forces and motives external to the particular State, and common to the whole country, or to great sections of it; and the growth of local parties, the emergence of local issues and development of local political schemes, are correspondingly restrained.

These considerations explain why the States, notwithstanding the original diversities between some of them, and the wide scope for political divergence which they all enjoy under the Federal Constitution, are so much less dissimilar and less peculiar than might have been expected. European statesmen have of late years been accustomed to think of federalism and local autonomy as convenient methods either for recognizing and giving free scope to the sentiment of nationality which may exist in any part of an empire, or for meeting the need for local institutions and distinct legislation which may arise from differences between such a part and the rest of the empire. It is one or other or both of these reasons that have moved statesmen in such cases as those of Finland in her relations to Russia, Hungary in her relations to German Austria, Iceland in her relations to Denmark, Bulgaria in her relations to the Turkish Sultan, Ireland in her relations to the United Kingdom. But the final causes, so to speak, of the recognition of the States of the American Union as autonomous commonwealths, have been different. Their self-government is not the consequence of differences which can be made harmless to the whole body politic only by being allowed free course. It has been due primarily to the historical fact that they existed as commonwealths before the Union came into being; secondarily, to the belief that localized government is the best guarantee for civic freedom, and to a sense of the difficulty of administering a vast territory and population from one centre and by one government.

I return to indicate the points in which the legal independence and right of self-government of the several States appears. Each of the forty-two has its own—

> Constitution (whereof more anon).
> Executive, consisting of a governor, and various other officials.
> Legislature of two Houses.
> System of local government in counties, cities, townships, and school districts.
> System of State and local taxation.
> Debts, which it may (and sometimes does) repudiate at its own pleasure.
> Body of private law, including the whole law of real and personal property, of contracts, of torts, and of family relations.
> Courts, from which no appeal lies (except in cases touching Federal legislation or the Federal constitution) to any Federal court.
> System of procedure, civil and criminal.
> Citizenship, which may admit persons (*e.g.* recent immigrants) to be citizens at times, or on conditions, wholly different from those prescribed by other States.

Three points deserve to be noted as illustrating what these attributes include.

I. A man gains active citizenship of the United States (*i.e.* a share in the government of the Union) only by becoming a citizen of some particular State. Being such citizen, he is forthwith entitled to the national franchise. That is to say, voting power in the State carries voting power in Federal elections, and however lax a State may be in its grant of such power, *e.g.* to foreigners just landed or to persons convicted of crime, these State voters will have the right of voting in congressional and presidential elections.[2] The only restriction on the States in this matter is that of the fourteenth and fifteenth Constitutional amendments, ... They were intended to secure equal treatment to the negroes, and incidentally they declare the protection given to all citizens of the United States.[3] Whether they really enlarge it, that is to say, whether it did not exist by implication before, is a legal question, which I need not discuss.

II. The power of a State over all communities within its limits is absolute. It may grant or refuse local government as it pleases. The population of the city of Providence is more than one-third of that of the State of Rhode Island, the population of New York city more than one-fifth that of the State of New York. But the State might in either case extinguish the municipality, and govern the city by a single State commissioner appointed for the purpose, or leave it without any government whatever. The city would have no right of complaint to the Federal President or Congress against such a measure. Massachusetts has lately remodelled the city government of Boston just as the British Parliament might remodel that of Birmingham. Let an Englishman imagine a county council for Warwickshire suppressing the muncipality of Birmingham, or a Frenchman imagine the department of the Rhone extinguishing the municipality of Lyons, with no possibility of intervention by the central authority, and he will measure the difference between the American States and the local governments of Western Europe.

III. A State commands the allegiance of its citizens, and may punish them for treason against it. The power has rarely been exercised, but its undoubted legal existence had much to do with inducing the citizens of the Southern States to follow their governments into secession in 1861. They conceived themselves to owe allegiance to the State as well as to the Union, and when it became impossible to preserve both, because the State had declared its secession from the Union, they might hold the earlier and nearer authority to be paramount. Allegiance to the State must now, since the war, be taken to be subordinate to the Union. But allegiance to the State still exists; treason against the State is still possible. One cannot think of treason against Warwickshire or the department of the Rhone.

These are illustrations of the doctrine which Europeans often fail to grasp, that the American States were originally in a certain sense, and still for certain purposes remain, sovereign States. Each of the original thirteen became sovereign when it revolted from the mother country in 1776. By entering the Confederation of 1781–88 it parted with one or two of the attributes of sovereignty, by accepting the Federal Constitution in 1788 it subjected itself for certain specified purposes to a central government, but claimed to retain its sovereignty for all other purposes. That is to say, the authority of a State is an inherent, not a delegated, authority. It has all the powers which any independent government can have, except such as it can be affirmatively shown to have stripped itself of, while the Federal Government has only such powers as it can be affirmatively shown to have received. To use the legal expression, the presumption is always for a State, and the burden of proof lies upon any one who denies its authority in a particular matter.[4]

What State sovereignty means and includes is a question which incessantly engaged the most active legal and political minds of the nation, from 1789 down to 1870. Some thought it paramount to the rights of the Union. Some considered it as held in suspense by the Constitution, but capable of reviving as soon as a State should desire to separate from the Union. Some maintained that each State had in accepting the Constitution finally renounced its sovereignty, which thereafter existed only in the sense of such an undefined domestic legislative and administrative authority as had not been conferred upon Congress. The conflict of these views, which became acute in 1830 when South Carolina claimed the right of nullification, produced Secession and the war of 1861–65. Since the defeat of the Secessionists, the last of these views may be deemed to have been established, and the term "State sovereignty" is now but seldom heard. Even "States rights" have a different meaning from that which they had thirty years ago.[5] . . .

The Constitution, which had rendered many services to the American people, did them an inevitable disservice when it fixed their minds on the legal aspects of the question. Law was meant to be the servant of politics, and must not be suffered to become the master. A case had arisen which its formulae were unfit to deal with, a case which had to be settled on large moral and historical grounds. It was not merely the superior physical force of the North that prevailed; it was the moral forces which rule the world, forces which had long worked against slavery, and were ordained to save North America from the curse of hostile nations established side by side.

The word "sovereignty," which has in many ways clouded the domain of public law and jurisprudence, confused men's minds by making them assume that there must in every country exist, and be discoverable by legal inquiry, either one body invested legally with supreme power over all minor bodies, or several bodies which, though they had consented to form part of a larger body, were each in the last resort independent of it, and responsible to none but themselves.[6] They forgot that a Constitution may not have determined where legal supremacy shall dwell. Where the Constitution of the United States placed it was at any rate doubtful, so doubtful that it would have been better to drop technicalities, and recognize the broad fact that the legal claims of the States had become incompatible with the historical as well as legal claims of the nation. In the uncertainty as to where legal right resided, it would have been prudent to consider where physical force resided. The South however thought herself able to resist any physical force which the rest of the nation might bring against her. Thus encouraged, she took her stand on the doctrine of States

Rights: and then followed a pouring out of blood and treasure such as was never spent on determining a point of law before, not even when Edward III and his successors waged war for a hundred years to establish the claim of females to inherit the crown of France.

What, then, do the rights of a State now include? Every right or power of a Government except:—

The right of secession (not abrogated in terms, but admitted since the war to be no longer claimable. It is expressly negatived in the recent Constitutions of several Southern States).

Powers which the Constitution withholds from the States (including that of intercourse with foreign governments).

Powers which the Constitution expressly confers on the Federal Government.

As respects some powers of the last class, however, the States may act concurrently with, or in default of action by, the Federal Government. It is only from contravention of its action that they must abstain. And where contravention is alleged to exist, whether legislative or executive, it is by a court of law, and, in case the decision is in the first instance favourable to the pretensions of the State, ultimately by a Federal court, that the question falls to be decided.[7]

A reference to the preceding list of what each State may create in the way of distinct institutions will show that these rights practically cover nearly all the ordinary relations of citizens to one another and to their Government.[8] An American may, through a long life, never be reminded of the Federal Government, except when he votes at presidential and congressional elections, lodges a complaint against the post-office, and opens his trunks for a custom-house officer on the pier at New York when he returns from a tour in Europe. His direct taxes are paid to officials acting under State laws. The State, or a local authority constituted by State statutes, registers his birth, appoints his guardian, pays for his schooling, gives him a share in the estate of his father deceased, licenses him when he enters a trade (if it be one needing a licence), marries him, divorces him, entertains civil actions against him, declares him a bankrupt, hangs him for murder. The police that guard his house, the local boards which look after the poor, control highways, impose water rates, manage schools—all these derive their legal powers from his State alone. Looking at this immense compass of State functions, Jefferson would seem to have been not far wrong when he said that the Federal government was nothing more than the American department of foreign affairs. But although the National government touches the direct interests of the citizen less than does the State government, it touches his sentiment more. Hence the strength of his attachment to the former and his interest in it must

not be measured by the frequency of his dealings with it. In the partitionment of governmental functions between nation and State, the State gets the most but the nation the highest, so the balance between the two is preserved.

Thus every American citizen lives in a duality of which Europeans, always excepting the Swiss, and to some extent the Germans, have no experience. He lives under two governments and two sets of laws; he is animated by two patriotisms and owes two allegiances. That these should both be strong and rarely be in conflict is most fortunate. It is the result of skilful adjustment and long habit, of the fact that those whose votes control the two sets of governments are the same persons, but above all of that harmony of each set of institutions with the other set, a harmony due to the identity of the principles whereon both are founded, which makes each appear necessary to the stability of the other, the States to the nation as its basis, the National Government to the States as their protector.

Notes

1. The case of Kansas immediately before the War of Secession, and the cases of the rebel States, which were not readmitted after the war till they had accepted the constitutional amendments forbidding slavery and protecting the freedmen, are quite exceptional cases.

2. Congress has power to pass a uniform rule of naturalization (Const. Art. i. § 8).

   Under the present naturalization laws a foreigner must have resided in the United States for five years, and for one year in the State or Territory where he seeks admission to United States citizenship, and must declare two years before he is admitted that he renounces allegiance to any foreign prince or state. Naturalization makes him a citizen not only of the United States, but of the State or Territory where he is admitted, but does not necessarily confer the electoral franchise, for that depends on State laws.

   In more than a third of the States the electoral franchise is now enjoyed by persons not naturalized as United States citizens.

3. "The line of distinction between the privileges and immunities of citizens of the United States, and those of citizens of the several States, must be traced along the boundary of their respective spheres of action, and the two classes must be as different in their nature as are the functions of their respective governments. A citizen of the United States as such has a right to participate in foreign and interstate commerce, to have the benefit of the postal laws, to make use in common with others of the navigable waters of the United States, and to pass from State to State, and into foreign countries, because over all these subjects the jurisdiction of the United States extends, and they are covered by its laws. The privileges suggest the immunities. Wherever it is the duty of the United States to give protection to a citizen against any harm, inconvenience, or deprivation, the citizen is entitled to an immunity which pertains to Federal citizenship. One very plain immunity is exemption from any tax, burden, or imposition under State laws as a condition to the enjoyment of any right or privilege under the laws of the United States. . . . Whatever one may claim as of right under the Constitution and laws of the United States by virtue of his citizenship, is a privilege of a citizen of the United States. Whatever the Constitution and laws of the United States entitle him to exemption from, he may claim an

exemption in respect to. And such a right or privilege is abridged whenever the State law interferes with any legitimate operation of Federal authority which concerns his interest, whether it be an authority actively exerted, or resting only in the express or implied command or assurance of the Federal Constitution or law. But the United States can neither grant nor secure to its citizens rights or privileges which are not expressly or by reasonable implication placed under its jurisdiction, and all not so placed are left to the exclusive protection of the States."—Cooley, *Principles*, pp. 245–247.

4. It may of course be said that as the colonies associated themselves into a league, at the very time at which they revolted from the British Crown, and as their foreign relations were always managed by the authority and organs of this league, no one of them ever was for international purposes a free and independent sovereign State. This is true, and Abraham Lincoln was in this sense justified in saying that the Union was older than the States. But what are we to say of North Carolina and Rhode Island, after the acceptance of the Constitution of 1787–89 by the other eleven States? They were out of the old Confederation, for it had expired. They were not in the new Union, for they refused during many months to enter it. What else can they have been during these months except sovereign commonwealths?

5. States rights was a watchword in the South for many years. In 1851 there was a student at Harvard College from South Carolina who bore the name of States Rights Gist, baptized, so to speak, into Calhounism. He rose to be a brigadier-general in the Confederate army, and fell in the Civil War.

6. A further confusion arises from the fact that men are apt in talking of sovereignty to mix up legal supremacy with practical predominance. They ought to go together, and law seeks to make them go together. But it may happen that the person or body in whom law vests supreme authority is unable to enforce that authority: so the legal sovereign and the actual sovereign—that is to say, the force which will prevail in physical conflict—are different. There is always a strongest force; but the force recognized by law may not be really the strongest; and of several forces it may be impossible to tell, till they have come into actual physical conflict, which is the strongest.

7. See Chapter XXII. *ante.*

8. A recent American writer well observes that nearly all the great questions which have agitated England during the last sixty years would, had they arisen in America, have fallen within the sphere of State legislation.—Jameson, "Introduction to the Constitutional and Political History of the States," in *Johns Hopkins University Studies.*

Unit Selections

Key Points to Consider

❖ Do you think that the current state of intergovernmental relations in the United States is satisfactory or unsatisfactory?

❖ Which level of government do you think is contributing the most to the welfare of Americans? Why?

❖ Under what circumstances do you think the national government should try to impose national standards on state and local governments? Under what circumstances do you think state governments should impose state standards on local governments?

❖ Should states and localities have responsibility for performing more tasks and for raising money to pay for them? Why or why not?

 **Links** **www.dushkin.com/online/**

These sites are annotated on pages 4 and 5.

Three levels of government—national, state, and local—coexist in the American political system. They not only survive alongside one another, but they also cooperate and conflict with each other in carrying out functions.

Legal bases for relationships among governments in the American political system include the United States Constitution, 50 state constitutions, court decisions by both state and federal courts, and state and national legislation. But legal guidelines do not prevent complications from arising in a system of government with three tiers. These three tiers of American government have often been likened to a layer cake: three layers in one overarching system of government. Still using the cake analogy, political scientist Morton Grodzins argued that a marble cake better represents the interactions of local, state, and national governments. According to Grodzins, these interactions are far less tidy than the model of a layer cake symbolizes.

Governments closest to the scene seem best able to handle certain kinds of problems, but at the same time higher, more "distant" levels of government often have access to better sources of revenue with which to finance government activities. Citizens give different degrees of loyalty and support to different levels of government, and competing ambitions of politicians at different levels of government can obstruct needed cooperation.

The formal relationship between the national government and the states is quite different from that between the states and their local governments. The national-state relationship is formally "federal" in character, which means that, in theory, the states and the national government each have autonomous spheres of responsibility. In contrast, the state-local relationship is not a federal one. Local governments are mere "creatures" of the states and are not on equal footing with their creators and masters. In practical terms, however, the national government has gained the upper hand in its dealings with the states, and in some areas localities are on almost equal footing with state governments.

Public school governance illustrates some of the complexities of intergovernmental relations in the American political system. Public schooling is usually viewed as primarily a local government function. But, as Grodzins pointed out, state governments play powerful roles by providing financial aid, certifying teachers, prescribing curriculum requirements, and regulating school safety and pupil health. The national government is also involved in public schooling. In the last 50 years, the United States Supreme Court and lower federal courts have made numerous decisions aimed at ending racial segregation in public schools. In addition, for several decades national government grants have helped finance various activities such as school breakfasts and lunches and special education programs. Even this brief review of local, state, and national involvement in one area, schooling, can show why Grodzins believed that a marble cake better reflects the reality of the American three-level system of government than does a layer cake.

Intergovernmental transfers of money are an important form of interaction among local, state, and national governments. "Strings" are almost always attached to money that one level of government transfers to another level. For example, when the national government provides grants to states and localities, requirements concerning use of the money accompany the funds, although the extensiveness and specificity of requirements vary greatly in different grant programs. Similarly, state governments aid local governments, and state money also brings strings of one kind or another.

Presidents and other government leaders often set forth proposals about how to structure relations and divide responsibilities among national, state, and local governments. President Reagan's "new federalism" was aimed at shifting greater responsibility back to the states and localities. The change in direction begun under Reagan continued under President Bush, and state and local governments had to operate in the context of what has been called "fend-for-yourself federalism."

Whatever changes in intergovernmental relations that the Clinton administration tried to make faded into obscurity with the coming of a Republican-controlled House of Representatives and Senate in January 1995. Newt Gingrich, the first Republican Speaker of the House of Representatives in 40 years, made shrinking the size of the national government and giving increased responsibilities to the states an important part of his campaign promises in the November 1994 congressional elections.

In the 104th Congress, the House of Representatives passed a number of bills fulfilling Gingrich's campaign promises. One such bill was designed to make it very difficult for Congress to mandate state and local governments to do something without providing the necessary funding. The welfare reform bill of mid-1996 rewrote the welfare system that began in the 1930s as part of the New Deal. At its core lay the devolution to state governments of all sorts of responsibilities for providing government assistance to the needy. While the national government remained responsible for funding the welfare system, state governments were given vastly increased responsibility for determining and implementing welfare policy. In the last two decades of the twentieth century, the United States may have begun a new era of intergovernmental relations that will result in substantial increases in the power and autonomy of state and local governments.

Selections in this unit treat various aspects of relationships among national, state, and local governments.

Intergovernmental Relations

Judicial Federalism: The Resurgence of the Supreme Court's Role in the Protection of State Sovereignty

Charles Wise, Indiana University

Throughout history, the courts have played a key role in determining the nature of the intergovernmental system in the United States. In particular, the Federal Courts have been the central arbiter in deciding between assertions of national authority and state claims to protection from federal encroachment. The Courts have been asked time and again to choose between Constitutional commands supporting the national government on the one hand and commands supporting state and local governments on the other. In the decades of the 1940's through the 1980's, more often than not, the courts decided the trade-offs in favor of national authority and thus significantly supported the expansion of national governmental power.

This trend in support of the Federal Government is important, in that it has played a crucial role in structuring our system of governance, altered our system of public administration, and constituted fundamental constraints on the ability of state and local officials to direct programs and operations to meet the expanded domestic policy agenda that has been devolved to state and local governments. The trend in favor of national authority had persisted for so long that some commentators concluded that the federalism principle had outlived its usefulness and was no longer a viable judicial doctrine (Choper, 1980, pp. 255 –256). Federalism supporters feared that the Supreme Court had reached the same conclusion and was formally signaling its abdication of any responsibility to protect state prerogatives.

Nonetheless, the worst fears of federalism supporters were not realized. The decade of the 1990's has brought a shift in the trend in federalism cases and brought the Supreme Court back to taking up a role as a protector of federalism. To understand why, it is necessary to scrutinize a series of cases decided from the opening of the decade. It began inauspiciously enough with an unobstrusive personnel policy case, *Gregory v. Ashcroft* (111 S. Ct. 2395,1991). In that case, state judges challenged Missouri's constitutional requirement that judges retire at age 70. Citing the Federal Discrimination and Employment Act of 1967 and the Fourteenth Amendment, Missouri supported its constitutional regulation through the Tenth Amendment of the United States Constitution, which reserves to the states all powers not explicitly granted to the federal government. The Court decided for Missouri, but what was more significant is that in doing so, it went on to engage in a lengthy review of past cases focusing on state political functions, and then went to extraordinary lengths to expound a general view of state sovereignty. Not content to stop there, the Court went on to equate the importance of a balance of power between state and federal governments with the separation of powers within the national government and stated that this constituted a "double security" for the people. The Supreme Court has followed *Gregory* with a series of decisions buttressing federalism. The cases that follow illustrate the nature and extent of the resurgence.

New York v. United States 505 U.S. 144 (1992)

Just one year after *Gregory*, the Supreme Court announced its decision in response to a challenge from two countries and the State of New York against the Low-Level Radioactive Waste Policy Act, which, among other things, mandated that states or regional compacts that fail to provide the disposal of all low level radioactive wastes generated in the affected states by January 1, 1996, must take title to the waste if requested by the generator or owner of the waste. The Court stated that this "take-title" provision offered the states a "choice" between two unconstitutional alternatives. The first choice, accepting ownership of the waste, would allow Congress to transfer radioactive waste from generators to state governments which was clearly unconstitutional. The second choice, regulating according to Congress's instructions, would command state governments to implement legislation enacted by Congress.

The Court emphasized that Congress exercises its conferred powers subject to the limitations contained in the Constitution and opined that just as Congress is constrained in the exercise of its powers by the First Amendment, so too is it restrained by the Tenth Amendment. This juxtaposition of the Tenth Amendment with the First demonstrates just how serious the Court is in emphasizing federalism, in that the Court has always been particularly vigilant in asserting its role in protecting First Amendment rights. The Court reminded us that "the Constitution protects us from our own best intentions: It divides power among sovereigns and among branches of government precisely so that we may resist the temptation to concentrate power in one location as an expedient solution to the crisis of the day." (505 U.S. 186). The Court concluded,

> States are not mere political subdivisions of the United States. State governments are neither regional offices nor administrative agencies of the Federal Government. . . . The Constitution instead 'leaves to the several States a residuary and inviolable sovereignty' (Federalist no. 39), reserved explicitly to the States by the Tenth Amendment. Whatever the outer limits of that sovereignty may be, one thing is clear: The Federal Government may not compel States to enact or administer a federal regulatory program (Ibid).

This conclusion clearly has broad implications at a time when the federal government looks increasingly at the states to implement and administer programs adopted by Congress.

While the Court reaffirmed there were incentives that Congress could use to encourage the States to choose to participate in federal regulatory programs, it was emphatic that clear limits based in the Constitution would limit Congress's reach.

United States v. Alfonso Lopez, Jr. 514 U.S. 549 (1995)

In this case, a twelfth grade student carried a concealed handgun into his high school and was later charged with violating the federal Gun Free School Zones Act of 1990. The Act forbids "any individual knowingly to possess a firearm at a place that [he] knows . . . is a school zone." The student appealed his conviction based on his claim that the law exceeded Congress's power to legislate under the Commerce Clause.

The Court reviewed its Commerce Clause decisions and observed that while its decisions in recent decades had greatly expanded the previously defined authority of Congress under the Clause, even those precedents confirm that this power is subject to outer limits (514 U.S. 556).

The Court stated that it had identified three broad categories of activity that Congress may regulate under its commerce power: (1) it may regulate the use of channels of interstate commerce, (2) it may regulate and protect the instrumentalities of interstate commerce, or persons or things in interstate commerce and (3) it may regulate those activities having a substantial relation to interstate commerce (514 U.S. 558). The Court observed that within the last category, its precedents had not made clear whether an activity must "affect" or "substantially affect" interstate commerce. The Court concluded that the proper test was "substantially affects" and that the Gun Free School Zones Act would have to meet that test.

The Government argued that the Act met the test because the costs of crime are substantial and through insurance are spread throughout the population, that fear of crime reduces the willingness of people to travel to areas perceived unsafe, and finally that guns in schools threaten the learning environment which in turn will lead to a less productive citizenry. The Court opined that these rationales were seemingly without limits on federal power. The Court concluded, "To uphold the Government's contentions here, we would have to pile inference upon inference in a manner that would bid fair to convert congressional authority under the Commerce Clause to a general police power of the sort retained by the States" (514 U.S. 567). The majority admitted that the Court's prior decisions had taken long steps down that road and suggested the possibility of additional expansion, but stated "we decline here to proceed any further" (514 U.S. 567).

The significance of this ruling is vast in that the Commerce clause has been the primary basis for regulatory legislation passed by Congress in multiple areas. Observers as far back as Justice Frankfurter have pointed out that the Commerce Clause has throughout the Court's history been the chief source of its adjudications regarding federalism. As the dissenters pointed out in this case, more than 100 sections of the United States Code including criminal statutes with at least 25 sections use the words "affecting commerce" to define their scope. The dissenters forecast that legal uncertainty they perceive introduced by this decision will restrict Congress' ability to enact criminal laws aimed at criminal behavior that seriously threatens economic as well as social well-being of Americans (514 U.S. 630).

Whether there will be greater uncertainty or not remains to be seen. It is clear however, that there is a majority on the Court ready to subject any congressional attempts at regulatory expansion to a stricter scrutiny than they have experienced in the recent past.

Seminole Tribe of Florida v. Florida, 116 S. Ct. 1114 (1996)

This is a case that has important implications for federalism and has significance for state and local governments beyond the context of the case itself. It concerns whether Congress can override the States' Eleventh Amendment immunity from suit by passing a statute to that effect. Such immunity is important, in that if it can be abrogated by an act of Congress, states' powers to actively regulate are significantly constrained by the threat of potential suits.

This case involved the Indian Gaming Regulatory Act, passed by Congress pursuant to the Indian Commerce Clause, which allows an Indian tribe to conduct certain gaming activities only in conformance with a valid compact between the tribe and the State in which the gaming activities are located. The Indian Commerce Clause, for these purposes, is indistinguishable from the Interstate Commerce clause, and thus the decision applies to the latter as well. Under the Act, the States have a duty to negotiate in good faith with the tribe toward the formation of a compact, and the tribe is allowed to sue a State in federal court in order to compel performance of that duty. In this case, the State moved to dismiss the complaint on the ground that the suit violated the state's sovereign immunity from suit in federal court under the Eleventh Amendment. The Seminole Tribe countered that the Supreme Court had previously held, in the 1989 case of *Pennsylvania v. Union Gas* (491 U.S. 1), that Congress has the power when legislating pursuant to Article I of the Constitution, to override States' Eleventh Amendment immunity from suit and did so in this case.

The Supreme Court reversed the 1989 *Union Gas* decision and held that the Eleventh Amendment prevents Congress from authorizing suits by Indian tribes against States to enforce legislation enacted pursuant to the Indian Commerce Clause. The Court found that *Union Gas* was wrongly decided, departed from the Court's federalism jurisprudence, and overruled it. More importantly, the Court declared that even when the Constitution vests in Congress complete law-making authority over a particular area (such as regulation of interstate commerce), the Eleventh Amendment prevents congressional authorization of suits by private parties against unconsenting states. The final result is that State sovereign immunity under the Eleventh Amendment takes precedence over congressional power under Article I of the Constitution. The projected far-reaching impact of this decision is predicted to give States greater protection against congressionally authorized suits by private parties in diverse areas of law.

Printz v. United States 117 S. Ct. 2365 (1997)

Provisions of the Brady Handgun Violence Prevention Act required the establishment of a national system for instantly checking prospective handgun purchasers' backgrounds and commanded the chief law enforcement officer of each local jurisdiction to conduct background checks on prospective purchasers. Two County sheriffs challenged this provision as unconstitutional.

The Court agreed with the Sheriffs and stated, "It is an essential attribute of the States' retained sovereignty that they remain independent and autonomous within their proper sphere of authority. . . . It is no more compatible with this independence and autonomy that their officers be 'dragooned' . . . into administering federal law, than it would be compatible with the independence and autonomy of the United States that its officers be impressed into service for the execution of state laws" (117 S. Ct. 2386). The federal government had argued that the provision was compatible with the Court's previous decision in *New York v. United States* both because no policy making on the part of the states was involved and/or because in this case the burdens on states are limited and are outweighed by the benefits. The Court rejected this reasoning and specifically stated that where in *New York* it held that Congress cannot compel the States to enact or enforce a federal regulatory program, it was now holding that Congress cannot circumvent that prohibition by conscripting State officers directly. The Court stated that the Federal Government may neither issue directives requiring the states to address particular problems nor command States' officers, or those of their political subdivisions, to administer or enforce a federal regulatory program. The principle is categorical and does not matter whether policy making is involved and no case by case weighing of costs and benefits is necessary.

City of Boerne v. P. F. Flores and United States 117 S. Ct. 2157 (1997)

The Catholic Archbishop of San Antonio applied for a building permit to enlarge a church in Boerne, Texas. The city zoning authorities pursuant to an historic preservation ordinance denied the permit and the Archbishop brought suit under the Religious Freedom Restoration Act of 1993 (RFRA). RFRA prohibits "government" from "substantially burdening" a person's exercise of religion even if the burden results from a rule of general applicability unless the government can demonstrate the burden (1) is in furtherance of a compelling government interest; and (2) is the least restrictive means of furthering that interest. The issue before the Supreme Court was whether in enacting RFRA, Congress had exceeded its enforcement power under the Fourteenth Amendment. This case is significant for federalism in that the Fourteenth Amendment perhaps even more than the Commerce clause has been the basis for extending the reach of national policy, and Congress has passed numerous laws pursuant to its enforcement power under the Amendment.

The Court found that Congress's power extends only to "enforcing" the Fourteenth Amendment and that the power is "remedial" as distinguished from "substantive." While the line between measures that remedy or prevent unconstitutional actions and measures that substantively change the Constitution is not easy to discern, the Court declared that the distinction must be observed. Further, there must be a congruence and proportionality between the injury to be prevented or remedied and the means adopted.

The Court found that the RFRA appears to be a substantive change in constitutional protections. Requiring a State to demonstrate a compelling interest and show that it has adopted the least restrictive means of achieving that interest is the most demanding test known to constitutional law. RFRA's sweeping coverage, the Court found, ensures its intrusion at every level of government, displacing laws and prohibiting official actions of almost every description and regardless of subject matter. The Court concluded that RFRA would require searching judicial scrutiny of state law resulting in the likely invalidation of many, and this is a considerable congressional intrusion into the States' traditional prerogatives and general authority to regulate for the health and welfare of their citizens.

The Court was most emphatic in discussing Congress' powers to legislate under the rubric of the Fourteenth Amendment, and made it clear that the Court itself would continue to determine limits on those powers according to its own responsibility to interpret the Constitution and to say "what the law is."

Some features of the above reviewed cases, taken as a whole, imply broad significance for the resurgence of federalism on the part of the Supreme Court. First, it should be noted that these are not narrow fact-bound decisions nor ones with precedents of limited applicability. Nor are they directed solely at specialized or segmented areas of statutory law. Instead, they are directed at what have served as some of the foundation stones of the expansion of national power. Cases reviewed here involve the Commerce Clause and the Fourteenth Amendment, and the majorities in these cases have taken particular pains to point out the need for limits on national power under these rubrics, and then have proceeded to set such limits. In doing so, they have by no means indicated that the limit setting is over.

Secondly, notable in several of these cases is the fact that the Court did not just address its previous precedents, but went back to "first principles" and took pains to lay out a philosophy of federalism that serves to indicate how fundamental an issue the majority in these cases considers the principles of federalism. Equating the Tenth Amendment with the First Amendment, and the vision of national and state power with the separation of powers between the branches in national government signals that the majority does not consider these transitory matters, and that it places a high priority on federalism. In doing so, the Court seems to be also reasserting its position as the protector of federalism and as the arbiter of the division of power between national and state governments.

Implications

These cases have important implications for the conduct of public administration in the United States. The Court's decision in *New York* and its emphasis and extension of the principles of *New York* in *Printz* make it clear that the Court is placing real limits on national regulatory and administrative schemes that seek to utilize the capacity of the states. The decisions in *City of Boerne* and *Seminole Tribe* create more space for state regulatory initiatives with a lesser threat of invalidation by means of national legislation. The decision in *Lopez* should give pause to those who would expand federal regulatory reach into areas traditionally left to the states.

The review of these cases is not meant to indicate that the Supreme Court is rolling back its previous decisions that have validated the expansion of federal power into many areas. Also, I do not foresee that the Court has now set out on a course which will almost always bring its decisions down on the side of the states. On the contrary, the Court will continue to engage in a balancing act that brings its decisions down sometimes on the side of the states and other times on the side of the federal government. Admittedly, these selected cases cannot provide a complete picture of the Supreme Court's federalism jurisprudence. (For a fuller explication of public administration related cases illustrating how the Supreme Court has treated these issues generally see Wise and O'Leary, 1992; and in a particular administrative area, see Wise and O'Leary, 1997). Nonetheless, federalism advocates appear to be in a far different position than they were immediately after the Court's decision in *Garcia*. Instead of abdicating its role with respect to issues of federalism, the Court has made it perfectly clear that it is back in the driver's seat as the Arbiter-in-Chief of federalism. The resurgence is real.

♦ ♦ ♦

Charles R. Wise is a professor of public affairs at Indiana University. He is a former managing editor of *PAR*. He has received the William E. Mosher and Frederick C. Mosher award three times for the best article, written by an academic, to appear in *PAR*. He is the immediate past president of the National Association of Schools of Public Affairs and Administration.

References

Choper, Jesse H. (1980). *Judicial Review and the National Political Process*. Chicago: University of Chicago Press.
Wise, Charles and Rosemary O'Leary (1997). "Intergovernmental Relations and Federalism in Environmental Management and Policy: The Role of the Courts." *Public Administration Review* 57(2): 150–159.
Wise, Charles and Rosemary O'Leary (1992). "Is Federalism Dead or Alive in the Supreme Court? Implications for Public Administrators." *Public Administration Review* 52(6): 559–571.

THE DEVIL IN DEVOLUTION

BY JOHN D. DONAHUE

The shift in government's center of gravity away from Washington and toward the states—a transition propelled by both popular sentiment and budget imperatives, and blessed by leaders in both major parties—reflects an uncommon pause in an endless American argument over the balance between nation and state. That argument got underway when the Framers gathered in Philadelphia to launch a second attempt at nationhood, after less than a decade's dismal experience under the feeble Articles of Confederation. The Constitution they crafted was a compromise between those who wanted to strengthen the ties among essentially autonomous states, and those who sought to establish a new nation to supersede the states as the locus of the commonwealth. While anchoring the broad contours of state and federal roles, the Framers left it to their successors to adjust the balance to fit the circumstances of the world to come and the priorities of future generations.

This moment of consensus in favor of letting Washington fade while the states take the lead is badly timed. The public sector's current trajectory—the devolution of welfare and other programs, legislative and judicial action circumscribing Washington's authority, and the federal government's retreat to a domestic role largely defined by writing checks to entitlement claimants, creditors, and state and local governments—would make sense if economic and cultural ties reaching across state lines were *weakening* over time. But state borders are becoming more, not less, permeable.

John D. Donahue is an associate professor at Harvard's John F. Kennedy School of Government.

Reprinted with permission from *The American Prospect*, May/June 1997, pp. 42–47. Adapted from *Disunited States*, by John D. Donahue, 1997, published by Basic Books, a division of HarperCollins Publishers, Inc., New York, NY. © 1997 by the American Prospect, P.O. Box 383080, Cambridge, MA 02138. All rights reserved.

From a vantage point three-fifths of the way between James Madison's day and our own, Woodrow Wilson wrote that the "common interests of a nation brought together in thought and interest and action by the telegraph and the telephone, as well as by the rushing mails which every express train carries, have a scope and variety, an infinite multiplication and intricate interlacing, of which a simpler day can have had no conception." Issues in which other states' citizens have no stakes, and hence no valid claim to a voice, are becoming rarer still in an age of air freight, interlinked computers, nonstop currency trading, and site-shopping global corporations. Our current enchantment with devolution will be seen one day as oddly discordant with our era's challenges.

The concept of "the commons" can help to cast in a sharper light the perils of fragmented decision-making on issues of national consequence. In a much-noted 1968 article in *Science*, biologist Garrett Hardin invoked the parable of a herdsman pondering how many cattle to graze on the village commons. Self-interest will lead the herdsman to increase the size of his herd even if the commons is already overburdened, since he alone benefits from raising an extra animal, but shares the consequent damage to the common pasture. As each farmer follows the same logic, overgrazing wrecks the commons.

Where the nation as a whole is a commons, whether as an economic reality or as a political ideal, and states take action that ignores or narrowly exploits that fact, the frequent result is the kind of "tragedy" that Hardin's metaphor predicts: Collective value is squandered in the name of a constricted definition of gain. States win advantages that seem worthwhile only because other states bear much of the costs. America's most urgent public challenges—shoring up the economic underpinnings of an imperiled middle-class culture; developing and deploying productive workplace skills; orchestrating Americans' engagement with increasingly global capital—involve the stewardship of common interests. The fragmentation of authority makes success less likely. The phenomenon is by no means limited to contemporary economic issues, and a smattering of examples from other times and other policy agendas illustrate the theme.

FAITH AND CREDIT

In the late 1700s, states reluctant to raise taxes instead paid public debt with paper money, with progressively little gold or silver behind it. Even states like Georgia, Delaware, and New Jersey that exercised some restraint in issuing paper money saw merchants lose confidence in their currencies, as the flood of bad money debased the reputation of American money in general. Half a century later defaults and debt repudiations by Pennsylvania, Arkansas, Florida, Illinois, and a few other states—which for the states concerned were unfortunate, but apparently preferable to the alternative of paying what they owed—polluted the common American resource of creditworthiness, and for a time froze even solvent states and the federal government out of international credit markets.

Presidential primaries, which are run state by state, provide another example. Each state prefers to be first in line to hold its primary (or at least early in the queue). In recent presidential election seasons—and especially the 1996 Republican primaries—states have wrecked the common resource of a deliberative primary process in a rational (but nonetheless tragic) pursuit of parochial advantage. California's primary in June 1992 had come too late to matter; anxious to avoid another episode of irrelevance four years later, it staked out March 26 for its vote. But several other states, whose *own* votes would be rendered superfluous once California's crowd of delegates was selected, rescheduled their primaries in response. A spiral of competitive rescheduling led to ugly squabbles as Delaware and Louisiana crowded New Hampshire's traditional first-in-the-nation franchise; a mass of state primaries ended up bunched right behind New Hampshire, and a grotesquely compressed primary season ensued. The outcome was clear by the first days of March, and California's primary—although held two months earlier than it had been in 1992—was just as irrelevant. Most voters perceived the 1996 primary season as a brief spasm of televised name-calling. Even supporters of the eventual nominee felt that Senator Dole, and the voters, had been ill served by the process.

Term limits for representatives and senators present a similar "commons" problem. Despite a flurry of term-limit legislation at the state level, anyone convinced that the United States should have a less-professionalized Congress may not want to count on state term-limit laws to accomplish the goal. If less-entrenched legislators make for better law—a plausible although not invulnerable proposition—

> States win competitive advantage by dumping costs.

then a citizen legislature is a common benefit for the nation as a whole. Yet an individual state is usually better off when represented by politicians with experience in the ways of Washington and a deep reserve of past favors on which to trade. Even if a majority of a state's citizens would like to see a Congress of fresh faces, they may well prefer to see *other* states restrict representatives and senators to a few years' service, while keeping their own old lions on the job.

The Constitution's "full faith and credit" clause, a court case in Hawaii, and the quadrennial uptick in political tawdriness brought an unusual sort of commons problem to center stage in 1996. The issue was whether the definition of "marriage" should be broadened to include same-sex unions. A handful of Hawaiian same-sex couples had asserted the right to have their relationships reckoned under state law as no different from heterosexual marriages, invoking provisions in the state constitution that bar sex discrimination in almost any form (including, the plaintiffs argued, restrictions on the gender of one's spouse). When a shift in the composition of Hawaii's supreme court made a seemingly lost cause suddenly viable, it dawned on advocates and opponents alike that if Hawaii legitimated same-sex marriage, those unions would have to be recognized nationwide. If any homosexual couple—at least those able to afford two tickets to Hawaii—could bypass more restrictive laws in their home states, the rapid result could be a national redefinition of what marriage means, without anyone outside Hawaii having any voice in the outcome.

National opponents of gay marriage staged a preemptive strike in the form of the Defense of Marriage Act, requiring the federal government to counter heterodoxy in Hawaii or anywhere else by declaring a *national* definition of marriage—one man, one woman, and that's that. Beyond excluding same-sex spouses from receiving benefits under any federal program, the act gave states the right to refuse recognition to other states' marriages. The Defense of Marriage Act raced through Congress and President Clinton quickly signed it (albeit without ceremony and literally in the middle of the night). Annoyed at being forced to alienate his gay supporters in order to stay wrapped in the family-values mantle, Clinton charged, no doubt correctly, that the bill's authors were driven by the partisan spirit of the election year. But whatever their motivations—and however one feels about same-sex marriage—they had a point: The definition of marriage in the United States should be settled by national deliberation.

There is an interesting historical irony here, however, Not so long ago, divorce was only a little more common, and only a little less out of the mainstream, than homosexual unions seem today. While the causes for its increase are many and complex, the pace was set in part by states' calculations of parochial advantage. Around the turn of the century legislators in several Western states—notably Nevada—passed liberal divorce legislation in part to encourage economic development. Unhappy couples facing onerous divorce laws in their home state could head West for a few weeks or months. There they could dissolve their union, while solidifying the local economy, in some striving desert town. Other states might have resisted the trend to more lenient divorce laws. But any couple—at least any able to afford a ticket to Reno—could bypass their home-state restrictions. If a legislature held the line it would only be subjecting its citizens to extra expense while sending money out of state.

The wholesale liberalization of American divorce laws is often seen as a mistake—if not from the perspective of men who can cast off unwanted obligations with minimal bother, at least from the perspective of women and, especially, young children who all too often are left economically stranded. Which raises a question: If states should be free to refuse recognition to marriages made elsewhere, on the grounds that another state's definition of marriage offends local morals, should they also be able to refuse to recognize out-of-state divorces? Suppose that Vermont, say, passed legislation toughening divorce laws and declaring Vermont marriages immune to dissolution by another state's laws. If the legislation survived constitutional challenge (which is doubtful, as it is for the Defense of Marriage Act's comparable provisions) there would be some definite advantages: More traditional states could wall themselves off as enclaves against unwelcome national trends; a potential spouse could signal the depth of his or her commitment by proposing a Vermont wedding. On the other hand, the United States would become a little bit less of a nation.

In one of the less glorious episodes in American history, this country attempted to define human slavery as an issue each state could settle on its own, according to its own economic and ethical lights. Northern states, however, eventually proved unwilling to accept the proposition that the moral commons could be so neatly subdivided. The Fugitive Slave Act required antislavery states to make room in their moral world for slaveholders to transport their "property" for use anywhere in the nation. The repercussions ultimately led to attempted secession, and then to the national abolition of slavery. The meaning of marriage may be another moral issue so basic that it must be dealt with through a national debate, protracted and painful as that will doubtless turn out to be.

ENVIRONMENTAL REGULATION

Antipollution law is perhaps the most obvious application of the "commons" metaphor to policymaking in a federal system. If a state maintains a lax regime of environmental laws it spares its own citizens, businesses, and government agencies from economic burdens. The "benefits" of environmental recklessness, in other words, are collected instate. Part of the pollution consequently dumped into the air or water, however, drifts away to do its damage elsewhere in the nation. If states held all authority over environmental rule-making, the predictable result would be feeble regulations against any kinds of pollution where in-state costs and benefits of control are seriously out of balance. Even in states whose citizens valued the environment—even if the citizens of *all* states were willing to accept substantial economic costs in the name of cleaner air and water—constituents and representatives would calculate that their sacrifice could not on its own stem the tide and reluctantly settle for weaker rules than they would otherwise prefer.

A state contemplating tough antipollution rules might calculate that its citizens will pay for environmental improvements that will be enjoyed, in part, by others. Even worse, by imposing higher costs on business than do other states, it risks repelling investment, and thus losing jobs and tax revenues to states with weak environmental laws. Congress explicitly invoked the specter of a "race for the bottom"—competitive loosening of environmental laws in order to lure business—to justify federal standards that would "preclude efforts on the part of states to compete with each other in trying to attract new plants." In a series of legislative changes starting in the early 1970s, the major choices about how aggressively to act against pollution were moved to the federal government. While aspects of enforcement remained state responsibilities—introducing another level of complications that continues to plague environmental policy—the trade-off between environmental and economic values moved much closer to a single national standard.

National regulation in a diverse economy does have a downside. States differ in their environmental problems, and in the priorities of their citizens. Requiring all states to accept the same balance between environmental and economic

values imposes some real costs and generates real political friction. Yet even if the tilt toward national authority is, on balance, the correct approach to environmental regulation, there is reason to doubt we got all the details right. Moreover, logic suggests that the federal role should be stronger for forms of pollution that readily cross state borders, and weaker for pollution that stays put. But federal authority is actually weaker under the Clean Air Act and the Clean Water Act than under the "Superfund" law covering hazardous waste. Toxic-waste sites are undeniably nasty things. But most of them are situated within a single state, and stay there.

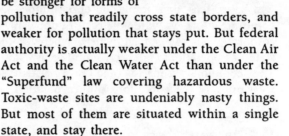

Pollution doesn't observe state borders.

CORPORATE CHARTERING

Few questions about the division of economic authority across our federal system have received as enormous an investment of intellectual energy as the state chartering of corporations. Since corporations can operate nationally, whatever their state of incorporation, state decisions on chartering have national implications. In the eighteenth and much of the nineteenth centuries, corporate charters were granted under far more stringent conditions than they are today, usually on the understanding that demonstrable public good would result from the corporation's activities. As corporations came to be seen less as agents of the public interest; as states came to presume, instead of demanding proof of, public benefits from business enterprise; and as some firms became sufficiently national to have meaningful choices about which state to call home, the specific terms of state chartering came to matter more. In 1896, New Jersey adopted aggressively liberal chartering rules, and became the legal home of choice for major corporations. New Jersey shifted to a somewhat tougher chartering law in 1913, however, and rapidly lost its hegemony to Delaware, which had altered its own incorporation provisions to mirror New Jersey's previous law. Delaware has tenaciously defended its dominant place in corporate chartering ever since.

Herbert Croly, the Progressive intellectual, considered state chartering a silly anachronism by 1909, arguing that "a state has in the great majority of cases no meaning at all as a center of economic organization and direction." Croly's call

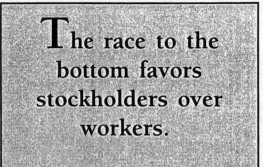

The race to the bottom favors stockholders over workers.

for national chartering was made "not because there is any peculiar virtue in the action of the central government, but because there is a peculiar vice in asking the state governments to regulate matters beyond their effective jurisdiction." States whose chartering rules appeal to managers win taxes, fees, and ample job opportunities for corporate attorneys, while the costs of unbalanced corporate law are spread widely, wherever the state has operations, sales, creditors, or investors. The commons scenario predicts a systematic weakening of the conditions of incorporation.

The phrase "race to the bottom" was introduced in 1933 by Supreme Court Justice Louis Brandeis—who also, interestingly enough, popularized the term "laboratories of democracy"—in connection with corporate chartering. Multistate companies, Brandeis said, sought charters "in states where the cost was lowest and the laws least restrictive. The states joined in advertising their wares. The race was one not of diligence but of laxity." The modern debate over the prudence of state chartering got underway in the early 1970s with an article by William L. Cary in the *Yale Law Journal* on the pernicious effects of interstate competition for corporate charters.

Some defenders of rivalrous state chartering argued that Delaware's advantage was not due to weak conditions of incorporation, but rather to its efficient procedures for chartering—streamlined administrative rule-making, courts dedicated to corporate law, a specialized private bar, and a tradition of depoliticizing corporate law made sustainable by the paucity of actual corporate *operations* within the state. But the more interesting rebuttal to the "race for the bottom" critics came from a group of scholars who emphasized the importance of market rationality in the crafting of corporate law. Ralph Winter, in an influential 1977 article, started by acknowledging that states compete to maximize their share of the nation's corporate charters, and that they do so primarily through loosening the conditions of chartering. But the race was to the *top*, not the bottom, Winter and like-minded analysts argued, because the goal toward which states raced, and the pace of their scramble, turn out to be set *not* by corporate managers but by investors.

The story goes like this: Corporations must attract capital. Investors will be more likely to commit their funds to firms whose charters require managers to do right by investors. And that story seems sound, so far as it goes. But this is not quite the end of the conversation. Interstate competition promotes laws that favor investors not because legislators are directly solicitous of shareholders, but because investors have leverage over managers, and managers have leverage over state policymakers. By this same logic, interests with a weaker claim on managers' devotion have no reason to expect that interstate competition will generate favorable results. For example, the dynamics of state competition for corporate charters are unlikely to generate a national pattern of laws that strengthens the hand of employees within the firm.

LEGALIZED GAMBLING

There has never been a time in America when a person determined to gamble could not find some action. Nor is *legal* gambling, for that matter, anything new. The Continental Congress fed and armed Washington's army, in part, with revenues from a lottery, and state-sanctioned games of chance financed the early growth of Harvard and other colleges. For much of this century, however, gambling has operated in the economic shadows. Except for the exotic enclave of Nevada, government's stance toward gambling ranged, until recently, from vigilant hostility to narrowly circumscribed tolerance.

This has changed with an astonishing speed and completeness. In 1988 Nevada and New Jersey were alone in allowing casino gambling. Eight years later there were around 500 casinos operating in 27 states, and some form of gambling was legal in all but two states. The total annual amount wagered legally in the United States is about $500 billion. (For a sense of scale, consider that America's entire annual output is in the range of $7,000 billion.)

Gambling brings some obvious benefits to the state that runs the lottery or hosts the casinos. It can generate relatively high-paying jobs even for workers without much training. It yields welcome revenues for the state treasury. (States took in $27 billion from lotteries in 1994, and had $9.8 billion in revenues left over after paying off winners and covering administrative costs. In 1994, taxes paid by casinos alone yielded $1.4 billion for states and localities.) Legalized gambling can also produce political benefits, most directly the rich lodes of campaign contributions available from a highly profitable industry that is so intensely dependent on political favor.

Yet there are costs as well. Some people will always gamble whether it is legal or not, but many more do so only when the law allows. Access to legal opportunities for gambling has been found to increase the number of people who develop a gambling problem. The consequences range from mild economic inconvenience to bankruptcy, embezzlement, divorce, and suicide. In 1995—ten years after their state launched a lottery, and four years after the first legal riverboat casino opened—nine out of ten Iowans indulged in gambling. One in twenty reported having a gambling problem, and Iowa social-service agencies were coping with a surge of collateral family and financial damage.

But shouldn't we leave it to officials in each state to tally up the expected costs and benefits and make decisions that sum to the right national policy? The logic of the commons makes this less than likely. If a state loosens its own restrictions on gambling, it gains the benefits in jobs, tax revenues, and political favor. It also suffers costs—but not *all* the costs. When citizens of *other* states buy the lottery tickets and visit the casinos, they leave their money behind when they return home, but take their gambling-related problems back with them. States that still ban gambling suffer much of the damage from the national trend toward legalization, but without sharing in the benefits.

Iowa, in fact, had maintained stringent anti-gambling laws until the mid-1980s. But as a growing number of Iowans played lotteries in neighboring states it became harder to resist proposals to revitalize a battered economy through riverboat casinos aimed at attracting out-of-state gamblers, especially from the prosperous, casino-free Chicago area. At first, Chicagoans did come, by the busload. But Illinois legislators, seeing gambling dollars heading down the interstate to Iowa, opted to allow riverboat gambling in their state, too. Iowa's initial liberalization law had tried to lower the risk of problem gambling by limiting the size of any one bet and the amount any person could gamble away in a single day. But when Illinois, Mississippi, and Louisiana introduced riverboats *without* any limits, Iowa lifted its own restrictions. In a similar way, after Montana allowed slot machines in taverns in 1985 neighboring South Dakota called and raised, allowing slot machines in bars *and* convenience stores.

By 1996 the only two states with no legal gambling at all were Utah, whose Mormon culture was uniquely resistant to the national trend, and Hawaii, where it is a good deal harder than in most other states for citizens to escape local restrictions by doing their gambling in the state next door. The federal government's absolute deference to the separate states began to bend that same year with legislation establishing a commission to examine the broader national impacts of gambling. A Nevada congresswoman denounced the bill as "the nose under the tent of Federal interference with the right of states to regulate gambling." She was entirely correct. But it is questionable whether exclusive state control over so massive a change in the legal economy's scope, with such sweeping implications for our culture, ever made much sense.

Not every issue, to be sure, can be cast as a commons problem. And even where state officials *are* tempted to pursue narrow agendas at the expense of national interests, it is not automatically true that the shared loss exceeds the advantages of state autonomy, or that an acceptable way can be found of safeguarding common interests without straining the framework of our federal system. There are two basic strategies for overcoming the confusion of incentives that trigger the tragedy of the commons. One is to fragment the commons into private holdings where property rights are unambiguous. The other is to maintain a polity that commands both the capacity and the legitimacy to give force to common interests. The debate over the future of America's federal-state balance can be seen, in a sense, as pivoting on this strategic choice. Devolution seeks to simplify incentives by subdividing the commons into separate plots. Federal reform requires accepting the challenge of balancing multiple interests within the national commonwealth.

Fixing the federal government is an intimidating proposition in the late 1990s. The trajectory of fiscal and political trends suggests that devolution will remain the focus of politicians' promises and citizens' hopes for some time to come. But the inherent limits of a fragmented approach to national adaptation will eventually inspire America to reappraise the ascendancy of the states. Not too far into the new century we will again collect the resolve to confront together our common fate. And we will once more take up, in the two-century tradition of Americans before us, the echoing challenge of George Washington's 1796 farewell address: "Is there a doubt whether a common government can embrace so large a sphere? Let experience solve it."

Powerless Pipsqueaks And the Myth of Local Control

ALAN EHRENHALT

The West has always believed in states' rights. Out beyond the Rockies, more than 2,000 miles from the seat of government power in Washington, it is an article of faith that political power and decision making should be concentrated close to home, where the elected officials are familiar and approachable folks who understand ordinary citizens and their needs. If there is one freedom Western lawmakers are willing to die for, it's freedom from interference by a meddling central government far away.

At least that's what they say. Whether they mean it is another question. You have to wonder when you look at the things some of these legislatures have actually been doing this year.

Consider Arizona, for example. The last of the contiguous 48 states to join the union, it has sometimes acted as if it thought that decision was a mistake. It kept itself out of the federal Medicaid program for more than a decade after every other state went in. Its former governor, Fife Symington, created a Constitutional Defense Council to protect it against federal tyranny. The Arizona House sends some of its most sensitive legislation to a committee on states' rights. And on and on.

A year or so ago, when the Clinton administration proposed a federal drunken-driving threshold of 0.08 percent blood alcohol, Arizona went ballistic. "We're doing what the legislature, the representatives of the people, wants, not what Washington, D.C., wants," a top state official said. "We don't need to be harassed by the federal government, especially when we're doing pretty damn good here."

That was a pretty clear statement of principle. But it doesn't exactly square with HB 2275, a bill that passed both chambers of the Arizona legislature overwhelmingly a few weeks ago. It prohibited cities and counties from enacting any ordinance relating to the transportation, possession, carrying, sale or use of firearms or ammunition. In other words, it stripped every locality in the state of its ability to write laws on what has historically been a local issue. Nine Arizona cities have ordinances restricting weapons in public places, some more than 20 years old; this law would have wiped out all of them.

You have to give the legislators credit for one thing—they were expanding the concept of states' rights. They were broadening it to include the right to treat their own local governments as powerless pipsqueaks.

How does a believer in "government close to the people" justify such a move? Creatively. One state senator described local gun laws, such as those restricting possession in public places, as "just a hardship on law-abiding people who go through the permit process." The House sponsor declared that the legislature had a responsibility to make gun policy uniform all over the state. Just when the state had acquired that responsibility was unanswered.

The legislation eventually died, in large part because its timing was horrible. HB 2275 reached Governor Jane Hull's desk the day after the Littleton massacre, and she vetoed it. She also showed some understanding of its blatant unfairness. "Just to wipe out the cities' ability to control their own destiny regarding guns... did not make any sense to me at all," the governor said. On the other hand, Hull said she would have signed a bill banning municipal lawsuits against gun manufacturers, so it wasn't entirely clear where she stood on the larger issue of state legislators kicking sand in the face of local government.

COLORADO IS another interesting case. The legislature there has spent much of this year debating schemes for emasculating local government on a whole variety of fronts. There were bills banning local ordinances against private ownership of assault weapons. There were bills limiting local power to make land use decisions. There were bills restricting cities' authority over their own employees. There was even a bill limiting the power of cities to use traffic-control radar. In the words of Sam Mamet, of the Colorado Municipal League, "One week we have legislators pretending to be planning directors; the next week they're pretending to be police chiefs. I have no idea what local control means anymore."

At times, Colorado's legislative leadership has been startlingly candid about its power grab. "We are real good as legislators at picking or choosing our mandates," admitted House Majority Leader Doug Dean. "Sometimes we'll trample all over local control if it suits our objectives."

It's clear enough why the pace of the power grab picked up this year. For years, Colorado had had Demo-

cratic governors who generally sympathized with local regulation, especially on guns and environmental issues, and vetoed or threatened to veto any efforts by the legislature to end-run local control. This year, with Bill Owens taking office as the first Republican governor in almost a quarter-century, that obstacle appeared to be eliminated.

The power grab hasn't been entirely successful. Owens vetoed one of the gun preemption bills in the wake of Littleton, and two others were withdrawn. A compromise was reached on property rights, and the personnel preemption was defeated. Still, there's a feeling among Colorado localities that they are under siege, mostly from legislators who have long complained about the tyranny of Washington. "Local control," Mamet says wearily, "now seems to mean controlling the locals."

The assault on local rights has spread to the Pacific Northwest as well. In Oregon a few weeks ago, the House and Senate both passed legislation rewriting housing policy in the city of Portland. That city has an ordinance requiring developers of low-income housing to offer their property to the city if they desire to leave the low-income field. They can decline the city's offer, but then they have to pay a fine of $30,000 for every unit they shut down.

Even those sympathetic to the public housing

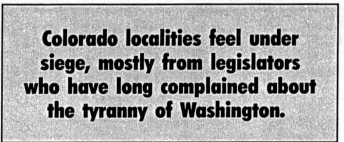

Colorado localities feel under siege, mostly from legislators who have long complained about the tyranny of Washington.

cause admit this ordinance is a little heavy-handed, but what the legislature did was even more heavy-handed. Its language would simply void the ordinance. "This is state government sticking its nose into an issue it has no business sticking its nose into," said one state senator who voted against the preemption. But it cleared both chambers overwhelmingly, forcing Governor John Kitzhaber either to veto it (and risk losing an override vote), sign it against his own better judgment, or find some way to force a compromise. Finally, the two sides did get together and made a deal, much to the governor's relief.

IF YOU ARE even a moderately cynical person, you may find yourself at this point asking a much broader question. Is there anybody in politics who *really* believes in states' rights—believes in it, that is, as a guiding principle, independent of what the issue of the moment happens to be? It is a very good question.

John C. Calhoun and the South Carolina nullifiers of the 1830s wrote more eloquently about states' rights than anybody in American history. They weren't doing it out of concern for the federal system—they were protecting slavery. States' rights served them as a means to an end, just as it later served the segregationists of the 1950s. The bottom line is that people compose lofty treatises on states' rights when the state they live in is getting pushed around. The outcome is more important than the principle.

One might say the same thing about devolution in general. Even those who argue most passionately in its favor usually have a deeper purpose they wish to accomplish. No doubt Ronald Reagan was being sincere in the 1980s when he urged that as many governmental functions as possible be pushed down to lower levels, where government is closest to the people. But what Reagan really wanted was for government to stop doing things, period—turn them over to the private sector. Dismantling federal bureaucracy was an instrument, not a goal.

While Reagan was preaching devolutionist principles in Washington, his favorite world leader, Margaret Thatcher, was finding ways to ignore them. Nobody was more forceful than Thatcher in denouncing the rigidity and stagnation of the British national state, and the injustice of its efforts to tyrannize innocent communities around the United Kingdom. But when militant leftists took over the Greater London Council, Thatcher knew exactly what to do. She shut the council down, and began making local decisions from Downing Street. When it came to devolution, she had all the ideological consistency of an Arizona state senator.

It is the way things have traditionally worked, and still do. Republicans swept to majority control of Congress in 1994 on a New Federalist platform that admitted Washington didn't have all the answers, and renewed Reagan's vow to return power and authority to the states. Three years later, scarcely any of the items on the agenda had been enacted, but Congress did take one bold step in the field of fiscal policy: It passed a law forbidding states to tax the transactions of the Internet industry for the next three years. Sometimes you just have to put theory aside and help the affluent in their hour of need.

In short, the more you think about the history of devolution and states' rights, the less surprised you should be about the antics in places such as Arizona and Colorado in 1999. They are behaving the way officeholders in all federal systems have behaved from time immemorial.

There's a word for this kind of thing, though. The word is hypocrisy. It doesn't hurt to bring it up every now and then.

Flunking local districts

Little Johnny still can't read—and states are demanding answers. When local school systems can't make the grade, the states are stepping in and taking over.

BY LEEANN TRACY

LeeAnn Tracy is a regional coordinator with CSG's States Information Center, Lexington.

After months of conflict and hostile debate, the Michigan Legislature in March agreed to turn over the Detroit public school system to the mayor's office. Mayor Dennis Archer quickly installed a new Board of Education on March 31 to take charge from the popularly elected board. Gov. John Engler first proposed the plan more than two years ago. The Legislature finally acted in the wake of continuing performance problems with the city's schools. In spite of a $1.5 billion school-renovation bond approved by voters in 1994, the city still only graduates about 30 percent of its students on time (compared to the state average of 76 percent). High dropout rates, crumbling facilities and board politics share the blame for poor student performance.

Detroit is not the only big city school system under fire. California is threatening a state takeover of the Oakland school system. The district's fourth graders ranked 49th on the 1998 National Assessment of Educational Progress. Even more troublesome, the majority of the students graduating can't read at a functional level. In response, Oakland Mayor Jerry Brown wants the state to give him control over the city's schools. In a recent interview, state Sen. Don Perata sponsor of the legislation, admitted, "Our schools continue to rank among the worst in the country and state. The district has not only refused to improve, it has downplayed and defended failure."

Taking the reigns

State or city takeovers such as the one in Detroit and the one proposed in Oakland are hardly unique. Currently, 23 states have enacted some form of takeover or intervention laws and at least nine other states have moved to take over poorly performing school systems. As education issues have been increasingly at

ishment system that targets accreditation. Delaware also subjects the system to local scrutiny if performance begins to flag. "This is a high stakes test," says Delaware Secretary of Education Iris T. Metts. "Now it carries a lot more weight to it, which is why you want to get the opinion of others."

Delaware leaves control of the schools with the local district but offers them the flexibility to recommend change in governance. Delaware's recent education reform also included an accountability measure that required the schools to reduce class size to receive funding for a "teaching unit" and more flexibility in using those funds. Metts, quoted in the summer edition of the CSG Eastern Regional Conference's *Nor'Easter*, maintained that "the next piece of the puzzle . . . is accountability— holding schools, school districts, teachers, parents and students themselves accountable for the success of Delaware's students."

Several other states, including Michigan, have assumed control of the failing school systems. "The Detroit board has a 20-year history of

the top of lawmakers' agendas, accountability has become a major concern. And while control of public schools has traditionally been given to local school boards, many state and local officials are finding that a takeover or even the threat of one may be their trump card.

According to The Education Commission of the States, the 23 states all use a series of "phased-in" actions that begin by warning the districts that are in trouble. Although the warnings usually mean extra resources or help from the state for the flagged district, this isn't always the case.

Making the grade

Education accountability is a two-fold process. First, states must establish academic standards students must meet. Once a state determines

its performance indicators, it uses them to measure the school's performance. According to the Education Commission of the States, there are four primary categories states use to create performance criteria: (1) student, including assessment scores, dropout rate and truancy; (2) professional staff measuring attendance, experience, and salary levels; (3) program—curriculum, climate, and parental involvement; and (4) expenditures and use of resources. Once the standards are in place, it's up to the school board to make sure schools meet them.

For some states, the problem occurs when a school district can't meet the performance measures. How do you handle a school district that consistently under performs? Some states, such as Delaware, devise a multilevel reward and pun-

Recent state takeovers of local districts

Connecticut, Hartford—1997
Illinois, East St. Louis—1994
Illinois, Chicago—1995
Kentucky, Pike County—1988
Kentucky, Letcher County—1994
Kentucky, Floyd County—1998
Maryland, Baltimore—1997
Massachusetts, Chelsea—1988
Massachusetts, Boston—1989, 1991
Massachusetts, Lawrence—1998
New Jersey, Jersey City—1989
New Jersey, Paterson—1991
Ohio, Cleveland—1995
Texas, Wilmer-Hutchins—1996
West Virginia, Logan County—1992
West Virginia, Mingo County—1998

Source: The Education Commission of the States

Performance indicators

There are some similarities in measurement criteria across the states. According to the Education Commission of the States, there are seven indicators that are used by at least 16 states.

- **Assessment scores** (41 states): AK, AL, AR, AZ, CA, CO, CT, DE, FL, GA, HI, ID, IL, IN, KS, KY, LA, MA, ME, MI, MO, NC, ND, NH, NJ, NM, NY, NV, OH, OK, OR, PA, RI, SC, TN, TX, UT, VA, VT, WA, WI

- **Dropout rate** (33 states): AK, AL, AR, AZ, CA, CT, FL, GA, ID, IL, KS, KY, LA, MA, MD, ME, MO, NH , NJ, NM, NV, OH, OK, OR, PA, SC, TN, TX, UT, VA, VT, WA, WI

- **Student attendance** (29 states): AK, AL, AR, CT, DE, IL, IN, KS, KY, LA, MA, MD, ME, MO, NC, ND, NH, NJ, NV, OH, OK, RI, TN, TX, UT, VA, VT, WA, WI

- **Expenditures and use of resources**—includes per-pupil expenditure (27 states): AR, CA, CT, DE, GA, HI, ID, IL, KS, LA, MA, MO, NC, ND, NH, NJ, NM, NY, NV, OH, OR, TX, UT, VT, WA, WI, WV

- **Graduation rate** (18 states): AK, AL, AZ, GA, IL, IN, KS, LA, ND, NH, NJ, NY, OH, OK, OR, TX, WA, WI

- **Student behavior**—includes discipline, truancy, expulsion, and/or suspension (17 states): AR, CA, DE, FL, ID, IN, KS, LA, MA, ME, NH, NV, OH, OK, RI, WA, WI

- **Transition** (16 states): AL, AR, AZ, CA, CT, GA, IN, KY, MO, ND, NJ, NM, NY, OK, WI, WV

failure," says Michigan Senate Majority Leader Dan DeGrow. "Clearly an overwhelming majority of people, both in the city of Detroit and the state, feel that it was time for a change."

In the driver's seat

Taking over a local school system is not without risks. Critics point out that replacing popularly elected school board members with appointed officials can hurt the process. While the Legislature debated the Detroit intervention, Michigan Rep. Keith Stallworth, who was opposed to the bill, pondered whether a governor should have the power to overturn a local election. "Many of the [former Detroit] school board members were elected in November. This bill was specifically designed to legislate some elected officials out of office .... This is a way to get rid of them."

There often is local opposition to takeover measures. School officials in neighboring Detroit school systems were strongly opposed to the takeover. A takeover in Detroit "will undermine local school boards, the very means through which the community expresses itself with respect to our elementary and secondary schools and students," the Oakland County, Mich., school board wrote.

Other districts were more blunt in their concerns over the intervention. "It wouldn't take much to make a small change to existing legislation and make it apply to other places," said Tony Derezenski, director of government relations for the Michigan Association of School Boards. "If Detroit can't stop this, what's to prevent it from happening in some smaller place?"

There are also questions of the effectiveness of the takeovers—they seem to be a mixed bag. Critics point to the Jersey City, N.J., school district, which, despite being taken over by the state Board of Education in 1989, still hasn't achieved the state standards in several areas, including assessment scores. Yet other states, such as Kentucky, which has an active history of intervention, claim improvements in student performance from the top down. Cleaning out the occasional corruption in Kentucky school boards, establishing clearer lines of organization and designing better management procedures were the initial goals of the state Legislature.

Looking ahead

What is the best way to hold school systems accountable? There doesn't seem to be any one answer to the problem. For states that prefer to use rewards rather than punitive measures, what happens when the rewards can't correct the problem? For states that assume control of local school systems, how long does the state want to maintain them? At what point is local ownership developed again?

That there have been fewer than 20 takeovers nationwide by only nine states in the last two decades proves that officials aren't eager to step in and assume control. There is the feeling that often the state is too far removed from the local societal problems, such as poverty or cultural indifference to education, to best address the problems. But that isn't to say that some states aren't willing to take a chance to fix a failure.

Unit Selections

Key Points to Consider

❖ If you were the head of an interest group, would you use different techniques in trying to influence a state government than in trying to influence a local government? What would the differences be?

❖ How do you think running for office in a small town differs from running for a seat in a state legislature, or running to be a member of Congress?

❖ Do you think people are more or less knowledgeable when they vote in state and local elections than in national elections? Why?

❖ Which level of government seems most responsive to citizens—national, state, or local? Why?

❖ Do you think citizens should be allowed to participate in policy making through the initiative and referenda processes? Why or why not? What do you think about allowing citizens to recall officials during their term in office?

DUSHKIN ONLINE Links   www.dushkin.com/online/

10. **Council for Ethics in Legislative Advocacy**
    http://www.lobbyistdirectory.com/indxcela.htm
11. **Direct Democracy Centerz**
    http://www.primenet.com/~conduit/
12. **PEJ Local TV News Project**
    http://www.journalism.org/LocalTV.htm
13. **U.S. Federalism Web Site**
    http://www.min.net/~kala/fed/edemoc.htm

These sites are annotated on pages 4 and 5.

The American political system is typically classified as a representative democracy. Top officials are elected by the people and, as a result, government is supposed to be responsive and accountable to citizens. Both the theory and practice of representative democracy are of interest to students of American politics. Political scientists study various processes that seem essential to the functioning of representative democracy: political parties, interest groups, election laws, campaign techniques, and so forth.

Attention is not limited to the national government; state and local governments are also examined to assess their responsiveness and accountability.

State and local governments operate under somewhat different institutional arrangements and circumstances than the national government. In many states and localities, voters can participate directly in the policy process through mechanisms known as *initiative* and *referendum*. In addition, some state and local voters can participate in removing elected officials from office by a procedure called *recall*. In many localities in the New England states, an open meeting of all local citizens, called a town meeting, functions as the local government legislature. These mechanisms provide additional avenues for citizens trying to influence state and local governments.

Generally speaking, party organization is strongest at the local level and weakest at the national level. Party "machines" are a well-known feature of the local political landscape in the United States, and colorful and powerful "bosses" have left their mark on local political history. While the heyday of bosses and machines is past, noteworthy examples of contemporary political machines still exist.

National elections, especially for the presidency, are usually contested vigorously by the two major parties and, over the long haul, the two parties tend to be reasonably competitive. This is less true in states and localities, because voters in some states and many localities are decidedly oriented toward one party or the other. Thus, in some states and localities, closer and more significant competition can occur within the nominating process of the dominant party than between the two parties in general elections.

Party labels do not appear on the ballot in many localities, and this may or may not affect the way elections are conducted. In "nonpartisan" elections, candidates of different parties may, in fact, openly oppose one another just as they do when party labels appear on the ballot. Another possibility is that parties field opposing candidates in a less than open fashion. As yet another alternative, elective offices may actually be contested without parties or the political party affiliations of candidates playing any part. One cannot assume that formally nonpartisan elections are accompanied by genuine nonpartisanship; nor can one assume that they are not.

One last feature of state and local political processes deserves mention here. While members of the Senate and House of Representatives in Washington, D.C., hold well-paid, prestigious positions, their state and local counterparts often do not. Many state legislators are only part-time politicians who earn the bulk of their livelihoods from other sources. This is also true of most general-purpose local government officials. In addition, most local school board members are unpaid, even though many devote long hours to their duties. That so many elected state and local officeholders do not get their primary incomes from their positions in government may well affect the way they respond to constituents. After all, while they and their families typically live in the community that they are representing, their livelihoods do not depend on being reelected. Selections in the first section of this unit focus on campaigns and elections. The second section covers the roles of interest groups, new technology, and news media in state and local politics. The third section treats referenda, initiatives, and recalls—three procedures that give voters in many states and localities a direct role in determining policies and overseeing the performances of elected officials during their terms in office.

REFORM GETS ROLLING

CAMPAIGN FINANCE AT THE GRASS ROOTS

BY ROBERT DREYFUSS

Last November, voters in Massachusetts and Arizona added the latest tiles in a growing national mosaic of state-based campaign finance reform efforts. It all began in 1996, when Maine voters passed a sweeping reform plan aimed at replacing special interest money with a system of voluntary public financing for state elections. In 1997, defying the conventional wisdom that politicians will never vote to replace the system of campaign contributions that elected them in the first place, the Vermont legislature passed a similar measure. Then in November 1998, two-thirds of Massachusetts voters opted for radical surgery rather than tinkering to cure their money-in-politics ills, putting into place a system modeled on the so-called "Clean Money" reform adopted by their New England neighbors. But the most consequential vote may have come the same day out West, when a bare majority of voters in the conservative but quirky state of Arizona proved that publicly financed elections were not merely the preserve of the liberal Northeast.

A pattern is emerging.

Quietly, with little fanfare and even less attention from the national media, a citizens' movement is making itself felt. With Congress stalling on ever more watered-down reforms of federal campaign laws, activists—a disparate coalition of labor unions, environmental groups, good-government reformers, women's and seniors' groups, and civil rights organizations—are targeting a dozen more states for Clean Money campaigns in 2000. They include a cluster of northwestern states—from Oregon to Washington to Idaho—along with Missouri, North Carolina, Wisconsin, and Michigan. Slowly but surely the

Reprinted with permission from *The American Prospect*, July/August 1999, pp. 39-43. © 1999 by The American Prospect, P.O. Box 383080, Cambridge, MA 02138. All rights reserved.

movement is gathering momentum from its victories. "After the votes in Massachusetts and Arizona last year, activists from five different states called and said, 'Can we do it here?'" says Ellen Miller, executive director of Public Campaign, the Washington, D.C.–based organization spearheading the national effort.

> **W**ith little fanfare, a citizens' movement is making itself felt. Activists are targeting a dozen states for Clean Money campaigns in 2000.

Along with Public Campaign, there is also a growing political infrastructure of foundations and funders, large and small, coming together to sustain the effort. In Montana, the National Institute on Money in State Politics is busily collecting campaign contribution data from state after state and transforming it into information that can be used by activists to illustrate the corrosive impact of money in state political races. Four regional organizations—based, respectively, in North Carolina, Wisconsin, Oregon, and Connecticut—provide guidance, training, and talent for the state-by-state efforts. National organizations, including the AFL-CIO and the League of Women Voters, have also lined up in support. Polls consistently show support for public financing of campaigns in the range of 60 to 80 percent.

But the ultimate fate of all these efforts remains uncertain. Less than half of the states allow the sort of ballot initiatives that succeeded in Massachusetts, Maine, and Arizona, and in some—such as Michigan and, of course, California—a campaign would involve enormous expenditures for media and public education. At the same time, despite the success in Vermont, an effort to pass radical campaign reform laws through state legislatures could easily get stuck in the kind of trench warfare that characterized the fight in Congress for a decade. There

are also serious questions over whether victories won in the political arena can be sustained in the courts, whether state legislatures will be able to tinker with or unravel new campaign finance regimes, and even whether continued funding can be assured for government-run campaign war chests. And even if these efforts are successful, none of the state-based reforms affect federal elections, where many of the most important decisions of national policy are made. Ultimately, those involved in the work say that in addition to creating a self-sustaining movement in the states, the goal is to use the leverage from state victories to get Congress unstuck. "In the end," says Miller, "we've got to bring it back to Washington."

VOLUNTEERS VS. MONEY MEN

So far, only a few dozen members of the House and a handful of senators are on record supporting bills that would establish public financing for congressional elections. But for different reasons, the victories in Massachusetts and Arizona last year have provided crucial evidence that the earlier actions in Maine and Vermont were not flukes.

The Massachusetts story shows that even in a fairly large state—which has a population three times the size of Maine's and Vermont's combined—it is possible to build and finance an organization that can push a public financing initiative over the top. In Massachusetts, a four-year organizing effort culminated in a stunning victory: 67 percent of the state's voters endorsed Question 2, the Massachusetts Clean Elections Law, sponsored by Mass Voters for Clean Elections (MVCE).

The measure, which takes effect with the 2002 state elections, provides state funds to candidates for the legislature, governor, and other statewide offices who voluntarily agree to fixed spending limits for their races. At the lowest end, a candidate for state representative would receive $24,000 in public funds, after first collecting a minimum of 200 contributions (ranging from $5 to $100) from registered voters in his or her district and agreeing not to spend more than $30,000 on the race. At the high end, a candidate for governor would have to raise 6,000 contributions of $5 to $100 and agree not to spend more than $3 million in order to become eligible for $2,550,000 in public funds. Other provisions of the law bar state parties from accepting unlimited amounts of "soft money" from national parties and provide additional matching funds for candidates whose

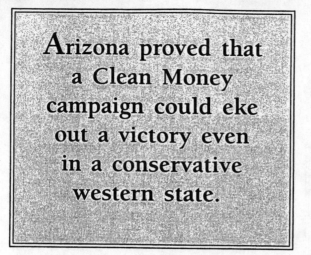

Arizona proved that a Clean Money campaign could eke out a victory even in a conservative western state.

opponents opt out of the system and spend money in excess of the specified spending limit.

More than 6,200 volunteers took part in the organizing effort on behalf of Question 2 in Massachusetts over the course of two separate signature-gathering drives and a high-energy election campaign; more than 65,000 petitions were signed on a single day, October 25, 1997, with a total of 130,000 collected by the December 1997 deadline. Backing the drive were the entire state congressional delegation, many state legislators, an advisory board of more than 60 business, political, and religious leaders and prominent citizens, and a broad coalition that included Common Cause, the League of Women Voters, the AFL-CIO, the American Association of Retired Persons (AARP), the Sierra Club, and a wide range of community groups.

In all, says David Donnelly, the veteran organizer who served as MVCE's campaign manager, the drive raised $1.2 million, which paid for a $475,000 television advertising blitz, $140,000 to collect signatures, and a staff of 17 full- and part-time workers. About half of the funds came from a handful of large ($100,000 or more) donors, including Public Campaign, with the rest coming from 2,000 individuals who gave in the $100 range and 5,000 more who contributed $35 or less. Though not lavishly funded, the campaign was professionally organized, with a hard core of 400 activists who, in turn, put together thousands of volunteers, a speakers bureau, a targeted direct mail campaign, and an aggressive presence at state and local events, including a ten-day bus tour that wheeled through dozens of towns in early October.

The organizers in Massachusetts took care early on to neutralize two potential sources of opposition: the American Civil Liberties Union (ACLU), which often opposes campaign finance reforms on First Amendment grounds, and the

business community. Organizers cultivated a relationship with the ACLU, sharing early drafts of the proposal and modifying the ballot measure—dropping, for instance, a provision that would have added matching funds to combat independent expenditures against a candidate who had opted into the system. Eventually, the ACLU voted to remain neutral. The Chamber of Commerce, too, decided to stay out of the fight, in part because the president of the Greater Boston chamber was a former politician who had been on record supporting partial public financing, and in part because the organizers succeeding in winning significant business support.

ACE'S HIGH

In Arizona, meanwhile, the victory of Proposition 200 showed that the Clean Money campaign could eke out a 51 to 49 percent victory in a conservative western state as well.

Getting off the ground in July 1997, the drive in Arizona from the start relied less on volunteers and grassroots organizers that it did on paid staff, paid signature-gatherers, and paid media. Funded largely from out of state—by foundations and by Public Campaign, which kicked in about $350,000, according to Miller—Arizonans for Clean Elections (ACE) spent $920,000 with a coalition roughly the same as the one in Massachusetts. Unlike in the Bay State, however, Arizona organizers faced determined opponents and negative editorials from leading newspapers, such as the *Arizona Republic*. "We had significant opposition," says Kaia Lenhart, now political director for Public Campaign, who ran the Arizona campaign in 1998. "We did not have the political establishment behind us. We had most of the elected officials campaigning against us. And we had hostile media." A month before the vote, an *Arizona Republic* poll showed Proposition 200 ahead 60 to 25, says Lenhart. But a month of anti-Proposition 200 work by a group called Citizens Against Dangerous Initiatives and its "Not With the People's Money" campaign, which bought significant radio advertising, brought the numbers down sharply, she says, by warning that Proposition 200 would encourage extremist candidates and would raise taxes.

In the end—with the help of volunteers organized by the League of Women Voters, in particular, along with students, Sierra Club members, and organizers from the Latino community—ACE managed a narrow win, turning out 200 volunteers on election day in Phoenix, Flagstaff, and Tucson. "We didn't have years to prepare in Arizona," says Lenhart. "We put this together in a fairly short time. And what it shows is that whether it's a liberal or conservative state, voters, given the chance to pass campaign finance reform, will."

THE DATA SHACK

Public Campaign, whose budget last year was $2.6 million plus a $600,000 Public Campaign Action Fund, hopes to increase its total spending for 1999 to around $4 million, two-thirds of which would go directly into state efforts. Meanwhile, coordinating the work of perhaps two dozen foundations and individual donors is the Piper Fund, which last year channeled about $1.8 million in grants to 53 organizations in 38 states working on campaign finance reform. Of that, about $700,000 went to support the work of four regional organizations that help make up the central nervous system of the emerging Clean Money organism—Northeast Action, Democracy South, the Western States Center, and the Midwest States Center. Another $300,000 went to the Montana-based National Institute on Money in State Politics, an informational clearinghouse often referred to as "the Data Shack."

"We're going like gangbusters," says Samantha Sanchez, who runs the Data Shack in Helena, Montana. From just a handful of states a few years ago, the Data Shack last year pulled in campaign contribution data from 40 states, often assembling the numbers from boxes of papers filed with state offices. State campaign records, laws, and disclosure rules are a patchwork of good, bad, and indifferent across the country, and in many states it has been difficult if not impossible for campaign reformers to make effective use of the numbers to prove their point about campaign finance abuses. But that may be changing: in Massachusetts, for instance, a team of 20 part-time data-gatherers is sorting through 70,000 records, at something like 15 cents per record. "We're doing the input from the last election," says Sanchez. "I've got data input people sitting at terminals putting this stuff into electronic databases." In Missouri, she says there are more than 100,000 records to go through; in Michigan, 150,000. Since 1996, the Data Shack's budget has quadrupled to about $800,000 in 1999.

Once it's digitized and sorted this data becomes an extremely potent tool in the hands of reformers. Available for electronic searches by reporters, academic researchers, and activists, the data can be sorted by politician, industry, and donor—making it much easier for the public to learn about how patterns of giving influence decisions on public policy. Margaret Gage, the Piper Fund's

director, says that activists in Ohio, Georgia, New Mexico, Massachusetts, and elsewhere are using the numbers to demonstrate the role of money in politics. "And the public gets it," she says.

BATTLEGROUND 2000

At this stage it's unclear exactly which states will be battlegrounds in 2000, but the states that have active coalitions in place include both those focusing on ballot initiatives and those coordinating lobbying efforts aimed at legislative action. One state likely to have a public financing measure on its ballot next year is Oregon, where organizers say they are making plans to raise $1.5 million and gather about 80,000 signatures by July 2000. Another is Missouri, where plans are underway for a petition drive this summer to gather up to 125,000 signatures to qualify for ballot status. Last year, after having already collected 120,000 petitions and raised about $500,000, Missouri organizers abruptly called off plans to make a run in 1998. "It was a very difficult decision," says Public Campaign's Lenhart, who was working in Missouri last year. "Raising money on this issue has been much more difficult than we expected." Ben Senturia, an organizer with the Missouri Alliance for Campaign Reform, says that the coalition just wasn't ready, especially since they expected stiff opposition from the Missouri Chamber of Commerce and the Associated Industries of Missouri. "It was clear that we needed to do some serious voter education," he says, "and to do that we needed either more time or more money." More than 45 organizations—including the AFL-CIO, AARP, League of Women Voters, Common Cause, the Reform Party and United We Stand America, various unions, environmental groups, farm groups, clergy, disability rights groups, and more—led by a steering committee called Missouri Voters for Clean Elections, are currently making plans to raise $1.5 million and build a network of grassroots volunteers.

Meanwhile, in North Carolina, with the help of Democracy South and Public Campaign, organizers are preparing for a multi-year campaign to win legislation modeled on the Clean Money reform plan, led by a coalition called North Carolina Voters for Clean Elections. Armed with polls showing that 66 percent of the state's voters support the measure, the coalition has hired a paid lobbyist and is organizing grassroots support, with plans to spend $500,000 a year for at least the next three years. Utilizing contribution data from the Data Shack, organizers plan to show how industries—including pig farmers, nursing home operators, and transportation interests—are using money to rig the system. "It's not a first tier issue for most people," says Peter MacDowell of Democracy South. "It's an issue that takes a little education." Much of that work, he says, will take place "below the radar," through house meetings and meetings with constituency groups, before moving to paid television and radio spots. "We realize that three-quarters of the effort has to be grassroots," he says.

In one sense, it's remarkable that in a single state like North Carolina organizers could envision spending half a million dollars a year on campaign finance reform. Yet the need to raise large sums of money to support campaign finance reform is more than a small irony tucked away in the effort to clean up our nation's politics. It's also a constant source of worry. Nationally, the movement is dependent, perhaps overly so, on foundations and other funders whose priorities often shift suddenly. The Schumann Foundation, long a backer of money-in-politics reform, has largely gotten out of it, leaving the field to others, like financier George Soros's foundations—and Soros, involved in everything from Eastern Europe to marijuana law reform, recently cut back significantly on his support for Public Campaign. "The financing for money-in-politics work has always been uncertain," says Miller, who adds that Public Campaign has recently hired a pair of fundraising experts to help state-based coalitions learn how to raise money, create lists, write pro-

posals, do direct mail, and organize house-party fundraising events.

Besides fundraising, organizers of the public financing drive are also confronting the challenges posed by special interest groups that thrive under the current system and by free speech groups like the ACLU. Legal challenges to Maine's 1996 law have already been filed by Maine Right to Life, and the ACLU is expected to mount a similar challenge. A similar legal challenge has been filed against Arizona's Proposition 200. In Massachusetts, the coalition is engaged in a legislative push to ensure that the state appropriates the necessary funds—about $13 million a year—to create the kitty of public money that would be made available to candidates in 2002. "What we've learned is that winning these victories is just the first step," says the Piper Fund's Meg Gage. "We still have to protect them from being whittled away." She estimates that Massachusetts alone will need $400,000 for its legislative work this year. "We're working with Maine, Vermont, and Massachusetts to implement these laws, which is a huge and very important task," adds Marc Caplan, director of Northeast Action. "If we can't get these laws to work, then we've won the battle and lost the war."

Robert Dreyfuss is a freelance writer based in Alexandria, Virginia, specializing in politics and national security issues.

How to Get Rid Of Excellent Public Officials

For some local governments, term limits are a cure worse than the disease.

BY CHARLES MAHTESIAN

The 3,600 citizens of Oneida County, Idaho, can count themselves fortunate to have the services of Stevin Brooks as public prosecutor. That's not just because of his legal talents—it's because he's the only lawyer in the county. If he hadn't agreed to take the job, it's not clear what they would have done.

Nor is it clear what will happen after he is gone. Given the heavy caseload and the $25,000 salary, Brooks isn't sure he'll run for reelection. But even if he does, it will only delay the inevitable. After two terms in office, he will be ineligible to continue serving—as will hundreds of other public officials in the state.

Dan Anderson, for example, is chief assessor of Nez Perce County. It's not what most people would consider a plum job, since it involves regular harassment from local homeowners who don't like their property assessments or didn't get their auto licenses on time. But Anderson likes the work, and the voters seem to like him. Or at any rate, there is no line of ambitious newcomers eager to succeed him. All three times his name has been on the ballot for county assessor, he has run unopposed.

Nevertheless, like Stevin Brooks, Anderson is making plans to leave public office—not because he wants to, or because he expects to become less popular, but because of a 1994 ballot measure limiting the terms of all elected officeholders, local as well as state. As of 2003, all county assessors, prosecutors, coroners, sheriffs, treasurers, mayors, school board trustees, highway dis-

trict members, cemetery board members and virtually every other public servant in Idaho will be prevented from seeking reelection if they have served eight years or more during the previous 15 years. County commissioners have it even worse. They are banned from the ballot if they have served six years or more during the previous 11, meaning some will be ousted beginning in 2001.

Idaho's term limit fever may be a little extreme, but it is far from unique. Since 1994, a watershed year for the term limits movement, the idea of forcing an end to elective careers has taken off not only in state government but in local government as well. More than 200 cities and towns in Colorado now restrict the number of years any official can hold local office. In Michigan, close to 30 cities limit city council terms. In Orange County, California, seven cities placed term limits on the ballot in 1996, and all seven passed them with 69 percent of the vote or more. All told, there are now 15 term-limited cities in Orange County alone.

Over the next decade or so, in every region of the country, thousands of local officials—from the highest offices to the lowest—will be slated for removal, some barred for life from ever holding the same office again.

For a considerable number of voters, this will be a reason to rejoice. But in places like Oneida and Nez Perce counties, where the candidate pool is not exactly overflowing, term limits are a cause for alarm, not just to elected officials such as Dan Anderson, who

stand to lose their jobs as a consequence, but to the communities faced with the task of replacing them. "What we did here," says Anderson, "was like that old Chinese saying about trying to swat a fly on your forehead with an ax."

The citizens of Idaho, it must be said, have spent a good bit of time and a considerable amount of tax money arguing over what exactly voters were trying to say when they approved the state's all-encompassing term limit initiative.

It's largely agreed by now that the main targets of the law were members of Congress. That purpose, however, was invalidated in 1995 by a decision of the U.S. Supreme Court. Still, the rest of the law was left untouched by the court, and it clearly includes state and local officeholders under its sweeping provisions. Term limit critics insist that this was mostly inadvertent, that voters had no idea the law extended all the way down to City Hall. "If I had a nickel for everybody who said, 'I didn't realize it would affect you,'" says Dan Anderson, "I could retire right now."

To Anderson and others like him caught in the term limit web, there is an obvious solution: ask the voters whether they really want all of their public servants forced out of office. And this fall, that will be attempted. The November election ballot in Idaho will include a four-line advisory proposition decoupling state and local term limits from the now-invalid congressional term limit law.

Reprinted with permission from *Governing* magazine, July 1998, pp. 25-26, 28, 30. © 1998 by Congressional Quarterly, Inc.

The measure on the ballot would not automatically repeal anything, but in the view of its supporters, it would send a message to the 1999 legislature to enact some form of "local option" clause, allowing voters in places such as Oneida County and Nez Perce County to exempt their local governments if they so choose. It's likely that some jurisdictions would exercise the option. Nine

Even Citizens for Federal Term Limits now recognizes that the one-size-fits-all statewide approach may have gone too far. Along with the Idaho Association of Counties, the organization crafted a bill to allow individual counties to opt out. "You can make a good argument for exempting the sheriff or especially the prosecutor," says state Representative Jeff Alltus, a staunch

expected to succeed them in running for the top county law enforcement slot, but term limits may alter that tradition.

As long as the assistants remain assistants, they do not have to worry about term limits, and in many instances, they are paid more than their elected bosses. So in order to ascend to the top slot, an ambitious assistant would be forced to take a pay cut and to give up a secure permanent position for one that must be vacated after two terms. That's hardly an encouragement to run.

'Who's going to want a job like county assessor? What kind of people are you going to get?'

Idaho counties, for example, voted against the term limit measure in 1994, but are currently stuck with it for their local governments anyway.

At the moment, though, prospects for passage of the advisory measure do not look very good. One reason is that it would challenge term limits for state legislators as well as local officials, and the public sentiment for doing that is not nearly as strong. "The state legislators are hiding behind the local officeholders in an attempt to rid themselves of their own term limits," says Stacie Rumenap, executive director of Idaho's Citizens for Federal Term Limits. "They have from now until 2002 to get them repealed, and they'll do anything they can." The current consensus in Idaho is that including state as well as local government in the decoupling measure will probably guarantee its defeat.

Whatever one may think of term limits for Idaho's state legislators, there are convincing arguments for relaxing them at the local level. A quarter of Idaho's counties don't even have full-time officeholders, let alone careerists. School board members perform their work without pay. For jobs such as prosecutor and assessor, incumbents often run unopposed, not because of the difficulty of defeating them but because no one else is interested in the job. "There are lots of uncontested races, particularly in those road districts, library districts and cemetery boards," says Senate Minority Leader Bruce Sweeney, who is retiring this year, "That indicates how tough it is even to find people who want the job."

Local leaders in much of the state say the same thing. "Who's going to want a job like county assessor?" asks Nez Perce County Commissioner J.R. Van Tassel. "What kind of people are you going to get? A real estate agent who couldn't cut it? Think about the demographics. You'll mostly get people who are retiring. . . . If you do it on a county opt-out basis, you could go to the voters and say, 'Hey, we're going to lose Betty.' "

term limits advocate who nevertheless supports local option. "If you term-limit your best guy out, he'll just go out on the defense side. Thus you could make the argument that criminals will get off."

Indeed, it's hard to make the case that many Idaho officials serving in any capacity are dangerously entrenched. In the Nez Perce County seat of Lewiston, for example, the past two decades have seen numerous recall efforts directed at city council members, including one that ousted five of the council's seven members in one shot. Last year, one councilman retired, and another incumbent was defeated along with the mayor. A fourth member of the council retired this past May. At the county level, the story has been much the same. In the last election, one of two Nez Perce commissioners up for a new term was defeated. This year, the county treasurer resigned to spend more time with her family.

Of course, frequent turnover in one city or county doesn't constitute an argument against local term limits. But it does highlight some misconceptions about the power of incumbency at the local level, and it serves as a reminder of the turnover incentives that are built into public service, particularly in rural communities or small cities such as Lewiston.

Certainly no one serves on the Lewiston city council for the money. In a town of 28,000, the job takes up too many hours to be considered part-time and, at $350 per month, it pays too little to be considered full-time. "When I was on the council," says John Taylor, who runs a Lewiston-based insurance company, "I was putting in at least 25 hours per week. Well, you still have to work at your business, so that's an incentive to leave or a term limit in itself."

Similar sentiments are beginning to circulate in Colorado, another state that caught term limit fever in 1994. There, most sheriffs will have to turn in their badges in 2002. Typically, their assistants might be

A growing number of cities and towns in Colorado have come to a similar conclusion. Unlike Idaho, Colorado's term limit law provides an opt-out mechanism for those places that choose to put it on the ballot. Already, 61 cities and towns have voted on an opt-out clause, and 35 have passed it, 19 of them this year alone. Five others have chosen to modify the law, staggering the order in which offices are affected or increasing the number of years before limits kick in.

Undoubtedly, some of those places held opt-out elections at the urging of incumbent officeholders who had a stake in the outcome. But others did it out of sheer necessity. It's no coincidence that all 19 of the Colorado municipalities that opted out this spring have populations of 3,000 or less. In rural Montrose County, "usually no one lasts more than two terms," says Cindy Bowen, the first commissioner ever to serve three.

The view from the big city is a little different. While Denver public officials wring their hands over what will take place in 2003, when a new mayor and an almost all-freshman city council will be sworn in, voters have shown no signs of remorse. Given the chance to opt out two years ago, they overwhelmingly rejected the idea.

Of course, you don't have to live in a city the size of Denver to believe in term limits. You don't even have to hate politicians. Back in Lewiston, former mayor and council member Delitha Kilgore insists that the officeholders who complain about term limits are being short-sighted. She herself has voluntarily retired as mayor twice, and she sees no problem in forcing others to do the same thing. "The more people you can get into local government, the better off the community is. Especially these days, now that there isn't the same spirit of civics and volunteerism that there used to be," she says. "With term limits, I don't think you'll have people running because they don't like someone or because they oppose something. You'll have people running because they support something like parks or libraries."

For all the hue and cry in Idaho, Colorado and elsewhere, the simple fact is that no one really knows what the ultimate impact of local term limits will be, and no one will know for several years. But there are a few places that started a little earlier down the term limits road, and they offer some instructive lessons.

Houston passed a term limits measure in 1991, and the effect on its city council was both swift and profound. Limited to just three two-year terms, officeholders quickly began showing a healthy concern for the prospect of forced retirement. Within a few years, several council members resigned in mid-term to pursue other offices, requiring a whole series of special elections. One of the more ambitious ladder-climbers filed her candidacy for another office on the same day she was inaugurated to the Houston city council.

From a policy perspective, the impact has been more subtle, but no less noticeable to those who watch the city's political scene. "People work on issues that are more popularized and short-term in focus," says political scientist Robert Thomas, the author of a book on Houston politics. "If you're talking about big-ticket items like a new convention center or a $250 million bond issue to improve streets, the council seems to go along with the mayor or public works people. But talk about a popularized issue like sex-oriented businesses, an issue that in dollar terms doesn't even compare, and they'll seize on it."

By the end of his own term-limited time in office last year, Houston Mayor Bob Lanier was complaining that local government—ostensibly non-partisan—had become more and more acrimonious as council members jockeyed for the partisan support they needed to leapfrog to the higher offices that are elected on a partisan basis.

For a while, it seemed that Lanier, who started out in political life as a term-limit supporter, might have the clout to overcome the obstacle. As the popular mayor neared the end of his third and final two-year term, his supporters began making noise about altering the law so that he might run again.

But they didn't want to change it themselves—one councilman testified publicly that such a move would be "political suicide."

Instead, the Houston council asked the Texas legislature to change the local limit to two four-year terms, giving Lanier at least two more years in office. Legislators, however, didn't want responsibility for modifying the limit any more than the local officials did. If Houston officeholders wanted to get rid of term limits, they argued, Houston officeholders ought to take the heat. So nothing was done, and Lanier left office on schedule, even though he would have won reelection overwhelmingly had he been allowed to run.

California's experience with local term limits dates back further, to a period before the issue became politically fashionable. As long ago as 1966, the state's first large-scale experiment was tried in the city of Santa Ana, in Orange County. Today, at least half the cities in Orange County have term limits, and local term limits have proven so popular that they have never failed at the polls.

Even after two decades, however, there remains a difference of opinion on what term limits in California have actually wrought. One study, by political scientist Mark Petracca of the University of California at Irvine, reported in 1993 that term limits had neither reduced the supply of candidate talent nor transferred power to lobbyists and appointed staff, as some had claimed. Three-quarters of Petracca's officeholding respondents said they thought term limits were indeed necessary at the local level. "If term limits were as bad and as unnecessary as opponents seem to surmise," Petracca says, "then there ought to be some tangible evidence of the damage they've wreaked."

Other scholars, however, claim that even if there isn't much evidence of damage, there is little reason to believe term limits have

accomplished anything either. In San Jose, one of the largest and earliest cities to enact a term limit law, political scientist Peter Haas studied the city council and noted a perceived decline in the council's power, as well as a musical-chairs game similar to the one that surfaced in Houston. Rather than attracting hordes of fresh-faced newcomers, Haas says, term limits in San Jose and nearby San Mateo County have merely served to recirculate many career-minded officials from office to office.

As for ridding the system of special-interest influence, Haas finds precious little support for that contention. "The cost of getting elected to city council keeps rising, regardless of term limits," says Haas. "They still have to raise money from the same kinds of moneyed interests. One could make the argument that moneyed interests are even more important now because in an open seat race, both sides have to raise money," and term limits mean many more open-seat elections.

Idaho, of course, has no city comparable in size to either Houston or San Jose—and few that even come close to reaching the size of the humblest Orange County suburb. Its cities and counties are unlikely ever to have to confront such problems as ladder-climbing officeholders or expensive campaigns for local office.

But the small-scale governments of Idaho will be facing a much more serious problem if they lose local officials for whom qualified replacements do not exist. Even those who support state and national term limits are willing to concede that that is something to worry about. By the time the voters realize it, though, they may find that it is too late. "I don't think the general public will recognize it for a while," says Lewiston's John Taylor. "We'll have to sacrifice a lot of competent officials like Dan Anderson before they recognize their folly."

MY LIFE AS A SCHOOL BOARD CANDIDATE: LESSONS LEARNED IN LOCAL POLITICS

ALLEN D. HERTZKE

Assistant Director **Allen D. Hertzke** ran for the Norman, Oklahoma school board. Although public office was not to be one of them, he found many rewards along the way. Now fully restored to academic life, he is involved in the Religion in Politics Section of the American Political Science Associ-ation, assembling twelve panels for the 1994 APSA convention.

I'm not sure when I actually began to think of running for the local school board. I do recall the thought teasing its way into my consciousness last summer. During little league baseball games, the bleacher talk turned to the schools. People were sharing experiences, comparing notes, commiserating. As a concerned parent and professor, perhaps I had something to offer.

In early December 1993 I took the plunge, filing as a candidate for the February election. In the next two months as a "participant observer" I learned a lot about the challenges and rewards of local politics. In an abbreviated form, the following are some of those lessons.

Lesson #1: THE DECISION TO RUN IS NOT A TRIVIAL THING.

There is something both exciting and daunting about walking into the election board and filing one's candidacy. I found myself thinking: Would I make a fool of myself? Where would I find the time to run a decent race? How would I get my regular work done? What would this do to family life? Would my candidacy put some friends and colleagues in an uncomfortable position? And, most importantly, what if I actually won?

Say what you will about it being "just" a school board race, becoming a candidate sparks a rather powerful chain of events. Filing for office, I had mounted a roller coaster. I lost sleep, my teaching suffered, and I missed a chapter deadline by over a month. Tired, I started taking vitamins and Ginseng. In the early days of the campaign there was arduous work to do with frustratingly little tangible result. "What have I gotten myself into?" was the feeling.

But as the campaign got rolling, as volunteers began to meet every Saturday in our house before canvassing, I also experienced the exhilaration of being the spark for something bigger than myself. I found my public voice, gained backers I respected deeply, and forged friendships with the kind of people who make a community work. What kept me going, indeed, was the realization that these fine people were going door to door for me in the middle of winter. If they could do that, I had a responsibility to do my best.

Lesson #2: IT AIN'T EASY BEING A CANDIDATE

I have worked in campaigns, written books, and lectured to four hundred students at a time. But running for the school board was one of the most intense, emotionally demanding, intellectually challenging experiences I've had.

In part this is because school board politics is intense, buffeted by deep clashing philosophies and profound equity issues. A veteran state senator explained it to me this way: "You are running for the toughest job there is, because if you mess with people's kids or their dogs you hit them where they live."

People demand a lot from prospective school board members. During the two month campaign, for example, we candidates attended six forums, answered four detailed questionnaires, shared two radio programs, met with the editorial staff of the local newspaper, and fielded numerous pointed questions over the phone from voters.

For a hotshot professor the experience in local democracy was humbling. I thought I knew the issues, but I had to go "back to school" when I got a questionnaire from a citizen's group with such fare as: What is your view of the Renzulli method of appropriate pacing? What is your understanding of a board member's liability under the Open Meetings Act? Then there was the League of Women Voters' question: What is your five-year goal for the Norman Public Schools? (*75 word limit!*). Now that requires some parsing.

Another thing I learned is that there is a profound difference between giving a lecture in a classroom and standing up in public and offering your views and vision. After my first forum with the other candidates one of my graduate students remarked, "Al, I've

Reprinted with permission from *Extensions,* Spring 1994, pp. 18–20. © 1994 by the Carl Albert Congressional Research and Studies Center, University of Oklahoma.

seen you lecture to hundreds of students, but tonight was the first time I've ever seen you nervous."

Yes, and then there was the TIME I WAFFLED. I learned just how hard politics can be one night when I appeared before the Republican Women's Club. Overconfident, I thought I was ready with tough answers on academic standards, self-esteem programs, sex education, and school-based clinics. Instead, the big issue of the night turned out to be a state constitutional question. On the basis of material I got from the "good government" types, I had told my volunteers I was in favor of the measure. But that night a speaker got up and blasted the amendment, to much whooping and cheering, giving examples of how voters elsewhere had used routine millage elections (to be eliminated by the amendment) to hold their school districts accountable. When the candidates were asked their position on the issue, the first three expressed their opposition, the fourth waffled so successfully that I thought he did too, and then it was my turn. I can only describe my answer as an *out-of-body-experience* in which part of me was watching as the other part was saying that perhaps we should defeat the measure.

That night I couldn't sleep. I thought to myself, "You gutless wonder—now what are you going to do?" I ultimately had to recant that waffling at the next forum, and I came away with a deeper understanding of why politicians act the way they do.

As the candidate, of course, I had to take full responsibility for what happened in the campaign. I'll never forget how, after a fitful night on election eve, I got a jarring phone call at 6:30 a.m.: "This is the election board and your signs are too close to the polling places. You need to remove them. So this is what being a candidate is like, pulling up yard signs during a sleet storm in the dark.

Lesson #3: LOCAL POLITICS IS REAL POLITICS

Looking back, I am struck by my own naivete. With only minimal discussions with a few close friends and without assessing the political landscape, I took the leap. I should have started much earlier, met with PTA officers and other community notables, and begun to build an organization prior to announcing. Which brings us to the lesson that school board politics is real politics. Running a credible race

for this hotly contested seat required name identification, organization, strategy, time, and money—just like any other campaign.

The cash economy, for example, has reached the school board level. Norman, Oklahoma is a city of about 80,000, and the district covered only a fifth of that. Turnout in previous elections was as small as 900 votes, so we weren't talking about a big area or population. But to run a minimally credible campaign took at least $2,000 and probably more. I spent $2,500 on brochures, a few newspaper ads, yard signs, voter lists, xeroxing, and a small bit of mailing. The winning candidate spent over $8,000 and the second-place finisher over $4,000.

The problem is that you have to spend some money to reach a threshold of credibility so you can raise more. And as all the literature says, the candidate must take the leadership in fund raising. Thus to my chagrin I had to divert precious time away from organizational work or door to door canvassing to write fund-raising letters. I hit up departmental colleagues, campaign volunteers, and old buddies from graduate school. It was hard, slogging work, and I was amazed that it paid off.

But money was only one part of the puzzle. In talking with other candidates, I found that we all struggled with the tasks of developing and sharpening a message, designing a strategy to get it across, and building an organization to achieve that goal.

Though all the candidates did pretty well by previous electoral standards, what none of us fully appreciated was that this wasn't a normal election. Not only were five candidates activating the local electorate as never before, but the eventual winner couldn't have been scripted as a more formidable candidate. His candidacy illustrates lesson #4.

Lesson #4: IT PAYS TO PAY YOUR DUES

Outside of the university community, I lacked public visibility. I had not paid my dues in the sense of being active in the PTA, serving on advisory committees, or attending school board meetings and speaking out. And though I ran a respectable campaign, that lack of visibility ultimately hurt me, especially in the compressed time of a short campaign.

The most formidable candidate, Mike Bumgarner, had clearly paid the most dues by extensive and visible in-

volvement in the community and in the public schools. As a minister with the largest church in town, Bumgarner's activities naturally placed him in contact with people in a variety of settings. But he had also spent untold hours as a school volunteer and had served as president of his school's PTA (unusual for an arena dominated by women). It also didn't hurt that he was from a well known Norman family (actor James Garner is one of the Norman Bumgarners). Gregarious and well liked, Mike was also backed by major establishment figures, including Democratic party insiders, who saw him as the perfect check on a possible "stealth candidate" from the Religious Right. He was organized, too, and at times it seemed to the rest of us that we were running against a machine. In some neighborhoods my volunteers found that practically everyone they knew had already been contacted by the Bumgarner organization.

Because of Bumgarner's strengths, the race took on a definite strategic shape. The only possible chink in Mike's armor was that he was perceived by some as the establishment's candidate at a time of rising discontent with the administration in some circles. But it was not clear that the majority felt that way, and the best any of Mike's opponents could hope for was to get into a runoff with him, unite the opposition, and eke out a win. I remember thinking that if Mike got only 40 percent of the vote, he might plateau there, and the second-place finisher would have the time and resources to overtake him in the runoff. But there were no tracking polls (thankfully) so none of us, including Bumgarner himself, knew exactly how it would come out.

The fog cleared on election day: Bumgarner received 1,211 votes (or 47 percent), followed by Kelly Lackey at 435 (17 percent), and myself with 389 (15 percent). Two other candidates received 10 and 8 percent respectively.

As I discovered, "real politics" did not end for me with the February election. Because no candidate had received a majority, a runoff was scheduled for April. Both Bumgarner and Lackey approached me with the same question: would I endorse? This forced me to do a lot of soul searching and strategic analysis. Irrespective of how I would personally vote, I knew I had a responsibility to those volunteers who had sat around the kitchen table, leaving it to go door to door in the middle of January for my campaign. I concluded that I couldn't speak for those who backed me, some of whom had strong reasons to vote for one or the other of the survivors. So I tried to play a constructive role, sharing my concerns and those of my backers with both candidates and hosting meetings for them.

Ironically, as a losing candidate I had become a more visible member of the community. Strangers congratulated me on the campaign; I was approached to serve on the parents advisory committee for the district. By running for the school board, in a sense, I have paid my dues.

Lesson #5: BEING A CANDIDATE ENLARGES ONE'S PERSPECTIVE

Everything I have just written suggests this final lesson. Almost daily during the campaign I was confronted with my own ignorance, and my learning curve shot up. I got to know the community and the people in it in a way I could never have imagined. I also gained an appreciation for how complex school board issues are. As a candidate I was in a unique position to hear from lots of different people, and I learned that there are endless currents and cross currents, not to mention strange bedfellows, in school board politics. From that experience I concluded that the culture wars thesis—that the struggle over public education pits Christian fundamentalists against secular school authorities—is just too simple, too Manichean. But that is another story.

The campaign was also a great experience for the family. My wife and I shared the expansive encounter with the community, and our boys got into the act. Patrick, my older son, had been something of a polling expert, predicting right from the start that I would place third. But on election night he wanted to see the results, so we hopped into the car and drove to his elementary school, the polling place for our own neighborhood. He knew the strategic situation well by then, that we were competing for the second spot, so he was excited when Precinct forty-three's results were posted: Bumgarner 140 votes, Hertzke 75, Lackey 48, and the others on down. Though other precincts did not come in so well, I will treasure that moment with my son, standing in the dark with sleet falling, reading my own name on the tally sheet, or the "ballot shower," as Walt Whitman described it, that constitutes the poetry of democracy.

Most of all, what I gained from the campaign was a platform to speak my mind, a chance to encounter what Hanna Arendt argued was the uniquely revelatory nature of public life, and an opportunity to taste what Aristotle viewed as the distinctive human experience—full citizenship.

WHO'S GOT CLOUT?

INTEREST GROUP POWER IN THE STATES

Who sways committee votes, who gets phone calls returned—in short,
who gets what they want from government—has always been
of interest to political observers.

By Clive S. Thomas and Ronald J. Hrebenar

The authors are political science professors, Clive S. Thomas at the University of Alaska in Juneau and Ronald J. Hrebenar at the University of Utah. This article is based in part on a chapter from Politics in the American States: A Comparative Analysis, *7th ed., Washington, D.C: Congressional Quarterly Press, 1999.*

At one time, especially from the 1930s to the early 1960s, five so-called "traditional interests"—business, labor, agriculture, local government and education—were virtually the only interest groups operating in state politics. But things have changed.

A major development in state capitals since the late 1960s has been the increase in the number and types of interest groups seeking to press their cases. The traditional groups have been joined by a plethora of so-called "new interests."

Our 50-state research project on interest groups—the Hrebenar-Thomas Study conducted over the last two decades using political scientists who are experts on politics in their own states—throws light on the essential

From *State Legislatures*, April 1999, pp. 30-34. © 1999 by the National Conference of State Legislatures. Reprinted by permission.

ingredients of interest group power: Is it just money or are there other reasons a group has political clout?

We've come up with a list of the 20 most effective interests as of the spring of 1998. We've also compiled the top 20 interests over the last two decades. These lists convey some interesting points and trends about the power of high-profile interest groups and lobbies.

The "new interests" range from environmentalists to women's groups to gay rights and victims' rights groups to hunting and fishing groups to anti-poverty and senior citizens' lobbies. The traditional groups have themselves increased and diversified. For instance, many individual cities, towns and special districts now hire their own lobbyists while remaining part of a state league of cities; and a host of businesses have their own lobbyists while remaining in a state manufacturers' or other trade association.

WHAT KIND OF POWER?

What exactly do we mean when we talk of interest group power? Do we mean the power of any group, well-known or not, to get what it wants? Do we mean the interest groups and lobbies that are considered by politicians and others to be the most effective in the state at large? Or do we mean the political clout of interest groups in general as a force in state politics compared with, say, parties, the governor, the legislature? All three are important to consider in trying to get a handle on interest group power. Our study looked at all three perspectives, but mainly focused on the sec-

ond—high profile groups and lobbies considered to be the most influential.

LOBBYING WITH SUCCESS

Of these three perspectives on power the only one that really counts is how successful any particular group is in getting what it wants. Some groups can be very successful in achieving their goals, but manage to keep a low profile in a state and not be singled out as powerful by public officials. It might be because the group is only occasionally active when it has an issue, such as an association of billboard owners working to defeat restrictions on the size of highway billboards. It could be an ad hoc group coming together on one issue and then disbanding when success is achieved, such as a coalition to defeat an anti-smoking ballot initiative or one to defeat a proposal for school vouchers. Or it could be that the group's issue is far from public view and of minor public concern, like dentists interested in the occupational licensing process, working with a department to write regulations. Rarely are dentists listed as among the most effective groups in a

WHO THE BIG ONES WERE

Up until the early 1960s most states were "run" or dominated by one or a handful of interest groups. In the late 19th and early 20th centuries, politics in all the 48 contiguous states were dominated by railroad interests. In California, it was the Southern Pacific; in North Dakota, Montana, Idaho and Washington, the Northern Pacific and the Great Northern; in Kentucky, the Louisville & Nashville Railroad; in Pennsylvania, the Pennsylvania Railroad; and in Maryland, the Baltimore & Ohio.

As late as the 1950s, Texas politics were dominated by the "Big Four"—oil, chemicals, the Texas Manufacturers Association and, again, the railroads. Maine's politics were long dominated by the "Big Three," electric power, timber, and textile and shoe manufacturing, while Iowa's politics were heavily influenced by agriculture and agribusiness interests (corn and hog farmers and farm machine manufacturers), truckers and the insurance industry.

The oil industry was dominant in Louisiana and Oklahoma, the Farm Bureau, county courthouses and utilities in many southern states—and the list goes on.

state, but they may be among the most successful groups in achieving their limited goals. Many groups involved in the regulatory process are successful because they "capture" their area of concern and have control of policymaking through the dependence of bureaucrats on their expertise. The last thing most of these groups want is public attention or to be singled out as effective.

This is not an easy aspect of group power to assess. Group leaders and their lobbyists are very reluctant to talk about their successes and failures.

REAL POLITICAL CLOUT

Our main concern, interest groups seen as powerful in the state at large, is the perspective on group power that most interests the press and the public, being, as they are, less concerned about the minutiae of government. Instead they focus on high-profile issues and questions such as "who is running the state" or who has "real political clout."

Of course we must be clear on what our lists of the 20 most effective interests now and over the past 20 years do and do not represent. They outline the interests that are viewed by policymakers and political observers as

THE ONES WITH CLOUT (SINCE 1980)

1	Teachers' organizations	12	State and local government employees (other than teachers)
2	General business organizations		
3	Utility companies & associations	13	Individual banks and financial institutions
4	Lawyers	14	Hospital associations and health care organizations (excluding physicians)
5	Bankers' associations		
6	General local government organizations		
7	Traditional labor associations	15	Realtors' associations
8	Insurance: general and medical	16	Environmentalists
		17	Universities and colleges
9	Manufacturers	18	K–12 education interests (other than teachers)
10	Physicians and state medical associations		
11	General farm organizations	19	Contractors, builders and developers
		20	Individual cities and towns

Source: The Hrebenar-Thomas study.

THE 20 MOST INFLUENTIAL INTERESTS IN THE 50 STATES IN 1998

Notes: This table is based on a ranking of individual interests in the 50 states conducted by political scientists from those states during the spring of 1998. Researchers ranked groups into "most effective" and "second level of effectiveness" categories. Rankings were calculated by allocating two points for each "most effective" ranking and one point for each "second level" placement and adding the totals. Where a tie in total points occurs, where possible, interests are ranked according to the number of "most effective" placements or the overall number of states in which they are effective. In some cases the totals for an interest add up to more than 50. This is because groups within an interest category sometimes appear within both the "most effective" and the "second level " category in a state. For example, utilities are ranked in both categories in North Dakota. Therefore, they are counted once for each category.

* Georgia, Maryland, Nevada and West Virginia.

** Teachers not ranked in Georgia.

***Hawaii, Illinois, Louisiana, North Carolina and Ohio.

Source: Compiled by the authors from the 1998 update and previous surveys of the Hrebenar-Thomas study. This table is based on information from a chapter by the authors in *Politics in the American States: A Comparative Analysis*, 7th ed., Washington, D.C.: Congressional Quarterly Press, 1999.

	Number of States Ranked:		
	Very Effective	Somewhat Effective	Not Effective
1 General business organizations (state chambers of commerce, etc.)	40	12	4*
2 Teachers' organizations** (predominantly NEA)	41	8	1
3 Utility companies & associations (electric, gas, water, telephone/ telecommunications, cable TV)	26	26	5***
4 Lawyers (predominantly trial lawyers & state bar associations)	26	14	12
5 Hospital associations/health care organizations (excluding physicians)	17	26	11
6 Insurance: general and medical (companies & associations)	21	16	13
7 General local government organizations (municipal leagues, county organizations, elected officials)	20	18	14
8 Manufacturers (companies & associations)	22	12	21
9 General farm organizations (mainly state Farm Bureaus)	17	18	16
10 Physicians/state medical associations	18	13	19
11 State & local government employees (other than teachers)	15	19	19
12 Traditional labor associations (predominantly the AFL-CIO)	14	21	15
13 Bankers' associations (includes savings & loan associations)	16	16	19
14 Contractors/builders/developers	11	13	28
15 Realtors' associations	11	12	27
16 K-12 education interests (other than teachers)	11	12	30
17 Gaming interests (race tracks/casinos/lotteries)	11	11	28
18 Individual banks & financial institutions	10	13	27
19 Environmentalists	7	19	25
20 Universities and colleges (public and private institutions and personnel)	6	19	26

the most effective in the states over the five years prior to the survey. And so they tend to be the most active groups or those with high profiles. It also may be that some observers confuse visibility with influence and list groups that might have little clout. The assessment should not be viewed as indicating that the groups near the top of the list always win or even win most of the time. In fact, they may win less often than some low-profile groups not listed. The ranking of an individual interest, however, does indicate its level of importance as a player in state politics in 1998 or since the early 1980s and its ability to bring political power to bear on the issues that affect it.

Comparing our findings over the years, what comes through most of all is that the types of groups that make the list and their ranking have stayed pretty consistent. When changes in ranking occur or new groups make the list, the changes appear to be most influenced by the prominence of particular issues at the time, as well as partisan control and the political complexion of state government. Gaming, health and insurance interests, for example, have steadily increased in perceived influence as lotteries and casinos, health care and tort reform have become issues in the states. Environmental and other liberal causes, as well as senior citizens' groups (not on either list), wax and wane in strength according to who is in power. This is also true of business and development interests, which have seen a boost in their rankings since the GOP successes in state elections in 1994. The biggest loser over the last 20 years is traditional labor, though white collar unions—particularly state and local employees—have risen to prominence and held on even as partisan control has changed.

Today, as over the past 20 years, two interests far outstrip any others in terms of their perceived influence and continue to vie for the top spot. These are general business organizations (mainly state chambers of commerce) and teachers (primarily state affiliates of the National Education Association—NEA). Despite the major expansion in group activity, few interests are considered to be effective in a large number of states. Only the top 13 show up as having power in more than half of the 50 states. The data confirm once again what researchers have known since the first study of state interest-group power in the 1950s. Business and the professions continue to be the most effective inter-

ests in the states (as they are in Washington, D.C.).

Some of these findings may seem fairly obvious, so why did we need a survey to discover the obvious? Because we now have hard evidence based on investigations in all 50 states to support what before were just "hunches" or personal observations. And while some things have been confirmed, like the power of business, some things, like a feeling among many that the "new interests" are taking over in the states, are quashed by our findings.

THE ROOT OF POWER

Our findings on the root of the power of individual groups and lobbies may, at first sight, also appear obvious. But again, we now have hard evidence across the states plus some new perspectives. We all know that money and numbers count, but without other factors like organizational skills to direct a lobbying campaign and good political timing, big bucks and numbers are of little use. The continued success and high ranking of NEA and state chambers are based on these organizations maintaining long-term insider relations with lawmakers and being able to enter into coalitions, rouse public interest and overcome the elements they lack to wield political clout in state capitals.

Our surveys reveal that the No. 1 element determining the political clout of a group is how much they are needed by politicians and government. This dependence could stem from campaign contributions (as with many business interests), running a state service like education (as with teachers) or simply a state's, and thus government's, dependence on an industry like Boeing in Washington state and coal in West Virginia. Some groups, such as victims' rights or the arts, may score short-term victories, but because government does not need them in the way it needs a major industry or teach-

WHAT DETERMINES INFLUENCE?

Internal Resources:

Political, organizational and managerial skills.
Financial resources.
Size and geographical distribution of membership.
Political cohesiveness.

Policy Goals and Potential Opposition or Support of Others

Whether lobbying focus is defensive or promotional.
The extent and strength of opposition.
Potential to enter into coalitions.

State Political Climate and Public Perceptions

Timing and the changing political agenda.
Partisan and ideological makeup of the executive and legislature.
Public perceptions of issues and groups.

Long-term Relations with Public Officials

The degree of necessity of group services and resources to public officials.
Relations between lobbyists and policymakers.

Source: The Hrebenar-Thomas study

ers, they will never exert long-term influence and be ranked among the most powerful in a state.

THE MAJOR PLAYERS

Our third and final perspective is that of the overall power of interest groups in a state. We know that in most states, interest groups were the major force for many years, dwarfing legislatures, governors and sometimes parties. This has changed a lot since the 1930s, but interest groups are still major players in policymaking.

The South has always been the region where groups have predominated, probably because of the weakness of any countervailing force like strong political parties. In contrast, the Northeast interest groups have been more constrained by other major elements in state politics, particularly strong parties, strong governors and generally more economic and social diversity. In our 1998 survey, the South remained the region with the most powerful interest group systems, followed by the West and the Midwest; the Northeast remains the region with the least powerful. These regional rankings are all unchanged from the early 1980s and probably even before that.

THE MORE THINGS CHANGE...

These findings on interest group power bring to mind the adage, "The more things change, the more they remain the same." Although this is partly true, a better way to look at it is that interest group and lobby power has reached a new stage of development as part of the constantly evolving state of politics in state capitals.

States are no longer dominated by one or a handful of interests, although some states still have a prominent interest—the Mormon church in Utah, chickens in Arkansas, gambling in Nevada, for instance. The last 30 years have seen a growth in both new and traditional interests.

There are more groups representing more people across the 50 states today than ever before. This increasingly crowded political playing field has made it more difficult to predict who will win and who will lose. It has forced the development of all sorts of new techniques on the part of traditional and new interests alike, such as "grassroots" lobbying and media campaigns, to try and meet the challenges. And most of these new techniques have democratized group activity.

On the other hand, some realities about interest group power, particularly of individual groups and lobbies, remain unchanged and probably will for generations to come. Since time immemorial, the possession of resources and a symbiotic relationship between a group and government has been at the root of power.

This largely accounts for the persistence of so-called "insider interests," particularly business, some of the professions and local governments. Most of the new interests do not yet have this symbiotic relationship. So despite the mushrooming of interests in state capitals, the groups considered powerful in 1998 are not that much different from 1978. There may be more players in the state capital political game, but the factors determining success are virtually unchanged.

The reality of what determines success has a host of implications for groups and state politics. Three are central. First, if the "outsider interests"—mainly the new interests—want to become "insiders," they need extensive resources— money, members and so on—and they need to build up a symbiotic relationship. Second, because some groups will never be able to do this, political inequality and uneven representation will always exist in state politics, as at the federal level and in any country, democratic or otherwise. In this regard, the populist sentiment among large segments of the population that money talks and some interests will always be more powerful than others is quite justified. And third, lobbying laws cannot even up the political playing field, but can only provide public disclosure of who's lobbying whom.

The Clamor of the Brave New World

It seemed like such a good idea—traditional cracker-barrel democracy with a 21st century sheen, the latest high technology hitched to an old and fundamental American tradition. But lawmakers are finding that e-mail can get mighty noisy.

By Garry Boulard

Suddenly and swiftly lawmakers are connected through computers, the Internet and e-mail with a vast universe of research and information available to voters both in their own districts and from places far away.

Senator
Bill Schroeder
Colorado

"I keep thinking about the future," remarked Senator Bill Schroeder of Colorado last year as the Colorado legislature was just laying the groundwork for going online. "By the turn of the century almost every legislative function will be computerized in our state and everywhere else. It is coming pretty fast, and I just want us in Colorado to be ready for it."

"It's a whole new world out there," agreed Raymond Brennan, the assistant secretary of the Michigan Senate, where the membership showed an early enthusiasm for high-tech democracy, going online as early as 1992. "We have to embrace it if we expect to stay competitive."

Garry Boulard, a free-lance writer in New Orleans, is a frequent contributor to State Legislatures. *His book,* Huey Long Invades New Orleans: The Siege of a City, 1934–1936, *was released by Pelican Publishing in August 1998.*

WHAT HAVE WE GOT INTO?

But now that the new world has arrived, many lawmakers are seeing another side to the wonders of the information age, and some are wondering what they have got into. Specifically, one of the most touted advantages of electronic democracy is also its greatest burden; it keeps lawmakers connected, on a moment's notice, with the people. And the people, thousands of them, hundreds of thousands of them, millions of them, are sometimes a very angry bunch with a whole lot to say.

Senator
Gerald Matzke
Nebraska

Consider this: In Nebraska a coordinated e-mail campaign last year resulted in members of the Legislature's Transportation Committee receiving hundreds of messages over a several-day period, sometimes as many as 300 messages per lawmaker a day, promoting passage of a particular bill. In response Senator Gerald Matzke complained about the "harassment and abusive practice" of inundating legislators with messages, the onslaught of which "denies other members of the public the benefits of e-mail to contact representatives." Another lawmaker, Senator Owen Elmer, was upset enough by the avalanche to go where few other lawmakers dare to tread,

From *State Legislatures,* May 1998, pp. 17–21. © 1998 by the National Conference of State Legislatures. Reprinted by permission.

Senator
Owen Elmer
Nebraska

calling for regulation of the Internet, "at least to the extent that we prevent abuse."

In Vermont, the state education department this year abruptly shut down an Internet forum designed to discuss a new school funding reform law, after some of the e-mail respondents began sending what were described as "harsh, sometimes abusive," messages.

Senator
Cheryl Rivers
Vermont

"I got some very angry e-mail, and not all of it was from my constituents," says Senator Cheryl Rivers, who was receiving up to 50 messages a day on the school law. One of those messages in particular was troubling, likening the law in question to Hitler's Final Solution. "It got a little out of control, and I decided I did not want to be a part of that type of discussion," Rivers said after the list serve was discontinued. "There were some people who mailed me all the time, several times a day. I could have spent my entire day answering e-mail, some of which was pretty extreme."

Assemblywoman
Debra Bowen
California

In California, Assemblywoman Debra Bowen, an enthusiastic backer of electronic democracy, admits to feeling overwhelmed by the amount of e-mail she receives. "We just don't have the staff time to answer every piece of e-mail that comes into our office," says Bowen, who can get up to 50 messages a day from constituents. But the California assemblywoman may have come up with a partial solution. In January she proposed a bill that would at least reduce

the amount of junk or "spam" she gets by requiring senders to attach an address or toll-free phone number that would allow recipients to get off their mailing list.

As for the rest of the e-mail, there is little Bowen can do except to wade through it: "The biggest downside to the immediacy of the Internet is that people who are e-mailing you expect an instant response," she adds. "And sometimes I just don't have the time to do that."

And who can forget the vociferous response among e-mail and Internet users three years ago to a proposed Conference of the States? It would have brought together representatives of each state legislature in one huge seminar designed to discuss common problems. Opponents of the conference got the idea that it was all a plot to federalize the states or somehow weaken state government. Throughout the spring and summer of 1995, legislatures across the country received hundreds of e-mail, Internet and faxed messages, often written in apocalyptic language, urging them to reject participation in the conference. Much of the opposition was orchestrated by former Colorado Senator Charles Duke who said he could connect with upwards of 100,000 people in a matter of minutes to flood a legislature with a coordinated response.

By the fall of 1995, organizers of the Conference of the States decided to scale back the proposed meeting, and one reason was certainly the amount and temper of the grassroots opposition it engendered.

Such results, depending upon your point of view and your fortunes thus far with public activism, embody either the worst mass hysteria or the best citizen participation that the new electronic democracy has to offer.

IT'S HERE TO STAY

But one thing is certain: Electronic democracy is not only here to stay, it is only going to become a larger, more engulfing thing as time goes by. And the old world when lawmakers could, for the most part, deliberate

quietly and without haste, has pretty much disappeared.

"This new world is a place where there are no barriers, no separations, and no moat between the legislature and the public forces," says Alan F. Rosenthal, professor of political science at the Eagleton Institute of Politics.

Rosenthal is worried about lawmakers like Nebraska's Matzke and Elmer and the roughly 700 angry e-mail messages they received. And he wonders how the modern deliberative process can withstand such high-tech pressures. "If you are a lawmaker and you get 700 messages in one day, you've got to take that seriously," he says, "whether it is orchestrated or not. It's not that these kinds of grassroots campaigns could not have taken place before now. It is just that the immediacy and the directness of a vote is today so close. There are less and less mediating factors, and that makes it much tougher for lawmakers to ignore a mass e-mail campaign, even if the campaign is wrongheaded."

At Harvard University, Jerry Mechling, the director of the program on strategic computing and telecommunications in the public sector, notes that this world is so new and has engulfed legislatures so quickly that no one is really certain of its final outcome.

"I don't think people know how much this has changed us," Mechling says. "In a true democracy you tend to believe that the more participation you have, the more voices that are heard, the more people are finding it worthwhile and meaningful to debate, the better that is going to be. So there is some hope that this is a good idea because it reduces the barriers and allows people to participate in politics."

At the same time, Mechling acknowledges that "people are nervous" about the full ramifications of an electronic democracy, because "we are trying to create venues and institutions that encourage deliberation. You don't want what is just on the very top of people's minds, you want what is there, but you also want them to

SPAM—NOT A TASTY TIDBIT

It's like those annoying telephone calls in the middle of supper. You know, the ones wanting to sell you subscriptions or solicit donations for charity. For a bona fide computer aficionado, the equivalent in aggravation is unwanted, junk messages that appear in private e-mail boxes.

This junk e-mail has been labeled "spam"—a term adopted from a Monty Python skit about gibberish that drowns out all other conversation and originally found in early usenet groups on the Internet—and it fills your computer with schemes to "get rich quick"—now sometimes labeled as "multilevel marketing." They still are basically the old pyramid schemes in electronic format. Junk e-mail also features the lose weight fast and chain letter scams as well as invitations to lurid sex sites.

More than annoying, spam can be expensive. It can cost a spammer about $20 to send out tens of thousands of junk messages that can cost millions to combat in terms of time, resources and money. Matrix News estimates that if it took five seconds to delete each spam message sent to 10,000,000 people (and, yes, that is possible at little cost for the spammer), it would waste 14,000 hours. Another computer vendor claimed to have lost $75,000 in salary and overhead because one employee was assigned to do nothing but fight spam for six months. And Internet service providers spend millions for extra bandwidth (the capacity a telecommunications firm has for carrying data), phone lines, personnel and software to keep unsolicited commercial e-mail from delaying messages or crashing their systems (which it has done—just ask the people at AT&T Worldnet). In short, spam clogs the system and requires time, effort and money to move it along or clear it.

With the burgeoning popularity of the Internet, legislators are hearing more and more complaints from their computer-literate constituents about junk e-mail.

Nevada was the first state to pass legislation to discourage spam. The law, which becomes effective July 1, 1998, requires that unsolicited e-mail be identified as an advertisement or promotion. Residents who receive unsolicited messages that do not comply with the law can go to court to prevent the advertiser from sending further messages and may recover attorney fees, costs and actual damages or damages or $10 per e-mail message.

Critics point out that advertisers can still send unwanted messages as long as they fit the labeling criteria.

Washington state passed a law in March that makes it illegal to forge headers, hijack other e-mail systems or otherwise "misrepresent the messages' point of origin." Because Internet service providers generally have strict rules against spam, most of those who mail out the junk use one or more of those methods to get their messages on the 'Net.

Several other states have introduced bills this session attempting to limit spam including Arizona, California, Kentucky and New Hampshire.

Four laws were introduced in Congress in 1997 aimed at slowing the flow of junk e-mail or at least requiring that it be identified as advertising.

Spam is frustrating, but it's not frightening. There are, however, messages that threaten or harass recipients. Several states—Alabama, Alaska, Arizona, Connecticut, Delaware, Michigan, Oklahoma and Wyoming—have made sending harassing electronic communications a crime. Washington is considering amending existing harassment and stalking laws to include e-mail.

—Janna Goodwin, NCSL

---

work down more deeply and resolve conflicts and tradeoffs."

ROLLING ELECTRONIC REFERENDA

The idea that legislatures of the future may be composed of little other than obedient lawmakers, laptops at the ready, faithfully following the wishes of their constituents according to that day's e-mail poll response, is enough to give anyone pause, and is not all that farfetched, according to Rosenthal.

Rosenthal and other school scholars forecast future electronic democracies with the public voting by computer on any number of issues, creating a kind of rolling electronic referend[um] aimed at the PC screen of the state lawmaker, who then must decide whether or not to vote accordingly. "And you can imagine the pressure any legislator would feel when you get any kind of vote result from your constituents."

A second, equally sobering scenario includes district voters viewing a particular committee hearing or floor debate over the state-run version of C-Span or live over the Internet and then sending their representative an e-mail to let them know what they're thinking. At that very moment. On the issue the lawmaker is right then debating.

"This way the legislator is getting an immediate feedback on the issue being discussed at that moment," says Rosenthal. "Now lobbyists do this all of the time. The lobbyist can stand in the rotunda and send a message to the legislator reminding him of their agreement or something."

But Rosenthal argues that the traditional relationship enjoyed by lawmakers and lobbyists across the country is manifestly different from anything currently going on between a representative and his frequently faceless e-mail correspondents. "The legislator knows the lobbyist, who that

Senator
Bill Finkbeiner
Washington

lobbyist is representing, whether or not the person is credible, what the political standing is of the organization the lobbyist represents ... but the legislator getting messages by e-mail on referenda votes has no idea who is behind it."

For Washington Senator Bill Finkbeiner, such arguments are academically interesting, but akin to gripes about the lack of color choices with

BE CAREFUL MEETING BY E-MAIL

Use of the computer for written conversation and discussion has grown exponentially over the past few years. And that popularity has opened an entirely new dilemma for lawmakers.

The popularity and ease of e-mail have led some critics to complain that it is being used to circumvent open meetings laws.

So far, concrete charges and resulting lawsuits have not reached the state level. But there are a growing number of local stories that warn the wary of the possible misuse of the new communications medium.

◆ Phoenix city council members debated issues and took straw votes via e-mail. After the local paper revealed the practice, the council spent $5,000 to upgrade the system so copies of e-mail posts could be kept in the clerk's office.

◆ A community college board in Maryland divested itself of computers because the county attorney informed members that e-mail would violate open meetings laws.

◆ In Florida, a majority of county commissioners agreed by e-mail to sell a site to a developer and withhold a public vote until after a September election. A lawsuit resulted, but was dropped when newly elected commissioners also voted to sell the site.

◆ Ann Arbor (Mich.) Mayor Ingrid Sheldon got a warning from the city attorney when she sent an e-mail to city council members seeking suggestions on ways to manage disruptive speakers at council meetings.

"It's just a modern version of telephone tag in which a city council would try to get around open meeting laws by deciding everything on the phone ahead of time," says Paul McMasters, a First Amendment expert with the Freedom Forum.

In one of the more unusual rulings, however, the North Dakota Attorney General Heidi Heitkamp ruled e-mail discussion by members of the North Dakota Board of Higher Education was legal, but similar messages over the telephone would be considered an illegal meeting. She based her decision on the fact that e-mail is considered a public record that can be scrutinized by the public.

But McMasters points out that an "after-the-fact" record of e-mail "is not much help when it comes to the First Amendment ability of citizens to petition government. If you don't know as you are sitting in a meeting that everything has been scripted, you can't react."

Other rulings have not been as lenient as the North Dakota decision. The Florida AG opined that a quorum cannot engage in "a simultaneous exchange of e-mail on a matter of public business." Public officials can send e-mail copies to as many people as they want, but no one can answer the post without breaking the law. The Kansas attorney general agreed, but added that one government official sending another an e-mail message was not illegal.

The Florida Legislature amended its Sunshine Law to include e-mail, faxes and other electronic communications. The Florida attorney general ruled that content—not format—determines whether a document is a public record or not. Legislation in Colorado provides state agencies with guidelines for classifying e-mail as public or private. Maryland's Public Information Act defines public record as including computerized records, and the attorney general has said that includes e-mail.

Electronic records are now subject to open records statutes in all states, but the status of electronic mail continues to be an issue. Proponents of including e-mail in the definition of public record argue that lawmakers should equate it to paper correspondence, which open records acts explicitly cover. Those who contend that e-mail is not a public record compare it to a telephone call. Telephone conversations are confidential and are not public records.

—Dianna Gordon

Henry Ford's Model T (they were all black) or the poor TV reception viewers got trying to watch Uncle Miltie in 1951. "It's all a moot point," he says. "For better or worse, all of these things—e-mail, the Internet, online information—are here to stay. We can't put the genie back in the bottle.

"Some lawmakers now and in the near future will use their computers and all of the new technologies available to them a lot, others won't," he continues. "But we are very close now to the point where you will not be able to get elected to a legislature without knowing how to use a computer as a daily tool."

In fact Finkbeiner, who has long been one of Washington's most ardent computer advocates, believes that lawmakers have only just entered a vast, startling, quick-changing new universe that will feature not only the input side of government, but its output as well, the part that will offer an array of government services needed for daily use by the citizens of the republic.

Such thinking is the fiber of what sustains Richard J. Varn, a former Iowa state senator and the current director of telecommunications for the University of Northern Iowa. Varn foresees an era emphasizing what he calls a "virtual service counter," where everything that people used to be able to get across the counter at their local, state or even federal government agency will soon be available by computer. "That means instead of making the trip to some government agency to get certain documents, even a license, you should be able to do it in an electronic format. It is just a matter of implementing the systems that let you do that."

Governments, big and small, increasingly are touting the miracle of the marketplace, privatization, and, at the very least, the need to provide services equal to or better than those of the private sector. And Varn believes the move toward computerizing virtually everything one could possibly need from government is not far away. "It would be like calling American Express, you can find out your account balance by punching in a few numbers," Varn explains. "We expect the rest of the world to work like that today, too. We expect services to be delivered to us that way. Government is supposed to be serving us, so why can't they serve us like everyone else does?"

AMBITIOUS EFFORTS IN MINNESOTA

For lawmakers, the more immediate future may be found in Minnesota, whose politics, says Steven Clift, "are probably the most online of anywhere in the country." Clift is one of the founders and guiding spirits behind an ambitious effort known as Minnesota E-Democracy and Democracy Online, two programs that promote ongoing vigorous dialogues between voters and their representatives through e-mail and the Internet.

For Clift, the democratic potential of the emerging technology is nothing less than revolutionary, no less important for the citizenry than the Bill of Rights or the abolition of slavery. Noting that in Minnesota most bills and laws are already on the Internet and that even some legislative committees have set up their own Web pages, Clift believes the next logical step is for integration.

"You could make it so that if you want to talk about a specific bill, you could go into a certain chat room or something and, at some point, lawmakers could hopefully become involved in that process too," Clift explains.

Clift's advocacy of an enhanced electronic interactivity between lawmakers and voters strikes a different chord from what is normally associated with activist members of the grassroots electronic democracy, at least as they have been generally portrayed in the press. Clift says he is not a bomb-thrower and is not automatically opposed to everything the government or a state legislature does.

In fact, he eschews the idea that the Internet and e-mail should be used only to represent voter outrage. "If all we do with all of this technology on the advocacy side is to raise

the din of protest," Clift offers, "then that would be like putting a big metal bar through the spokes of governance. The Internet should not be a way to just flood the system with protests. It should be a way for the forces of society to find each other and duke things out on their own, to really learn from one another and to have a meaningful dialogue with our elected representatives."

Clift also believes there are thousands more Internet users like himself out there, people who do not fall into the far edges of political extremes, but who are interested in how their government works and in enhancing democracy through increased citizen participation.

Clift may be right. A recent study by Virginia pollster Frank Luntz revealed that most citizen activists who are Internet users—up to 65 percent of them—dubbed "digital citizens" or "netizens," were either political independents or slightly inclined to vote Democratic or Republican. Those who identified themselves as either strongly Republican or strongly Democratic accounted for no more than a third of the total.

Luntz also produced another finding that contradicts popular prejudice: His Digital Citizens were confident and optimistic. The overwhelming majority expects the future to be better for their children and believes that they control change, not the other way around.

Given such statistics, it is not surprising that when the Virginia legislature's Joint Commission on Technology and Science recently posted draft legislation on the Internet the response was, according to Diana Horvath, director of the commission, "overwhelmingly moderate and reasonable."

"We ended up posting roughly six bills for public comment, and we got a lot of good comments from people through the e-mail, from practitioners and other agency people, from folks who had studied the stuff and really had good comments on the legislation," Horvath says. "It was a good

experience and something I would want to continue."

As for the e-mailers who had nothing good to say about anything, Horvath responds: "The benefits of electronic interactivity, as far as I can see, far outweigh its problems. If you get a few nutballs, it's still worth it."

CHANNELING NUTBALLS

Indeed, some electronic democracy students believe the only way state legislatures will be able to transform being wired into a positive experience is to learn how to channel nutballs. "That's how large corporations do it," says Harvard's Mechling. "They put more channelized bureaucratic procedures into their networks. When people before were allowed to use e-mail to complain about software bugs, it generated

Representative
Jim Morrison
Kansas

an avalanche of over-the-transom communications. They could not listen to them all, so they reinstituted a procedure that all communications, even electronic ones, had to go through a hierarchical filtering system."

Representative Jim Morrison of Kansas likes that idea a lot. "How do you think Microsoft handles 500,000 sources of e-mail a day? They are immediately sent to various departments, based upon content, subject line and source of origin."

Morrison, who may hold something of a record among state lawmakers for first clicking on to the Internet as long ago as the mid-1970s, believes his fellow legislators need to look at all of the wonders of the electronic democracy and make them their own. He is a particularly big defender of his right to trash any message he doesn't feel like being bothered with. "Use a filter, period," Morrison instructs. "A filter allows you to identify e-mail if it comes from a specific point of origin, for example from known spammers who come

Senator
Jon Bruning
Nebraska

from certain service providers, and, if you want to, you can put it on a kill list or trash it. You never have to see it. That's your right."

Others, such as Nebraska Senator Jon Bruning, who was among those flooded with e-mail messages during last year's Transportation Committee debate, says he is a "big fan" of electronic communication, "but when an e-mail is personally addressed to me it has a lot more effect than one that is spammed. If somebody purposely sends me 600 e-mails and the sender doesn't even have an idea of who I am or really what the issue is, I am probably not going to pay a lot of attention to it."

On the other hand, if the e-mailer is a constituent with a concern about service or questions and opinions about issues under consideration by the Nebraska Senate, Bruning says, "I take it very seriously, read them and even respond. To me it's a positive experience."

And for almost everyone in public life, the electronic democracy experience is certain to become more frequent.

As of last year, there were more than 30 million PC users in the United States surfing the 'Net. That number is expected to surpass the 100 million mark at the beginning of the new century.

Even in tiny Colby, Kan., the home of Jim Morrison, there are

USE AND ABUSE OF E-MAIL

During a recent seminar at Tulane University on the use and abuse of e-mail and the Internet, an agitated member of the audience stood up and issued an impassioned warning: "Never, never put anything in e-mail or over the Internet that you wouldn't want millions of people to read. Your messages and words can end up in very odd places. It's important to be discreet."

Washington Senator Jeanne Kohl knows what he means. Last year, after responding to an Internet message that opposed a football-soccer stadium bill she was sponsoring, Kohl was surprised to find out where her remarks went. "The individual," Kohl says, "ridiculed my response and sent it to all legislators and legislative staff. The same thing has been done to other legislators as well."

On another occasion, fighting over a different bill, Kohl's Internet e-mail remarks to a correspondent were taken out of context, read aloud during a public rally and then re-sent over the Internet with "remarks purported to be mine, but incorrect and with embellishments," she relates.

Meanwhile, the Internet e-mail of Vermont's Senator Cheryl Rivers is being collected by a constituent who has candidly warned her not to change her position on any of the issues she has discussed in e-mail. He says he has "more than 50 messages addressed by me that he could use at any moment against me if I ever publicly say anything that does not agree with those e-mail positions," she says.

"He even told me that if he was in public life he would never use e-mail because it is too easy to trap someone," Rivers laughs.

But how e-mail and Internet messages are ultimately used is a legitimate concern of lawmakers, Rivers continues, noting how easy it is for a skilled opponent to take a few words or a sentence and give them new meaning. "Just be careful. Everything you say can come back on you. It's one of the dangers of our new era."

Despite the abuses, Kohl and Rivers are ardent users of e-mail, answering their messages themselves and using it to communicate with staff. Pennsylvania Representative Harry Readshaw and Minnesota Senator Michelle Fischbach have found other helpful uses for the technology.

Readshaw used e-mail and the Internet to publicize and gather support for a bill he was pushing to help renovate the monuments at Gettysburg. "It's a national effort," says aide Jay Purdy. "Many of the monuments came from regiments and legislatures in other states. E-mail and the Internet were key to getting the word out across the country."

Fischbach used the Internet to run a paid ad in support of her bill to eliminate her state's motor vehicle registration tax. Her "Ax the Car Tax" electronic ad was a first by a state legislator, according to Shawn Towle, publisher of *Checks & Balances*, the online magazine that ran her ad. Readers could click to see the full text of Senator Fischbach's bill, go to her Web page and send e-mail to committee chairs who were dealing with the tax cut proposal.

"Using these new technologies to reach the public is going to become even more important in the future," Senator Fischbach says.

more than 700 Internet subscribers in a town of 6,000 people. And that number is growing. "Up to 20 percent of the people in this district have e-mail, and three years ago it was zero percent," Morrison reveals.

"Before it is all over, the entire city could be connected. And any of those people could reach me in a moment if they wanted to. That's the future we're all going to have to get used to."

MORE NEWS, LESS COVERAGE?

A huge study last year showed that despite the shift in power from Washington to the states, newspapers were cutting back on the number of reporters assigned to the statehouse beat.

BY GARRY BOULARD

It seems like an idea whose time has come: a Web site for journalists, constituents and lawmakers devoted in its entirety to state legislative news.

"We've been on line since Jan. 25, and so far we're seeing about 3,000 readers a day," reports Ed Fouhy, editor of Stateline.org, which is being produced by the Pew Center on the States.

"We are not interested in sheer numbers. This is not a mass media site where we are competing with the Associated Press or CNN," continues Fouhy. "But even so, the response we've gotten has far exceeded our expectations."

Just as impressive, the average visitor to the new site, according to Stateline's own detailed in-house readers' surveys, sticks around for nine to 10 minutes—an eternity in Web space.

Fouhy believes such responses indicate a yawning hunger across the country for news coming out of the state capitals, particularly during a time when because of devolution there is more news to report.

"We've seen a great deal of power and money going back to the states in recent years," Fouhy says, "which naturally means that the states themselves will be creating more news. But even more than that, the states finally have the *authority* to do things they've been saying for a long time they should be doing for themselves. That in itself makes them newsworthy."

If the birth of Stateline.org reflects the shift of power from Washington to state capitals—perhaps the most important story of the 1990s—it also is indicative of a far less certain, and much more tentative response on the part of the press as to where government news comes from today.

"We're hearing all kinds of things on that question," says Gene Roberts, a professor of journalism at the University of Maryland and a long-time working reporter for such papers as *The New York Times* and the *Philadelphia Inquirer*.

"On the one hand, newspapers want to make the claim that they provide their readers with the most comprehensive coverage possible," says Roberts. "But it also is true that there have been cutbacks in much of the state coverage, and this has proved to be a sore point with many of the larger papers."

Roberts should know. In 1998 he helped compile a massive study funded by the Pew Center and released by the *American Journalism Review* that showed clearly that many papers across the country were reducing their state coverage and cutting back on the number of reporters assigned to roam the marble halls of state capitols.

EMPTY DESKS

The study pulled no punches: "Coverage of state government is in steep decline," it said.

Garry Boulard, a free-lance writer in New Orleans, is a frequent contributor to State Legislatures.

 From *State Legislatures,* June 1999, pp. 14-18. © 1999 by the National Conference of State Legislatures. Reprinted by permission.

"In capital press rooms around the country, there are more and more empty desks and silent phones. Bureaus are shrinking, reporters are younger and less experienced, stories get less space and poorer play, and all too frequently editors just don't care."

The industry's response to the study was overwhelmingly negative. Newspapers across the country denied that they were shortchanging readers, or that reducing their staff presence at the legislatures meant a reduction in the amount or scope of coverage.

Other papers argued that the study shortchanged them by failing to count the many special reporters they send to cover the legislature for singular topics such as science or environmental issues. "But we were not aware of any health care reporters coming to any capital and staying for weeks at a time," explains Roberts. "We counted only the correspondents who stuck with it day in and day out."

Even so, the industry criticism of the study continued, proving at the very least that a nerve had been touched.

"I guess some people got mad," laughs Reese Cleghorn, president of the *American Journalism Review* and dean of the college of journalism at the University of Maryland, "so that means the study had an effect. And it should have had an effect because it is something the papers should be embarrassed about."

The study also went beyond the numbers. It dug into the very marrow of how papers decide whether or not a legislative story is worth covering. And more often than not, researchers for the Pew report found that many editors today just don't give a hoot about legislative reporting.

"They say 'Don't do the procedurals, don't do the subcommittees, wait until something goes to a full committee,'" continues Cleghorn, "even though what happens at the subcommittee level may be the most important part of the legislative process."

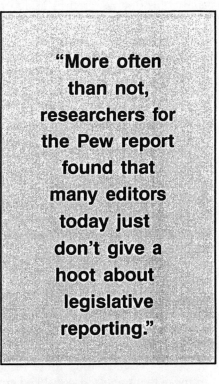

"More often than not, researchers for the Pew report found that many editors today just don't give a hoot about legislative reporting."

BIG PICTURE REPORTING

This so-called "big picture" reporting is not without its critics.

Dave McNeely, political columnist for the *Austin American Statesman* and a well-known advocate for increased statehouse reporting among the nation's papers, thinks following and writing about what happens to a bill as it pushes its way to final passage is the most interesting part of the process. It's what provides readers with a tangible view of where power resides in any given legislative session, he says.

"A lobbyist friend of mine once told me there is only one way to pass a bill and that is through the House and Senate, ending when the governor signs it," says McNeely. "But there are 476 ways to kill a bill and knowing where those spots are and what the process is, is crucial to both lobbying and reporting."

Jack Wardlaw, who reports on the Louisiana Legislature for *The Times-Picayune* in New Orleans, says what happens to a bill in a committee or subcommittee can provide substance and shape that might alter the meaning and intent of the final legislation. "That's why it's important to report on the progress of a bill all the way

through, particularly when it is something that the people care about anyway. If you don't, you're really doing the public a disservice."

But even worse than failing to report on the ups and downs of certain legislation is a much larger, and far less tangible, attitude on the part of many papers today concerning government reporting in general: "They don't like it," says Professor Roberts. "We were amazed to discover just how many editors today are philosophically opposed to governmental coverage in general. It is just in the air. Some newspaper companies and editors even go so far as to simply believe that state government and all government news is a big turn-off to readers, so they want to stay away from it."

Former Pennsylvania Speaker of the House and frequent press critic Bob O'Donnell sees all of this as inevitable: "You have to look at the press as a business, and until you do that you are not going to understand the story."

O'Donnell argues that the frequently aired declarations from the press that they are here to serve and fight for the public's right to know are basically nothing more than a lot of smoke and noise.

"Those kinds of statements are essentially self-serving," charges O'Donnell. "Informing the citizenry is not their main goal, making a buck is. And when you see it that way—that this is nothing more than a business looking for a market, and if reporting on lifestyles instead of the legislative process is what gets them their market—all of this begins to make much more sense."

ENTERTAINING NEWS

Alan Rosenthal of the Eagleton Institute of Politics at Rutgers University has his own take: "Papers want to find stuff that connects with their audience, things that affect their personal lives, news that is more entertainment-oriented.

"That makes it kind of hard to sell that story about the legislature discussing energy deregulation. People just don't see what it has to do with them," he says.

But Rosenthal says he can't but wonder if a shrinking state press corps is such a bad thing: "Given the nature of the coverage, I am not really all that devastated."

Industry insiders say the primary reason for the decrease in state coverage is found in the results of the many readers' surveys that papers regularly conduct. These are surveys usually commissioned by a paper or publishers' group and intended to gauge public satisfaction or the lack of it with a given newspaper. Should the front page type be bigger or smaller? Would you like to see more or fewer graphs and color? How about the amount of sports reporting and the number and variety of cartoons?

But the answers to such surveys are oftentimes colored by the manner in which questions are asked and their context. And sometimes the survey results can be downright contradictory. In 1990 some 63 percent of the readers of *The Orange County Register* in Santa Ana, Calif., said in a survey that they would read the paper more if fewer of the stories from the front page "jumped" to an inside page.

In response, the *Register* began to run shorter stories, half of which began and ended on the front page. Goodbye to those annoying jumps. Then in 1997 came another survey for the same paper, and it showed that 59 percent said they wanted to read longer stories in the newspaper, and would be *more* likely to read the *Register* even if a story from the front page jumped to an inside page.

Similar surveys repeatedly indicate that readers dislike meaty government pieces, whether of the reporting or analytical variety, prompting publishers and editors to cut such coverage.

But the problem with such marketing research is that it is anything but solid or sure. "Much of it is subjective, unscientific and amenable to manipulation," contends the *American Journalism Review* in another epic study, this one released in March on how reader surveys are conducted. "Its heavy reliance on focus groups constitutes a serious weakness. Its results always depend on the question asked. And questions of interest to serious journalists (for instance, what's the impact of challenging a community's cherished assumptions?) are almost never explored."

Perhaps the landmark readers' survey was sponsored by the Newspaper Advertising Bureau and the American Newspaper Publishers Association in the late 1970s. Comments from some 3,000 respondents indicated that readers wanted more attention paid "to their personal needs, help in understanding and dealing with their own problems in an increasingly complex world."

Newspaper publishers and editors across the country took those results to mean that people also disliked governmental reporting, beginning the long drive to lessen coverage on the national, state and local levels. And even though the two principal authors of the 1978 Newspaper Readership Project later argued that their findings had been taken out of context, the trend has clearly continued.

FEWER REPORTERS

As of 1998, according to the Pew study, virtually every major newspaper had pulled back on its statehouse reporting. In some 27 states, there were fewer reporters covering state news than just six years ago, while only 14 states could report increases. Part of the decline is due to the collapse of the United Press International news service, which was once a major presence in virtually every state capital.

Other statehouse reporters were lost to mergers or the closings of such papers as the *Baton Rouge State Times,* the *Nashville Banner,* the *Phoenix Gazette* and the *Arkansas Gazette.*

The giant Gannett and Knight-Ridder newspaper chains have reduced their statehouse reporting staffs by more than 14 percent followed by smaller decreases at the Newhouse and MediaWatch chains.

But individual papers such as *The Albuquerque Journal, The Charlotte Observer* and *The Times-Picayune* have seen moderate gains in the number of reporters assigned to the state legislatures.

"Our statehouse staff has actually increased in recent years," says McNeely of the *Austin American Statesman.* But in a state that has seen an abnormal amount of press closings, including the *Houston Post,* the *Dallas Times Herald* and the *San Antonio Light,* the surviving papers in these big Texas markets, according to McNeely, "don't do as much state reporting as they used to mainly because they don't have the competition they once did. There's a lack of incentive."

Ironically, as many in-state papers have cut back on their statehouse reporting, national papers such as *The New York Times, The Wall Street Journal* and *The Washington Post* have increased their state staffs.

The New York Times, in fact, has emphasized increased statehouse reporting on its national pages, a move that Robin Toner lauds as a move in the right direction. "The *Times* today takes the states incredibly seriously. And, what with welfare and more of the important stuff getting kicked out to the states as opposed to being dealt with exclusively in Washington, this is the kind of coverage we should be providing."

Toner, who was the chief of correspondents for the national desk at the *Times* and is now covering policy news in Washington, comes to her interest in state news naturally: She covered the West Virginia and then Georgia legislatures when she began her career as a journalist in the late 1970s. She now says she cannot imagine tackling Washington without the experience she gained at the state legislative level.

"There is a certain rhythm to covering a legislative body that is transferable," says Toner. "And that helped me immensely when it came to trying to understand Washington."

STRINGERS HELP

The New York Times does not maintain a presence in every one of the state capitals, but it does employ an elaborate network of stringers and paid correspondents who keep the regional bureaus and the national desk back in New York abreast of statehouse events. If a story is particularly important, the *Times* will send in one of their heavy hitters to cover it at the statehouse.

"You don't see much of them unless there is a big story unfolding with true national interest," says Wardlaw of the *Times-Picayune*. He remembers the explosive abortion rights debates that took place in the Louisiana Legislature during the early 1990s, which attracted staff reporters from the *Times*, the *Los Angeles Times* and *The Washington Post*, far and above their usual stringers. "They ganged up on us then," says Wardlaw.

Similarly at *USA Today*, columnist Rich Wolf, who willingly said adios to writing about Washington in favor of emphasizing the states, does not actually visit each and every one of the state capitols, nor does he write about them all. But his net is wide if he can spot a trend.

"That's the best thing about this business," explains Wolf. "So often there will be five or six or eight states tackling something like welfare reform or term limits at the same time. That is perfect for my column because then I can write about as many states as possible with this one topic and compare and contrast the things they are doing."

The New York Times, says Toner, uses the same approach. "I think we are looking for patterns: Is what is happening in Oklahoma also happening in Texas and Missouri? And are we going to be the first to pick up on it?"

Although on many days the *Times* does indeed reach deep into the

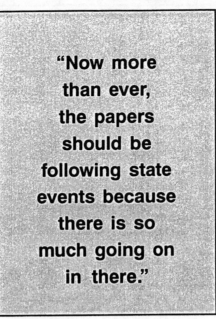

"Now more than ever, the papers should be following state events because there is so much going on in there."

South through its Atlanta bureau or out West with the desk in Los Angeles, the paper obviously continues to emphasize its coverage of states nearest to its circulation base: New Jersey, Pennsylvania and Connecticut in particular. "If they are a state legislative paper," says Rosenthal, "that legislature is in Albany."

Although no one argues that the increased attention of the *Times* and other national publications will compensate for the cutbacks in statehouse reporting on the part of the other big city and capital city dailies, statehouse reporting advocates are fighting back.

OCTOBER SEMINAR

In October, the editors of the *Colorado Springs Gazette*, in conjunction with the Pew Center as well as several other sponsoring groups (including NCSL), will host a three-day seminar designed to examine the state of statehouse reporting. The idea, says Steve Smith, managing editor at the *Gazette*, is partly to talk about "the possibility of organizing ourselves into some sort of professional organization that would

help perpetuate the craft of statehouse reporting."

With more than 400 statehouse reporters from around the country already signed up for the conference, Smith says the meeting could also serve to symbolize the commitment that at least this part of the press feels toward "quality legislative coverage." Whether or not their publishers will be listening is another matter.

Meanwhile the editors of the massive Pew study that got everyone charged up in the first place are hoping to find funding for a second study that may show marginal increases in the number of reporters covering state capitols.

"The evidence is only anecdotal at this point," says Professor Roberts. "But from what we've been hearing, many of the papers who reduced their staffs by 1996 and 1997 have turned around and hired new reporters to cover the legislatures. We just don't know at this point if the new gains are enough to make up for the old losses. Probably not. But at least it's a step in the right direction."

For Fouhy at Stateline.org the idea that any news organization could ignore or choose not to cover the states is inconceivable. "Now more than ever, the papers should be following state events because there is so much going on in there," he says. He notes by way of illustration that the states recently were earmarked for more than $30 billion in federal money that was once used to fund more than 100 jobs and vocational training programs.

"So the obvious question now is what are the states going to do with that money? How will they do anything different? What new ideas will they come up with?" Fouhy continues.

"How can any paper not want to cover stories like this?"

California, Here We Come

Government by plebiscite, which would have horrified the Founding Fathers, threatens to replace representative government

by Peter Schrag

Peter Schrag writes frequently on education and politics. His article in this issue appears in somewhat different form in his book *Paradise Lost: California's Experience, America's Future,* published by The New Press.

This June marks the twentieth anniversary of the passage of Proposition 13, the California voter initiative that has in many respects had a political and social impact on this era—not just in California but across much of the nation—almost as profound and lasting as that of the New Deal on the 1930s, 1940s, and 1950s.

The effect on California—which had been well above the national average in what it spent to educate its children, to provide free or nearly free higher education to every person who wanted it, for highway construction, and for a range of social services for children and the needy—was traumatic. Cutting local property taxes by more than 50 percent and capping the tax rate at one percent, Proposition 13 and the various initia-

tives that followed in its wake forced California to a level of spending far below the national average for such things as K-12 schooling, public-library services, the arts, and transportation. The respected journal *Education Week* said last year of California schools, "a once world-class system is now third rate." Even with a booming economy, California remains in the bottom third among the states, and far below the other major industrial states, in what it budgets per pupil.

Just as important, the march of ballot initiatives, the attack on legislative discretion, and the related acts of "direct democracy" that Proposition 13 helped to set in motion—involving taxes and spending, affirmative action, immigration, school policy, environmental protection, three-strikes criminal sentences, term limits, campaign reform, insurance rates, and virtually every other public issue—continue with unabated force, in California and beyond. In November of 1996 voters in twenty-three states were polled on a total of ninety initiatives, the most in more than eighty years (a decade ago there were forty-one), on everything from hunting rights to gam-

bling to logging regulations to sugar production to the legalization of medical marijuana use (which was approved in Arizona and California).

This June, as if to honor the anniversary of Proposition 13, Californians will again confront a large array of sometimes nearly incomprehensible ballot measures, among them yet another one on term limits and one that would all but end bilingual education. Each proposed reform further restricts the power of the legislature and local elected officials to set priorities, respond to new situations, and write budgets accordingly. When half of the state's tax-limited general fund must, under the terms of one initiative, be spent on the schools; when a sizable chunk must, under the mandate of the state's three-strikes measure, be spent on prisons; and when lesser amounts must, under the terms of still other initiatives that have been approved in the past decade, be spent on the repayment of bonds for parkland and transportation projects, the amount left over for everything else shrinks with Malthusian inevitability—as does the state government's capacity to cope with changed circumstances.

From *The Atlantic Monthly*, March 1998, pp. 20, 22, 30–31. © 1998 by Peter Schrag. Reprinted by permission.

When cities and counties are prohibited from raising property-tax rates beyond Proposition 13's one percent, and when it is difficult to raise other revenues without a vote of the electorate (in many instances a two-thirds vote) or of the affected property owners, local control is drastically reduced.

Just as inevitably, public policy is increasingly distorted by the shifting of costs from the general fund to the Byzantine system of fees, assessments, and exactions that local governments have devised in their attempts to get around tax limits and other restrictions. This reinforces the larger shift from a communitarian to a fee ethic—in the support of parks and playgrounds, in the construction of new schools, and in financing a range of other services that used to be funded entirely from general taxes. As one California letter writer complained to a newspaper, why should citizens contribute to "the methodical pillaging and plundering of the taxpayer, forcing those who have no kids to pay through the nose for someone else's"?

Direct democracy is an attractive political ideal, as close to our own experience as the New England town meeting. It has never worked, however, in large, diverse political communities, and the belief that electronics, direct mail, and televised slogans can replace personal engagement has so far looked far more like fantasy than like anything derived from hard political experience. In the case of the initiative, the new populism—unlike the reform movement that wrote the initiative into the constitutions of nineteen states around the turn of the century—seems to want greater engagement in government less than it wants an auto-pilot system to check government institutions with little active involvement by the citizenry beyond occasional trips to the polls to vote on yet more initiatives.

California sparked the anti-government, anti-tax mood that has gripped the nation for most of the past two decades, and it remains the most extreme illustration of that mood, a cautionary tale for those enamored of plebiscitary democracy. But it is now hardly unique. Virulent anti-institutionalism, particularly with respect to government, has become a prevailing theme in our national political discourse. A decade after Ronald Reagan left office, his facile dismissal of government as "the problem," not the solution, remains a talk-show staple, a

posture that serves to exonerate both civic laziness and political ignorance. And this attitude, which has become banal toward representative government, now also encompasses the related institutions of constitutional democracy: the courts, the schools, the press. Voting and serious newspaper readership are declining together. The communitarian civic ideal that they represent is giving way to "markets," a fee-for-service ethic, and the fragmented, unmediated, unedited exchange of information, gossip, and personal invective.

Nothing in California's initiative process presents the downside or the implications of any issue.

The media—new and old alike—may ensure against the power of Big Brother to dominate communications, but they also proliferate shared ignorance at an unprecedented rate: what used to be limited to gossip over the back fence is now spread in milliseconds to a million listeners during the evening commute, and to thousands over the Internet. And at the fringes are the militias and the "patriots," collecting weapons and supplies, training in the hills, and hunkering down against the black helicopters and the coming invasion of United Nations troops. That kind of ignorance and extremism, the new media, and the surrounding paranoia about government have all become commonplace in the past decade. Oliver Stone's *JFK* and the videos promoted by Jerry Falwell about the alleged murder of Vincent Foster work the same territory.

Tracy Westen, the president of the foundation-funded Center for Governmental Studies, in Los Angeles, has constructed a "digital scenario" for the election of 2004—a not altogether wild fantasy about thirty-five California voter initiatives on various subjects, all of

which have been circulated for "signatures" online, along with a spectrum of arguments pro and con, available at the click of a voice-activated mouse, from every conceivable source. In combination with a number of new elective offices, including drug commissioner and gay-rights commissioner, those measures contribute to a total of 200 ballot decisions for each voter to make.

Among Westen's futuristic initiatives is one urging Congress to approve an amendment to Article V of the U.S. Constitution such that the language guaranteeing every state a "Republican form of government" is modified to permit the states to replace representative democracy with direct democracy. Westen points out that most of the technology for this politopia—individually targeted campaign ads, interactive "discussions" with candidates, electronic voting—already exists. Since "state legislatures seem to be fighting more and doing less . . . and leaving the real legislation to the people," the scenario continues, "it seems the trend toward 'democracy by initiative' is inevitable." A few years ago the Canadian fringe Democratech Party wanted to submit all government decisions to the public through electronic referenda. An official Democratech statement said,

> Representative government assumes that the people need to elect someone to represent them in a faraway legislative assembly. But with modern, instantaneous communications, the people can directly make their own decisions, relegating politicians to the scrap heap of history.

THREE years ago *The Economist* mused about the possible benefits of replacing representative democracy with Swiss-style direct democracy, in which the voters "trudge to the polls four times a year" to decide all manner of plebiscitary questions. This process would prevent lobbyists and other special interests from buying the outcome, because "when the lobbyist faces an entire electorate . . . bribery and vote-buying are virtually impossible. Nobody has enough money to bribe everybody."

California shows that the process of bedazzling voters with sound bites, slogans, and nuanced bias works as effectively in the initiative process as it does in electoral politics. Offers that sound like something for nothing (a 50 percent property-tax cut, or a guaranteed level of education funding, or a state lottery offering a payoff for schools as well as for the lucky winners) may not be bribes, but they are the nearest thing to them. And when they work at the ballot box, their effects may last far longer than those of conventional legislation.

The larger danger, of course, is precisely the nondeliberative quality of the California-style initiative, particularly in a society that doesn't have the luxury of slow alpine trudges during which to reflect on what it's about to do. Nothing is built into the process—no meaningful hearings, no formal debates, no need for bicameral concurrence, no conference committees, no professional staff, no informed voice, no executive veto—to present the downside, to outline the broader implications, to ask the cost, to speak for minorities, to engineer compromises, to urge caution, to invoke the lessons of the past, or, once an initiative is approved by the voters, to repair its flaws except by yet another ballot measure (unless the text of the initiative itself provides for legislative amendment). Indeed, if the past decade of initiatives in California demonstrates anything, it is that the majoritarianism essential to the ethos of direct democracy almost inevitably reinforces an attitude of indifference if not hostility toward minority rights. All these dangers would be exacerbated, of course, by electronic or other forms of absentee balloting, whereby voters would no longer be required to go to the local school or church or social hall and encounter their fellow citizens participating in the same civic ritual—and thus be reminded that they are, after all, part of a larger community.

To say all that, probably, is merely to say awkwardly what the Framers of the Constitution said better in Philadelphia, what Hamilton, Madison, and Jay said in *The Federalist*, and what scores of delegates said in 1787–1788 at the various state conventions leading up to ratification, even before the Terror of the French Revolution: unchecked majorities are a danger to liberty almost as great as oligarchs and absolute monarchs.

AMONG the most common measures, put on the ballot by the organization U.S. Term Limits in fourteen states and passed in 1996 by voters in nine, is the "Scarlet Letter" initiative, also known as the "informed voter" initia-

tive, which instructs a state's elected officials to support a constitutional amendment limiting members of the House of Representatives to three two-year terms and members of the Senate to two six-year terms, and which requires state election officials to indicate on the ballot next to the name of each congressional incumbent and each member of the legislature whether he or she "disregarded voters' instruction on term limits." It also requires nonincumbents to indicate whether they have signed a pledge supporting the amendment; those who have not will be similarly identified on the ballot. For Paul Jacob, who heads U.S. Term Limits, no compromise is acceptable. The watchword is "No Uncertain Terms" (which also happens to be the name of the organization's newsletter).

> *Ballot initiatives reduce the power and accountability of legislatures—and thus the ability to govern.*

Jacob's very inflexibility helped to derail a more moderate term-limits amendment when it came up in the House (for the second time) early last year. It would have allowed six two-year terms in the House and two six-year terms in the Senate. By denouncing it as a sellout, U.S. Term Limits helped to ensure that no term-limits amendment was approved, and thus that the organization would enjoy a long, healthy life. The large turnover in Congress in 1994 probably took enough steam out of the movement to reduce its chances of success, but not enough to end it.

The Scarlet Letter initiative is probably unconstitutional. (U.S. Term Limits is now asking individual candidates to pledge to serve no more than three terms in the House or two in the Senate.) In Arkansas, one of the nine states that passed it in 1996, the state supreme court struck it down, as a violation of the procedures set forth in the U.S. Con-

stitution for amendment. Because the drafters of the Constitution, in the words of the Arkansas court, "wanted the amending process in the hands of a body with the power to deliberate upon a proposed amendment ... all proposals of amendments ... must come either from Congress or state legislatures—not from the people." The U.S. Term Limits measure was "an indirect attempt to propose an amendment ... [that would] virtually tie the hands of the individual members of the [legislature] such that they would no longer be a deliberative body acting independently in exercising their individual best judgements on the issue."

There are scattered indications that the rabid anti-government fervor of the early nineties may have peaked. (One of those indications, in the view of Nancy Rhyme, who tracks the issue for the National Conference of State Legislatures, is that only nine passed the Scarlet Letter initiative.) Certainly, term limits are not likely to be written into the Constitution any time soon.

But the issue will not go away, either in national politics or in the eighteen states that now have term limits for their legislatures written into their constitutions or otherwise written into law. On almost the same day that term limits failed (again) in the House early last year, the Scarlet Letter, funded largely by U.S. Term Limits and a handful of out-of-state term-limits organizations, qualified for the next California ballot. (U.S. Term Limits kicked in about $300,000 to the campaign to qualify the California "informed voter" measure but won't, of course, disclose where its money comes from. The organization is willing to provide a list of its National Finance Committee members, all of whom are said to have contributed more than $1,000, but will not specify which among them are its largest contributors.) A few months later the long-established California organization Field Poll reported that voter support of term limits, which stood at roughly two thirds, remained just as strong as it had been in 1990, in the months before California approved term limits for legislators and other state officials.

NOR has the initiative process lost its allure. Twenty-four states have some form of initiative in their constitutions, most of them dating from the Progressive Era. Recently there have been moves in a number of other states—including Rhode Island and Texas—to write the initiative process into their constitutions.

The pressure does not come from Hispanics or other newly active political groups, who tend to vigorously oppose these constitutional changes as openings to yet more measures like California's Proposition 187—which, until it was blocked by a federal court, sought to deny schooling and other public services to illegal immigrants. Rather, the impetus is from Ross Perot's United We Stand America and other organizations that are overwhelmingly white and middle-class. And in the states that already have the ballot initiative, there is increasing pressure to use it, sometimes generated by the dynamics of political reform itself. In California, political officeholders, from the governor down, have become initiative sponsors as a means of increasing name recognition and raising or stretching political campaign funds. And as initiatives circumscribe the power and discretion of legislatures, often the best way of responding to new circumstances—and sometimes the only way—is through yet

another initiative. The result, for better or worse, is an ongoing cycle of initiative reform, frustration, and further reform.

Yet despite all the unintended consequences and the inflexibility of the initiative and other devices of direct democracy, they seem to have one thing in common, whether they are used by liberal environmentalists or by tax-cutting conservatives: they are the instruments of established voter-taxpayer groups, particularly the white middle class, against urban politicians and political organizations that represent the interests and demands of minorities, immigrants, and other marginal groups. At the turn of the century the Yankee establishment in Boston and other cities sought to create political institutions and devices to dilute the power of the upstart Irish. In its impulse and spirit the current pressure for plebiscitary solutions driven by the general electorate, in which the white middle class can still dominate, is not all that different.

The celebratory history of direct democracy centers on its inclusiveness, but in our politically more sophisticated

(and no doubt more cynical) age there is a need to understand that defense of the initiative may be less disinterested than it seems. The groups that embrace and cheer it are not just "the people" fighting "the interests" or "the politicians," much less battling "Satan" and "Mammon," as the editor of the Sacramento Bee put it in the heyday of the Progressives. They are often established political interest groups trying by extraordinary means to further a cause or repulse the advances of other groups. More important, each initiative reduces the power and accountability of legislatures—and thus the general ability to govern, meaning the ability to shape predictable outcomes. And whereas the initiative may well further the Jeffersonian objective of tying government down, and thus preventing mischief, it also vastly reduces the chances that great leaders, and the visionary statecraft with which they are sometimes associated, will arise. In the battle over the initiative the Framers would be the first to recognize that our politics, rather than being too conservative, are in the Burkean sense not nearly conservative enough.

DIRECT DEMOCRACY WORKS

Voter initiatives can be costly and confusing, but letting people direct legislation is at the core of democracy.

BY CHARLES M. PRICE

As predictable as swallows returning to San Juan Capistrano in the spring, after every California election a host of pundits, professors and politicians weigh in with bitter criticism of the state's initiative process. These critics say there may have been some justification for the initiative historically when state legislatures were

Charles M. Price is a political science professor at California State University-Chico. These views are his own.

unresponsive, but no longer. Indeed, Professor Alan Rosenthal of the Eagleton (SGN, January 1995) calls initiative lawmaking "sloppy democracy."

Let's consider some of the standard criticisms of the initiative and then explain how defenders of the initiative might rebut them, based on California's recent direct democracy experiences.

• *The initiative has become a plaything of the special interests instead of being a tool used against special interests.*

Special interests have sponsored many initiatives lately, but so have public-interest lobbies that promote the common good. On the 1996 California general election ballot, Common Cause and the League of Women Voters sponsored the campaign-finance reform initiative. Ralph Nader's CALPIRG wrote a campaign-spending initiative. Doctors and pro-marijuana groups touted the medical use of marijuana. In short, special interests do not have a monopoly on the initiative process.

• *California politicians increasingly are writing and sponsoring initiatives to gain favorable publicity for their campaigns and partisan advantage.*

Since the 1970s, state elected officials have gotten into the initiative process in a big way. Their knowledge of fund raising and campaigning makes them formidable proponents. Ambitious politicians can generate favorable publicity by using the initiative process.

Insurance Commissioner Chuck Quackenbush wrote the 1996 initiative concerning uninsured motorists and drunk drivers. Gov. Pete Wilson has written or sponsored a number of initiatives. Since voters have the final say on propositions and politicians of both parties write or sponsor them, elected officials have every right to promote initiatives. This is not a problem.

• *Qualifying initiatives is the exclusive province of mercenary, professional petition firms, that collect signatures for a fee.*

Virtually all special-interest and politician-inspired initiatives use paid petitioners to collect signatures. Public-interest groups often collect many signatures through the efforts of unpaid volunteers. Of course, even volunteer efforts are costly (perhaps $400,000 to $500,000 to qualify a statute initiative). There are

Reprinted with permission from *State Government News*, June/July 1997, pp. 14–15, 35. © 1997 by the Council of State Governments.

expenses for printing petitions and for the salaries of coordinators who organize the volunteers. The state allows 150 days for signature collection. There would be less need for paid petitioners if there was more time to collect signatures. Of the 24 initiative states, only Oklahoma and Massachusetts have a shorter circulation period than California.

• *Initiative drafters sometimes fail to spell out all of their contingencies in their text.*

Lawmaking by the Legislature is more effective, but initiatives emerge when gridlocked legislators cannot resolve a policy issue. Politically savvy attorneys draft most initiatives that make it to California's ballot. They carefully craft their measures to avoid attacks on weak points and withstand court challenges. The worst scenario for initiative proponents is to have opponents attack a measure's text for vagueness, drafting errors or oversights. Wilson's budget powers and welfare-reduction reform in 1992 did not explain whether the Legislature could override spending cuts when the governor operated under special emergency powers. Opponents defeated the measure by exploiting that point.

• *Many initiatives are unconstitutional from the get-go.*

Since 1960, about one-half of voter-approved initiatives have been declared unconstitutional in whole or in particular sections by state and federal courts. Initiatives approved last November—campaign-finance reform, ending affirmative action and medicinal marijuana—face legal challenges. Laws approved by the Legislature and governor are far less likely to face a legal challenge and/or be declared unconstitutional. California courts have been reluctant to challenge popularly ap-

People want the right to vote on legislation.

proved initiatives, even those that appear to violate the single-subject requirement. This has been true whether liberals or conservatives dominate the state court. Federal courts seem more willing to challenge populist initiatives. The point is one never knows how the court will rule.

• *Misstatements and half-truths permeate initiative campaigns.*

Lies and distortions characterize many initiative campaigns. The fact is, initiative campaigns are no better and no worse than candidate campaigns. Both have protection under the First Amendment's free-speech provision.

Many of the same people who run candidate campaigns also work on initiatives. In the past, campaign committees used generic names to disguise their proponents. That has changed, however, since the passage of Proposition 208 in November. Campaign advertisements and literature now must identify major financial backers.

• *The side with more money invariably wins the initiative battle.*

Having more money is helpful but not critical. The side with the most money wins about two-thirds of the time. However, insurance companies spent $56 million in 1988

on their no-fault initiative. Their opponents spent $26,000 and won with 76 percent of the votes. Tobacco companies spent more than $18.5 million on Proposition 188 in 1994 while their opponents spent a little more than $1 million. The result: the tobacco industry lost, netting only 20 percent of the votes.

The case for initiatives

With all these drawbacks, one might consider: Why has the initiative process been with us since 1911? Why not reform it drastically or eliminate the process? Foremost, Californians would rather vote on major policy issues affecting their lives—even if they grouse about having to vote on so many difficult issues—than trust their legislators to do the right thing.

Rooted deeply in the initiative process is a suspicion about politicians and their intentions. One noted pollster, Mervin Field, reports that 66 percent of Californians think the initiative is a "good thing"; most of the rest believe it has good and bad aspects, and only a few totally oppose the process. Public and media pressure have defeated all efforts to make qualifying initiatives more difficult. It is a sacred cow for most Californians.

If the state did not have initiatives, popular laws such as campaign finance and lobby reforms, tobacco-tax increase, property-tax relief, the open primary and the state lottery probably never would have made it out of the Legislature. Whether these ideas are good or bad is another matter. Certainly, fine-tuning reforms could improve the process, but the core should remain fixed. It is what the public wants, and that is what democracy is all about.

Grassroots Charade

The voter initiative process was designed to give ordinary citizens leverage against powerful interests. These days, though, it's mostly the powerful that use it.

BY CHARLES MAHTESIAN

After California's Proposition 226 suffered a stunning rejection at the polls last May, disconsolate conservative activists could be found muttering to themselves, demoralized by the unexpected loss of an important ballot initiative that at one time seemed headed toward easy victory.

Prop 226, a so-called "paycheck protection" measure that would have required unions to get annual permission from members before using their dues for politics, began with a seemingly insurmountable lead. Early polls showed that even among union members, two-thirds supported the idea. But by the end of the spring campaign, after labor blanketed the state with negative television ads and poured millions into an aggressive and well-organized turnout effort, the lead had vanished. The measure lost by a margin of 53 to 47 percent.

Democrats and unions crowed over their victory, calling rejection of Prop 226 a humiliating loss for California Governor Pete Wilson, who had contributed money from his personal political action committee, lent his name to a mail appeal for petition signatures and paid for automated phone calls in support of the measure.

The governor and his allies knew different. Prop 226 was a humbling defeat for union foes, but not necessarily for Wilson. For one thing, he burnished his conservative credentials,

which will prove helpful if he enters the presidential race two years from now. Besides, Prop 226 afforded him the advantage of sticking a thumb in the eye of his longtime nemesis, the California Teachers Association. The governor, it turns out, gained in stature simply by waging the battle. "If anybody is a hero of this Dunkirk," said one prominent Republican consultant in the aftermath, "it's Wilson."

Wilson himself knew it better than anyone because over two terms in office, he has made an art out of leveraging the initiative process for political gain. Today, he is probably the best known initiative proponent and practitioner in the country, having utilized it both as a speaking platform and as a weapon with which to bludgeon his political enemies and legislative opponents.

Even as far back as his first successful run for governor in 1990, Wilson recognized the power of the ballot initiative. That year, he polished his crime-fighting reputation by hitching his gubernatorial campaign to Proposition 115, known as the Crime Victims Justice Reform Act.

And that was just the beginning. In 1992, when the legislature failed to enact his proposed welfare cuts, Wilson sponsored Proposition 165, a measure allowing welfare cuts in a time of state financial emergency. Proposition 187, an initiative denying most public benefits to illegal immi-

David Clark illustrations

grants, jump-started his struggling re-election campaign in 1994. Two years later, an initiative that called for an end to most government affirmative action programs formed the cornerstone of his brief presidential run.

Now, even as Wilson prepares to leave office, he is still using the process to advance his interests. In this month's general election, he's backing two more initiatives: a juvenile crime measure and a wide-ranging educa-

tion reform package that is already giving fits to his long-time adversaries in the education establishment.

Wilson, of course, is not the first California governor to take his case to the initiative forum, nor will he be the last. But it is probably fair to say that this is not what progressive reformers envisioned back in 1912, when California first established the voter initiative. Back then, the initiative was designed not for use by

elected officeholders but for use against them, a populist tool to wield against the business lobbies that possessed a stranglehold on the state policy-making arena.

Today, though, it is officeholders such as Wilson and a new set of special interests that tend to be the driving force behind initiatives and referendums. In Mississippi, it is Republican Governor Kirk Fordice who is back-handing his enemies and advocating

71

a favorite issue by pursuing a term-limit initiative that the Democratic legislature is determined to stop. "It's become obvious for politicians that there is mileage to be gained by being identified with an issue in terms of fundraising, name recognition, or particularly if a politician is of one party and the legislature is controlled by another," says Charles Price, a professor at California State University-Chico who is an expert on ballot initiatives.

If there is any state that rivals California as an initiative hothouse, it is Oregon, where as many as 57 proposed voter initiatives were circulating at one point this past spring. So it should come as no surprise that Oregon is the site of another evolution of the initiative form.

For the past five years, as head of Oregon Taxpayers United (the group that sparked the state's property-tax revolt nearly a decade ago), Bill Sizemore has tied the state political establishment in knots. First, he sponsored two 1994 initiatives that called for a public vote on all new or increased taxes and required that public employees increase their pension contribution. Next came two more measures in 1996, one opposing light rail and another, known as Measure 47, that cut property taxes a

second time. Last year, Sizemore successfully backed another proposal, this one known as Measure 50, rewriting the tax laws yet again.

This month, Sizemore is offering another initiative to the voters, but with a twist: He, too, will appear on the ballot—as the Republican gubernatorial nominee. For someone whose prior experience with elected office consisted of unsuccessful bids for Portland city council and the state legislature, Sizemore's political ascent is remarkable. Within a span of five years, his success as an anti-tax, initiative provocateur has been so complete that he can no longer realistically be considered an outsider.

"He's a clear example of someone who's used the process to increase his name recognition and notoriety," says M. Dane Waters, president of the Initiative and Referendum Institute, an organization that supports the initiative process. "The sole reason he's even in a position to run for governor is because of his work on initiatives."

Purists in the Oregon anti-tax movement look upon this with some dismay; they trace Sizemore's metamorphosis back to Measure 50, the 1997 initiative that repealed Measure 47. In their view, Measure 50 was

nothing less than a betrayal. For starters, Sizemore collaborated with legislative leaders to craft the replacement tax-relief measure, which was designed to rewrite the flaws in Measure 47. Worse still, anti-tax activists contended, Measure 50 hardly even resembled the measure it was supposed to replace.

Sizemore, however, has never looked back. On the day after the replacement initiative won approval last year, he upstaged everyone by turning up at the Secretary of State's office with documents in hand for three new initiatives.

While that gave him a head start on his run for governor this year, he is learning some painful political lessons now that he is on the inside. His campaign has struggled amid criticism that he is spending too much time on initiative management and not enough on his bid for office. Meanwhile, the view from inside the political fishbowl is turning out to be entirely different from the one he was accustomed to. When he was merely an initiative bombthrower, his personal life went unscrutinized. Now, thanks to a searing report in Portland's *Oregonian* newspaper, his extensive business debts and failures have been revealed to the entire state.

While Bill Sizemore and Pete Wilson have discovered the promise and peril of the initiative process as a vehicle for advancing causes, the most deeply entrenched interest groups have discovered its value as a means of thwarting them. In the Prop 226 battle, organized labor managed to neutralize the California Chamber of Commerce, a seemingly certain supporter of the measure, by threatening to retaliate with three tax-related counter-initiatives designed to hit business where it hurt. Labor strategists correctly surmised that business taxes were of greater importance to the Chamber than the notion of paycheck protection. Faced with a choice between supporting a measure the group liked, versus losing the tax breaks it loved, the Chamber decided to sit on its hands during the campaign.

THE INITIATIVE STATES

States allowing ballot initiatives

Source: Book of the States

In Nevada, "paycheck protection" advocates ran into a similar roadblock. When a judge invalidated the paycheck proposal there this summer, the state Republican Party played a key role in ensuring that it was not revived in time for the November ballot. The GOP, divided between one camp that adamantly wanted the measure on the ballot and a more moderate wing led by gubernatorial nominee Kenny Guinn, agreed not to pursue a court appeal. In return, Republicans received a promise from labor activists that they would not offer a competing ballot measure.

This non-aggression pact was, in large part, influenced by neighboring California's experience with the issue earlier in the year. By the time that campaign ended, Californians had been told that Prop 226 posed a threat to their pensions and benefits, constituted a gross invasion of their privacy and would somehow lead to an increase in crime. Having witnessed that across-the-border spectacle—and the pro-union voter turnout sparked by it—Nevada Republicans didn't have the stomach to take on the fight. Given a choice between capturing the governorship and passing the initiative, the state party settled for pragmatism over principle.

Whatever view one might have on initiatives such as this, it's a bit of a stretch to portray them as populist weapons in the hands of citizen activists. They are more like doomsday weapons whose use by interest groups is controlled by a complex process of mutual deterrence. If this is grassroots democracy, it is being played out on artificial turf.

Of course, special interests have had a role in initiative campaigns since they began exactly one century ago, when South Dakota became the first of 24 states that would eventually adopt the system. If there was a turning point in the evolution of the initiative, though, it came in 1978, the year California's Proposition 13 sparked a nationwide tax revolt and a sharp rise of interest in the initiative as a policy-making instrument.

Prior to Prop 13, for example, California voters had passed judgment on 153 measures over a span of 66 years. Now, an average of 70 initiatives are filed in the state every two years. Not all of them make the ballot, and even fewer still pass muster with voters, but the fact remains that close to 30 initiatives have been approved at the California polls over the past decade, enacting substantive policy changes in areas that stretch from education to insurance to taxes to the environment. Elsewhere, the story has been much the same. In Colorado, 15 initiatives went before the voters in the 1980s. More than twice that number will appear on the ballot during this decade.

In 1998 alone, voters in 17 states are going to the polls to vote on as many as 65 different questions. They range from medical use of marijuana to hog farm regulation, campaign finance to the rights of adoptees and animals. Some of the most contentious issues discussed this year in legislatures will also go before the electorate, including abortion, physician-assisted suicide, affirmative action and term limits.

But while the initiative process is more vigorous than ever, the true citizen initiative is becoming a thing of the past, not only in California and Oregon, but virtually everywhere that statewide voter initiative or referendum is authorized. Most of the current campaigns are marked by little grassroots participation of any meaningful sort. "We're not seeing as many public interest campaigns anymore," says Charles Price. "A great majority of the initiatives on the ballot come from special interests with an ax to grind."

That certainly was true of last year's catfight in Wyoming, which found dentists on one side and denturists, who make and repair false teeth, on the other. After posting several initiative victories in other Western states, denturists decided to try a ballot proposal that would have brought them under Wyoming's den-tal practice act, and thus given formal legitimacy to their services. It's hard to argue that there was a popular groundswell of support for the denturists, or against them either. Few voters even knew the argument was taking place. But both sides fought it out with every weapon they had. Ultimately, the denturists gave up the fight before the issue came to a vote, charging that the Secretary of State's office had subverted the initiative process by distorting the official ballot language.

One might argue that the initiative process is an odd place to decide matters of dental regulation: a legislature would seem the appropriate venue for such a dispute. The Wyoming denturists, on the other hand, insisted that they had no choice but to take the measure to the ballot—because they couldn't get a fair hearing at the state-house. "Every legislator has a dentist. But they don't have a denturist, which means dentists can explain to their legislators why they are right. So we don't have a chance," says Brett Kandarian, chairman of the American Academy of Denturitry. "But when you take it to the people, they understand."

Recent years have witnessed similar ballot clashes, both between relative special-interest small fry, such as in Wyoming, and between lobbying titans, as when trial lawyers butted heads with insurance companies over California tort law. Four years ago in Massachusetts, big retail chains faced off with their smaller competitors. Last year, chiropractors backed a measure to require insurers to cover their services in the state of Washington. Whatever the organized interest might be, whether it's casinos, utilities, timber companies, teachers, banks, hunters or environmentalists, the odds are that it is, has been or expects to be on the ballot with a proposal whose passage it favors.

That's because the initiative process, as it has developed, enables virtually any group with a moderately sized budget to bring its cause before the voters. A burgeoning initiative industry has generated political consultants to design the campaign, direct-mail consultants to inundate voters with literature, lawyers to handle the endless litigation and paid signature-gatherers to rake in the requisite petition signatures.

Today, it takes at least $1 million

Prop. 42,871,15-6,930,013,256

David Clark illustration

to place an initiative on the California ballot. In neighboring Oregon, the total amount spent merely to qualify initiatives for the ballot more than doubled between 1992 and 1996, from $1.8 million to $4 million. Since 1990, total spending on initiative campaigns in Oregon has also doubled, from $10.4 million to $20.9 million, and is far outpacing the growth of statehouse lobbying expenditures.

This fact alone says something profound not just about the initiative but about its impact on the legislative process. Organized money moves inexorably toward where the action is, and these days, that place is the ballot as often as it is the statehouse.

For an interest group, the voter initiative offers distinct advantages over traditional lobbying practices. There are no hostile committee chairmen to strangle legislation. Gone is the long and arduous process of shepherding the bill to enactment. Best of all, initiatives allow the injection of unlimited amounts of cash into a one-shot, do-or-die, six-month-long popularity contest fought according to a lenient

set of rules. Unlike campaign financing for elected offices, initiative financing places few restrictions on the way proponents or critics spend their money.

The gaming industry, for one, likes its chances under that kind of format. In Florida, supporters of legalized casinos continue to try for statewide approval, despite three previous rejections—including one that cost them $17 million in cash and contributions in 1994. "Initiative and referendum is a wonderful populist tool when the legislature is not responsive, but what's happened is that special interests are using the process in some troubling ways," says Sally Spener, executive director of Florida Common Cause. "There is a minute and insignificant number of contributions from average Floridians, and millions and millions from gaming interests who would get rich from casino gaming here."

Initiative critics point to the story of how California got a state lottery as one of the most troubling of all. It happened nearly 15 years ago, but it remains fresh in the minds of many who consider it a watershed in initiative history.

Prior to 1984, polls had long registered high levels of support for a lottery in California, but not nearly enough to persuade lawmakers to act. The horse-racing industry, on the other hand, was steadfastly determined to keep the idea buried in a legislative committee.

Organized money goes where the action is, and these days, the action is on the ballot.

Kelly Kimball, the former head of a Los Angeles-based petition-signature-gathering company, found a way to break the logjam. In an attempt to gin up some business in what promised to be a slow year for his firm, Kimball took the idea of a lottery initiative to an industry that had as much to gain from the scheme as the horse tracks had to lose from it—the makers of lottery equipment. He persuaded Scientific Games Inc., a Georgia-based company, to kick in more than $2 million for a campaign to take the issue to the ballot. On Election Day, the pro-lottery effort won in a cakewalk. To this day, Scientific Games holds the ticket-making contract.

Kimball says the initiative industry has taken off since those early days. "People began to realize that a good initiative campaign will earn you as much money as a presidential campaign can," he says. "Once they saw that, they began thinking, 'Hey, I could become a millionaire overnight.'"

To a growing chorus of critics and reformers, California is the perfect symbol of a process spiraling out of control. To true believers, on the other hand, recent developments are merely a sign of the system's health. "The more money put into an initiative campaign, the more interest it generates," says Dane Waters. "Basically 600 initiatives and constitutional amendments have been put into law because of the initiative and referendum process over a period of 100 years. Compare that to tens or hundreds of thousands of bills that have been enacted by legislatures over the years that people know nothing about."

The majority of ballot initiatives, Waters points out, are rejected by voters. And in any case, he says, with initiative campaigns at least the entire process is out in the open—unlike the sometimes clandestine route bills take before becoming law. "Say there's $10 million poured into a California initiative. That $10 million is in the sunlight as compared to $10 million spent to lobby the legislature," he says. "There's a better chance of influencing 150 legislators in Sacramento than influencing 5 million voters in California with the same amount of money."

Pete Wilson aside, most elected officials have yet to be convinced of the merits of a freewheeling initiative process. Many, in fact, are doing their best to keep it under wraps. Florida Governor Lawton Chiles has repeatedly called for limits on the process, echoing sentiments voiced in every state that currently uses it. In Oregon, nearly 80 initiative-related bills alone surfaced last session in the legislature, almost all aimed at reining in some aspect of the enterprise. For its part, the state's employment department weighed in with a 1997 ruling that paid signature-gatherers must be treated like employees—rather than independent contractors—a costly decision for petition-management firms and one that ultimately strikes a blow against initiatives.

Restrictive legislation has passed in states that have been inundated with initiatives, and it has passed in others, such as Wyoming, where initiative action has never been especially intense. But few of the restrictions passed so far have amounted to much, other than to make the price of participating that much more expensive. Most have tinkered with the qualification requirements or tried to regulate the activities of paid signature-gatherers. Some states have attempted to ban out-of-state signature-gatherers, or to require them to wear identifying badges. Understandably, the pro-initiative forces don't like it.

"These are all clearly designed to make the process more difficult," says Dane Waters. "Throughout the history of the initiative process, there has been a legislative assault, but it's really taken off over the past four to six years."

Unit Selections

Key Points to Consider

❖ Compare and contrast the positions of president of a school board, elected chief executive of a small town, city manager, mayor of a large city, state governor, and president of the United States.

❖ How does your state constitution compare with the United States Constitution—in length, subjects covered, ease of reading, and your familiarity with it?

❖ Is it better to have well-paid and prestigious, elected positions as in the national government, or less well paid, part-time elected posts as are common in local governments and many state legislatures? Which makes for better government?

❖ Do you think that it is a good idea to let citizens participate directly in the policy process by means of initiatives, referenda, or town meetings? Or should legislating be left to elected representatives? Why or why not?

❖ In 1990, three states—California, Colorado, and Oklahoma—passed referenda establishing "term limits" for their state legislatures. Since then, many other states have followed suit. What effects on the functioning of the state legislatures in these states do you expect term limits to have? Do you think it is a good idea to limit the number of terms or length of years that individuals can serve in one house of a state legislature? Why or why not?

DUSHKIN ONLINE Links   www.dushkin.com/online/

14. **Americans Back in Charge Foundation**
    http://www.abic.org
15. **Center for the American Woman in Politics**
    http://www-rci.rutgers.edu/~cawp/cawpfs.html
16. **Council on Licensure, Enforcement and Regulation**
    http://www.clearhq.org
17. **EMILY's List of Women in State Legislatures**
    http://www.emilyslist.org/news/st_legis/ak.htm
18. **National Conference of State Legislatures**
    http://www.ncsl.org/index.htm
19. **NGA Online**
    http://www.nga.org

These sites are annotated on pages 4 and 5.

Government institutions are to state and local political systems what skeletons are to people. They shape the general outlines of policy processes in the same way that bones shape the outlines of human bodies. For state and local governments, as well as for the national government and most governments everywhere, institutions are critical factors in the governing process. There are important state-by-state variations in executive, legislative, and judicial structures and in the degree to which citizens have access to the policy-making process. In "strong governor" states, chief executives hold substantially greater appointive, budgetary, and veto powers than in "weak governor" states. The roles of parties, committees, and leaders differ among state legislatures, as does the degree of "profession-alization" among legislators themselves. The roles of state court systems vary according to the contents of state constitutions as well as state political and judicial traditions. In some states, the state's highest court plays a role that is roughly comparable to that of the United States Supreme Court at the national level. The highest courts in most states, however, are generally less prominent. States also differ in whether judges are elected or appointed. With respect to policy making and government as a whole, some states allow for direct citizen involvement through the devices of initiative, referendum, and recall, while others do not. Many of these structural details of state governments are spelled out in each state's written constitution, although state constitutions generally do not play as prominent or symbolically important a role in state government as the United States Constitution does in national government.

Local governments do not incorporate the traditional three-branch structure of government to the extent that state and national governments do. Legislative and executive powers are often given to a single governing body, with the members choosing one of themselves to be the nominal chief executive. For example, school boards typically elect their own board "president" to preside over meetings, but they hire a professional educational administrator, called a superintendent, to manage day-to-day affairs. What is true of school districts also applies to many other local governments. In contrast, the structures of some "strong mayor" cities do resemble the executive-legislative arrangements in national and state governments. The traditional notion of an independent local judiciary as a "third branch" does not easily apply at the level of local government. Local courts, to the extent that they exist, do not restrain the other branches of local government in the way that state and national courts are empowered to restrain their respective legislative and executive branches. As with state judges, some local judges are appointed and some are elected.

This unit on institutions is organized along traditional legislative, executive, and judicial lines. The first section treats state and local legislatures, which include town meetings, city and town councils, school boards, and, of course, state legislatures. The second section turns to governors and local government executives, while the third and last section treats state and local courts.

LIVING WITHIN THE LIMITS

The way legislatures run, the way lawmakers conduct business, our very concept of representative democracy is likely to be shaken up by term limits. In this first article of a three-part series, State Legislatures examines the recent history of the term limits movement and the maturation of American state legislatures.

By Karen Hansen

"The branch of government which holds the most hope, I think, for bringing society together is the legislative branch. Computer technology cannot replace the importance of men and women coming from many different societal backgrounds to meet and deliberate, to learn from each other and do consensus building. The executive branch isn't in a position to do that. The judicial branch is not. That's why I find term limits so troubling, because I think term limits attack the heart of what is a good representative process."

–Paul Hillegonds
Michigan Speaker of the House, 1995–96

Term limits are one of the decade's most popular political ideas. And they have taken the states by storm. Well-financed, well-orchestrated and well-planned, the term limitation movement has won over voters in 20 states. Citizens in those states are beginning to learn if this experiment in democracy delivers on its promise–a more responsive, effective and energized government–or whether it is the wrong prescription.

A new characteristic now distinguishes states: those with term limits and those without. Twenty states are term limited–they prohibit their members by constitution or law from running for reelection beyond a prescribed term. No state legislature to date has swept out all the incumbents and voted in new lawmakers under term limits. But the clock is running. In 2008, limits will be fully implemented in all the states that passed them. Legislators in California and Maine were the first to find themselves out of work as lawmakers, not in an election defeat, but because of term limits. The houses in Arkansas, Colorado, Michigan, Montana, Oregon and Washington and the California Senate will be the next to replace incumbents after the 1998 elections. There will soon be a time when entire chambers have members with fewer than six years' experience.

THE RUSH OF THE 1990s

The rush to limit terms began in 1990. The early successes in California, Colorado and Oklahoma provided momentum in the following five years. In 1992, 14 initiatives were certified and placed on the ballot and every one passed.

With the exception of Utah, where the Legislature imposed limits on itself, and Louisiana, the only state where the Legislature itself

Karen Hansen is editor of State Legislatures *magazine.*

CHRONOLOGY OF LEGISLATIVE TERM LIMITS

1781
Articles of Confederation limit representation to "three years in six."

1787
New Constitution for federal Congress has no limitations set on representatives or senators.

1951
Twenty-second Amendment to the U.S. Constitution limiting presidential terms to two four-year terms is approved.

1978
U.S. Senate Judiciary subcommittee holds hearings on congressional term limits. No action taken.

1988
GOP platform includes plank advocating congressional term limits.

1990
Oklahoma, California, Colorado pass term limits on state elected officials. (Colorado's provisions also include federal lawmakers.)

1991
April
California Legislature challenges Proposition 140, which includes term limits for state lawmakers, in state Supreme Court.

October
California Supreme Court upholds term limits.

November
Washington state fails to pass term limits.

December
California Legislature appeals term limits case to U.S. Supreme Court, which declines to hear it.

From *State Legislatures*, June 1997, pp. 13–19. © 1997 by the National Conference of State Legislatures. Reprinted by permission.

VETERAN LAWMAKERS DISCUSS TERM LIMITS

In the summer of 1995 and again in January 1996, NCSL and the Milbank Memorial Fund invited a group of veteran legislators to consider the implications of term limits on the legislative institution. *State Legislatures* is publishing a three-part series of articles based in part on the discussions of these lawmakers.

The participants were:

John J. H. Schwarz—The Michigan Senate president pro tem, Schwarz chaired the NCSL-Milbank discussions. A surgeon, he has served 11 years in the Legislature. He was mayor of Battle Creek and a city commissioner before his election to the state Senate.

"Term limits will empower lobbyists, bureaucrats, professional legislative staff and governors (even those who are term limited themselves). Term limits both trivialize and marginalize the legislature. The people's representatives are neutered. The people lose—large impersonal government wins."

Jane Campbell—Elected to six terms in the Ohio House of Representatives, Campbell was majority whip and assistant minority leader. She served as president of NCSL in 1995 and is now vice president of the Cuyahoga Board of County Commissioners.

"Term limits were a dramatic prescription that I don't think solve the problem. People wanted more responsive governments, and term limits were presented as a mechanism for that. As soon as they passed, however, we began losing talented members because they couldn't make a career here."

Larry Campbell—Currently president of The Victory Group in Eugene, Ore., Campbell served as speaker of the Oregon House from 1991 to 1995. He was the House Republican leader for eight years and served as a state representative from 1979 to 1995.

"All states have a pressing need to take actions that contribute to maintaining legislatures as co-equal branches of government. This need, however, is greatly increased in term-limited states."

John Dorso—Elected in 1984, Dorso is the majority leader in the North Dakota House of Representatives. He also is vice chairman of the legislative council.

"The people of North Dakota have rejected term limits because we are a citizen legislature. We are open and accountable to the people of our state. They know us and trust us."

Art Hamilton—The minority leader of the Arizona House of Representatives since 1981, Hamilton has served in the Legislature since 1973. He was president of NCSL in 1992–93. He is a public affairs representative for Salt River Project.

"There is a clear loss of collegiality and much more contentiousness between the House and the Senate."

Paul Hillegonds—Currently president of Detroit Renaissance, Hillegonds served as speaker of the Michigan House of Representatives, co-speaker, and Republican leader during his 18-year legislative career.

"Will term limits truly make government more responsive and accountable to the people? I remain very skeptical and concerned."

Bobby Hogue—Speaker Hogue is the only the fourth person in the history of Arkansas to serve more than one term as speaker. He has served in the legislature since 1979.

"While the negative impact of term limitation is clear to me, I am not willing to devote my energy to fighting its repeal. I am more interested in developing a positive response. This involves creating a legislative branch of government in which new members are trained well and given the resources needed to participate quickly and fully in the process."

Phillip Isenberg—A lawyer and college professor, Isenberg served 14 years in the California Assembly, where he was assistant speaker pro tem. Isenberg was mayor of Sacramento and a member of the city council.

"State legislators spend far too much time worrying about term limits and predicting that if they are adopted, disaster is around the corner. To be honest, we won't have a clue about the impact of term limits for 10 to 15 years."

John McDonough—A member of the Massachusetts House, McDonough was elected in 1985. He is an adjunct professor of public health at the Boston University School of Medicine.

"If someone suggested term limits for partners in law firms, corporate directors, medical department heads—people would think you were crazy. There's a real lack of appreciation of the need for institutional memory for legislative bodies. And loss of that institutional memory is one of the most damaging things about term limits."

Joyce McRoberts—Currently regional director for the Idaho Department of Health and Welfare, McRoberts was elected to the state Senate in 1989. She was named assistant majority leader in 1991 and majority leader in 1993.

"In Idaho where every year we pass significant water laws that are critical to keeping our own water in our own state, we are losing two legislators who are national experts in water law because of term limits. We will never have their institutional knowledge again."

Thomas Norton—A professional engineer, Norton has been president of the Colorado Senate since 1992. Norton was elected to the Colorado House in 1986 and to the Colorado Senate in 1988.

"The effect of term limits on a legislative institution can be positive if leaders create changes that encourage optimum member participation and training in legislative management and procedural issues. Leadership also needs to redefine the role of staff to better serve legislative members."

Raymond Rawson—A dentist and college professor, Rawson was elected to the Nevada Senate in 1984. He has served as assistant majority floor leader and assistant minority floor leader.

"Term limits remind me of the difference between modern warfare and indiscriminate warfare. The winnowing process without term limits is discriminate—the bad get weeded out. But term limits indiscriminately target the good with the bad."

Michael Wagner—Elected to the South Dakota House of Representatives in 1988, Wagner was assistant majority leader. He left the Legislature in 1996 to consult for the Advisory Board Company in Washington, D.C.

"One of the reasons state legislatures traditionally have been more effective than Congress on some issues is because legislators have to live with each other over time. Now term limits are ripping that very fabric."

Don Wesely—Elected in 1978, Wesely was the third youngest person to serve in Nebraska's Unicameral Legislature. He currently serves as chairman of the Health and Human Services Committee. He is a senior research associate with Aliant Communications.

"In Mexico, they've had term limits since about 1910 and there's a movement to get rid of them. What they've found is they didn't work because people who were very good could only serve three or six years."

put term limits on the ballot, citizen groups have spawned successful petition drives to curb the time lawmakers may serve. These have not been undertaken in isolation, however. National advocacy groups such as U.S. Term Limits, Americans for Limited Terms and Americans Back in Charge have coordinated initiative campaigns and encouraged similar ballot language in many states.

A DIVERSE GROUP OF STATES

Forty-two percent of the American population lives in the 20 term-limited states. The states are geographically, economically and politically diverse. Their legislatures are full-time, part-time and citizen. Their populations are large—California, Florida, Massachusetts, Michigan, Ohio—and small—Montana, South Dakota, Utah, Wyoming. They are located in the East, South, Midwest and the West. Their economies are agricultural, industrial, high tech, tourist, petroleum- and mining-based. They have large budgets, and relatively small ones.

Of these 20 states, 14 have constitutional limits on service (Arizona, Arkansas, California, Colorado, Florida, Louisiana, Michigan, Missouri, Montana, Nevada, Ohio, Oklahoma, Oregon and South Dakota). Limits in the remaining six (Idaho, Maine, Massachusetts, Utah, Washington and Wyoming) are statutory. The issue was brought to the ballot by citizen initiative in 18 states. Alaska, Illinois, Mississippi and North Dakota are the only remaining states that permit citizens to place measures on the ballot that have not enacted term limits.

The states vary significantly. California, Massachusetts, Michigan and Ohio all have full-time legislatures with both central and partisan staffs and lawmakers who are paid higher annual salaries than their peers in other states. They meet year-round. Arizona, Colorado, Florida, Louisiana, Missouri, Oklahoma, Oregon and Washington, on the other hand, are part-time legislatures, but they are nevertheless well-staffed and comparatively well-paid. Florida, for example, is a large state with a large professional staff, but its Legislature meets only two months of the year. Colorado is constitutionally limited to 120 session days per year. The term-limited states with part-time legislators, low pay and small staffs are Arkansas, Idaho, Maine, Montana, Nevada, South Dakota, Utah and Wyoming. Arkansas, Montana, Nevada and Oregon meet only every other year. In three of these states, House members will meet in session only three times before term limits force them out of office.

The men and women serving in these 20 legislatures are responsible for budgets that range from $94 billion in California to $1.7 billion in South Dakota. They are writing some of the most significant legislation in the history of the states as Congress turns over programs formerly administered by the federal government, and they are doing it without the benefit of legislative historical perspective and institutional memory.

"That's what has been the beauty of representative government. We have an enormously diverse society, and we've been able to stay together as a country because we have representative bodies that have found ways to reach consensus across geographical and philosophical lines," says former Michigan Speaker Paul Hillegonds, now president of Detroit Renaissance, a corporate alliance dedicated to revitalizing the city. "That process is enhanced by personal relationships and this thing I call institutional memory—people who have been through issues on a periodic basis and have a better understanding when the same issue arises again."

Former Speaker
Paul Hillegonds
Michigan

Representative
John McDonough
Massachusetts

Senator
Don Wesely
Nebraska

1992

November

Fourteen ballot initiatives limiting state or federal officials pass in Arizona, Arkansas, California, Florida, Michigan, Missouri, Montana, Nebraska, North Dakota, Ohio, Oregon, South Dakota, Washington and Wyoming.

1993

November

Maine passes limits on state officials. It becomes the first state to make limits retroactive.

1994

March

Arkansas Supreme Court rules that voters cannot restrict eligibility of federal candidates, but upholds limits for state lawmakers.

Utah Legislature passes term limits on itself.

May

Nebraska Supreme Court overthrows 1992 term limits initiative on a signature technicality.

October

U.S. Supreme Court agrees to hear appeal of Arkansas Case. (U.S. Term Limits vs. Thornton)

November

Alaska, Idaho, Maine, Massachusetts, Nebraska and Nevada voters approve term limits measures for state lawmakers. Colorado voters extend limits to local officials. A ballot initiative in Utah does not pass, but a law passed by the Legislature in March 1994 remains in effect.

1995

May

U.S. Supreme Court rules on Thornton, arguing that individual states may not limit terms in Congress.

CALIFORNIA TERM LIMITS
DECLARED UNCONSTITUTIONAL

Just as California's legislative term limits were about to finish the job the voters started more than six years ago, a federal judge in April struck down the law as unconstitutional.

Federal District Judge Claudia Wilken, however, suspended her own decision pending an appeal, leaving 27 termed out lawmakers in limbo, wondering whether a final decision will be reached before the 1998 elections.

Legislators were divided over whether to place a new term limits measure on the ballot, possibly in a special election this year or let the appeals run their course. Governor Pete Wilson, who would have to call a special election if there is to be one, said he was not inclined to do so.

"I respect the will of the people of California who enacted term limits," Senate President Pro Tem Bill Lockyer said. "However, sometimes even the will of the voters is constrained by the right of free speech and association guaranteed by the United States Constitution. I am convinced that we can reconcile the two by enacting a term limits law which, without a lifetime ban, would be constitutional."

California's term limits, enacted by voters in 1990, limit members of the Assembly to three, two-year terms and cap Senate service at two, four-year terms. Once members reach those limits they must leave office and can never run again.

The November 1996 elections marked a watershed, for it was then that the last of the 80 Assembly members in office when term limits were approved were forced to retire. Nine state senators remain from the 1990 class and will be forced out next year if term limits remain in effect.

Wilken, appointed to the bench in 1993 by President Clinton, ruled that the law's lifetime ban violated the right of voters to choose candidates with extensive legislative experience. She said it also infringed unduly on the right of citizens with legislative experience to seek office. And she said the structure of the law, as interpreted in an earlier case by the state Supreme Court, required her to strike it down entirely rather than simply remove the offending provision.

Term limits themselves, Wilken said, need not be found unconstitutional. But their goal—limiting the power of incumbency—could be achieved by requiring

legislators to sit out for a period rather than banning them for life, she said.

"Because California's extreme version of term limits imposes a severe burden on the right of its citizens to vote for candidates of their choice, and because it is not narrowly tailored to advance compelling state interests, it violates the First and 14th Amendments to the United States Constitution," Wilken wrote.

The decision came in a case filed in 1995 by then-Democratic Assemblyman Tom Bates and several constituents. Their lawyer, Joseph Remcho, praised the ruling and predicted it would withstand review by the 9th District Court of Appeals and, if necessary, the U.S. Supreme Court.

"I think the ninth circuit can and should have this decided by the end of the year," Remcho said. "We're going to ask them to move very quickly."

Attorney General Dan Lungren, who is running for governor in 1998, will defend the law on appeal. Lungren offered no quick legal analysis of Wilken's ruling, but criticized her for overturning "the clear will of California voters."

Several legislators, meanwhile, suggested calling a special election for November to allow voters to decide the issue before the 1998 campaign season gets under way. Among them was Democratic Assembly Speaker Cruz Bustamante, who also said he would suggest adding at least one more term to the limit, which would allow him to serve beyond 1998. Lockyer, who was planning to run for attorney general next year, issued a similar statement.

Republicans, however, generally urged caution on going to the voters with a new term limits law before the appeals are exhausted. Assembly Republican Leader Curt Pringle said he feared that a special election would "restart the clock" for legislators who are approaching their limit. That, he said, would be a "phony fix."

And while there were suggestions of a possible deal linking a new term limits law to the creation of an independent redistricting commission, which Republicans would like, Governor Wilson was cool to the idea of a special election.

"I don't know if that would be quicker or if it would be better," Wilson said.

—*Daniel Weintraub*
Sacramento bureau chief
Orange County Register

October

Louisiana voters pass a referendum proposed by the Legislature that sets term limits on state lawmakers.

November

Mississippi fails to pass a term limit initiative for state office holders.

1996

February

Nebraska Supreme Court utilizes *Thornton* to overthrow limits approved in 1994.

Maine federal district court denies a request brought by the League of Women Voters for a preliminary injunction against the term limits law.

September

Maine Supreme Court rules that term limits are constitutional under the state constitution.

October

Arkansas Supreme Court strikes down a proposal requiring ballots to indicate whether candidates back term limits legislation. Despite this ruling, the court allows the measure to remain on the ballot.

November

Voters in nine states (Alaska, Arkansas, Colorado, Idaho, Maine, Missouri, Nebraska, Nevada and South Dakota) pass "inform and instruct" measures requiring ballots to note whether candidates support term limits legislation. Such measures fail in Montana, North Dakota, Oregon, Washington and Wyoming.

North Dakota fails to pass an initiative limiting state legislative terms.

1997

January

The first three chambers to be entirely "termed out"—the California Assembly, the Maine House and Senate—convene for their annual sessions.

"I think institutional memory is very important, to have people who remember as far back as possible to avoid mistakes and to have people who were eyewitnesses to what has happened before," says Massachusetts Representative John McDonough. "It doesn't have the same impact on people's thinking to have a written document that says this is what happened versus having someone stand up in a caucus or on the floor and say, 'Wait a minute, I was here, and this is what really happened.' It makes a very, very big difference."

There are 7,424 state legislators in the United States; 2,615, or 35 percent, serve under term limits

"It's just knowing the history and the context—why something didn't happen," says Senator Don Wesely of Nebraska. "Maybe those reasons have changed, and that helps you fashion better solutions to problems. To take that away, in my view, is reinventing the wheel."

LEGISLATURES UNDER CHALLENGE

"Today, state legislatures are among the most revitalized and changed institutions in America with a vastly increased capacity to govern," says William T. Pound, executive director of the National Conference of State Legislatures.

The ability of legislatures to create and shape programs has never been greater than it is now. Yet they also are under challenge as never before. Public perception, the citizen initiative, the demand to maintain government programs in a tax restricted environment are but a few of the difficulties facing legislatures today. And the movement to limit terms is among the most serious.

Almost every national policy innovation can be traced back to the states. Old age pensions created by state legislatures were the model for the federal Social Security Act. States created programs to compensate workers who were injured on the job. Today, all but three states have workers' compensation plans. And more recently, state legislatures have effected health reform even as Congress and the president struggled with increasing access to health insurance. The federal Health Insurance Portability and Accountability Act of 1996 nationalized many of the reforms already enacted in the majority of states. State legislatures have streamlined Medicaid, increasing coverage and stabilizing costs, while the federal government continues to debate whether to hand the program in its entirety to the states. State legislatures have reformed welfare and provided the inspiration for congressional action.

Progressive and creative social policy and institutional innovations in the states rival the very best of federal legislation:

- Oregon passed one of the most comprehensive health programs in the nation, increasing by 60 percent the number of people covered by Medicaid by guaranteeing health coverage for all people living below 100 percent of the poverty level. The state also created a high-risk pool for people with pre-existing medical conditions and a health insurance purchasing pool for small businesses.
- Florida enacted one of the nation's first managed competition approaches to health care reform—Florida Health Access—that allowed small businesses to purchase health care at group rates, providing access to health insurance to more than 17,000 employers and more than 76,000 people who had gone without it. The Florida plan has become a model for the nation.
- Michigan scrapped its school finance system, replacing local property taxes with a 2-cent increase in the state sales tax and other state taxes, and provided substantial new funding to improve the poorest schools in the state.
- In a special session that was the first of its kind in the nation, Colorado passed a tough new ban on kids possessing guns and created a new penal system for hard core offenders.
- Massachusetts prohibited HMOs from restricting communication between providers and patients about various medical procedures.
- Congress and the Environmental Protection Agency modeled the 1993 Clean Air Act Amendments on California's innovative air quality program that allows emissions trading in polluted areas and encourages the use of electric cars.

These states share creativity in public policy. But they also share another bond: Their terms are limited.

TURNOVER—ALREADY A REALITY

Term limits' promise—and appeal—is to oust the entrenched and bring in the new—new people, new ideas, new ways of doing things. By forcing turnover, the argument goes, term limits ensure that public policy, not politics and the personal gain of politicians, is the outcome of government. Scrapping the seniority system means that no single person can have a stranglehold on a leadership position, a committee chairmanship or a district.

There are 7,424 state legislators in the United States; 2,615, or 35 percent, serve under term limits. There is clearly a belief among voters who supported term limits that they were the only way to get rid of superannuated veterans. But natural turnover and the ballot box achieve the same end.

Statistics from the National Conference of State Legislatures illustrate that state legislatures change through natural turnover every decade without term limits. Turnover in state legislatures is, on average, 20 percent every two years. In 10 years, theoretically, everybody is new. A study of turnover in state legislatures between 1987 and 1997 showed actual turnover to be 72 percent for the nation's state senates and 84 percent for houses. The statistics for leadership turnover are even more impressive: From 1990 to 1997, 86 percent of senate presidents, house speakers and majority and minority leaders changed.

Total membership turnover is much higher in state legislatures than in Congress. According to the Congressional Research Service, the re-election rate for House incumbents has fallen below 70 percent only three times since the turn of the century and has averaged more than 90 percent since 1950.

By comparing actual turnover rates in the 1990s with the enforced turnover under various term limitations, it is evident that some states get to 100 percent more quickly than others—and even faster than term limits require. Statistically, membership in lower chambers of Louisiana, Nevada, Montana, Idaho, Oklahoma and Utah would naturally turn over in about six years, while the term limitations in those states range from eight to 12 years. On the other hand, natural turnover in the Ohio, California and Michigan houses takes about 18 years. Their term limitations are stringent—eight years in Ohio, six in California and Michigan.

But voters who passed term limits may not really want drastic change. In Michigan, a state that overwhelmingly passed one of the nation's most severe term limit laws in 1992, only one seat changed parties in 1994, tilting a previously tied chamber to the Republicans for the first time in 25 years. The Legislature had had its most productive session in years, according to the former speaker of the House, and the public showed its approval by returning all but one member to office.

STATE LEGISLATIVE TURNOVER 1987–1997

STATE	Total Senate	Senate New Members	Turnover (percent)	Total House	House New Members	Turnover (percent)
Alabama	35	24	69%	105	74	70%
Alaska	20	17	85	40	36	90
Arizona	30	28	93	60	55	92
Arkansas	35	20	57	100	75	75
California	40	31	78	80	80	100
Colorado	35	27	77	65	54	83
Connecticut	36	30	83	151	119	79
Delaware	21	13	62	41	19	46
Florida	40	31	78	120	95	79
Georgia	56	45	80	180	132	73
Hawaii	25	21	84	51	42	82
Idaho	35	26	74	70	51	73
Illinois	59	34	58	118	90	76
Indiana	50	29	58	100	64	64
Iowa	50	39	78	100	84	84
Kansas	40	33	83	125	110	88
Kentucky	38	31	82	100	72	72
Louisiana	39	33	85	105	80	76
Maine	35	35	100	151	149	99
Maryland	47	28	60	141	94	67
Massachusetts	40	34	85	160	119	74
Michigan	38	26	68	110	84	76
Minnesota	67	41	61	134	99	74
Mississippi	52	41	79	122	86	70
Missouri	34	22	65	163	130	80
Montana	50	39	78	100	84	84
Nebraska	49	35	17	NA		Unicameral
Nevada	21	11	52	42	32	76
New Hampshire	24	20	83	400	340	85
New Jersey	40	24	60	80	63	79
New Mexico	42	31	74	70	47	67
New York	61	29	48	150	95	63
North Carolina	50	40	80	120	92	77
North Dakota	49	33	67	98	82	84
Ohio	33	20	61	99	61	62
Oklahoma	48	30	63	101	83	82
Oregon	30	22	73	60	52	87
Pennsylvania	50	26	52	203	150	74
Rhode Island	50	38	76	100	75	75
South Carolina	46	28	61	124	100	81
South Dakota	35	31	89	70	61	87
Tennessee	33	19	58	99	76	77
Texas	31	25	81	150	116	77
Utah	29	24	83	75	65	87
Vermont	30	26	87	150	127	85
Virginia	40	26	65	200	64	64
Washington	49	39	80	98	88	90
West Virginia	34	28	82	100	90	90
Wisconsin	33	24	73	99	72	73
Wyoming	30	26	87	60	50	83
Total	1,984	1,433	72	5,440	4,258	84

Source: National Conference of State Legislatures, May 1, 1997.
o=Political party other than Democratic, Republican or Independent
v=Vacancy
L=Libertarian

TERM LIMITS' NEW INCARNATION: THE SCARLET LETTER

The 1996 election saw a lot of term limit activity on the ballot—but with a new wrinkle. The "scarlet letter."

In this case, the sign of disgrace is a designation on the ballot that the candidate has refused to sign a "pledge" or otherwise does not support congressional term limits. In 14 states last November, citizens voted on measures to limit congressional terms, even though the U.S. Supreme Court in 1995 ruled such limits unconstitutional. Each of these measures contained the so-called "inform and instruct" or "pledge" provision. They passed in nine states: Alaska, Arkansas, Colorado, Idaho, Maine, Missouri, Nebraska, Nevada and South Dakota; and failed in five: Montana, North Dakota, Oregon, Washington and Wyoming.

But in the first of several challenges against "inform and instruct" measures, the Arkansas Supreme Court ruled that state's initiative unconstitutional, and the United States Supreme Court in February, without comment, let the ruling stand, casting doubt on the constitutionality of all such measures.

In February, the South Dakota Legislature repealed the "inform and instruct" initiative approved by citizens three months earlier. That measure would have required the South Dakota congressional delegation to support an amendment to the U.S. Constitution limiting members to three two-year terms in the U.S. House and two six-year terms in the Senate. Failure to support that exact amendment would have resulted in a notation next to their names on the ballot stating "disregard voters' instructions on term limits." A similar label would have been placed next to the names of nonincumbents who refused to sign a pledge supporting the constitutional amendment.

"Folks, I really haven't seen anything quite this incredible or onerous to me in all of my terms in the Legislature," said Representative Linda Barker, chief sponsor of the repeal legislation.

Within a month, South Dakotans for Term Limits filed documents for a new petition drive. The group needs 15,581 signatures to place on the 1998 ballot an initiative reversing the Legislature's action repealing the 1996 initiative.

"The people of South Dakota are not going to be blunted in their efforts to bring change to Washington, D.C.," said Jerry Munson, co-chairman of the term limitation group.

What makes the scarlet letter measures controversial is not whether legislative bodies support term limits or not, but whether individual lawmakers have the constitutional right to vote freely on the matters before them. And further, whether it is constitutional to use ballot measures to require state legislatures to call for a constitutional convention.

State Supreme Courts in unrelated cases in California, Maine and Montana have ruled that it is not. A federal district court in May temporarily halted Nebraska's law. In the Maine case, the federal judge called the inform and instruct law "intentionally intimidating." Other cases relating to scarlet letter laws are pending in Colorado and Idaho.

And court challenges to the initial term limits laws persist. A federal district court judge in California has already ruled that state's term limits law unconstitutional (see "California Term Limits Declared Unconstitutional"). Legislators in Arkansas are challenging their law in federal district court. Michigan, with a term limits law identical to California's, is weighing the possibility of a challenge. Washington leaders from both sides of the aisle are considering a challenge to their law limiting legislative terms. In Washington, the Legislature could itself overturn the limits because they are statutory rather than constitutional.

—*Nancy Rhyme, NCSL Leaders' Center*

February

U.S. district court judge in Maine rejects constitutionality challenge to the Maine term limits law.

The U.S. Supreme Court lets stand the ruling of the Arkansas Supreme Court on the constitutionality of voter initiatives as a method for amending the U.S. Constitution.

1997

February

The South Dakota Legislature repeals the "inform and instruct" initiative passed by the voters in 1996.

April

A federal judge in California rules that lifetime limits for legislative service imposed under Proposition 140 is unconstitutional. She suspends implementation of the ruling for the 1998 elections, pending the results of an appeal.

Arkansas legislators mount a challenge to their state's term limits law using arguments similar to those presented in the California case.

May

A federal district court temporarily halts Nebraska's inform and instruct law.

A federal judge throws out Maine's inform and instruct law calling it "intentionally intimidating."

Source:

Nancy Rhyme,

George Peery,

NCSL

But that option is no longer available to Michigan citizens.

"In 1999, there will be 67 new legislators out of 110 in the Michigan House," Hillegonds says. "The court of public opinion will have to decide how we feel about those we had and how the new group is performing."

The court of public opinion clearly had its say in other states in 1994 when voters accomplished through the ballot box what term limits will impose on state legislatures beginning in 1998. That Election Day knockout punch was the largest mid-term election sweep of the century. Republicans not only took control of Congress for the first time since the Eisenhower era, but made huge gains in state legislatures. When the final count was taken, Republicans, who held the majority in eight legislatures going into the election, had taken control of 19. The number of new state legislative seats told the story: Republicans, 472, Democrats 11. The voters had spoken more persuasively and personally than they did in approving term limits.

Democrats went into the 1996 election the underdog for the first time in 36 years. With the net switch of some 100 seats from a total of 5,989 seats up for election, they won the majority in eight legislative chambers that were formerly controlled by the GOP or were tied. Republicans, on the other hand, won three chambers controlled by the Democrats before the election and maintained the numerical hold on legislatures they had in 1995. Six of the 11 chambers that switched party control are in term-limited states. Once again, the public effected change through the ballot box.

AN IDEA REVISITED

Term limits are a new idea with old roots. The Continental Congress limited the terms of its representatives to "three years in six" in the Articles of Confederation. But then members of the Constitutional Convention in 1787 ultimately determined that the people should decide who represented them and for how long. In the 1990s, a frustrated public, encouraged and directed by well-financed and well-orchestrated term limitation campaigns, took aim at Congress for what it perceived as gridlock, abuses of political power and privilege, the influence of lobbies, and the failure to deal effectively with issues of crime and the economy. Of the first term limitation initiatives in California, Colorado and Oklahoma—passed in 1990—only Colorado attempted to limit federal as well as state legislative terms. Subsequent initiatives in 21 other states also targeted federal lawmakers.

Today, the terms of legislators in 20 states are limited. Those of Congress are not. The U.S. Supreme Court in May 1995 ruled that states may not put restrictions on federal lawmakers other than those spelled out in the Constitution. Writing for the Court in *Thornton vs. Arkansas,* Justice John Paul Stevens stated: "If there is one watchword for representation of the various states in Congress it is uniformity. Federal legislators speak to national issues that affect the citizens of every state .... The uniformity in qualifications mandated in Article I provides the tenor and the fabric for representation in Congress. Piecemeal restrictions by states would fly in the face of that order."

So for the moment, at least, America's experiment with limiting terms will be conducted in the states. Are term limits good medicine for the ills of democracy? Will term limits make representative government less effective or more? What effect will term limits have on the legislature's ability to enact a responsible state budget, to hold the executive branch accountable, to "solve problems" and to pursue "good government"?

Women in the Legislature: Numbers Inch Up Nationwide

ON THE MOVE: WOMEN IN STATE LEGISLATURES 1976-1999

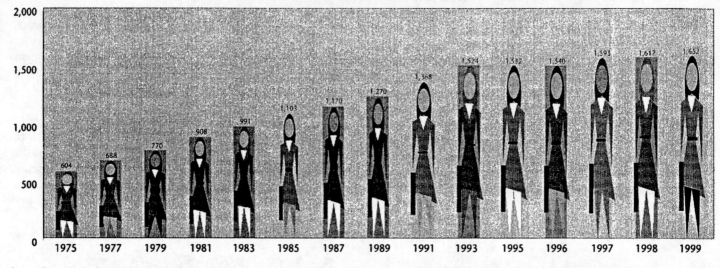

Source: Center for the American Woman and Politics (CAWP), National Information Bank on Women in Public Office, Eagleton Institute of Politics, Rutgers University.

It was that old good news, bad news scenario for women in the '98 election.

On the bonus side, Washington state has set a record for all legislatures in the United States. When lawmakers there are sworn in this month, almost half—41 percent—will be women, a first for women in the states. In Arizona—another first. And it truly was the "year of the woman." Women virtually took over the state, winning the top five offices—governor, secretary of state, attorney general, treasurer and superintendent of public instruction. The sweep is the first in U.S. history. Thirty-two women will be serving in the Legislature, down by one from the 1996 elections.

There also are a record number of women in the Nevada Legislature—23, five in the Senate and 18 in the Assembly. That surpasses the old record of 22 in 1995.

On the down side, women are nowhere near parity with their male counterparts, except in Washington. In Michigan, women were unable to increase their numbers from 31 in the House. Former Representative Maxine Berman blames term limits. "This was the first time since at least 1982, when I was elected, that we didn't add to the number of women.

"That's directly because of term limits," she said. Although 16 women were elected, she added that it was "on the backs of 16 other (incumbent) women whose opportunity was taken away. It means we're going to have to struggle to hold our own."

In Kentucky, the number of women in the Senate doubled—but you can still count them on one hand. Two more female senators were elected, bringing the total to four. Women represent 11.6 percent of the 138 members of the state General Assembly with 16 in the House (up three from last year). Kentucky still ranks 48th in the nation for elected female representatives

where most states average 21.8 percent female members in their legislatures.

In Montana, a record number of women will serve, but men still outnumber them 3 to 1. The 1999 session will involve 38 women out of 150 members, which beats the previous 1995 record of 36. There are eight women in the Senate.

WOMEN AS LEADERS: VIVE LA DIFFERENCE

Women have invaded the male bailiwick that is the state legislature,
and even the crusty old die-hards admit they're doing a pretty good job.

By Garry Boulard

For years lawmakers wanting to get business done in the Connecticut House of Representatives inevitably found their way to the ornate, antique-filled speaker's office in the old Capitol building. There they would take part in the ancient, but necessary, art of negotiation, lobbying and horse trading.

Sometimes there was even the whiff of cigar smoke in the air.

But when former Majority Leader Moira Lyons was elected to the speakership on the opening day of this year's session, it seemed to some that a grand tradition had come to an abrupt end.

"A male friend of mine asked, 'How should we act around you now?'" recalls Lyons, who was first elected to the state legislature in 1980. "He went on, quite seriously, to tell me that with the guys, 'we put our feet up on the desk, smoke a cigar... and make deals.'" Lyons, who is known for being direct, said she had a quick response: "I told him he has known me for 15 years, why did he or anyone have to treat me differently now?"

Life in the Connecticut legislature moves on. Both female and male lawmakers are still welcome in the speaker's office, with or without cigars.

But that such a thought was even voiced underlines the sometimes uneasy relationship many women legislative leaders have with their still predominantly male chambers and raises some questions: Are women leaders really the same as the men? Can they truly lead in the confident, commanding ways of their male predecessors?

The answer to both questions is no. And that's the good news.

"Women approach leadership positions in an entirely different manner than the men do," says Mary Hawkesworth, director of the Center for Women and Politics at Rutgers University's Institute of Politics. "Some of the research I've gone through indicates that women are very good at consensus building, but they tend not to be as prone to power plays. They are good at bringing people together and helping bridge groups with divergent views to help them arrive at a consensus." The political scientists call it the "collaborationist model."

"Yes, I think that is so," agrees Oregon's Speaker Lynn Snodgrass, who, like Lyons, took over the House leadership in early 1999. "Perhaps I'm not what the public might see as the typical insider leader, a beefy guy with a cigar or something, but I am very comfortable with negotiating. That, to me, is what public service is all about."

Known for her quiet and calm demeanor, "I have a very long fuse," Snodgrass says, the new Oregon speaker is nonetheless well regarded for the swift and efficient way in which she makes decisions. "I don't agonize forever over what needs to be done," she says. "And once the decision is made, I move on."

Arizona Senate Majority Leader Lori Daniels, in a state that has seen women this year take over the top five state-wide government positions from governor on down, thinks women in leadership tend to posture less. "There may be more long-winded speeches or political points to be made when you only have men,"

Garry Boulard, a frequent contributor to State Legislatures, *is a free-lance writer from New Orleans.*

Connecticut Speaker Moira Lyons says women lawmakers are getting high rankings because they listen more carefully to what people say.

Representative
Lori Daniels
Arizona

TOP WOMEN LEADERS 1999

Speaker of the House

Moira K. Lyons, Connecticut
Donna Sytek, New Hampshire
Jo Ann Davidson, Ohio
Lynn Snodgrass, Oregon

Senate President

Drue Pearce, Alaska
Brenda Burns, Arizona
Toni Jennings, Florida
Mary Kramer, Iowa
Lorrine Wojan, Washington

Majority Leader

Lori Daniels, Arizona House
Barbara Flynn Currie, Illinois House
Chellie Pingree, Maine Senate
Linda Melconian, Massachusetts Senate
Barbara Lisk, Washington House (co-leader)
Lynn Kessler, Washington House (co-leader)

Minority Leader

M. Adela Eads, Connecticut Senate
Barbara Marumoto, Hawaii House
Wendy Jaquet, Idaho House
Jane Amero, Maine Senate
Emily Swanson, Montana House
Alice Costandina (Dina) Titus, Nevada Senate
Kate Brown, Oregon Senate
Kitty Piercy, Oregon House
Gilda Cobb-Hunter, South Carolina House
Shirley Krug, Wisconsin Assembly
Louise Ryckman, Wyoming House

Oregon Speaker Lynn Snodgrass is regarded for the swift and efficient way she makes decisions.

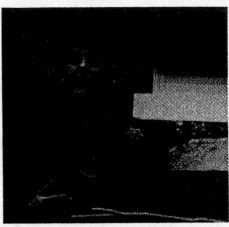

Florida Senate President Toni Jennings was elected to lead the Senate for an unprecedented second term.

Daniels laughs. "I know I am willing to listen to all of the different points of view, but, in the end, I want to see some sort of resolution."

Representative Donna Sytek New Hampshire

New Hampshire Speaker of the House Donna Sytek thinks women have confidently assumed leadership roles because in recent years they have done just about everything else. "Women have been doing the heavy lifting in legislatures for years," says Sytek, who is serving her second term as speaker and her 12th as a member of the New Hampshire legislature.

"We have been effective advocates for a variety of causes, committee chairmen, caucus leaders, whips and majority leaders," she continues. "This experience has established a comfort level among our peers that has allowed us to overcome the last hurdle and attain the top jobs."

Sytek adds that the emergence of women is not as revolutionary as it is evolutionary: "I don't think there has been a seismic shift in the attitudes of legislatures. Rather, it has been a gradual transformation, reflective of the evolution of opinion by the people who elect us."

Observing the Washington Legislature, which has had more than a third of its committees headed by women and currently leads the nation in percentage of women law-makers, Seattle political consultant Cathy Allen noted a tangible difference from the way a mostly male legislature might work. "Women tend to have longer meetings, some would say they belabor the issues, they ask more questions, there's more public involvement," Allen said of the women leaders in an interview with the *Christian Science Monitor.* "They study the effects [of proposals] on as many different kinds of people as possible."

All of which should make women leaders, all things being equal, even more effective than their male counterparts. But all things aren't equal, according to Cindy Simon Rosenthal, a professor of political science at the University of Oklahoma.

The fact that state legislatures remain a world created by men, where men in the vast majority of legislatures still represent vast majorities of the members, works against the onward and upward progress of the women.

"The legislative process was built and created by men, it is part of a larger male culture," says Rosenthal, who has called women the "second sex" in state legislatures. "Plus, despite their recent progress, women still remain the distinct minority in every state legislature. Just that factor alone has a dramatic impact on the way women try to do their business. The women have to cater to or respond to the male majority."

And sometimes they may be doing so as the only woman in the room.

"I know that feeling," acknowledges Elizabeth "Libby" Mitchell, the former speaker of the House in Maine, "to be the only woman in a room or in a meeting of high-powered men. Every woman in every state legislature has gone through it, and it really is something you have to go through. You have to be confident enough not to let those kinds of situations bother you, which is one more pressure women leaders have to put up with that the men don't."

So, to be a woman in leadership means it's lonely at the top.

"Well, it is the kind of thing that makes you feel alone," agrees Snodgrass in Oregon, "but not really lonely. You feel alone using the skills you have been given and not being able to have any sense of camaraderie with another woman legislative leader whom you can compare yourself with and feed off of. The men, I think, do that all the time. It is much less likely to happen if you are a woman."

PERSONALITY TYPE MAY EXPLAIN LEADERSHIP DIFFERENCES

The different ways that male and female legislators make decisions can be explained to some extent by differences in personality traits. And as our legislatures draw more and more female lawmakers, new leadership styles are emerging.

Women legislators often say that they are more concerned about how their decisions will affect different kinds of people. They tend to be more compassionate and empathetic with voters, less confrontational and more consensus oriented. They say they are also more interested in issues directly affecting people than in abstract ideas.

These traits represent key distinctions of the "feeling" preference on the Myers-Briggs personality test. Two-thirds of all women use "feeling" traits when making decisions compared with about two-thirds of all men who prefer "thinking" traits. This is the only area in which clear gender differences are found.

The Myers-Briggs test was developed by Katherine Briggs and her daughter Isabel Briggs Myers, who through years of testing and study, identified four basic aspects of human personality and 16 different personality types. Everyone fits into one of these types. One dimension of our personality deals with how we make decisions and come to conclusions. The two different ways of making decisions are by thinking or feeling.

Thinkers prefer making decisions that make sense logically and pride themselves on being objective, analytical and applying impersonal analysis to issues, according to Myers-Briggs research. Thinkers tend to favor confrontation to allow the clash of ideas to result in greater clarity. Feelers, on the other hand, prefer making decisions based on human values and the needs of people. They pride themselves on their ability to be empathetic and compassionate and tend to emphasize harmony and consensus building.

As Paul Tieger and Barbara Barron Tieger write in *Do What You Are*: "Everyone uses both preferences. Thinkers do have emotions and personal values, and feelers can be perfectly logical. However, each of us uses one process more naturally, more often and more successfully than the other." Even though thinking may be considered a more rational approach to decision making, both styles are rational and effective, they just use different criteria in the process.

Women leaders may even be at a disadvantage when it comes to something as simple as talking.

"Men interrupt much more often when a woman is speaking," says Lyn Kathlene, a professor of political science at the University of Nebraska who has done research on the conversational dynamics between men and women in state legislatures.

"I have seen cases where a male legislator would get up to introduce a particular measure, and he would be greeted with respectful silence," continues Kathlene. "But a woman lawmaker doing something as simple as her introductory remarks could easily be interrupted several times by her male counterparts with questions and clarifications."

Is this bad?

"Well, it is not a case of bad or good," Kathlene says. "But when people interrupt someone else, they usually succeed in ultimately changing the tone and even substance of the discourse."

And the very newness of assuming power is in itself a burden for women, says Speaker Lyons, because that usually means there is no previous tradition for women to draw upon.

"By and large, we are new to the work force in any significant numbers," says Lyons. "So we are new to understanding how you are supposed to network and build relationships. It is still very much a part of a learning process for most of us, and out of that process comes the confidence you build to help make future success more likely."

Colorado Senator Norma Anderson, the former House majority leader and now a state senator, is blunter: "What it really boils down to is that the women leaders have

Senator Norma Anderson Colorado

---

to work harder than the men to get anything accomplished. It will probably not be as hard for the next group of women coming up in the next decade, but that's just how it has been up to now."

Harder work. And less confrontation.

Oregon Senate Democratic Leader Kate Brown sees it this way: "I just don't think there is any question that the women legislative leaders have been much more inclined to stay away from the kind of partisan wrangling that men get involved in," Brown says. "It is not really natural for women to seek confrontation that way. But because they seem to me to be less interested in confrontation, they have more energy left for direction, for coming up with solutions."

Senator Kate Brown Oregon

Oftentimes, those solutions have been in the area of the so-called "women's issues," such as health care, child care and education. But even here, women leaders have learned to tread gently because some of their male counterparts are sick of these same issues. Brown remembers one male lawmaker telling her he voted for a "feminist, far left" bill she drafted. He didn't seem happy. The bill in question? "It was a health care bill," Brown laughs. "What did that have to do with feminism?"

Yet it is undeniable that women, both members and leaders, have put more emphasis on such issues.

"It makes sense that women will embrace those kinds of issues, at least initially, because women come to the legislatures with different perspectives than men," says Connecticut's Lyons. But Lyons thinks any attempts to pigeonhole women lawmakers as always being of a certain legislative persuasion is dangerous. "You are going to see an increasing number of women lawmakers involved in a whole array of issues. That is certainly how I see my job as speaker."

Toni Jennings, the Florida Senate president, may best illustrate today's emerging woman leader simply because her legislative priorities have long included matters beyond social policy.

"My background was in business," Jennings says, remembering that when she first came to the Florida Legislature in 1976 she was not sure if she was more burdened by being a woman or being a Republican in this once-solid Southern yellow dog Democratic state.

"In those days the men would put women members on some education or human services committee while they did all of the big stuff," Jennings remarks. "I refused to let anyone do that to me." Instead Jennings from the outset worked on issues like unemployment and workers' compensation reform. She believes the hard-earned respect she eventually won from her male colleagues as she negotiated with them over nuances in tax policies, tort reform and labor issues confirmed that she had made the right decision in her legislative priorities.

But then she had a price to pay with women.

"On more than one occasion, I was severely criticized by different women's groups for not focusing more on women's issues," Jennings says. "And I got angry over it. I told them if the economy is not an issue that affects women, where half of our work force is composed of single women and women who have to support families, then I did not know what a woman's issue is."

Norma Anderson agrees with that approach. "I never let anyone tell me I had to deal with only certain types of legislation because I was a woman," Anderson reflects. "I was interested in things like taxation policy and economic issues from the start."

Anderson believes that as more women are elected to state legislatures across the country and emerge as leaders, it is less likely they will be relegated to only certain types of committees.

In Maine, where women have long held leadership positions in higher percentages than the national norm, Elizabeth Mitchell believes the common perception of the woman lawmaker will soon undergo a major change. "I think you will increasingly find that the women are as interested in balancing the budget and tax matters as the men," she says. "And there may be more conservative Republican women in state legislatures in the years to come who have different views on those same issues."

But to make things even more challenging, some women leaders believe that even an increase in the number of women is no guarantee that there will be more female leaders. "We talk about men who have a gender bias when it comes to electing women to power," says Speaker Snodgrass. "But there are women out there who have the same kinds of problems, women who do not like to have other women as their leaders. And it can be just as difficult to deal with a woman who does not want a woman leader as it is a man."

And in some chambers when the female membership does reach what is called a "critical mass," the male membership, like components in an energy lab test, grows more recalcitrant. "There have been cases where the men simply dug in their heels more when they've seen larger numbers of women around them," says Rutgers' Hawkesworth. "A whole host of gender-based obstacles were put in the women's way, making it obviously much harder for women leaders to lead."

Yet despite such challenges, the number of women members, as well as leaders, continues to grow. Today there are 1,652 women state lawmakers, an all-time high, up 35 seats from just last year alone. Since 1989, women's numbers in state legislatures have increased by 400. And in an unexpected twist, the term limits movement has actually helped women gain power in many places simply because powerful male incumbents have had to give up their offices. "You're seeing some state legislatures where the turnover rate is about 25 percent," notes Brown in Oregon.

"With that many people coming and going, women not only have a much better chance of getting elected, but now the playing field has been leveled in terms of women having a real chance to rise to leadership positions," she adds.

Others think a weakened party system, once the clubhouse of the men, has allowed more women to come to the fore, particularly in the states with some of the highest percentages of women lawmakers, Arizona, Nevada, Colorado and Kansas.

An increase in the overall number of women members, which, on balance, is expected to increase the numbers of women leaders, may also be accelerated by recent major shifts in the way voters perceive women. For decades, notes Lyons in Connecticut, voters were unwilling to trust women with important public office because they were unsure of their reliability. Now on the reliability question, "women get much higher rankings than men do," Lyons says.

"I really believe this: When women begin campaigning, they almost always come across well because they just tend to listen more carefully to what people say. They are usually very concerned about the issues, and voters see this and like it. These are exactly the qualities that voters today want," Lyons continues.

Still, until women approach membership parity with the men, and no one expects that to happen any time soon, their leadership styles may continue to reflect either their minority status or a basic gender difference as leaders or both.

The new women leaders in the legislature say they are confident they can do as good a job, or better, than their male predecessors. But expect the leadership offices to be quieter places, with fewer grand speeches and less yelling, they say, with more questions and time to fully hear all opposing views.

Women do place a greater emphasis on the effects of legislation and—despite criticisms—issues like health care, child care and education will continue to dominate their agendas.

Women leaders also intend to solidify their gains by appointing even more women to top posts. "After I became speaker (the speaker here makes all of the important chairmanship positions), I did what I could to get more women in the top leadership positions as well as making them chairmen of certain committees," says Lyons. "I really wanted to get women in those positions, but I still focused on the person's ability. I don't know what would have happened if it hadn't worked out that way, but it did."

Ultimately, thinks Rutgers' Hawkesworth, the example that women leaders make will lead to future success.

"Some people think women in leadership positions are there only as tokens," she says. "But you cannot be a token leader. You have to be the leader of your party, you have to move legislation and build consensus, which requires real skills. And you have to serve as a statewide figure beyond your own constituency."

At such a high level of unending decision making, adds Hawkesworth, "a token will not last very long. Only true leaders do."

Legislative Party Caucuses: Open or Closed?

Should party "haggling and strategizing" be kept private? Or do these discussions fall under state open meeting provisions?

By Brenda Erickson

Controversy surrounds the question of whether legislative caucus meetings should be open to the public and press or restricted to members.

In Montana, the courts decided. District Court Judge Thomas Honzel ruled in June that the public has a right to know what happens during political party meetings at the Legislature. "Clearly, legislators gather at caucuses to discuss the public's business," he wrote. "When they do so, the public has a right to observe their discussions and to be informed about what happens at those meetings."

No one event triggered the court battle to open party caucuses in Montana, but after the 1994 election the same party (Republicans) controlled the governor's office, the Senate and the House of Representatives for the first time in many years. Caucuses were being held with greater frequency, and there was a perception by the press that policy decisions were being made behind closed doors. So, 22 news organizations sued to force open the meetings.

Honzel's first ruling, which came in 1996, was split. He said caucus meetings held before the Legislature met should be open, but he allowed party caucuses held during session to be closed. The news groups appealed to the state Supreme Court which ordered Honzel to reconsider his decision and decide one way or the other. Thus the June ruling this year.

The Society of Professional Journalists views the decision as a victory for open government. According to its president Fred Brown, who is political editor of *The Denver Post,* the ruling "will allow some much- needed sunshine into an area of public policymaking that should not be kept dark."

However, around the Montana Legislature, there are other viewpoints.

"The ruling adversely affects the ability of legislative caucuses to plan coherent strategy," says Senate Minority Leader Mike Halligan. "With other people in the room, I think there will be more political posturing than candid conversation.

"As a leader, I am concerned about this," he continues. "If members aren't giving candid, personal opinions, leaders may make decisions that don't accurately represent caucus views."

House Minority Leader Vicki Cocchiarella also fears that caucus dynamics will change. "This

Representative
Vicki Cocchiarella
Montana

Senator
Mike Halligan
Montana

was the only time that party members could freely vent and share ideas. I'm not sure where this will happen now." Both Cocchiarella and Speaker of the House John Mercer believe that caucuses may not meet as often. "Fewer meetings mean less brainstorming among veteran and freshman legislators," Cocchiarella adds. "And that will be unfortunate since we're getting ready for term limits."

"But I'm more concerned that the recent court ruling gives additional clout to lobbyists," says Speaker Mercer. "Caucus meetings used to be one of the few places closed to lobbyists, where legislators could get away."

Halligan agrees, "The Legislature must ensure that the open caucuses are as free as possible from special interest influences."

Speaker
John Mercer
Montana

Party caucuses are the principal partisan vehicle in most state legislatures. Generally, they operate in three primary areas—legislative organization, information gathering and dissemination, and policy formulation.

However, the role and power of party caucuses vary from state to state and even from chamber to chamber. For example, the Nebraska Unicameral is nonpartisan, so there are no

Brenda Erickson tracks legislative rules and procedures for NCSL.

From *State Legislatures,* October/November 1998, pp. 12-13. © 1998 by the National Conference of State Legislatures. Reprinted by permission.

political caucuses. The Alabama, Arkansas, Louisiana and Mississippi senates do not have active partisan caucuses. In the Alabama House and Texas Senate and House, partisan caucuses are informal; they are not sanctioned, funded or staffed by the legislature. In other legislatures, the political caucuses are much more clearly defined. Statutes or chamber rules refer to them. Even Democratic and Republican staffs exist.

Caucus meetings are no exception to the variety in legislative processes. In *Cole vs. State*, the Colorado courts determined that the sunshine law, which applies to the Colorado General Assembly, also includes legislative caucus meetings at which public business is discussed. However, in *Abood vs. League of Women Voters and Anchorage Daily News*, the Alaska Supreme Court ruled that the courts could not enforce the open meetings act against the Alaska Legislature due to the separation of powers among the three branches of government. The sep- aration of powers doctrine also was used by the Florida Supreme Court in deciding *Moffitt vs. Willis*, which dismissed a civil action pending in a lower court. In the lower court case *(Miami Herald Publishing Co. vs. Moffitt)*, 16 Florida news- papers claimed that private legislative meetings violated federal and state constitutions, state laws and legislative chamber rules.

In Arizona, Utah and Wisconsin, the open meeting law covers the legislature, but legislative party caucuses are specifically exempted. In practice, however, the caucuses in these states are open more often than not.

Senate President Brenda Burns Arizona

"Sometimes closed caucuses are considered more productive than open ones when working on highly charged issues," says Arizona Senate President Brenda Burns. "But open caucuses are in the best interest of the public that we serve. It lets people see their government at work."

Across the nation, over 56 percent of legislative chambers reported always or usually closed caucus meetings, while about 35 percent are always or usually open. This changed from 1988, when about 45 percent reported closed caucuses and 41 percent, open.

STATUS OF LEGISLATIVE CAUCUS MEETINGS

	Republicans Democrats	
STATE	**SENATE**	**HOUSE**
Alabama	N/A	Closed
Alaska	Usually closed Usually open	Usually closed Usually open
Arkansas	N/A	Usually closed
California	Usually closed	Closed
Colorado	Open	Open
Connecticut	Usually open	Closed
Delaware	Closed	Usually closed
Florida	Usually open	Usually open
Georgia	Usually open	Usually closed
Hawaii	Closed	Closed
Idaho	Closed	Closed
Illinois	Closed	Usually closed
Indiana	Closed	Closed
Iowa	Closed	Usually closed
Kansas	Open	Open
Kentucky	Open	Open Usually open
Louisiana	N/A	Closed
Maine	Usually closed Usually open	Usually open
Maryland	Usually open	Usually open
Massachusetts	Usually closed Closed	Closed
Michigan	Usually open Usually closed	Usually closed
Minnesota	Usually open	Usually open
Mississippi	N/A	N/A
Missouri	Closed	Closed
Montana	Open*	Open*
Nebraska	N/A	Unicameral
Nevada	Closed	Usually open
New Hampshire	Closed	Usually closed
New Jersey	Usually closed	Closed
New Mexico	Closed	Usually closed
New York	Usually closed	Closed
North Carolina	Usually closed	Closed
North Dakota	Open	Open
Ohio	Closed	Closed
Oklahoma	Closed	Closed Usually closed
Oregon	Closed	Closed
Pennsylvania	Closed	Closed
Rhode Island	Usually open No response	Usually open
South Carolina	Usually closed	Open
South Dakota	Closed Usually open	Usually closed Open
Tennessee	Open	Usually open
Texas	Closed	Closed
Utah	Usually open	Usually open Open
Vermont	Usually open	Usually open
Virginia	Closed	Usually closed
Washington	Closed	Closed
West Virginia	Closed	Closed
Wisconsin	Usually open	Usually open
Wyoming	Closed Usually open	Closed Open

*At this time, the Montana Legislature has not decided whether it will appeal the court ruling that requires open meetings. Meanwhile, they are open.

Source: NCSL, August 1998.

Choosing among delectable homemade pies is sometimes the most difficult decision to make at traditional New England town meetings.

Town Meeting Time

Photos and text by John Nordell
Staff photographer of The Christian Science Monitor

STRAFFORD, VT.

AS MOUTH-WATERING smells waft from casserole dishes warming atop a wood stove, the people of Strafford, Vt., open their town meeting with the Pledge of Allegiance: " . . . with liberty and justice for all." "We hope," a voice murmurs, audible enough to elicit chuckles.

This year on Town Meeting Day in Vermont—an official state holiday that falls on the first Tuesday in March—more than 100 residents of this rural town gathered to speak their minds and

"New England is the only place in the world where town meetings take place."

—Joseph Zimmerman, political scientist at the State University of New York at Albany

vote on issues such as the town budget, a dump-truck purchase, and the selection of town officers.

"Everyone is responsible for the issues, to make sure things are running well," says Strafford resident John Freitag, after voting on the eight articles on the meeting's agenda.

For hundreds of years New Englanders have gathered in open town meetings

TWO CENTURIES LATER: Residents of Strafford, Vt., stream out of the historic Town House after a recent meeting. Construction on the building began in 1799 and the first town meeting took place two years later. Heat was added in the 1830s, but the only restroom is still a corner outhouse.

like this one, debating issues large and small—sometimes with rancor—thereby participating in a direct form of democratic government practically unique to these former colonies.

"Aside from a few rural areas in Switzerland, New England is the only place in the world where town meetings take place," says Joseph Zimmerman, a political scientist at the State University of New York at Albany and author of "The New England Town Meeting: Democracy in Action."

The first town meetings sprang up in the Massachusetts Bay Colony around 1629. The original towns were religious settlements and their townsfolk were called on to make important decisions. The first order of business was to build a church, which also served as a town hall, and hire a minister. Out of

SPEAKING UP: In this rural town of 901, 148 registered voters show up, speak their minds, and vote on issues such as the town budget, a dump-truck purchase, and the selection of town officers.

> **"It's great to see everyone after a long winter. It's a great community gathering. It really starts off the spring."**
>
> **—Strafford resident Laurie Berkenkamp**

necessity, a new form of self-government was created: a direct democracy by which people gathered to make their own laws and decisions affecting their town.

Poet James Russell Lowell, writing in the late 19th century, observed: "Puritanism, believing itself quick with the seed of religious liberty, laid, without knowing it, the egg of democracy."

To these early settlers' brethren back in Europe, still under the rule of kings, the town-meeting forum for making choices about a community's destiny would have been unthinkable. Bear in mind that this formation of direct democratic government by religious pioneers predated the American Revolution by roughly 150 years.

In the small, tightly knit New England communities, the town meeting evolved into both a cherished form of government and an important yearly community gathering.

Now, more than 200 years after the shot heard round the world, the future of open town meeting hangs in balance.

Declining interest and rising populations have caused some New England towns to shift from open town meetings to a format where interested people meet to debate the issues one day and show up to cast ballots another.

Further diluting the spirit of direct democracy is the representative town meeting, where residents elected by the voters decide the town's business.

In some growing towns, it would be impossible to fit all the voters in one hall. Due to swelling ranks of newcomers from cities who don't know about town meetings and often don't have the interest to invest hours in meetings that can meander into arcane discussions, some have dropped town meetings altogether in favor of elected councils.

"Town meeting is really on its last legs in Rhode Island," says Mr. Zimmer-

man, "due to a lack of interest and the increased services provided by the state." Despite the move away from town meetings in the faster-growing New England towns, Zimmerman concludes: "It's safe to say that in small rural towns, town meeting is well established with deep roots and will last another hundred years. It would be very hard to dig up the roots."

Steve Jeffrey, director of the Vermont League of Cities and Towns, is less optimistic: "We're worried. We've seen a decline in participation, just as we've seen a decline in participation in state and federal elections. Perhaps it's because people have money in their wallets and the school budgets have passed."

However, Mr. Jeffrey adds, "if there's a big issue, everybody shows up and there's tremendous participation. Participating and being at town meeting is the lifeblood of local government."

Back at the recent Strafford meeting is Laurie Berkenkamp, who alternately holds, nurses, and plays with her infant son, Simon. She attends town meetings because "everyone has a chance to be heard on equal ground."

She continues, "It's great to see everyone after a long winter. It's a great community gathering. It really starts off the spring."

The Gulf of Government

BY DONALD F. KETTL

A few weeks ago, House Speaker Newt Gingrich laid out his policy agenda for the coming year. He challenged local schools throughout the country to teach the Constitution and Declaration of Independence. He recommended that legislators read the works of management gurus Peter Drucker and W. Edwards Deming. He called for a commission to devise a long-term solution to Social Security.

That same week, as it happened, Wisconsin Governor Tommy G. Thompson, a fellow Republican, laid out his agenda. Like Gingrich, he focused much of it on education. He had good reason to do that. As he spoke, Milwaukee's school system had just been labeled one of the nation's worst by *Education Week*, which noted that, on a typical day, one of every four students is missing from class.

Thompson sent a stunning shot across the bow of Milwaukee's public school district. He set four tough standards for the district's performance. If the school district fails to meet those standards within two years, he said bluntly, "it will be dissolved." He pledged to shut down its operations and turn its management over to a state board.

Not only that, but Thompson made it clear he was willing to risk sharing power to get the problem solved. If Milwaukee's school responsibilities do go to a state board, only one of the three members will be a gubernatorial appointee. The other two will be appointed by Milwaukee's Democratic mayor and by the state school superintendent—both of whom have battled with Thompson in the past.

The difference between those two speeches is pretty hard to miss. Two conser-

Donald F. Kettl is director of the University of Wisconsin's Robert M. La Follette Institute of Public Affairs and of the Brookings Institution's Center for Public Management.

vative Republicans, both in key positions of leadership. One is dealing in symbolism, and the other is taking action. One is choosing politics, the other pragmatism. And that is as good a measure as any of the gulf that is opening up these days in American federalism: the gulf between the pragmatism of governors and mayors and the symbolic ideology that prevails along the Potomac.

In the nation's best-run states and cities, it's hard to find a distinctly Republican or Democratic theme shaping this new approach to policy problems. From Republican Mayor Stephen Goldsmith's massive privatization of Indianapolis' public services to Democratic Mayor Michael White's transformation of Cleveland, a new generation of state and local officials is defining success simply as getting things done.

Some of this growing gulf between Washington and the states comes from the fact that Washington is doing less and less of the high-profile work every year. It runs the air-traffic control system, inspects the safety of meat, guards the borders, mails Social Security checks, and collects taxes. It conducts foreign policy and national defense. But a search for where the action is in American politics would lead even Inspector Clouseau to the states.

This isn't to suggest that the federal government has become entirely marginal. It plays an important role (to say the least) in banking, and in collecting money for Medicare, Medicaid, welfare and a host of other transfer programs. But in managing the programs, it relies increasingly on contractors (for such things as Medicare and toxic waste cleanup) and on state and local governments (for programs ranging from Medicaid to mass transit). The federal government moves money and builds partnerships. But it is not the primary problem-solver any more.

To further complicate the federal government's role, much of the real work of the federal bureaucracy happens in the back

rooms and side channels of the contracting and intergovernmental systems. EPA is hammering out new regulatory-reform pilot projects with the states. The Department of Health and Human Services is trying to connect immunization programs with local schools. Throughout the federal government, hundreds of detailed regulatory actions and tens of thousands of meetings—but only rarely major congressional policy debates—are what shape the federal government's domestic policy stewardship.

The success of this stewardship depends on how well the subtle regulatory changes and coordinating meetings work. Along the Potomac, where thousands of ears bend for news of presidential scandals or major new policy pronouncements, such details are just not the stuff of politics. What the federal government actually does to help most domestic programs work rarely attracts the attention of congressional committees and seldom draws more than yawns from the Washington media.

So the truth is that not only is Washington increasingly insulated from the real action, but the Potomac community is increasingly isolated from what little action the federal government genuinely initiates. In speaking to their myopic constituency, federal elected officials like Newt Gingrich and Bill Clinton are increasingly tempted to promote symbols rather than substance. They are far removed from the big action and can't grasp the real levers of power. Most of the time, they aren't even looking for them.

Meanwhile, mayors and governors are quietly revolutionizing American federalism and American politics, putting their bets on results over rhetoric and on pragmatism over partisanship. The states are no longer just the laboratories of American democracy. They are its shop floor. They are where most of what gets done in government actually gets done.

ASSESSMENTS

It Pays to Know Where the Bodies Are Buried

ALAN EHRENHALT

If there's one thing I've learned from experience, it's that experience is overrated. How many times have you turned on a football or basketball playoff, listened to the announcers blather on about the importance of playoff experience, and then watched the battle-tested veterans get flattened by a collection of rank rookies? Experience is a lousy standard to use in picking a winner on the field. You almost have to be a sportscaster not to notice that.

By and large, the same principle holds in most fields of endeavor. You need a certain amount of experience to perform competently, but at some point, it ceases to be the most important credential. Forty years of practice doesn't make anyone the best candidate to represent you in court, remove your appendix, teach you piano or cater your wedding. If you think it does, you'll make the wrong choice more often than not.

But like all household truths, this one has its exceptions. If you look around carefully, you will probably notice that there are a few important jobs that still seem to be handled best by somebody who's been around the track a few times. The evidence of the past few years would suggest that governing a state is one of those.

To govern effectively—or to dismantle government—brains and ideology aren't enough.

Not long ago, as a way of avoiding more productive work, I took out a piece of paper and made a list of the "best" American governors of the 1990s. Here, in no particular order, are the ones I came up with: Ned McWherter of Tennessee, George Voinovich of Ohio, Roy Romer of Colorado, Tommy Thompson of Wisconsin, John Engler of Michigan and Zell Miller of Georgia.

I don't pretend there's anything objective about such a list, or that I'm the most qualified person to draw one up. But I have no particular axe to grind, and I tried as best I could to leave my own pet causes out of it. I was looking for governors who (1) set out a coherent policy agenda and accomplished most of it or (2) projected a consistent image of competence and authority.

All six of these contenders passed one or the other of these two tests. McWherter launched the nation's most innovative and widely copied health care and housing programs, and Miller rewrote his state's civil service law and steered through a nationally admired higher education funding program. Thompson and Engler took office vowing to reorganize state government along market-friendly lines, and to a great extent both of them accomplished it.

Voinovich and Romer don't fit so neatly in the innovation category, but I included them under the second criterion, as prudent and sensible managers who leave no doubt that somebody capable is in charge. Romer has demonstrated his negotiating skill in tough situations time after time, while Voinovich has proved to be exemplary at bringing labor and management together in an efficient administration.

I DIDN'T DRAW MUCH from this exercise in the way of partisan or ideological conclusions. McWherter, Romer and Miller are moderate Democrats, Voinovich is a moderate Republican, and Thompson and Engler are identified with the GOP right. You can argue that the activist left isn't represented on my list, but maybe that's because it hasn't elected many governors in the past decade.

But there's one interesting thing that all these governors have in common: On the day they were sworn in, they had served in government for a very long time.

McWherter spent 18 years in the Tennessee House of Representatives, 14 of them as its speaker. Romer was a state legislator for eight years and state treasurer for 10. Voinovich was a legislator, a county auditor, a county commissioner, and then a three-term mayor of Cleveland. Miller spent four years serving in the Georgia Senate and 16 years presiding over it as lieutenant governor. And each of them started young; all except McWherter made it to public office by the age of 30.

But the most interesting cases are Thompson and Engler. Both took office as sworn enemies of careerist government and bloated bureaucratic payrolls. But both had spent their entire adult lives in public office. Thompson was elected to the Wisconsin Assembly at age 24, the year he got his law degree. Engler was in an even greater hurry: He won his first term in the legislature at 22, before he had even graduated from college.

To critics on the left, the careers of Thompson and Engler have always been monuments to the hypocrisy of conservatives who bash government while making a living from it for decades on end. But there's a more benign and ultimately much more interesting point to make about these two conservative Republican careerists. They are tangible proof that a lifetime in public office is the best preparation for virtually anything you want to do in government—and that includes dismantling it.

Just why that should be so is an interesting question. Governing a state is difficult, but so are litigation and surgery, and they don't seem to demand experience in quite the way that being a governor does. There are brilliant brain surgeons fresh out of residency, and superb trial lawyers who have just been promoted from associate. There have been decent 32-year-old governors, too, but it's pretty clear that in recent years the truly superior ones, the ones who have placed their stamp on a state government and changed it permanently, have tended to come into power after an uncommonly long political apprenticeship.

The reason is that governing a state is not only difficult, but difficult in its own peculiar fashion. It involves threading one's way through a maze of complex institutions and personalities, bending them to one's will, and doing that without the benefit of any real instruments of autocratic power. It's a job for which creativity, intelligence and stamina alone are almost never enough.

The very best governors seem to know things that are very difficult to pick up anywhere else but in state government. They know how the legislature works, and who the pivotal members are, and how they can be flattered, cajoled, shamed and bullied. They are accustomed to bureaucratic inertia, but they have seen it conquered a few times over the years. They know they can appeal to the voters to rally support for a cause, but they also know they can't do it very often without wasting their credibility. In short, they know things that you aren't likely to know just because you are smart. Those who haven't mastered them tend to fail, no matter how much leadership ability they may have demonstrated in other lines of work.

I HAVEN'T MADE any list of the "worst" governors to go with my roster of the best, but I think I know what the ideal candidate for gubernatorial failure in the 1990s looks like. He's a successful self-made businessman, disdainful of government and uncomfortable with politics, accustomed to having his way in the private entrepreneurial world. He doesn't know many legislators, or want to know them. His main interest in the bureaucracy is in humbling it. He has no desire for a long career in politics—he just wants to come in, straighten things out and return to private life before he's contaminated. He's very smart, and articulate. He's just not very smart about the things governors need to know.

Gary Johnson, the Republican governor of New Mexico, is an extremely intelligent man. He became a multimillionaire in the construction business by the time he was 40, and in 1994 decided to put his talents to work

The best governors know things that are difficult to pick up anywhere else but in government.

in Santa Fe, shaking up the state and rearranging its affairs on a businesslike basis. Three-and-a-half years into his term, he has succeeded mainly in establishing a condition of almost permanent warfare with the legislature, the bureaucracy and the court system, and vetoing nearly half the bills sent to his desk for signature.

You can't say that Gary Johnson hasn't made his presence felt on the New Mexico political scene. What you can say is that he hasn't exactly succeeded at establishing authority or enacting an agenda.

Nobody seems to realize that more than Johnson. "My whole life," he said a few months ago, "I've been a success because I possess a lot of really good ideas, and I'm able to implement those ideas." As governor, he admitted, "none of my good ideas get anywhere."

Some of Johnson's defenders say that is because he is too conservative, and others insist it is because he is too blunt, eccentric and temperamental. More likely, though, it is for a much more humdrum reason: He didn't spend the years between age 25 and 40 prowling the corridors of power in state government, figuring out where the bodies were buried. The difference between a Gary Johnson and a John Engler isn't brains or ideology, it's just preparation.

OF COURSE, all the preparation in the world is no guarantee of success in running a state, any more than it is in running anything. Peter Wilson in California and Lawton Chiles in Florida both had spent more than two decades in public office when they arrived on the gubernatorial scene in 1990, and yet it would be difficult to classify either of them among the most successful governors of the past decade.

But at the very least, a life spent in politics immunizes any new governor—any chief executive in government at any level—against the dangerous illusion that he possesses more power than he really does. You may recall the rude awakening Harry Truman predicted for Dwight Eisenhower just before leaving office: "He'll sit here and he'll say, 'Do this! Do that!' And nothing will happen. Poor Ike—it won't be a bit like the Army. He'll find it very frustrating."

You might argue that Eisenhower, notwithstanding his profound lack of political experience, ended up doing pretty well for himself. I agree with that. On the other hand, Eisenhower had the advantage of being a national hero. Not many governors have anything similar in their background to call upon. For them, 20 or 30 years in the trenches of state politics is as good a substitute as they are likely to find.

Roaring forward

The father of the nation's biggest change in social policy in 50 years has more ideas to share.

BY ELAINE STUART

Expect the unexpected from the innovator who brought the nation welfare reform. After turning the 60-year-old failed welfare system on its head, the irrepressible governor of Wisconsin isn't slowing down.

Gov. Tommy G. Thompson says, "I have a million ideas. I get about 100 ideas a day. One is good."

One idea attracting national interest is school choice. Under Thompson's leadership, Wisconsin became the first state to pass a law giving vouchers to low-income students to attend any private school, regardless of its religious affiliation. The Wisconsin Supreme Court in June 1998 upheld the program. The U.S. Supreme Court Nov. 9, 1998, allowed the decision to stand, giving heart to choice supporters elsewhere.

Citing Thompson's welfare and education reforms, former Ohio Gov. George Voinovich, now a U.S. sena-

tor, says, "Gov. Thompson is one of the most active and effective governors in the whole nation." Thompson earned his stripes on the national scene in numerous trips to Capitol Hill advocating welfare flexibility for states.

Of Thompson's influence on federal welfare reform, Ed Fouhy, executive director of the Pew Center on the States, says, "He's the father of the most important change in national social policy since Medicare."

Closer to home, Thompson, 57, has won the hearts of Wisconsin voters. They elected him to an unprecedented fourth, four-year term with 59 percent of the vote in November. They had plenty of reasons—Wisconsin's unemployment rate is below the national average, and its poverty rate is the fifth lowest in the nation. While Wisconsin already has the nation's second highest health insurance rate at 92 percent, Thompson is seeking a federal waiver to expand health insurance to all state residents. He's also delivered tax cuts and educational improvements. Thompson's high national profile has attracted speculation in recent years about a presidential or vice presidential candidacy—but Thompson denies presidential plans.

Thompson is in the forefront of yet another emerging national issue—work force development. Speaking at the annual meeting of The Council of State Governments in De-

cember, Thompson challenged state officials to "Build Tomorrow's Workforce." Thompson, the Council's new president, said the aging of the baby boom generation and the expanding economy are leaving employers pinched for enough workers. He urged states to engage employers, labor leaders, educators and local governments in planning "to make sure everyone in America has a good job." Everyone, he says, includes young people, retirees, migrant workers and people with disabilities.

In Wisconsin, Thompson is unwrapping a program called "Pathways to Independence" that would allow people with disabilities to keep their Medicaid and Medicare health coverage while working. The disabled often don't work because of fear of losing their health coverage, which is literally their lifeline.

Thompson, as he did in welfare reform, began seeking federal waivers for the work force program a year ago. As Thompson told CSG delegates, "States are doing the heavy lifting and changing lives. . . . I think the biggest problem we face is trying to get Washington to give us more authority."

Success breeds success

Congress followed Wisconsin's lead in replacing the 60-year-old Aid to Families with Dependent Chil-

Wisconsin fast facts

Legislature: Senate, 33; Assembly, 99
Capital: Madison
Largest city: Milwaukee
Total area: 56,153 square miles
Population: 5.1 million
Statehood: May 29, 1848
Nickname: The Badger State
Motto: Forward

Gov. Tommy Thompson rode his Harley to the nation's Capitol to celebrate Wisconsin's Sesquicentennial.

dren program in 1996 with the Temporary Assistance to Needy Families program.

"I started welfare reform in this country in 1987, before anyone was thinking about it seriously," Thompson says. "As the saying goes, success has 1,000 parents and failure but one. Everyone now is the father and mother of welfare reform in Wisconsin. There's enough credit to go around."

As proof, Thompson has the waivers he received from the Reagan, Bush and Clinton administrations. "Learn-fare," the first pioneering reform in 1987, required children ages 6 to 19 to attend school or their families' benefits were reduced. Wisconsin Assembly Speaker Scott Jensen, who was then Thompson's chief of staff, says, "From each program, we learned something and we used that

experience to form the great reform of W-2. It really is the program the rest of the nation's welfare reform is patterned after."

Successes paved the way for more waivers. In September 1997, Wisconsin became the first state to end welfare. The "Wisconsin Works"—or W-2—program replaced the entitlement system with a system that requires participants to work, lets them earn wages and learn skills. As of October, fewer than 10,000 families out of the state's population of 5 million people remained on the W-2 caseload.

"People are better off working under W-2 than under the apathetic welfare system. They have more money, they have more opportunity and they have greater self-esteem," Thompson says. In October, he appointed an independent committee

of national experts to evaluate W-2 and use the results to improve the program.

Thompson, a Republican, has shown remarkable success in getting legislation passed, even when both houses of the Legislature were in Democratic hands. "He's a very practical and pragmatic politician," Jensen says. "He's not an ideologue. He's a Main Street Republican, who says, 'Let's make government work.'"

John O. Norquist, the Democratic mayor of Milwaukee, praises Thompson's lead on welfare reform and the state's school voucher program, which is targeted in Milwaukee. He says, "Almost all Democrats support school choice because we want strong schools."

Thompson believes in breaking the mold to get results. He says, "If you believe in the status quo,

Thompson is a popular politician in Wisconsin.

you should not be a governor or a legislator."

Overcoming the odds

Thompson ran for governor in 1986 because he was frustrated after 20 years in the Assembly minority, including serving as minority leader

Thompson took his fellow governors on a ride at NGA in Milwaukee.

and on all major committees. "I could never get anything passed," he said. "After 20 years I was tired of getting stomped on."

No one gave him a prayer in the governor's race, but he took more than half the vote in the GOP primary over five other contenders and swept the general election.

"I've been underestimated all my political life at every juncture," he says. He won by outorganizing and outcampaigning everyone else. Thompson's willingness to buck the tide showed up in his embrace of the Republican Party while a student at the University of Wisconsin, where he graduated in 1963. "Everyone was so liberal that I rebelled and became a conservative." He started "Collegians for Goldwater" in 1963.

Then in what Thompson calls "the greatest summer of my life," he won a scholarship to study on Capitol Hill. Lecturers included then Attorney General Bobby Kennedy, cabinet officials and—his hero—Barry Goldwater. Most exciting of all was Teamsters' leader Jimmy Hoffa, who lambasted the federal investi-

gation of the union. Thompson says, "I was the only one of 500 students to give a standing ovation. He was a going machine."

The fiery labor leader set Thompson on fire. The political science graduate, who had planned a military career, decided to enter politics instead. Back in Madison to attend law school, Thompson worked as a messenger at the state Capitol, then as an aide to the Senate Judiciary Committee while tending bar to earn money. He planned to serve four years as a JAG officer in the Air Force after graduation. With a summer school class to finish in 1966 to graduate, he decided to establish himself before he left by running for his district's House seat. Thompson borrowed $600, bought a $100 car and knocked on every door in the district. He surprised even himself by winning against a nearly 20-year incumbent. Then in 1986 after his unpredicted gubernatorial win, Thompson caught everyone off guard by persuading Senate Democratic Majority Leader Tim Cullen to join his administration. Thompson says, "I said you can spend your time undercutting me or you can join my administration as a cabinet officer and develop a bipartisan agenda."

Public office: Governor of Wisconsin

Family: Wife, Sue Ann; three children, Tommi, Kelli and Jason

Education: B.S. 1963, J.D. University of Wisconsin

Profession: Attorney

Military: Served in Wisconsin National Guard and the Army Reserve

CSG ties: President of The Council of State Governments

Posts: Past chairman, National Governor's Association, Republican Governors Association and Education Commission of the States

Thompson signs an accord with U.S. Coast Guard and U.S. Environmental Protection Agency officials on state-federal responsibilities in emergencies.

He learned to work hard at the insistence of his store keeper father. At age 6 he cleaned eggs brought in by local farmers to earn money for a bike. While he hates eggs to this day, he says, "My father taught me to be tough and hardworking."

Jensen says, "If anyone strolls in the governor's office, they'll see that everyone is 20 to 25 years old—because he (Thompson) wears them out." Jensen recalls his days with the governor began at 7:30 a.m. and often ended with a phone call from the governor at 11:30 p.m. "He's an extraordinarily hard worker."

Thompson admits, "I'm a workaholic as all my staff will tell you. I have great staff and I'm hard on them."

To get Thompson to relax, several of his motorcycle-riding friends challenged him to take up the sport several years ago. He agreed to go on a Superior to Madison ride, although he never had touched a bike. Much to his surprise, the morning of the ride, a half-dozen TV trucks showed up to record the event. Not wanting to expose his motorcycle ignorance, Thompson got on his new Harley, accidentally killed the motor, restarted it, fumbled for the gears, popped the clutch and, out of control, headed straight toward a TV

Cullen opted to become head of Human Services and helped push the first welfare initiatives through the Democratic Legislature. In designing welfare reform, Thompson invited a dozen welfare mothers to lunch at the governor's mansion. Jensen says it was a typical move for Thompson. "He mulls ideas over and insists on talking to many more people than most governors would."

Thompson also reached out to get school choice adopted. He teamed up with urban African-American legislators, who had been supporting all-black urban schools. Thompson convinced them that segregated schools, even for a good cause, wouldn't pass constitutional muster. The first school choice law, passed in 1990, provided vouchers for nonsectarian private schools in Milwaukee. Thompson says Democratic Rep. Annette Polly Williams, who authored the 1990 law, disagrees with expansion of the program to religious schools.

"I don't know if it's going to work," Thompson says of the expanded vouchers. He adds that Milwaukee now has a great opportunity to succeed because of the choices available to students there. A July poll showed more than 60 percent of Wisconsin residents supported school vouchers.

Jensen says of the unlikely coalition, "A small-town, rural Republican governor and central-city minority legislators started school choice to improve education."

Relaxing on a Harley

Thompson's outgoing manner has won him the affection of many in Wisconsin. He regales audiences by saying his hometown of Elroy, population 1,500, is so small, you can dial a wrong number and still talk more than 30 minutes. Thompson says his mom, a schoolteacher, gave him her gregarious Irish nature and passed on a streak of human kindness.

Thompson talks with former Secretary of State Henry Kissinger at NGA.

Thompson has reached out to African-Americans in welfare reform and school choice decisions.

Thompson's wife of 30 years, Sue Ann, plays an active role on the state and national scene, including delivering remarks to the Legislature as part of the governor's annual message. The first lady, a sixth grade teacher, helped create the Governor's Office for Family Literacy to coordinate literacy efforts. A breast cancer survivor, Mrs. Thompson has traveled nationwide promoting breast cancer awareness and launched a women's health initiative in Wisconsin.

As for his future, Thompson says, "I made the commitment that this is my last election (as governor). I don't care about anything but doing what's right."

Doing what's right means Thompson will be as hard driving as ever, pushing through an ambitious agenda of tax reduction and simplification, educational improvement, health reforms and work force strategies. Jensen says, "He's a tireless reformer, continuously searching for ways to make things better."

Thompson plans to keep Wisconsin moving forward. He brags at national conferences of state officials that he takes back ideas to implement in Wisconsin and advises them to do the same. He told CSG delegates, "Let the best practices bubble up from the states and share our ideas."

Thompson is ready to do what it takes to keep the forward motion going. He says, "I'm a hard driver. I want to do it, then go onto the next fight and get it done. I've had to fight a lot of odds, but there's always some way to accomplish the task."

truck. Miraculously, he missed the truck.

In a high-profile ride, Thompson joined more than 200 Harley-Davidson motorcycle riders on a 1,350-mile road trip to Washington, D.C., in June to celebrate Wisconsin's Sesquicentennial. Appropriately, Wisconsin is the home of Harley-Davidson and the site of the company's world headquarters.

This August, Thompson was his congenial best hosting in Milwaukee the National Governors' Association, which he once chaired. Declaring he was in charge of fun, Thompson invited his fellow governors and their wives to a bike ride and arranged for the conference delegates to view Milwaukee's world famous circus parade. An unashamed booster of all things Wisconsin, Thompson welcomed the governors by saying, "Wisconsin is the state where Harleys roar, eagles soar and Packers score." A football autographed by Packers quarterback Brett Favre rests on his office desk.

Conservative Governors and The Joy of Spending

ALAN EHRENHALT

Anybody who has followed Connecticut politics in the past year has every reason to suspect that a bizarre plot has been unleashed on the state: Some fiend has kidnapped the conservative governor and installed a liberal look-alike in his place. The man currently working out of the big office in Hartford bears a striking resemblance to John Rowland, and even his voice sounds about the same. But he's been governing more like Hubert Humphrey.

The first sign that something was amiss came last February, when the man who insists he is Rowland unveiled his 1998 education agenda. Just a year earlier, the governor had been his familiar old self, calling for a 10 percent cut in higher-education funds and trying to get rid of a program that awarded cash grants to top-performing schools. All of a sudden he was coming forward with a five-year, $500 million, 20-point program to invest in teachers, computers and capital construction. Instead of canceling the achievement grants, he proposed to triple them.

Then he started behaving even more strangely. The budget Rowland sent to the legislature was stuffed so full of generous initiatives that it violated the state spending cap, adopted in 1991 and never breached before. To get the budget approved, the administration had to prepare a "Declaration of Extraordinary Circumstances," even though it was hard to tell just what the emergency was supposed to be.

All through the spring and summer, Democrats and cynics offered an easy explanation for what was going on: Rowland was simply passing out money to guarantee his reelection in November. The new commitment to schools was nice, said the chairman of the Senate education committee, but the state shouldn't have to wait "every four years for John Rowland to have an epiphany that education is important."

A few weeks ago, however, it became unmistakably clear that the governor was suffering from something more than campaign fever. Sounding expansive and jubilant at a state capitol rally, and speaking live on television all over the state, he announced that the New England Patriots pro football team had agreed to move from Boston to Hartford, and at a bargain price of only $375 million in state bonds to subsidize roads, parking and other infrastructure to support the stadium that would be built in Hartford's downtown. Rowland emphasized that the bonds would be paid for by taxing ticket sales and player salaries, not by hitting up the general public. On the other hand, if the luxury boxes don't bring the Patriots' owners at least $175 million, the state has promised to make up the difference, so the public still could be out a chunk of money in the end.

"There's no one more cautious than I am," the new-model Rowland assured the crowd. "But let's seize the moment. Let's make it happen. . . . Today we have a chance to redefine ourselves.

IT'S HARD TO TELL whether he was most concerned about redefining the state, the city or himself. But you can't attribute his deal with the Patriots entirely to political expediency. At the time of his announcement, the election was over. The governor had just won a second four-year term with 63 percent of the vote. Obviously, some other factor was at work.

There's one other relatively simple way to explain how Connecticut's Scrooge candidate of 1994 turned into the incumbent Santa Claus of 1998. Four years ago, Connecticut, like every other jurisdiction in New England, was suffering from budget problems. Now, it is flush with money. At the time Rowland submitted his budget last spring, the books showed a surplus of more than $300 million. By the time he announced the Patriots' move, the surplus was closer to $500 million and still continuing to climb. You can't ignore the obvious: Governors spend money when there is money in the treasury to spend.

On the other hand, there's more than one way to deal with a surplus. You can give it back to the taxpayers. You can put it into the rainy day fund. Connecticut did both of these things on a small scale last year. Or you can use extra cash to pay down some of your long-term debt; Rowland's state has about $13 billion worth of indebtedness of various kinds. But Rowland didn't want to do that, and neither did the Democratic legislature. They were more than happy to indulge and endorse the Republican governor's surprising new fondness for spending money.

I'm not saying this was a bad decision. Connecticut, like every other state in this country, has a big backlog of public needs that have been deferred too long, and if you don't address them in good times, you probably will never address them at all. I don't even quarrel with the subsidy for the Patriots. I know what it means for a city to have a professional football team. I wish we had one here in Washington.

BUT I DO THINK there's a larger point to be made here on the whole subject of governors, budgets and conservatism. It's a rare governor, however stingy he might consider himself, who can make it through an entire term without discovering just how enjoyable the expenditure of state money can be.

I would never try to claim, for example, that George Pataki, the governor of New York, is anything but a conservative. In his approach to taxes, to bureaucracy, to social issues, to just about every aspect of public policy, he marks a clear departure from Mario Cuomo, his liberal Democratic predecessor.

But you wouldn't know that to look at the numbers. Last year, when Pataki sent the legislature a budget that called for overall spending increases of 8 percent, he was proposing the biggest boost in a decade and a bigger one than Cuomo had sought in 10 of his 12 years in office. Pataki wanted more money for just about everything: $518 million more for school aid, $41 million in arts grants to local communities, a hefty 11 percent increase in mass transit funding. The Conservative Party, which had backed Pataki enthusiastically in his first campaign in 1994, accused him of taking a "left fork."

It didn't turn out to be a hard left. The legislature threw in $800 million on top of the governor's recommendations, and Pataki vetoed that. The budget that finally became law during the summer was somewhat tighter than the one Pataki had proposed in January. Still, it's fair to say that New York doesn't exactly have the skinflint chief executive it seemed to be getting in 1994.

I don't think the crucial factor in loosening gubernatorial purse strings is ideology. I think it's ambition. All governors, all chief executives of any sort, find themselves after a couple of years pondering what their place in history will be. Even the most conservative among them ultimately conclude that they would like to be remembered for something more tangible than tax rebates and dexterity in using a red pencil. One Connecticut lobbyist reported that Rowland showed the Patriots' owner a set of plans for the rebuilding of downtown Hartford, and then turned to him and said, "This is my legacy, and you can be part of it."

The truth is that virtually any signature program a governor chooses to build a reputation on invariably costs lots of money. George W. Bush, running for his second term in Texas last year, based most of his campaign on the need to improve education, and to improve it in the most traditional-sounding way: by putting an end to the social promotion system by which teenagers graduate from high school without knowing how to read.

But ending social promotion without creating some new strategies for helping kids learn isn't very appealing in political terms, let alone in public policy terms. So Bush threw in a two-year, $203 million reading-skills initiative aimed at third-grade pupils. His Democratic challenger called that woefully inadequate, and said a real attack on the problem would cost more like $2 billion over two years. Bush disputed that. But wherever the truth lies, it's inescapable that a full-fledged attack on childhood literacy problems will force the governor—and seeming presidential front-runner—to err on the side of being a spender, not a skinflint.

Bush's brother, newly elected Florida Governor Jeb Bush, managed to cast aside his earlier reputation for stinginess even before taking office. His 1998 campaign platform sounded like the blueprint for building a Great Society in the Sunshine. Bush promised to create an "Office of Urban Opportunity" under his personal direction. Twenty specially designated "front-porch communities" would shape action plans to revive inner-city neighborhoods and distribute $50 million over 10 years to developers of low-income housing. Bush's Democratic opponent accused him of "planning to create a large bureaucracy and throwing more money at it." But if so, it didn't seem to bother the voters. Jeb Bush, like his brother, like Pataki, and like John Rowland, was an easy winner in 1998.

Jeb Bush appears to have learned at the very outset what some of his fellow conservatives found out more slowly. The American people consider themselves fiscal conservatives. They believe in low taxes, frugal management and a government that lives within its means. They like the idea of a state treasury with plenty of money in it. But as Groucho Marx might say, they don't mind seeing the governor take it out once in a while.

If you didn't care for this column, you almost certainly will not enjoy Democracy in the Mirror, *a new collection of Alan Ehrenhalt's Assessments essays available from Congressional Quarterly Books (800-638-1710).*

Nobody In Charge

When everyone seems to be running a city, there's a good chance it isn't being run at all.

BY ROB GURWITT

IN THE END, LARRY BROWN HAD LITTLE CHOICE but to resign as city manager of Kansas City, Missouri. By late June, when he finally agreed to give up his office atop the city's oddly graceful, Depression-era skyscraper of a city hall, Brown was a man beset, openly mistrusted by the council and sniped at by employees. His imminent departure was a universal assumption within local political circles.

There are those in Kansas City who, in hindsight, trace Brown's downfall to his 1994 arrest for drunken driving, which they contend cost him the respect of city staff. Others point to his decisions last year to give his top aides large pay raises and to send them to California's Napa Valley for taxpayer-supported training sessions—steps that turned into public-relations nightmares. By April, when a city council majority lambasted his proposed budget and yanked funding from his efforts to transform city government, it was just a matter of time.

But the truth is that the seeds of Brown's departure were sown at the beginning, at the very moment he was hired. Never short on ambition, Brown wanted nothing less than to assert the authority of the city manager to run Kansas City government as he saw fit. Instead, encountering more and more resistance the harder he tried, Brown learned a painful and expensive lesson: Nobody runs Kansas City. And a complex array of political forces is organized to keep it that way.

Power rests everywhere within the community—in the corporate boardrooms, with neighborhood developers and community organizations, within city agencies, on appointed boards, with the city council, in the hands of the mayor and in the office of the city manager. Building consensus on any issue is a time-consuming, frustrating process, and it is made harder by a structure that deliberately impedes the clear-eyed exertion of political will. Yet, as Brown discovered, so many people have a vested interest in the status quo that—for a city

manager, at least—trying to change this state of affairs may be impossible.

This is a schizophrenic moment in the political history of America's big cities. For many of them, even some that were once branded ungovernable, the 1990s have brought a restoration of managerial competence, symbolized by New York's attack on crime, Cleveland's downtown revival, Chicago's school reform crusade and Philadelphia's return from the brink of bankruptcy.

All of the surging cities of this decade have had leaders with the ability to articulate and then enforce their priorities. These may be, as in New York, Chicago and Philadelphia, strong mayors in both the structural and political sense. Or they may be, as in Phoenix, a dynamic and widely admired city manager working with an elected council. But, in every case, there is a palpable sense that someone is in charge, setting an agenda about what is needed to make them attractive places to live and work.

Meanwhile, however, another set of cities, symbolized by Kansas City, Cincinnati, Miami and Dallas, among others, is stuck at the opposite end of the scale—mired in bickering, divided responsibility and long-standing political confusion. Nobody is in charge in these places. And it seems to take forever for anything to get done.

For the most part, these cities never fell quite as far as the Philadelphias and Clevelands of America. As a result, they have not been forced to look as hard at remaking local government. But, in the end, they will have no alternative. In the coming years, the struggle for urban viability will be hard enough, even under the best of circumstances. The fragmented cities will be at a profound disadvantage.

And they may finally be realizing it. In Kansas City, in the wake of Brown's resignation, popular but constitutionally weak

From *Governing* magazine, September 1997, pp. 20–24. © 1997 by Rob Gurwitt. Reprinted by permission.

Mayor Emanuel Cleaver has begun talking about the need to give more authority to his successors. In Cincinnati, there have been nine attempts during the past decade to give the mayor more control, and another—with the quiet backing of the current mayor, Roxane Qualls, and the city's business leadership—is in the works. Dallas, shocked by a decade of political incivility following generations of close-knit cooperation, is openly debating where it went wrong, and what sort of governmental structure it might need to set things right. The forces backing change in all of these cities seem to agree that, although there may be no one formula for success in urban government, there is a recipe for failure, and it is the absence of leadership.

At first glance, it might seem odd to include Kansas City anywhere near the top of the list of troubled American cities. The regional economy is doing just fine, with unemployment in the metropolitan area below 4 percent. The city itself has seen new employers—Gateway 2000 and Harley-Davidson among them—set up plants in town. According to U.S. Census Bureau estimates, Kansas City actually has grown in population since 1990—although pretty much all of that growth has been in the long-annexed rural and suburb-like reaches north of the Missouri River.

Mayor Cleaver has embarked on a revitalization effort that includes creating a jazz hall of fame and a Negro Leagues baseball museum. Several of the city's leading businessmen are hoping to launch a huge hotel and entertainment complex on a dormant parcel of downtown land. And a committee that draws from both sides of the Missouri-Kansas state line is overseeing the resurrection of Kansas City's famous beaux arts Union Station as a hands-on science center.

Still, beneath the glowing press releases, there is trouble. Kansas City faces the same disquieting trends as other depressed central cities. "Projections show an increase in the number of jobs in the core, but as a share of the region's jobs, Kansas City's will either not increase or will decline," says David Warm, of the Mid-America regional council. "Most of the jobs, wealth and people are locating at the edges of the region. So there is the same clear and continuing pattern of decline in the center, disinvestment in the inner-tier suburbs and rapid growth on the edges that you see elsewhere." In the competition with its suburbs, in other words, Kansas City is, at the moment, losing.

On the day he announced Larry Brown's resignation, Emanuel Cleaver made it clear that there is another competition that weighs on him as well. Pressed by reporters about what he thought of a governmental structure that, in essence, makes him merely the most prominent member of the city council, Cleaver could not hold back his frustration. "Kansas City is now a big-league city," he said, "and when the mayor of the city sits around with the president and CEO of a major corporation trying to get them to relocate here, the mayor is at a disadvantage, because other mayors can cut the deal at the table. We are at a disadvantage in many instances when we are out competing."

The fact is, running Kansas City is mostly a matter of indirection. Mayors and city managers have to deal not only with a set of department heads who historically have had great room to pursue their own priorities, but also with circumstances that couldn't be better designed to water down their authority. The police are funded by the city but controlled by a state board. Libraries are under a separate board. Economic development, which is much of what Cleaver has been about in recent years, is under the control of the Economic Development Corp., which has become a sort of independent dealmaker for the city. The schools have been answerable to a federal court for 20 years, foster care services are in court hands as well, and the housing authority is in receivership. No one who wants to get things done in Kansas City, in other words, can do it directly.

The fragmented cities are entangled in rivalry and personal politics.

As you might expect, many Kansas Citians have grown to like this state of affairs—it leaves each player within city government, along with those who try to affect it, with a fair degree of autonomy. It also means, though, that when their agendas differ, the city looks rudderless. "When communities have well-organized voices or a broad community ethic that's widely shared," says the head of one organization in Kansas City, "when there's a strong leader with clear ideas and directions, when there are well-organized plans and a well-organized and directed civic leadership that pursues those plans, that's when you get a healthy politics of ideas. Kansas City is not there at the moment. . . . The city is up for grabs."

In the year or so leading up to Brown's forced resignation, there were at least three distinct sets of priorities being laid out in city hall. Cleaver's had to do with bringing in new economic development, redeveloping Kansas City's historically black neighborhoods and tackling the issue of race relations head-on. The city council was focusing on how to pay for the city's infrastructure needs and shoring up basic services to residents. With all this going on, Brown was maneuvering to redesign the entire process by which Kansas City government worked. In retrospect, there was no way he could have succeeded.

In his defense, Brown was doing pretty much what the council had said it wanted when it hired him, back in 1993. Its members had asked for someone to bring Kansas City government in line with the movement toward cost containment and quality service that other cities had been pursuing. "We wanted someone to take charge and run the city wisely and economically and efficiently," says George Blackwood, the council's mayor pro tem. "We said, 'We're out of control. Get good people, get the job done, let's create a lean, mean fighting machine.' "

Brown's response was a process he called "transformation." Part of his goal was to introduce the notions of customer service and efficient, responsive bureaucracy that have taken hold elsewhere. But he also set out to break down the barriers that, over the decades, had grown up among departments that had become accustomed to being treated as sovereign entities. Most important, Brown wanted to reestablish the city manager's authority over the day-to-day running of the organization. Over the years, not only had department heads grown accustomed to following their own lead but city council members also had grown accustomed to making requests directly of department heads and even mid-level managers. The result was a city organization in which the right and left hands often didn't keep track of each other.

Brown made every effort to deal with this problem. As it turned out, though, few of his efforts sat well with others in city hall. Although some departments and lower-level managers responded to the service-oriented freedom Brown offered them—the city's fire department being, perhaps, the leading example—others resisted; they found sympathetic ears on a council that already saw Brown cutting off its direct pipeline to city departments.

The council was especially vulnerable on this point because there was no real leadership pushing it to embrace the principles that "transformation" was supposed to instill; indeed, there was no particular leadership pushing it in any direction at all. A set of scandals during the past few years—four council members have been indicted on corruption charges—has created an ominous level of mistrust, turning the council into a set of 12 independent players who may come together around specific priorities—fixing the city's decaying infrastructure or backing neighborhood services—but otherwise prefer to be seen as individuals, not as a collective municipal leadership. "It is not an individual responsibility of each member to be responsible for the next," says Ken Bacchus, whose six-year tenure makes him one of the council's senior members.

Given those circumstances, council members' political legitimacy has rested, in large part, on their day-to-day involvement in city government; it was Brown's difficulty grasping the importance they placed on this that, more than anything else, undermined him. The budget he submitted to the city council this spring is a good example: It was essentially all text, a budget designed to get the council to think about policy without worrying about particular line-items. As a matter of theory, this should be all a council needs from a city manager in order to pass judgment on the general direction city government is headed. But as Cleaver points out, "Politics 101 is, Don't call the politicians stupid. His statement, as I interpreted it, was, 'You guys set policy, I'll worry about the rest.' Well, in 1997, politicians don't fade into the woodwork. That ain't going to happen anymore." When it became clear that Brown had no intention of setting aside his priorities in favor of the council's and the mayor's—that, indeed, there was no way to reconcile them—he left.

There are those in Cincinnati, too, who have become increasingly impatient with a political process that treats issues crucial to the city as though they were mice let loose among a swarm of cats. "I think that the city of Cincinnati is an essentially scandal-free, well-managed city with a work force of good, dedicated people," says Nick Vehr, a recently retired Republican councilman. "But . . . things get mired down in endless political debate and a kind of bureaucratic morass that pounds them to a pulp before they can be implemented."

Cincinnati, too, is a council-manager city. Unlike Kansas City, however, its mayor isn't even elected separately. Instead, he or she is simply the council member who gets the most votes in the general election. Because no one actually runs for mayor, and because the mayor is no more powerful than any other member of the city council, there is very little political accountability in Cincinnati. The result, says Zane Miller, a political scientist at the University of Cincinnati, is an "absence of coherent leadership."

"The city bounces from problem to problem," agrees John Fox, editor of *City Beat*, Cincinnati's local alternative weekly newspaper. "The bottom line is city government becomes a reactionary body rather than a proactive body that says, 'Here's our vision for where we're going in the next 10 years.' "

This is not necessarily for lack of trying. For two years, in fact, administrative staff worked with the council to develop a strategic planning process that was to produce a clear set of priorities on which the city manager could focus. In a series of sessions with the council, however, city hall's vision of the future became muddier, not clearer. Rather than establish a handful of priorities with a few "action steps" attached to each, council members decided they had dozens of priorities. The "strategic plan" sank under its own weight.

Visiting Cincinnati, one does not get a sense of a city at loose ends. Its long-neglected riverfront is about to become a new focus for city life as two sports stadiums—one for the football Bengals, the other for the baseball Reds—are built there. Main Street, which was pretty much derelict 10 years ago, now has become a restaurant- and bar-filled entertainment zone at night. Parts of the neighborhood known as Over-the-Rhine, which was essentially a ghetto sitting on downtown's heels, are rapidly being gentrified. A new department store is going up on a prime downtown parking lot that many had despaired would never be replaced. "If you look ahead 10 years," says Al Tuchfarber, director of the Institute for Policy Research at the University of Cincinnati, "you're going to see a very revitalized downtown and riverfront."

Yet, the good things that are taking place in Cincinnati are taking place more in spite of city government than because of it. The revitalization of Over-the-Rhine might have materialized years ago had the city not set up barriers to redevelopment there. The new department store on Fountain Square West took a decade to materialize because the council spent most of that decade squabbling over just how the land ought to be used.

Perhaps the most troubling example of the city's problems, though, is the stadium deal. Given a deadline by the Bengals to come up with a plan that would keep the team in town, the city—after much hairtearing—essentially punted. The financing deal was finally put together by surrounding Hamilton County, which, with three county board members, can move much more quickly. In exchange, the county will own the stadiums. "It wasn't until we shifted authority to the county," Nick Vehr says, "that the sports franchises seriously began negotiating to stay in this town. . . . I think there's a general perception in this community that the ability to manage the future no longer resides, as it did in the past, in city hall."

There are, to be sure, plenty of people in both Kansas City and Cincinnati who believe that their cities are better off precisely because power is so fragmented. "The successful person negotiates coalitions and puts them together on a given issue," says one former Kansas City government staffer, "and that's not a bad thing. With coalition-building, there's some kind of consensus reached. Maybe it takes longer and demands more skill, but maybe the stuff that results is more durable."

It can also, of course, be argued that forceful leadership is hardly a panacea for American cities. If it were, neither Detroit under Coleman Young nor Washington, D.C., under Marion Barry would have fallen into the disrepair both cities now struggle against.

But for a much larger number of cities these days, it is fractured leadership—not abused personal power—that constitutes the main political problem. In Miami, for instance, the fiscal insolvency and corrupt practices of its former city manager and finance director flourished in no small part because each major player in city government was content to go his own way—the manager pursued his own political goals, each city commissioner was wrapped up in his own pursuits, the finance director was given a free hand, and the business community and many onlookers were convinced that the city itself did not matter. There was, simply put, no one in charge who cared about Miami as a whole.

Dallas, meanwhile, has been an exhibit of fragmentation for the entire decade of the 1990s. Once, it was a prime example of the opposite: a place where decisive mayors and city managers worked quietly and efficiently with a single-minded business establishment to set clear community priorities. Thirty years ago, when Mayor Erik Jonsson felt he needed a blueprint for long-term urban planning, he simply rounded up 80 civic leaders, spirited them off to a country club for a weekend and returned with a short list of major goals for the 1970s—most of which were implemented.

But that Dallas power structure eventually succumbed to its own weaknesses. It was so tightly controlled, so exclusive and so overwhelmingly affluent, male and white that it bred long-standing resentments among the groups in town that felt left out of its processes. When the establishment expired, it set in motion a long period of chaos during which the newly enfranchised elements jostled for power without paying much attention to the interests of the community as a whole.

In 1991, under court pressure, Dallas switched from a council whose members were elected at-large to a district-by-district system. Ever since then, the council's deliberations have been one long bout of factionalism—ethnic, ideological and geographic. Presided over by a mayor with little formal power, the council has drifted from one crisis to another.

Recently, some of the tumult on the council has quieted down amid Mayor Ron Kirk's efforts to build a consensus around long-term plans for the city. At the same time, however, the school board threatens to explode under the pressure of racial feuding—for the most part between African-Americans and Hispanics—and much of the rest of the city's political leadership is finding it difficult to avoid being dragged into that battle.

Insolvency and corruption flourished in Miami in part because each major player was allowed to pursue his own political goals. There was no one in charge who cared about Miami as a whole.

In may be too much to say that all fragmented cities are alike these days, but all of them seem to be a little like Dallas, Cincinnati and Kansas City: so enmeshed in rivalries and personal politics that they are having trouble living up to their potential—or even seeing clearly just what that potential might be. If they are to remain competitive when it comes to attracting businesses, rebuilding the public schools and drawing middle-class residents back to their neighborhoods, they somehow need to rely upon leaders who can help them coalesce around coherent visions of where they're going. Such people clearly exist in all of these cities; the only question is whether they will be allowed to emerge.

"Leaders shackled by unreasonable restrictions are forced to engage in compromises and deal-making that slows forward movement and inhibits development of wide-ranging vision," the editor of the *Kansas City Star*'s editorial page wrote not long ago, in a commentary that just as easily could have been applied to Cincinnati and any number of other places casting about for direction these days. "The way Kansas City's government now works," Rich Hood wrote, "there are so many safeguards built in to prevent dramatic leadership (or risky gambles that might not pay off) that we too frequently witness government by paralysis."

WATCHING THE BENCH

Justice by Numbers

Mandatory sentencing drove me from the bench

Lois G. Forer

Lois G. Forer, a former judge of the Court of Common Pleas of Philadelphia, is the author, most recently, of Unequal Protection: Women, Children, and the Elderly in Court.

Michael S. would have been one of the more than 600,000 incarcerated persons in the United States. He would have been a statistic, yet another addition to a clogged criminal justice system. But he's not—in part because to me Michael was a human being: a slight 24-year-old with a young wife and small daughter. Not that I freed him; I tried him and found him guilty. He is free now only because he is a fugitive. I have not seen him since the day of his sentencing in 1984, yet since that day our lives have been inextricably connected. Because of his case I retired from the bench.

Michael's case appeared routine. He was a typical offender: young, black, and male, a high-school dropout without a job. The charge was an insignificant holdup that occasioned no comment in the press. And the trial itself was, in the busy life of a judge, a run-of-the-mill event.

The year before, Michael, brandishing a toy gun, held up a taxi and took $50 from the driver and the passenger, harming neither. This was Michael's first offense. Although he had dropped out of school to marry his pregnant girlfriend, Michael later obtained a high school equivalency diploma. He had been steadily employed, earning enough to send his daughter to parochial school—a considerable sacrifice for him and his wife. Shortly before the holdup, Michael had lost his job. Despondent because he could not support his family, he went out on a Saturday night, had more than a few drinks, and then robbed the taxi.

There was no doubt that Michael was guilty. But the penalty posed problems. To me, a robbery in a taxi is not an intrinsically graver offense than a robbery in an alley, but to the Pennsylvania legislature, it is. Because the holdup occurred on public transportation, it fell within the ambit of the state's mandatory sentencing law—which required a minimum sentence of five years in the state penitentiary. In Pennsylvania, a prosecutor may decide not to demand imposition of that law, but Michael's prosecuting attorney wanted the five-year sentence.

One might argue that a five-year sentence for a $50 robbery is excessive or even immoral, but to a judge, those arguments are necessarily irrelevant. He or she has agreed to enforce the law, no matter how ill-advised, unless the law is unconstitutional.

I believed the mandatory sentencing law was, and like many of my colleagues I had held it unconstitutional in several other cases for several reasons. We agreed that it violates the constitutional principle of separation of powers because it can be invoked by the prosecutor, and not by the judge. In addition, the act is arbitrary and capricious in its application. Robbery, which is often a simple purse snatching, is covered, but not child molestation or incest, two of society's most damaging offenses. Nor can a defendant's previous record or mental state be considered. A hardened repeat offender receives the same sentence as a retarded man who steals out of hunger. Those facts violate the fundamental Anglo-American legal principles of individualized sentencing and proportionality of the penalty to the crime.

Thus in Michael's case, I again held the statute to be unconstitutional and turned to the sentencing guidelines—a state statute designed to give uniform sentences to offenders who commit similar crimes. The minimum sentence prescribed by the guidelines was 24 months.

A judge can deviate from the prescribed sentence if he or she writes an opinion explaining the reasons for the deviation. While this sounds reasonable in theory, "downwardly departing" from the guidelines is extremely difficult. The mitigating circumstances that influence most judges are not included in the limited list of factors on which "presumptive" sentence is based—that an offender is a caretaker of small children; that the offender is mentally retarded; or that the offender, like Michael, is emotionally distraught.

So I decided to deviate from the guidelines, sentencing Michael to 11-and-a-half months in the county jail and permitting him to work outside the prison during the day to support his family. I also imposed a sentence of two years' probation following his imprisonment conditioned upon repayment of the $50. My rationale for the lesser penalty, outlined in my lengthy opinion, was that this was a first offense, no one was harmed, Michael acted under the pressures of unemployment and need, and he seemed truly contrite. He had never committed a violent act and posed no danger to the public. A sentence of close to a year seemed adequate to convince Michael of the seriousness of his crime. Nevertheless, the prosecutor appealed.

Michael returned to his family, obtained steady employment, and repaid the victims of his crime. I thought no more about Michael until 1986, when the state supreme court upheld the appeal and ordered me to resentence him to a minimum of five years in the state penitentiary. By this time Michael had successfully completed his term of imprisonment and probation, including payment of restitution. I checked Michael's record. He had not been rearrested.

I was faced with a legal and moral dilemma. As a judge I had sworn to uphold the law, and I could find no legal grounds for violating an order of the supreme court. Yet five years' imprisonment was grossly disproportionate to the offense. The usual grounds for imprisonment are retribution, deterrence, and rehabilitation. Michael had paid his retribution by a short term of imprisonment and by making restitution to the victims. He had been effectively deterred from committing future crimes. And by any measurable standard he had been rehabilitated. There was no social or criminological justification for sending him back to prison. Given the choice between defying a court order or my conscience, I decided to leave the bench where I had sat for 16 years.

That didn't help Michael, of course; he was resentenced by another judge to serve the balance of the five years: four years and 15 days. Faced with this prospect, he disappeared. A bench warrant was issued, but given the hundreds of fugitives—including dangerous ones—loose in Philadelphia, I doubt that anyone is seriously looking for him.

But any day he may be stopped for a routine traffic violation; he may apply for a job or a license; he may even be the victim of a crime—and if so, the ubiquitous computer will be alerted and he will be returned to prison to serve the balance of his sentence, plus additional time for being a fugitive. It is not a happy prospect for him and his family—nor for America, which is saddled with a punishment system that operates like a computer—crime in, points tallied, sentence out—utterly disregarding the differences among the human beings involved.

The mandatory sentencing laws and guidelines that exist today in every state were designed to smooth out the inequities in the American judiciary, and were couched in terms of fairness to criminals—they would stop the racist judge from sentencing black robbers to be hanged, or the crusading judge from imprisoning pot smokers for life. Guidelines make sense, for that very reason. But they have had an ugly and unintended result—an increase in the number of American prisoners and an increase in the length of the sentences they serve. Meanwhile, the laws have effectively neutralized judges who prefer sentencing the nonviolent to alternative programs or attempt to keep mothers with young children out of jail.

Have the laws made justice fairer—the central objective of the law? I say no, and a recent report by the Federal Sentencing Commission concurs. It found that, even under mandatory sentencing laws, black males served 83.4 months to white males' 53.7 months for the same offenses. (Prosecutors are more likely to demand imposition of the mandatory laws for blacks than for whites.)

Most important, however, as mandatory sentencing packs our prisons and busts our budgets, it doesn't prevent crime very effectively. For certain kinds of criminals, alternative sentencing is the most effective type of punishment. That, by the way, is a cold, hard statistic—rather like Michael will be when they find him.

Sentenced to death

In the past two decades, all 50 state legislatures have enacted mandatory sentencing laws, sentencing guideline statutes, or both. The result: In 1975 there were 263,291 inmates in federal and state prisons. Today there are over 600,000—more than in any other nation—the bill for which comes to $20.3 billion a year. Yet incarceration has not reduced the crime rate or made our streets and communities safer. The number of known crimes committed in the U.S. has increased 10 percent in the last five years.

How did we get into this no-win situation? Like most legislative reforms, it started with good intentions. In 1970, after the turmoil of the sixties, legislators were bombarded with pleas for "law and order." A young, eager, newly appointed federal judge, Marvin Frankel, had an idea.

Before his appointment, Frankel had experienced little personal contact with the criminal justice system. Yet his slim book, *Fair and Certain Punishment*, offered a system of guidelines to determine the length of various sentences. Each crime was given a certain number of points. The offender was also given a number of points depending upon his or her prior record, use of a weapon, and a few other variables. The judge merely needed to add up the points to calculate the length of imprisonment.

The book was widely read and lauded for two main reasons. First, it got tough on criminals and made justice "certain." A potential offender would know in advance the penalty he would face and thus be deterred. (Of course, a large proportion of street crimes are not premeditated, but that fact was ignored.) And second, it got tough on the "bleeding heart" judges. All offenders similarly situated would be treated the same.

The plan sounded so fair and politically promising that many states rushed to implement it in the seventies. In Pennsylvania, members of the legislature admonished judges not to oppose the guidelines because the alternative would be even worse: mandatory sentences. In fact, within a few years almost every jurisdiction had both sentencing guidelines and mandatory sentencing laws. Since then, Congress has enacted some 60 mandatory sentencing laws on the federal level.

As for unfairnesses in sentencing—for instance, the fact that the robber with his finger in his jacket gets the same sentence as the guy with a semiautomatic—these could have been rectified by giving appellate courts jurisdiction to review sentences, as is the law in Canada. This was not done on either the state or federal level. Thus what influential criminologist James Q. Wilson had argued during the height of the battle had become the law of the land: The legal system should "most definitely stop pretending that the judges know any better than the rest of us how to provide 'individualized justice.' "

Hardening time

I'm not sure I knew better than the rest of you, but I knew a few things about Michael and the correctional system I would be throwing him into. At the time of Michael's sentencing, both the city of Philadelphia and the commonwealth of Pennsylvania were, like many cities and states, in such poor fiscal shape that they did not have money for schools and health care, let alone new prisons, and the ones they did have were overflowing. The city was under a federal order to reduce the prison population; untried persons accused of dangerous crimes were being released, as were offenders who had not completed their sentences.

As for Michael, his problems and those of his family were very real to me. Unlike appellate judges who never see the individuals whose lives and property they dispose of, a trial judge sees living men and women. I had seen Michael and his wife and daughter. I had heard him express remorse. I had favorable reports about him from the prison and his parole officer. Moreover, Michael, like many offenders who appeared before me, had written to me several times. I felt I knew him.

Of course, I could have been wrong. As Wilson says, judges are not infallible—and most of them know that. But they have heard the evidence, seen the offender, and been furnished with presentence reports and psychiatric evaluations. They are in a better position to evaluate the individual and devise an appropriate sentence than anyone else in the criminal justice system.

Yet under mandatory sentencing laws, the complexities of each crime and criminal are ignored. And seldom do we ask what was once a legitimate question in criminal justice: What are the benefits of incarceration? The offenders are off the streets for the period of the sentence, but once released, most will soon be rearrested. (Many crimes are committed in prison, including murder, rape, robbery, and drug dealing.) They have not been "incapacitated," another of the theoretical justifications for imprisonment. More likely, they have simply been hardened.

Sentence structure

Is there another way to sentence criminals without endangering the public? I believe there is. During my tenure on the bench, I treated imprisonment as the penalty of last resort, not the penalty of choice. And my examination of 16 years' worth of cases suggests my inclination was well founded. While a recent Justice Department study found that two thirds of all prisoners are arrested for other offenses within three years of release, more than two thirds of the 1,000-plus offenders I sentenced to probation conditioned upon payment of reparations to victims successfully completed their sentences and were not rearrested. I am not a statistician, so I had my records analyzed and verified by Elmer Weitekamp, then a doctoral candidate in criminology at the Wharton School of the University of Pennsylvania. He confirmed my findings.

The offenders who appeared before me were mostly poor people, poor enough to qualify for representation by a public defender. I did not see any Ivan Boeskys or Leona Helmsleys, and although there was a powerful mafia in Philadelphia, I did not see any dons, either. Approximately three fourths of these defendants were nonwhite. Almost 80 percent were high school dropouts. Many were functionally illiterate. Almost a third had some history of mental problems, were retarded, or had been in special schools. One dreary day my court reporter said plaintively, "Judge, why can't we get a better class of criminal?"

Not all of these offenders were sentenced to probation, obviously. But I had my own criteria or guidelines—very different from those established by most states and the federal government—for deciding on a punishment. My primary concern was public safety. The most important question I asked myself was whether the offender could be deterred from committing other crimes. No one can predict with certainty who will or will not commit a crime, but there are indicators most sensible people recognize as danger signals.

First, was this an irrational crime? If an arsonist sets a fire to collect insurance, that is a crime but also a rational act. Such a person can be deterred by being made to pay for the harm done and the costs to the fire department. However, if the arsonist sets fires just because he likes to see them, it is highly unlikely that he can be stopped from setting others, no matter how high the fine.

Imprisonment is advisable even though it may be a first offense.

Second, was there wanton cruelty? If a robber maims or slashes the victim, there is little likelihood that he can safely be left in the community. If a robber simply displays a gun but does not fire it or harm the victim, then one should consider his life history, provocation, and other circumstances in deciding whether probation is appropriate.

Third, is this a hostile person? Was his crime one of hatred, and does he show any genuine remorse? Most rapes are acts of hostility, and the vast majority of rapists have a record of numerous sexual assaults. I remember one man who raped his mother. I gave him the maximum sentence under the law—20 years—but with good behavior, he got out fairly quickly. He immediately raped another elderly woman. Clearly, few rapists can safely be left in the community, and in my tenure, I incarcerated every one.

Yet gang rape, although a brutal and horrifying crime, is more complicated. The leader is clearly hostile and should be punished severely. Yet the followers can't be so neatly categorized. Some may act largely out of cowardice and peer pressure.

Fourth, is this a person who knows he is doing wrong but cannot control himself? Typical of such offenders are pedophiles. One child abuser who appeared before me had already been convicted of abusing his first wife's child. I got him on the second wife's child and sentenced him to the maximum. Still, he'll get out with good behavior, and I shudder to think about the children around him when he does. This is one case in which justice is not tough enough.

By contrast, some people who have committed homicide present very little danger of further violence—although many more do. Once a young man came before me because he had taken aim at a person half a block away and then shot him in the back, killing him. Why did he do it? "I wanted to get me a body." He should never get out. But the mandatory codes don't make great distinctions between him and another murderer who came before me, a woman who shot and killed a boy after he and his friends brutally gang-raped her teenage daughter.

I found this woman guilty of first-degree murder, but I found no reason to incarcerate her. She had four young children to support who would have become wards of the welfare department and probably would have spent their childhoods in a series of foster homes. I placed her on probation—a decision few judges now have the discretion to impose. She had not been arrested before. She has not been arrested since.

Of course, the vast majority of men, women, and children in custody in the United States are not killers, rapists, or arsonists. They're in prison for some type of theft—a purse snatching, burglary, or embezzlement. Many of these criminals can be punished without incarceration. If you force a first-time white-collar criminal to pay heavily for his crimes—perhaps three times the value of the money or property taken—he'll get the message that crime does not pay. As for poor people, stealing is not always a sign that the individual is an unreasonable risk to the community. It's often a sign that they want something—a car, Air Jordans—that they are too poor to buy themselves. Many of them, if they are not violent, can also be made to make some restitution and learn that crime doesn't pay.

Of course, to most of us, the idea of a nonprison sentence is tantamount to exoneration; a criminal sentenced to probation has effectively "gotten off." And there's a reason for that impression: Unless the probationer is required by the sentencing judge to perform specific tasks, probation is a charade. The probationer meets with the probation officer, briefly, perhaps once a month—making the procedure a waste of time for both. The officer duly records the meeting and the two go their separate ways until the probationer is arrested for another offense.

When I made the decision not to send a criminal to prison, I wanted to make sure that the probation system I sent them into had teeth. So I set firm conditions. If the offender was functionally illiterate, he was unemployable and would probably steal or engage in some other illegal activity once released. Thus in my sentencing, I sent him to school and ordered the probation officer to see that he went. (I use the masculine pronoun deliberately for I have never seen an illiterate female offender under the age of 60). I ordered school dropouts to get their high school equivalency certificates and find jobs. All offenders were ordered to pay restitution or reparations within their means or earning capacity to their victims. Sometimes it was as little as $5 a week. Offenders simply could not return to their old, feckless lifestyles without paying some financial penalty for their wrongdoing.

Monitoring probation wasn't easy for me, or the probation officers with whom I worked. Every day I'd come into my office, look at my calendar, and notice that, say, 30 days had passed since Elliott was let out. So I'd call the probation office. Has Elliott made his payment? Is he going to his GED class? And so on. If the answer was no, I'd hold a violation hearing with the threat of incarceration if the conditions were not met within 30 days. After I returned a few people to jail for noncompliance, both my offenders and their probation officers knew I meant business. (Few probation officers protested my demands; their jobs were more meaningful and satisfying, they said.)

Of course, probation that required education and work and payment plans meant real work for criminals, too. But there was a payoff both the probation officers and I could see: As offenders worked and learned and made restitution, their attitudes often changed dramatically.

Time and punishment

My rules of sentencing don't make judgeship easier; relying on mandatory sentencing is a far better way to guarantee a leisurely, controversy-free career on the bench. But my rules are, I believe, both effective and transferable: an application of common sense that any reasonable person could follow to similar ends. What prevents Americans from adopting practical measures like these is a atavistic belief in the sanctity of punishment. Even persons who have never heard of Immanuel Kant or the categorical imperative to punish believe that violation of law must be followed by the infliction of pain.

If we Americans treated crime more practically—as socially unacceptable behavior that should be curbed for the good of the community—we might begin to take a rational approach to the development of alternatives to prison. We might start thinking in terms not of punishment but of public safety, deterrence, and rehabilitation. Penalties like fines, work, and payment of restitution protect the public better and more cheaply than imprisonment in many cases.

Mind you, sentencing guidelines are not inherently evil. Intelligent guidelines would keep some judges from returning repeat offenders to the streets and others from putting the occasional cocaine user away for 10 years. Yet those guidelines must allow more latitude for the judge and the person who comes before him. While some states' sentencing laws include provisions that allow judges to override the mandatory sentences in some cases, the laws are for the most part inflexible—they deny judges the freedom to discriminate between the hardened criminal and the Michael. Richard H. Girgenti, the criminal justice director of New York state, has long proposed that the legislature give judges more discretion to impose shorter sentences for nonviolent and noncoercive felonies. This common-sense proposal has not been acted on in New York or any other state with mandatory sentencing laws.

Current laws are predicated on the belief that there must be punishment for every offense in terms of prison time rather than alternative sentences. But when it comes to determining the fate of a human being, there must be room for judgment. To make that room, we must stop acting as if mathematic calculations are superior to human thought. We must abolish mandatory sentencing laws and change the criteria on which sentencing guidelines are based.

Why not permit judges more freedom in making their decisions, provided that they give legitimate reasons? (If a judge doesn't have a good reason for deviating—if he's a reactionary or a fool—his sentencing decision will be overturned.) And why not revise the guidelines to consider dangerousness rather than the nomenclature of the offense? If we made simple reforms like these, thousands of non-threatening, nonhabitual offenders would be allowed to recompense their victims and society in a far less expensive and far more productive way.

You may be wondering, after all this, if I have a Willie Horton in my closet—a criminal whose actions after release privately haunt me. I do. I sentenced him to 10 to 20 years in prison—the maximum the law allowed—for forcible rape. He was released after eight years and promptly raped another woman. I could foresee what would happen but was powerless to impose a longer sentence.

And then there are the other cases that keep me up nights: those of men and women I might have let out, but didn't. And those of people like Michael, for whom justice shouldn't have been a mathematical equation.

Bench Press

Its legislative gains undone by unsympathetic state supreme courts, the business lobby is bringing its political resources to bear on judicial elections.

BY CHARLES MAHTESIAN

You would think that these would be heady days for the Ohio Chamber of Commerce. The legislature and the governor's mansion are safely ensconced in business-friendly Republican hands. Better still, two years ago the business community finally achieved the legislative victory that had eluded it for years—a comprehensive tort law that limits personal injury, malpractice and other awards in civil suits. By all measures, this should be a time for the Ohio business lobby to rest on its laurels.

The truth is, business interests are biting their fingernails in Columbus. The statehouse may be secure, but a few blocks away, the Supreme Court of Ohio is not. And that just happens to be where the fate of their prized tort package lies right now, awaiting judgment by the seven-member high court. If it is overturned, the millions of dollars business has spent to elect sympathetic officeholders will have amounted to very little.

While there is no way of knowing which way the court will decide, there are some hints, and from where the Ohio chamber sits, those hints are not encouraging. For starters, the case took an unusually direct route to the high court, bypassing a lower court review. Legal motions favored by supporters of the new law have gone unheeded by the supreme court. And if the past is any indication, the court is not apt to show any deference to the legislature when it comes to so-called tort reform. The last time the General Assembly passed a similar bill, in 1987, the court overturned every major provision of that law.

What troubles the chamber most, however, is what the organization's own research on the habits of the high court seems to foreshadow. An evaluation of more than 150 business-related decisions spanning the past decade concluded that three of the seven justices had repeatedly ruled against business interests and a fourth had lined up against the business-favored position nearly 80 percent of the time. Not coincidentally, the chamber likes to point out, between 1992 and 1996 those four justices received nearly

$800,000 in campaign contributions from the lobby that would like to gut the tort law—the Ohio trial lawyers.

The chamber has been cataloguing and chronicling the high court's views on everything from torts to taxes, including employment law, the environment, product liability, insurance, medical malpractice and workers' compensation. This new gambit is, in part, a defensive maneuver. The big corporations, small businesses, manufacturers, farmers, doctors, hospitals, retailers, nonprofits, trade and professional associations that comprise Ohio's business community are determined that the latest effort to rein in civil lawsuits not meet the same fate as the 1987 version.

There's not much they can do now that hasn't already been done. But the chamber and its allies can make sure they are never again in a position to worry, by beginning with the three court seats on the 1998 ballot. The business lobby is actively pursuing the election of judges who are perceived to share similar views—or at least those less inclined to override the will of the legislature. This fall will be a test of their determination, with two of the justices that the chamber considers the least friendly up for reelection.

Ohio is just one of an increasing number of states where business is seeking to recalibrate the scales of justice. Similar business-backed initiatives, in various stages of gestation, are under way in virtually every state where judges are elected to the bench or face the voters in retention elections.

Of course, there's nothing new about an interest group throwing its political weight—and campaign contributions—around in an effort to influence the outcome of judicial elections. Nor is there a lack of precedent for the same application of pressure—albeit behind the scenes—in states where judges are appointed rather than elected.

Organized labor and particularly the trial lawyers in virtually every state where judges are elected have long supported and even groomed candidates for election. In 1994, for example, the two trial lawyer- and union-backed Democratic nominees for the

Michigan supreme court outspent their opponents by a margin of more than 2 to 1. Two years later, attorneys at one Michigan law firm alone contributed more than $100,000 to the preferred candidate's coffers—he was a former president of the state trial lawyers' association.

The emerging interest of business forces in who sits on the bench is to some degree a response to the trial lawyer, labor and other traditionally Democratic lobbies, which, having lost control of various statehouses, are now taking the fight to the courthouse on a wide range of issues. "The plaintiffs' bar has been involved in a concerted manner in judicial politics," says Charles McConville, the political director for the Ohio Chamber of Commerce. "We are showing our members for the first time that the people who are making a living out of suing their businesses are the ones electing these judges. This is a wake-up call."

So in state after state where business helped elect Republican legislative majorities or governors only to find their resulting legislative gains undermined by unsympathetic courts, efforts have begun in earnest to try to help business-friendly candidates win election to the states' highest courts. An initiative every bit as sophisticated as Ohio's is operating under the auspices of the Michigan Chamber of Commerce, sparked by the state high court's stripping of late 1980s workers' compensation reforms and the chamber's interest in preserving recently enacted liability and regulatory reforms. "It is no longer enough to win in the legislative arena only to lose it in the judiciary," says Robert LaBrant, general counsel and senior vice president for political affairs for the Michigan Chamber of Commerce. "The business community has to change its attitude about getting involved in judiciary races and put as much priority on the state supreme court as in legislative races."

In Illinois, where the state supreme court overturned a sweeping 1995 tort package in December, still-seething business interests are beginning preparations for an all-out

Reprinted with permission from *Governing* magazine, August 1998, pp. 18-23. © 1998 by Congressional Quarterly, Inc.

blitz in 2000, when three high court seats will go before the voters. "The court's actions have opened everyone's eyes," says Edward Murnane, president of the Illinois Civil Justice League, a business-backed tort reform group. "In the business and health care community, there was a strong reaction."

After years of ceding the judicial arena to those who practiced before it, the business lobby, in increasing numbers, is coming to the conclusion that it can no longer afford to do so. "We have a very activist judicial system across the country. More and more judges are deciding issues that were once decided legislatively," says Jim Weidman, manager of state media relations for the National Federation of Independent Business, the small-business lobby. "Look at all the school finance cases. They are essentially writing the tax laws. That's very different than 10 or 15 years ago. In the past, you would think that once the law passed, that was it. Now it's the court that seems to hold the veto pen, rather than the governor."

While it is still too early to gauge the long-term impact of business' foray into judicial elections, it almost certainly is leading to a proliferation of campaign spending. In the lone 1992 North Carolina high court contest, for example, political action committee contributions totaled less than $3,000. Two years later, with banks, utilities, small business and insurance companies in the hunt for two seats, PAC donations amounted to 15 times that figure.

W hat has only recently become clear in North Carolina has been commonplace for more than a decade in several other states. Nobody who has lived through the judicial wars in Texas or Alabama would be surprised to hear that business is taking an active interest in who gets elected to the state courts. During the 1980s, the Texas supreme court won notice as perhaps the most notorious appeals court in the nation, controlled by a trial lawyer-backed majority whose scandalous fund-raising practices landed them an unwanted appearance on network television's *60 Minutes.* Soon after their ignominious national TV debut, Texas voters elected a new slate of "reform" candidates.

A decade later, it turns out, the court is still heavily influenced by an interest group. But it's a different interest group. Thanks to a concerted effort by corporate interests, the court now boasts a pro-business majority and is raising money almost as ferociously as before. It used to be that the court drew ridicule for its close ties to personal-injury lawyers. Today, that same court is under fire for its friendliness to insurance companies and the medical community. The only real difference between now and then is that there are no questions of illegality these days—although there are plenty of questions about propriety. According to a recent report by a consumer

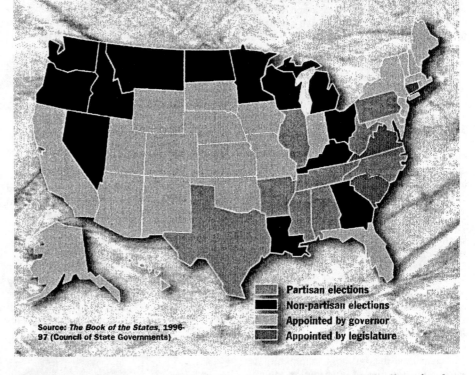

The Route to the Highest Bench

Justices of more than half of the nation's state supreme courts are appointed, in all but a handful of states by the governor. But in many of those states, even appointed judges eventually have to face the voters in retention elections.

Partisan elections
Non-partisan elections
Appointed by governor
Appointed by legislature

Source: *The Book of the States, 1996-97* (Council of State Governments)

group known as Texans for Public Justice, 40 percent of the $9.2 million in campaign funds raised by the seven justices elected since 1994 came from contributors with connections to cases before the court.

In Alabama, a state widely recognized in business circles for its own peculiar brand of "jackpot justice"—a derisive term used to describe the tendency of local juries to award generous punitive damages—the high court has descended into particularly low repute, largely due to soap-opera-like elections where candidates serve as foils for the Alabama Trial Lawyers Association or the state Business Council. In one of its most recent episodes, the bitterly contested campaign for chief justice came down to a difference of just 300 votes out of 1.1 million cast. The dispute over the winner went all the way to the U.S. Supreme Court before business-backed challenger Perry Hooper Sr. was certified to take office.

Until recently, Texas and Alabama were considered aberrations—quirky examples of partisan judicial elections gone terribly wrong, as well as prime arguments in favor of "merit selection" (appointment) of judges. Now, however, as a result of a growing number of acrimonious judicial elections, more states may be inadvertently moving toward those models than away from them. Cham-

ber of Commerce-backed efforts in places such as Ohio and Michigan are less shrill and more thoughtful than the heavier-handed approaches in Alabama and Texas, but in those two states and others where the business agenda has been thwarted by court rulings, the idea of a full frontal assault on the judiciary is beginning to look more and more appealing to those in the private sector.

Business interests, of course, are not the only ones spoiling for a fight with the judiciary. The more staid chambers of commerce are joined by a combative array of business-funded front groups, tort reform coalitions, anti-tax activists, free-market and social policy shops that view both the federal and state courts as activist, unaccountable institutions with little regard for conservative causes.

W hether or not the courts are nests of activist policy makers is a matter of interpretation. But it is undeniable that, over the past two decades or so, the state high courts have become more assertive policy players than at any time before. For many of them, it has been an unavoidable fate. Nearly every contentious legislative issue is litigated these days, flinging political grenades ranging from tort reform and workers' compensation to school finance and school choice into the courtroom.

That is what led the Michigan Chamber of Commerce to reassess its traditional political strategy. Stung by the state supreme court's dismantling of workers' comp reforms and determined to pick up a decisive fourth seat on the seven-member court, the chamber aided in the creation of an independent political action committee designed to level the judicial playing field in 1996.

In the year preceding the 1996 elections, various business PACs were asked to raise $170,000 for a committee known as Justice for Michigan Citizens. JFMC then sought to identify an additional 200 businesspeople, who themselves would pledge to raise $2,500 for the committee, followed by an additional $2,500 for each of two supreme court candidates in 1996. All told, the target amount for the 1996 elections was about $1.5 million, a large chunk of which was actually raised. JFMC even prepared a formula for business PACs to follow, based on the size of their individual election-cycle budgets. The suggested donation for high court campaign involvement ranged from 6 to 15 percent of each PAC's budget.

The result of this initial foray was mixed: Business-backed incumbent Chief Justice James Brickley won reelection, but business failed to pick up a vacant seat. Still, Justice for Michigan Citizens caused fits for the opposition—the state Democratic party unsuccessfully brought suit against the entity, alleging that JFMC constituted an illegal second political action committee for the Chamber of Commerce.

Persuading the business community to warm up to the idea of contributing to judicial campaigns was not easy at first. The Michigan chamber had to patiently explain how the judiciary affected a broad range of issues related both to individual workplaces and to the state's general economic climate. More was at stake than excessive jury awards, frivolous lawsuits, product liability and workers' comp. Control of the judiciary had a direct impact on nearly every priority of the business coalition, including issues such as charter schools, redistricting, environmental regulation, and various types of union political activities that only peripherally affect the bottom line but go a long way toward establishing what economic development professionals like to call a "competitive business climate."

Elsewhere, a similar scenario is playing out—sometimes aided by impeccable timing. As the Ohio chamber's initiative geared up last year, a 1997 school funding decision threatened to raise sales taxes, a frightening prospect for small businesses. This past May, a high court ruling that said cities could tax telephone company profits raised the specter of a broad range of new municipal taxes, ranging from levies on gasoline and alcohol to taxes on other utilities.

In Wisconsin, the Metropolitan Milwaukee Association of Commerce informed its membership prior to a 1997 high court contest that its top education reform item—school choice—hung in the balance, and indeed it did. The victor in that election, Justice Jon Wilcox, sided with the majority in a 4-2 decision this past June upholding a state law allowing tax dollars to be used to send children from low-income families to religious schools. Wilcox, it is worth noting, was also the beneficiary of a last-minute anonymous mass mailing by a secretive Republican-backed group that spent $135,000 to send out nearly at least 350,000 postcards on his behalf.

So far, most of business' attention around the country has been focused on supreme court campaigns. That stands to change beginning in November. The growing practice of rating judges according to their rulings on business decisions is expanding in many states to include cases handled by the lower courts. In Illinois, three appellate court contests already have been targeted for expenditures, along with a handful of selected circuit court elections. "Law is established in many cases by the appellate courts," says Edward Murnane. "We view it as just as important as the state supreme court in many respects."

And there is one additional reason to pay attention to the lower courts, one that has not escaped notice of politically savvy business operatives. "The state Court of Appeals serves as the farm team for the state high court," explains Michigan's LaBrant.

One appellate court judge who knows all too well the power of the business lobby is Oklahoma's Keith Rapp. In his view from the Court of Civil Appeals bench, the full-scale, business-backed electoral blitz aimed at him in 1996 was nothing more than a crude attempt at political strong-arming. "This is an attempt by people involved in litigation to get results indirectly that they couldn't accomplish directly," says Rapp. "They are trying to intimidate the judiciary."

That year, Rapp was blindsided by a last-minute blitz of close to $150,000 in eye-catching, full-page newspaper ads. For judges such as Rapp, prohibited by judicial canon from discussing their positions on issues, it is nearly impossible to reply in kind. "The court can't defend itself. It's simply interpreting the letter of the law," says Seth Andersen of the American Judicature Society. "If judges could defend themselves more openly, they'd tell you that they don't want to take on these hot-button issues, but that the legislature threw it into their laps because they didn't have the proper will to handle it."

In Rapp's case, the ads began appearing five days before Election Day, timed too late for him to respond. His 41 percent rating by Citizens for Judicial Review, a group funded by oil, gas, banking and insurance interests,

How are these seven justices affecting your bottom line?

1997 BUSINESS EVALUATION OF THE SUPREME COURT OF OHIO

P.a.C.E.
Political and Candidate Evaluations

"The Ohio Chamber's Pro-Business Approach to Government"

Last year, the Ohio chamber sent out a 36-page study examining the voting records of state supreme court members. Three high court seats are on the ballot this year.

among others, was hard enough to explain to voters. But the pointed content of the ads was nearly impossible to counter. One contained a collage of newspaper headlines drawn from the nation's most notorious tort cases—including the infamous McDonald's spilled-coffee case. It hardly mattered that Rapp had nothing to do with that case, which was decided in another state.

"It's really sinister, because most people don't understand how judges have to rely on precedent or apply case law. They're not in a position to make decisions based on whether a decision is pro-business or anti-business," says Clark O. Brewster, president of the Oklahoma Trial Lawyers Association. "I might disagree with the way a judge interprets the law or a decision, but I don't attack the judge's intellectual honesty. Their approach is that unless your decision favors banking or insurance, you're anti-business."

Fortunately for Rapp, voters saw the ads for what they were. He won retention easily. Still, a restless assortment of Oklahoma business-backed research groups and PACs are undoubtedly registering an impact. One sure sign came in 1995, when the trial lawyers' association agreed to a legislative compro-mise that dissuaded the business lobby from pursuing a sweeping tort reform initiative.

Why would a powerful statehouse interest group like the trial lawyers knuckle under to an upstart pressure group? For one thing, the plaintiffs' bar knew the opposition had deep pockets. But they also were well aware that the personal injury lawyers could never win a public relations battle that revolved around issues such as contingency fees, medical malpractice and, of course, the McDonald's coffee case.

In most states, the trial lawyers, along with organized labor, are indeed defending themselves, as well as some of the judges who are in the crosshairs. In states such as Oklahoma, Alabama and Florida, where judges are being evaluated by lawyer surveys conducted by an Oklahoma-based firm—rather than from a survey of court decisions, as it is done in Ohio and Michigan—state bar and trial lawyer associations are warning members not to respond. They contend that the results are likely to be unreliable and will be used to support a single-issue agenda. In Florida, the trial lawyers' association went so far as to distribute a toll-free phone number established by the Florida affiliate of a Washington, D.C.-based anti-tax group known as Citizens for a Sound Economy, and encouraged attorneys and their staff to call in an effort to run up the opposition's phone bill.

The judiciary, too, is fashioning its own measured response to ratings efforts and mounting criticism. In Oklahoma at least, the state supreme court has appointed a committee to study the idea of ratings and to determine whether the judiciary is in need of independent evaluation.

Anything that would remove the influence of any interest groups attempting to influence the direction of court decisions—whether business, trial lawyers or labor—would be welcome, says the American Judicature Society's Andersen. "The danger is that when the judiciary is dragged into the muck of partisan elections, you'll have single-issue partisan groups determining the outcome or having a strong hand in the outcome of elections," he says. "One year you'll have a judge who is friendly to, say, the teachers' unions, and then there will be a backlash and then another judge who is friendly to, say, business interests will be elected and then there will be another backlash. But the only constituency a judge should have is the law."

Ideas & Trends

When the Verdict Is Just a Fantasy

The $2.9 Million Cup of Coffee

By WILLIAM GLABERSON

HERE'S another story about America's out-of-control courts: Southern Pacific Railroad was so besieged by frivolous lawsuits in one Texas county that it ripped up 28 miles of track and shut down operations in the early 1990's.

Like similar anecdotes in almost every state, the tale of the disgusted railroad has been repeated for years in Texas. It even made its way into a conservative research center's report as proof of what most people believe anyway: havoc is being wreaked and jobs lost by an irrational legal system.

But, like many legal horror stories, it may not have been 100 percent true. "It was kind of a coincidence of timing," said Mark Davis, a spokesman for Union Pacific, which merged with Southern Pacific in 1996. "Southern Pacific was studying that line to be abandoned anyway."

For years across the country, accounts of bizarre jury verdicts and huge damage awards (like the McDonald's customer who spilled coffee on herself and collected $2.9 million) have been used to prove that the courts are wacky or worse. But increasingly, some political scientists, legal scholars and consumer advocates are suggesting that outlandish examples have created a distorted picture of the legal system.

Huge punitive damage awards, for example, have become everyday events, right? Actually, a study of courts in the nation's 75 largest counties conducted by the National Center for State Courts found that only 364 of 762,000 cases ended in punitive damages, or 0.047 percent.

O.K., but isn't it true that more and more liability claims are filed every year? Actually, a study of 16 states by the same center showed that the number of liability suits has declined by 9 percent since 1986.

Well, didn't that McDonald's coffee drinker laugh all the way to the bank? Maybe, but she was 81 years old, the coffee was scalding and she needed skin grafts for third-degree burns. And she settled for about $600,000 after a judge reduced the 1994 jury award.

Marc Galanter, a law professor at the University of Wisconsin, described these popular stories about the courts as "legal legends" in the Arizona Law Review last year. The label is sticking and some scholars and consumer advocates are starting to systematically challenge their accuracy.

They say legends like the one about the Texas railroad have been used to maximum effect by a national business-supported movement to make it harder for plaintiffs to win lawsuits under tort law, which governs civil injury claims. Just last week, the Alabama Legislature passed sweeping tort law changes, including a bill that would put a cap on punitive damages awarded by juries. Virtually every state has considered similar measures since the mid-1980's, and most have passed some measures to limit lawsuits.

"The story of tort reform across the country is that it is one of the most carefully developed and exquisitely executed political campaigns ever," said Andrew F. Popper, a law professor at American University in Washington who is an expert on personal injury law and identifies himself as a supporter of consumer rights.

One advocate's distortion, of course, is another's innocent spin. David Shaffer, president of the Public Policy Institute, a New York business group pushing for lawsuit limits in New York, said examples of ostensible outrages are used by consumer advocates as well as business groups. "It's done on both sides," he said. "The trial lawyers drag in pictures portraying some person who has been a victim of a terrible accident."

EVEN if there are occasional exaggerations, some business lobbyists say, there are enough large verdicts to intimidate corporations into large settlements and inhibit innovation by making companies fearful of bringing out new products that might attract lawsuits. The possibility of huge jury awards and the expense of battling suits, they say, combine to keep useful products off consumers' shelves.

But some lawyers and academics argue that consistently far-fetched accounts of court rulings have warped the debate about the legal system. And shrewd public relations by business and other groups pushing to limit lawsuits may only be part of the reason.

Unusual or big verdicts make news, said Michael W. McCann, a political science professor at the University of Washington. Professor McCann and William Haltom of the University of Puget Sound in Tacoma, Wash., found in a study that the large McDonald's verdict got extensive front-page coverage in 1994. But only about half the newspapers carried articles when the judge later reduced the punitive damages to $480,000.

In similar research, Oscar G. Chase, a law professor at New York University, found in a survey of cases in the New York area that the average verdict reported by The New York Times in 1989 was $20.5 million. But including the much larger number of cases that did not attract media attention, the average verdict was really $1.1 million.

"Policy makers," Mr. Chase said in an interview, "can't reliably use their impressions from reading the press about issues like whether the court system is out of control."

The problem, some legal experts say, is that policy makers do rely on such impressions. In his law review article, Professor Galanter traced the long afterlife of an infamous 1986 case involving a Philadelphia psychic who won a $1 million verdict. She had claimed she had an allergic reaction to medical treatment and lost her psychic powers.

The story of the psychic's verdict was widely circulated. Eventually, Professor Galanter found, it found its way into a 1991 report of the President's Council on Competitiveness, which referred to such bizarre cases as "almost commonplace" but did not disclose that the psychic's verdict had been reversed and that she had collected nothing.

Business groups say they are at a disadvantage in a public relations war that often spotlights alarming accounts of supposedly risky products, dangerous drugs and cancer-causing chemicals. "Emotions are stirred more when people are frightened for their own safety than they are by large damage awards that are not going to be paid out of their own money," said Victor E. Schwartz, a Washington lawyer who lobbies for businesses on tort issues.

But consumer groups say accounts of ostensible outrages in the courts seem more methodically misleading than reports about product dangers. A recent report by Citizens for Corporate Accountability and Individual Rights, a New York consumer group, said the Public Policy Institute had "misreported and misused" every case it described in its efforts to show that the New York courts were out of control.

"They usually don't mention that the defendant did anything wrong,"

said the consumer group's executive director, Joanne Doroshow, a former associate of Ralph Nader.

One supposedly outrageous case the Institute cited in a report last year involved an award of $650,000 given by New York City to the family of a drunk driver who was killed in an accident while driving the wrong way on a parkway. The Institute did not disclose that the court said the city's signs "virtually invited wrong-way entry," the consumer group said.

ASKED whether the report was misleading, Mr. Shaffer of the Public Policy Institute said anecdotes were less important than the harmful impact of the overall legal system on corporate innovation. "It is impossible," he added, "to include complete information about everything."

True or false, legal legends do make effective debating points. In a series of interviews recently in Texas, several leaders of a movement to end "lawsuit abuse" mentioned the case of the railroad that abandoned Matagorda County in Texas because of excessive lawsuits.

Richard W. Weekley, a Houston businessman who is a leader of Texans for Lawsuit Reform, said in a recent interview he had used the railroad story for years in speeches as an example of legal craziness. Audiences are horrified, he said. "People sit there and say, 'Why is a railroad tearing up 28 miles of track?'" Mr. Weekley said.

In response to an inquiry from a reporter, Mr. Davis, the railroad spokesman, said "Litigation was last on the totem pole" among reasons for ceasing operations in Matagorda County. "Traffic was down to one freight car a year."

Unit 5

Unit Selections

Key Points to Consider

❖ Do you prefer city or suburban life? What do you imagine are the key differences between city and suburban life?

❖ Do you share the pessimism of many people about the ability of local governments in major urban areas to cope with contemporary urban problems? Why or why not?

❖ Would it be desirable for suburban local governments to raise property taxes and provide better public transportation, more frequent garbage collections, and better recreational facilities? Why or why not?

❖ Would major metropolitan areas be better served if they each had only one metropolitan-wide local government instead of the large number of local governments that currently exist in each metropolis? Why or why not?

 ## Links — www.dushkin.com/online/

20. **ICMA: International City/County Management Association**
    http://www.icma.org/information/othersites/
21. **Innovation Groups**
    http://www.ig.org
22. **National Association of Counties**
    http://www.naco.org/links/counties.cfm
23. **National League of Cities**
    http://www.nlc.org

These sites are annotated on pages 4 and 5.

More than three-quarters of Americans live in cities or in surrounding suburban areas. In these densely populated settings, local governments face great challenges and opportunities. One challenge is to provide a satisfactory level of services such as policing, schooling, sanitation, water, and public transportation at a cost that taxpayers can and will bear. An accompanying opportunity is the possibility of helping to create a local setting that improves the lives of residents in meaningful ways. The challenges and opportunities occur amid a formidable array of urban and suburban problems: crime, violence, drugs, deterioration of public schools, racial tensions, financial stringencies, pollution, congestion, aging populations, decaying physical plants, breakdown of family life, and so forth.

Cities are the local government jurisdictions that generally exist where there is high population density. Major metropolitan areas usually have a large city at their center and a surrounding network

suburbs because people live there with their families and commute to and from the central city to work. Others have more of an independent economic base. Local governments in suburbs have often emphasized "quality education" (i.e., good schools), zoning plans to preserve the residential character of the locale, and keeping property taxes within tolerable limits. Generally speaking, suburbs have a greater proportion of whites and middle-class people than cities have.

One problem facing suburban governments today stems from aging populations. Older people need and demand different services from the young families that used to occupy suburbia in greater proportions. It is not always easy to shift policy priorities from, for example, public schooling to public transportation and recreational programs for the elderly. A second problem is structural in nature and relates to the overlapping local government jurisdictions in suburban areas—school districts,

of suburbs under a number of smaller local government jurisdictions. In smaller metropolitan areas, a single county often encompasses both the center city and the surrounding suburbs. Smaller cities may themselves be part of suburban rings, or they may exist independently of major metropolitan areas, with their own smaller network of surrounding suburbs.

Cities of all sizes generally provide more services to local residents than other kinds of local government jurisdictions. Thus, city residents generally expect their city governments to provide water, a sewer system, public transportation, a professional firefighting force, public museums, parks and other recreational areas, and various other amenities associated with city life. By contrast, local governments in rural areas are not expected to provide such services. Local governments in suburban areas typically provide some but not all of them. With the greater range of services provided in cities come higher taxes and more regulatory activities.

Like cities, suburbs come in various shapes and sizes. Some are called bedroom or commuter

sanitation districts, townships, counties, villages, and boroughs. The maze of jurisdictions often confuses citizens and sometimes makes coordinated and effective government difficult.

The goals of small suburban local governments, one or more counties, and the central city government in a single metropolitan area often come into conflict in such policy areas as public transportation, school integration, air pollution, highway systems, and so forth. Sometimes common aims can be pursued through cooperative ventures between suburban and city governments, through counties, or through creation of metropolitan-wide special districts. Sometimes, through annexation or consolidation, a larger unit of general-purpose local government is formed in an attempt to cope with metropolitan-wide issues more easily.

Selections in this unit mainly treat city and suburban governments and the problems and opportunities faced in metropolitan areas. Cities and suburbs, of course, typically face different sets of problems. Even so, it is important to note that not all cities face similar problems; nor do all suburbs or all counties.

CAN CITIES ESCAPE POLITICAL ISOLATION?

BY KAREN M. PAGET

CITY PROSPECTS

In the past three decades, most cities outside the Sunbelt have experienced economic contraction, population decline, and increasing concentrations of poverty. For some, like Detroit, the descent has been catastrophic. Dozens of smaller, once vibrant manufacturing and commercial cities like Newark, Cleveland, Buffalo, and St. Louis face similar conditions. Three decades after the wave of urban conflagrations countless neighborhoods that once housed a productive lower middle class still look as if 1968 happened yesterday. Others, such as New York, Chicago, and Los Angeles, tell tales of two cities—glittering economic resurgence coexisting with deepening deprivation.

The loss of good blue-collar jobs, the flight of the middle class to suburbia, and the urban concentration of minorities and the poor are not a new story. What is relatively new, however, is the political isolation of cities and a related decline in federal and state aid. Public policy once recognized that cities faced a terrible mismatch between local resources and local need. But cities today have more expensive social problems, a stressed local tax base, and less intergovernmental help. "The contraction of aid has been so dramatic that Washington's loss of interest in urban affairs is one of the signal stories of the great transformation to the New Federal

Order," says urban scholar Peter Eisinger of the University of Wisconsin's Robert M. La Follette Institute of Public Affairs.

This new reality reflects the conjuncture of several factors. The bipartisan commitment to budget balance, coupled with an aversion to raising taxes, has constrained federal outlay across the board. Within this general climate of fiscal scarcity, the sanctity of Social Security and the bipartisan collusion to avoid cutting defense have imposed disproportionate cuts on the discretionary portion of the budget, which includes urban aid. In this zero-sum game, as a National League of Cities analysis observes, the reduced funds flowing to cities

go into a local "shark tank where they will compete directly against each other—the growth in any one program important to cities will only come at the expense of another."

The fiscal isolation of cities also reflects a political deterioration. Many older suburbs, as well as rural small towns, face similar economic and social problems. But where cities were once central to a broader coalition that believed in social remediation through public outlay—whether for rural development or urban antipoverty—cities are now increasingly on their own.

Is there any prospect for reversing these trends, or are cities doomed to go it alone for the foreseeable future?

Why have city voices been so muted politically, even among Democrats who rely on urban voters? Can one imagine the revival of a public spending coalition that would unite voters from cities, less affluent suburbs, and needy rural areas? Or is this strategy doomed by the politics of budget balance?

A great urban awakening occurred in the 1960s. Intergovernmental aid, which previously had favored suburbs and rural development, began rising—and flowing increasingly to cities. With the War on Poverty and the Great Society, federal policy sought to compensate for the disparity between urban problems and urban resources. Though Richard Nixon's New Federalism changed the form of the funding to block grants often funneled through states, the stream of federal money continued.

According to the Advisory Commission on Intergovernmental Relations (ACIR), an immensely useful research body crippled by the Reagan administration in the mid-1980s [see sidebar, next page], in 1957 cities at the center of metro areas got just 19 percent of their total expenditures from intergovernmental aid, compared to 26 percent for suburban and rural communities in the same metro areas. By 1970, intergovernmental aid had increased dramatically to 31 percent for cities and 33 percent for adjacent communities. By the peak in 1977, center cities were depending on federal and state aid for fully 44 percent of their outlays, outpacing nonurban areas, which were getting 41 percent.

State governments also became more conscious of the need to redistribute resources to fiscally stressed cities. Frank Mauro, director of the Fiscal Policy Institute near Albany, recalls the successful 1969 campaign waged by New York City Mayor John Lindsay and five upstate mayors to alter formulas that had biased state education aid against urban areas. The mayors' success in achiev-

ing formula changes has been gradually reversed in the last two decades, first by changing the aid criteria in ways detrimental to cities, and then by outright cuts. "What was understood so much better then [in the 1960s] was that there was a mismatch between resources and needs, and that the higher level of government had the broadest tax base," Mauro says.

DEFINING DEVOLUTION DOWN

Since the late 1970s, there has been a sharp reversal. Both the amount of intergovernmental aid and the share going to center cities have declined. Aggregate data comparable to the ACIR's earlier series are not available, since ACIR scaled back its publications during the 1980s before finally being effectively eliminated at the end of fiscal year 1996. But "The Collapse of Urban Aid" (below) suggests the magnitude of the cuts in aid to cities.

According to a study by the U.S. Conference of Mayors, between 1981 and 1993 funding of community development block grants, urban development action grants, general revenue sharing, mass transit aid, employment, and the various programs of the Economic Development Administration fell by a total of 66.3 percent in real dollar terms.

During nearly two decades of federal disinvestment, state aid to cities has also declined. Economists Howard Chernick of Hunter College and Andrew Reschovsky of the University of Wisconsin at Madison estimate that state aid to local government, as a portion of local revenues, dropped from 25.4 percent to 21.2 percent of local revenues between 1977 and 1992.

"Devolution," in Republican hands, has not just meant giving lower levels of government greater responsibility, as Nixon's New Federalism did, but a dramatic cut in resources. Richard Nathan, a longtime scholar of federalism, observes that today's proposals stand the original principles of devolution of program responsibility on their head. In a 1996 speech to California legislators, Nathan noted that Nixon's New Federalism was based on "the theory that income transfer programs should be centralized, and other programs should be converted into block grants."

Nixon's proposed family assistance program would have had the federal government take over welfare. In health care, Nixon proposed requiring employers to provide insurance to their employees. Even Ronald Reagan's proposals partly reflected similar principles. Reagan's proposed "swap" would have had the federal government take over

THE COLLAPSE OF URBAN AID

Federal Funds for Cities, 1981–1993
(in billions of constant 1993 dollars)

Program	Fiscal Year 1981	Fiscal Year 1993	Percentage Real Cut
Community Development Block Grant	$6.3	$4.0	−36.5%
Urban Development Action Grant	0.6	0	−100.0
General Revenue Sharing	8.0	0	−100.0
Mass Transit	6.9	3.5	−49.3
Employment and Training	14.3	4.2	−70.6
Economic Development Administration	0.6	0.2	−66.7
Assisted Housing	26.8	8.9	−66.8
Clean Water Construction	6.0	2.6	−56.7

Source: U.S. Conference of Mayors, *The Federal Budget and the Cities* (1994).

Medicaid and the states take over Aid to Families with Dependent Children. Thus, Republicans as well as Democrats once recognized that a state or local tax base was insufficient to provide necessary social supports to its citizenry, and that only the federal government was large enough to raise and redistribute adequate resources.

FALLING AID, RISING NEED

If these cuts in aid to cities had occurred against a backdrop of broadly rising prosperity, they would be less painful. But in the past two decades, poverty has become more concentrated and more urban. The Annie E. Casey Foundation's recent report, "City Kids Count," assessed how children were faring in the nation's 50 largest cities. Using ten key indicators, ranging from low birth weight to school dropout rates and unemployment figures, the report found: "For every measure the average value for the 50 cities shows that kids living in large cities are more likely to be worse off than kids in the nation as a whole," and that poverty rates for children in cities are increasing disproportionately.

"Between 1969 and 1989, the child poverty rate in the 50 largest cities increased from 18 to 27 percent, while the national child poverty rate grew from 15 to 18 percent," the foundation reported. The percentage of children living in distressed neighborhoods in the 50 largest cities increased between 1970 and 1990 from 3 percent to 17 percent. These averages understate the condition of the most distressed cities. For instance, the percentage of children under age 15 living in Detroit's distressed neighborhoods increased from 3 percent in 1970 to 37 percent in 1980 to 62 percent in 1990. Several cities, including Buffalo, Cleveland, and St. Louis, now have 40 percent or more of children under 15 living in distressed neighborhoods. Twenty years earlier, these percentages were all 10 percent or less.

The decline in federal housing aid illustrates how shifts in federal spending patterns compound urban poverty. Since the 1930s, Washington has invested in housing for the poor, either directly with construction grants or through mortgage interest subsidies, and more recently with vouchers. This policy had bipartisan support, acknowledging that poor households, especially in cities where real estate is costly, simply cannot afford market rentals. Even the Reagan administration approved an average of 80,000 new subsidized housing units annually. Few if any new subsidized housing units are included in the current budget, and Washington is actually shedding subsidized units as old mortgages are paid off and public housing projects are downsized.

These budget figures do not take into account the level of unmet need. The number of affordable housing units—defined as a unit that a low-income household can afford without spending more than 30 percent of its income on rent—is shrinking nationwide, while needs are increasing. Using 1993 Housing and Urban Development (HUD) data, the Center on Budget and Policy Priorities estimates there is currently an affordable housing gap of approximately five million units. Comparable 1970 HUD data showed roughly 700,000 units in excess of low-income need.

There is often an important, interactive relationship between two or more federal programs. For instance, ending "welfare as we know it" will end the ability for some unknown number of low-income individuals to pay their rent—just as subsidized housing is becoming more scarce. As welfare reform bites, voluntary agencies dealing with the homeless report huge increases in the number of homeless people seeking shelter.

Shoot the Messenger

By AMY D. BURKE

The Advisory Commission on Intergovernmental Relations (ACIR) is probably one of the least known victims of federal downsizing, but the effect of its elimination at the end of September 1996 was significant. Without the ACIR, local, state, and federal officials have less contact with each other, and there is a shortage of data about the impact of federal programs on state and local governments.

At a time when local and state governments are being called upon to pay for more of their services with less support from Washington, the only government agency charged with evaluating the impact of government policies and programs on states and localities has been zeroed out. Though the ACIR was resuscitated last spring to conduct a study for the government's commission on gambling, it is now a mere shadow of its former self, with little hope of being permanently reauthorized.

From its creation in 1959 through 1996, the commission provided a wealth of information about the fiscal well-being of state and local governments. Often the ACIR was the only place people interested in urban policy could look to for data about city versus suburban fiscal resources. The commission's members included governors, mayors, state legislators, county officials, and members of Congress—all of whom served two-year terms. As a non-partisan group, the commission earned a reputation for producing accurate and unbiased reports. "They were scrupulous in terms of getting people from both parties and all levels of government to literally just shine a light about what is going on," according to David Liebshutz, the associate director of the Center for the Study of the States at the Rockefeller Institute of Government in New York.

According to the *Flint* (Michigan) *Journal*, one agency, Love, Inc., reported a 44 percent rise in the number of people seeking food or clothing between July 1996 and July 1997 despite a generally improving economy. Since cities house a disproportionate number of welfare recipients, they will experience most of these multiple effects, all of which make cascading claims on city budgets.

LOST POLITICAL CLOUT

Disinvestment trends in the face of growing poverty are not simply the consequence of scarce resources. They reflect a steady loss of power by cities, in both Congress and state legislatures. While suburban population growth is an old story, its political effects are relatively recent—and intensifying. Suburbs have become the battleground for swing voters, often at the expense of policies that benefit cities.

Suburbanites were a majority of presidential voters for the first time in 1992. In that election, Clinton narrowly beat George Bush among suburban voters, 41 to 39, with Perot getting 21 percent. In 1996, President Clinton increased his suburban vote, winning 47 percent to Dole's 42 percent and Perot's 9 percent. Fourteen states, including California and Flor-

ida, have populations with suburban majorities. In 1996, Clinton won 13 of the 14, and his wins included suburban districts that had not been won by a Democrat since the 1960s.

This capacity to carry the suburbs may be good partisan news for the Democrats, but it carries an ominous message for cities. The grain of truth in the battle for "suburban soccer moms" lies in the gender breakdown for 1996, and illustrates just how critical women voters have become: While suburban men vote 62 percent Republican to 37 percent Democrat, suburban women, by contrast, voted Democratic, 53 to 47. While women have emerged as a key Democratic bloc, the battle for the swing suburban female vote reinforces the general suburban tilt of presidential politics and the impulse to neglect urban voters.

Congressional Democrats, however, ran behind Clinton. In 1994, when they lost control of the House, Democrats lost suburban voters to Republicans, 43 percent to 57 percent. In 1996, a comeback year for Democrats, Clinton won the suburban vote by five points, but House Democrats lost the suburbs by four points, 48 to 52. Democrats may yet be competitive in the suburbs—but at the expense of policies that address cities.

Until the Republicans took control of Congress in 1994, central city representatives, though declining in number, had one huge advantage. Largely Democrats with safe seats and hence seniority, they controlled a disproportionate number of leadership positions. That advantage, of course, depended on Democratic control of Congress, and was wiped out in 1994. Central city representation fell from 30.5 percent to 10.1 percent of committee and subcommittee chairs, while suburban representatives increased their leadership positions from 43.7 to 69.7 percent.

Politically, cities are trapped in a vicious circle. It is a staple of political science literature that lower income voters are less likely to vote because they feel less of a sense of efficacy and have less confidence that politics will make a difference. This dynamic has intensified in recent years. The political system has delivered less to cities—and urban voters have reciprocated. So while cities have lost population, they have lost even more voters. Voting turnout has declined generally in recent years, but most sharply among the poor. New York's fifteenth and sixteenth districts, representing Harlem and the South Bronx, had turnouts of 33 and 29 percent in 1996. A few miles away, the third and fourth

---

ACIR studies took a comparative look at state and local patterns of spending and taxation. By spotlighting fiscal disparities, ACIR became a force for greater equalization of resources. The commission was the first government agency to support the idea of general revenue sharing. The ACIR also raised awareness about the plight of cities by revealing the financial isolation of urban areas. And many experts, such as Oliver Oldman, a professor emeritus at Harvard University's law school, believe that the ACIR had an enormous impact on the operation of state and local governments because it enabled them to operate with an understanding of each other's fiscal resources.

But during the 1980s, as the federal debt and deficit grew—and as Ronald Reagan implemented his so-called new federalism—the ACIR fell out of political favor. By the mid-1980s, House Republicans began targeting the commission for elimination. "We were on a list of a number of small agencies that it was felt the government could do without," explains Bruce McDowell, the ACIR's director of government policy research at the time it closed down, so "ACIR lost about half of its funding and staff during the eighties." In the late 1970s, the ACIR had a staff of 50. By 1994, that number had dwindled to 14.

The elimination of ACIR reports has left a void—both of data and of inter-

governmental communication. "We were an ombudsman and a significant provider of information," says Charles Griffiths, the current executive director of the commission, adding that "we still get requests for the old publications." Finally, it should be noted that not only did the ACIR gather and distribute valuable information, but it did so for free. The few groups that have stepped forward to carry on with the publication of certain ACIR studies will now charge for the reports, meaning the information will reach fewer people. And without a federal agency to publish the data, state and local officials will be further isolated from Washington at the very time they need it the most.

districts, on suburban Long Island, had turnouts of 58 and 55 percent. According to Curtis Gans, director of the Committee for the Study of the American Electorate, the sharpest decline of all has occurred among voters earning under $15,000, with a 20 percent decline between 1990 and 1994 alone.

Cities are experiencing a parallel loss of clout in state legislatures as well because of similar population shifts. Prior to the Supreme Court decision in *Baker v. Carr* (1962), which required legislative districts to roughly reflect population size, state legislatures

Wealth and Turnout

Votes Cast in 1996 Presidential Election as Percent of Voting-Age Population

57%

42%

Twenty Richest Congressional Districts

Twenty Poorest Congressional Districts

Source: N.C.E.C. and 1990 Census

were dominated by rural interests, and cities were vastly under represented. While *Baker v. Carr* forced a more equitable distribution of seats, by the time its effect was felt, suburbs, not cities, were the beneficiaries. In many states, the full political impact was delayed, because longtime control of the legislature gave Democrats critical influence in the reapportionment process. In 1994, Democratic representation in state legislatures was at its lowest level since before *Baker v. Carr*, and rebounded only slightly in 1996.

Consider Chicago and New York. In 1950, according to Margaret Weir

of the Brookings Institution, 69.5 percent of people in the greater Chicago metro area lived in the center city, Chicago. By 1990, that figure had dropped to 31.9. New York City's comparable population share fell from 81.1 percent in 1950 to 63.9 percent in 1990.

"For much of the postwar era," Weir observes, "Chicago was able to exercise power in the state legislature by striking bargains with downstate rural Republicans and Democrats, and the suburbs were generally left out of such deals." While that coalition had been unraveling for awhile, "the final blow was the 1991 redistricting that eliminated the city's advantage in the legislature." After the 1992 elections, the suburbs held the majority of seats in the house, 37 percent, compared to Chicago's 19 percent, and 37 percent in the Senate, compared to Chicago's 15 percent. Suburban representatives immediately exercised their muscle by denying Chicago a major economic development project and by slashing general welfare assistance for the urban poor, 80 percent of whom lived (in 1992) in Chicago.

Likewise, New York City's influence in Albany traditionally relied on the sheer number of city voters. According to Weir, the consequences of New York City's shrinking electorate became evident during Governor Mario Cuomo's tenure. Cuomo "spoke out in favor of the city's interests and occasionally proposed such policies as state takeover of Medicaid and more aid for urban school districts, but . . . was often criticized for not following through in the legislature," which had already become suburbanized. By contrast, Republican Governor George Pataki, Cuomo's successor, was elected "on a wave of support from upstate voters . . . who were deeply antagonistic to state spending, which they believed favored the city at their expense."

Two reporters for the *Buffalo News*, Sue Schulman and Jerry Zremski, spent months investigating why the upstate cities of Buffalo,

Syracuse, Rochester, Niagara Falls, Schenectady, Troy, and Utica were faring so badly. Buffalo typifies the dynamics of urban fiscal and political decline. Buffalo has had massive population loss (46 percent since 1950), accompanied by a loss of federal and state aid. Federal aid dropped from 26 percent of the city's budget in 1980 to 14 percent in 1995. In the same period, state aid dropped from 24 percent to 18 percent. Buffalo is so broke that the city is selling off assets and exploring a merger with Erie County.

Schulman and Zremski concluded that reapportionment, which redrew legislative district lines in accordance with suburban population shifts, compounded Buffalo's loss of political influence. Today, only one state legislator out of ten in the state assembly and senate who represent parts of Buffalo represents exclusively the city; the other legislators who represent part of Buffalo have a majority of suburban voters in their districts, and frequently vote against legislation sought by city officials. The *Buffalo News* quotes public opinion polls indicating suburbanites believe Buffalo "should take care of its own problems."

In a recent paper, political scientists Harold Wolman of the University of Maryland at Baltimore County and Lisa Marckini of Wayne State University examined changes in central city, suburban, and nonmetropolitan congressional districts between 1964 and 1994. The drop in districts with a majority of central city voters, while evident (18 percent), is not nearly so dramatic as the growth of majority suburban districts (228 percent) and the drop in nonmetropolitan seats (54 percent decline).

Wolman and Marckini explored the relationship between place and liberal attitudes and found a consistent correlation, with representatives from cities the most liberal, from suburbs less so, and from nonmetropolitan areas the least. That finding is not unexpected, but Wolman and

Marckini also found that place itself made a difference, independent of party affiliation or other factors: "Something about representing a central city, apart from the actual constituency characteristics of the district and party affiliation, had a discernible impact on voting."

THE SEARCH FOR ALLIES

There are essentially two available possible strategies for reversing these trends: either the development of new forms of regionalism, which would broaden cities' fiscal and political bases, or the revival of even broader coalition politics. David Rusk, former mayor of Albuquerque, has written a provocative book, *Cities without Suburbs*, in which he argues that "the real city is the total metropolitan area—city and suburb." He classifies American cities into two categories: elastic and inelastic. Elastic cities either have vacant land to develop within their city limits or can expand by annexing adjacent land. Inelastic cities can do neither. Thus, elastic cities can capture some of the regional growth that occurs beyond their boundaries, while inelastic cities mainly reap the social costs.

Inelastic cities, Rusk reports, have everything from greater concentrations of poverty, more segregation, and greater urban-suburban income gaps, to lower bond ratings. Inelastic cities, unable to grow, do not just not remain static; they "start shrinking," losing their people, tax base, and fiscal capacity. Inelastic cities lacking development land, or amenities to attract or renew a middle class, lose most of their middle class to adjacent suburbs. Thus, the city of Detroit is in near-terminal decline, while surrounding suburbs are healthy and even affluent.

Rusk identified 24 cities as having "passed the point of no return," those with major population loss (20 percent or more), a disproportionate minority population (typically 30 percent or more), and average income levels of less than 70 percent of suburban income levels. These cities simply cannot "escape the grip

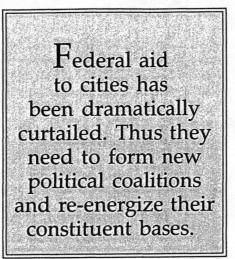

Federal aid to cities has been dramatically curtailed. Thus they need to form new political coalitions and re-energize their constituent bases.

of ghetto poverty solely by their own efforts." Further, he argues, "no city past the point of no return has ever closed the economic gap with its suburbs by as much as a single percentage point." Yet many of these poorest cities are surrounded by some of the wealthiest suburbs. Therefore, regional economic development is an insufficient strategy to help these cities.

Rusk advocates metropolitan or regional solutions as the key to coping with dwindling growth, diminished fiscal capacity, and growing concentrations of poverty. If cities can annex suburbs, as New York and Boston did around the turn of the last century—or make an equivalent claim on tax base and economic resources—then the fruits of growth can be distributed more evenly. While a few cities, such as Indianapolis, have recently succeeded in annexing suburbs, most suburbs neither wish to be annexed nor to share their tax base in other ways. Commuter taxes and other proposals to allow cities to capture suburban tax bases are mostly political nonstarters. The more that suburbs become politically ascendant, the less chance such proposals have.

Another strategy has been proposed by Myron Orfield, an urban planner and state legislator from Minnesota. Orfield is a leading proponent of metropolitan

government, having sponsored and passed legislation that yokes together the fate of center cities and suburbs. Until a decade ago, Orfield writes in his book, *Metropolitics: A Regional Agenda for Community and Stability*, the Twin Cities were thought to be "immune to urban decline inner-suburban decay, urban sprawl—and the polarization that has devastated and divided older, larger regions." But, as the 1980s unfolded, all the patterns that describe Chicago, Detroit, and Milwaukee developed in Minneapolis-St. Paul. Orfield says education is always a bellwether of a downward spiral. Between 1982 and 1994, the Twin Cities' percentage of children on free or reduced-cost lunch went from 33 percent to 52 percent. School enrollment went from 34 percent to 59 percent minority, and "both central cities lost one-third of their preschool white children." Crime rates grew, including a 1995 murder rate that was "higher than New York City."

Concluding that there was "no federal urban policy left," Orfield introduced legislation to give greater taxing capacity to a previously created Metropolitan Council. Through an ingenious use of mapping, Orfield showed fellow legislators a geographical distribution of social and economic problems, including the increased concentrations of poverty and racial segregation. He also mapped the geographical distribution of state and federal subsidies. Not surprisingly, the maps revealed that those suburbs with the most wealth and resources received significant government subsidies, while many working- and middle-class suburbs, or "inner-ring" suburbs, shared many of the same needs and social problems of the Twin Cities, but had fewer government resources.

Orfield concluded that a regional tax could produce a substantial increase in resources for affordable housing. Again through the use of mapping techniques, he demonstrated that most of the suburbs that ring the Twin Cities (roughly 80 percent) would be net beneficiaries of such a regional tax; that is, they would receive back more than they contributed to a common pool. Only a handful of the wealthiest suburbs, such as Edina or Eden Prairie, would experience a net loss.

Since 1993, a legislative majority has twice approved Orfield's proposed regional property tax on assessed values over $200,000. The Republican governor, Arne Carlson, vetoed it both times. Whether or not the Orfield-inspired coalition will hold hasn't been tested a third time, and likely won't be until there is a different governor.

National economic studies confirm that the economic health of cities and their suburbs is closely tied together, though casual empiricism displays dynamic suburbs ringing decaying cities. What is important is that Orfield proposes a commonality based on self-interest, not altruism. Politically, a coalition of the central city with inner-ring or less affluent suburbs is the polar opposite of the more typical dynamic where a few central city representatives fight suburban legislators over scarce resources. An Orfield-style coalition broadens the urban base to include needed suburban allies. Orfield is convinced that the potential for new political coalitions is not limited to the peculiarities of the Twin Cities or the progressivism of Minnesota, and is helping to advise Cleveland, Chicago, Philadelphia, and Portland, Oregon. In fact, Orfield says every organizer needs to have the following slogan taped to his or her desk: "It's the older suburbs, stupid."

Some elements of Orfield's overall argument are controversial, especially his contention that inner-city poverty is more pathological because it is so concentrated. And some of his remedies face more political opposition than his proposal for a regional tax. Orfield supports transportation and housing policies that literally move people from the inner city to the suburbs where jobs are going begging. Such plans re-

quire dispersing low-income housing throughout the region—just the kind of proposal that draws objections from both sides of the racial divide. Racial and ethnic populations often view with suspicion efforts to break up culturally cohesive neighborhoods, even if poverty-stricken; in some cases, dispersal threatens minority political power. Conversely, white suburbanites remain hostile to an influx of racial minorities.

While states could authorize cities to diversify their tax base, they seldom have granted this authority. Wealthy potential taxpayers can usually find friends in the legislature. In one stunning case, a state legislature withdrew its authorization for a city to tax itself in order to provide for low-income housing, even though state coffers weren't out a penny. Washington state legislators passed legislation that enabled Seattle to impose a real estate tax on property transactions. It was short-lived because realtors and developers, who hate this tax, complained to their legislative friends. City representatives, shy of allies, watched as the state revoked its permission.

NEW POLITICAL COALITIONS

American history suggests the basis of a broader coalition politics. For all the difference between urban progressives and rural populists, the basis of their alliance was economic. They expressed a common antagonism against "the interests," who ranged from railroad owners, bankers, and grain dealers to timber and mining corporations. Party alliances, in turn, were backed by the institutional strength of both urban labor and rural farmer's unions, the fullest expression of which is Minnesota's Democratic Farmer-Labor Party (DFL). Throughout the West and Midwest, this alliance produced both progressive Republicans and liberal Democrats, such as Republican George Norris of Nebraska, and Democrats Warren Magnuson of Washington,

George McGovern of South Dakota, and Frank Church of Idaho.

Even today, North Dakota's Byron Dorgan, Iowa's Tom Harkin, and Minnesota's Paul Wellstone are beneficiaries of this (albeit now considerably weakened) tradition. What's missing today is the mass organizational base that sent such representatives to Washington (and to state capitals). The rural social underpinning of this political alliance is substantially gone, with the demise of small farmers as a major political force, the weakening of unions, and the reduction of federal outlay as a source of economic development. In its place, Samantha Sanchez, who tracks money in Western states sees a rise of rural conservative populism ("black helicopter types") often allied with corporate interests such as the "wise use movement" financed by extractive industries to counter environmentalists [see Samantha Sanchez, "How the West Is Won: Astroturf Lobbying and the 'Wise Use' Movement," *TAP*, March-April 1996.]

So long as the political problem is narrowly defined as cities versus the suburbs, little progress toward rebuilding political coalitions can be made. But the persistence of rural poverty and the growing diversity of suburbs may contain the seeds of new political alliances. A dramatic example of change in suburban demographics is the election of Loretta Sanchez to the House of Representatives from Orange County, one of the most conservative areas in the country. In 1996, she replaced Robert "B-1 Bomber" Dornan, who, as of this writing, is still protesting her narrow victory.

This review of the growing fiscal and political isolation of cities suggests one more political price of the bipartisan obsession with budget balance and tax reduction. It is hard to imagine a new public spending coalition in which cities share, if public spending itself is off the table. The old spending coalition included outlays that were place-specific (urban renewal, public housing, rural electrification, public works, farm supports) as well for the broad citizenry (Social Security, Medicare.) Some of the latter programs, such as Head Start, Medicaid, and food stamps, were targeted to the poor and hence benefited the urban poor. Public spending, as a function of government, had broad legitimacy, and cities were considered legitimate claimants. The shift in political power to the suburbs now inhibits the role of place-specific remedies.

There are obvious limits to public spending. But other advanced democracies spend at least ten percentage points more of their gross domestic product than the United States does, and with it they purchase a more equitable society. To restore a spending coalition that cares about urban problems, cities and their advocates need to move on all fronts—to pursue the regional strategies commended by people like Orfield, to restore links with coalition partners, and to energize a constituent base.

For the most part, progressive organizations have had their base in central cities, which are now politically isolated. With the exception of environmental and good-government groups, few progressive organizations seriously pursue the suburbs. Beyond regional alliances, any renaissance of advocacy on behalf of cities requires a broader national agenda that renews the legitimacy of public outlays.

Karen M. Paget has consulted on state and local fiscal issues for the Ford Foundation and the Twentieth Century Fund, and is the author of "The Battle for the States," in *The New Majority*.

How to save our shrinking cities

WITOLD RYBZYNSKI & PETER D. LINNEMAN

The first half of the twentieth century saw the widespread emergence of large cities in the United States. In 1900, there were only six cities with more than half a million inhabitants; only 50 years later, there were 17 such cities. Much of this urban growth was stimulated by two world wars and the government-supported expansion of war-related industries, most located in big Northeastern and Midwestern cities. The largest cities also benefited from the fact that for more than a decade after the Second World War the United States was the only country in the world with its manufacturing facilities intact.

It was inevitable that eventually things would change. Europe and Japan rebuilt themselves and challenged the dominance of U.S. urban manufacturing. The previous rapid growth of large cities began to level out, and new urbanization patterns emerged. One of these patterns was a change in the kind of cities Americans chose to live in. We differentiate between small cities (100,000 to 500,000 inhabitants) and large cities (more than 500,000 inhabitants). In 1900, eight million Americans lived in large cities as compared to less than five million in small cities.

Over the next 50 years, the total population of the large cities increased at a faster rate than that of the small cities, and, by 1950, the large cities were home to more than 26 million people, compared to about 13 million for the small cities. However, after 1950, this pattern began to reverse, and the total population of small cities grew more quickly. By 1990, for the first time in the twentieth century, more Americans lived in small cities than in large ones. This situation is likely to continue for some time. For example, between 1980 and 1990, the total population of the small cities increased by a remarkable 17.3 percent, compared to 6 percent for large cities, and 9.7 percent for the nation as a whole.

An earlier version of this article appeared in the Warton Real Estate Review, *Fall 1997.*

Forces of change

What drove this reversal? The growth of small cities and the decline of large cities in the postwar period resembled the contemporary restructuring of the steel industry, where new small plants replaced old large mills. Technological advances made the old steel plants obsolete and took their toll on large cities. The confluence of river and barge commerce, railroads, and the telegraph fueled urban centralization throughout the nineteenth century. In the early 1900s, these forces were reinforced by the efficiencies of scale in urban infrastructure technology, such as water supply, sewage treatment, and streetcars. However, the post–World War II period witnessed the predominance of car and truck commerce, the expansion of air travel, the evolution of modern telecommunications, and massively improved efficiencies in the provision of sewer- and water-treatment facilities. All of these changes facilitated urban decentralization. Air conditioning opened up large parts of the country to year-round occupancy, just as heating technologies had done centuries before. Entertainment and communication technologies, including television, the VCR, and the personal computer, greatly reduced the sense of cultural inferiority and isolation that historically characterized life in small cities. Now, a small city with an airport and access to an interstate highway became just as good a place from which to conduct business as the downtown of a large city. Land economics allowed residents of small cities to enjoy larger (and newer) homes while still being able to see their favorite sports team, watch first-run movies, and enjoy concerts on cable TV.

These technological changes were fueled by the evolution of increasingly efficient capital markets. Capital markets actively sought out, and provided capital to, the best businesses, even if they were not in the biggest cities. Examples include: The Limited (Columbus, Ohio),

From *The Public Interest*, Spring 1999, pp. 30-44. Originally published in *Wharton Real Estate Review.* © 1999 by Witold Rybzynski & Peter D. Linneman. Reprinted by permission.

WalMart (Bentonville, Arkansas), Microsoft (Seattle), and Turner Broadcasting (Atlanta). In addition, the municipal bond market increasingly provided equal access to capital (for public infrastructure) to cities and communities that had previously been too small to tap this source.

In older cities, an aging infrastructure imposed increasingly high capital and operating costs. In contrast, smaller cities had recently installed new infrastructure with low maintenance and operating costs. Older cities flourished when they were the newest, cheapest, and most modern. The mantel has now passed to a new set of cities and suburbs.

However, not all large cities were equally affected by these trends. Of the 77 cities with current (1990) population in excess of half a million, 51 actually grew by an average of 539 percent between 1950 and 1990. The nine largest of these (Los Angeles, Houston, San Diego, Dallas, Phoenix, San Antonio, San Jose, Jacksonville, and Columbus) grew from 1950 to 1970, and continued to grow during the next two decades. Nevertheless, 26 of the 77 cities shrank (by an average of 24 percent) between 1950 and 1990. Moreover, these shrinking cities include some of the largest in the country. Seven of the largest cities that declined (New York, Chicago, Philadelphia, Detroit, Baltimore, Washington, D.C., and Boston) have been doing so steadily since 1950. Indianapolis, Milwaukee, and Memphis declined in population between 1970 and 1990, although they grew between 1950 and 1970. Only one major city, San Francisco, reversed its 1950–70 decline during the following two decades.

Two facts stand out about the decline of the largest cities. First, the population losses have been significant. Chicago, New York, and Detroit have each lost about half a million people each since 1970 while Philadelphia has lost more than 350,000 over this period. Second, this decline is neither merely recent nor episodic. The cities that are shrinking have been doing so steadily for the last half of this century, and, according to the recent U.S. Census figures, the decline continues to the present day.

Some of the population increases in the growing cities have been the result of the aggressive annexation of surrounding cities and towns. Since 1950, the fastest growing seven major cities (Phoenix, San Jose, San Diego, Jacksonville, Houston, Dallas, and San Antonio) have each at least doubled their areas through annexation. In the case of Phoenix and Jacksonville, the increase in area has been more than twentyfold. Some of the urban growth, especially in California, Texas, and Florida, has been due to immigration. In fact, were it not for the steady flow of immigrants, cities like New York, Chicago, and Washington, D.C., would have experienced massive population losses.

Against this backdrop of the decline of the largest cities and the growth of our smaller cities, it is imperative to remember that every metro area has experienced population growth since 1950. Thus, although the cities of St. Louis, Cleveland, and Detroit lost about half their populations between 1950 and 1990, their metro areas each notably expanded. Similarly, while the city of Philadelphia lost about half a million people during this period, Philadelphia's metro area grew by more than a million. This means that the cities that shrank did so not because they were part of dying regional economies but, rather, in spite of strong regional growth.

Vertical cities and horizontal cities

The cities that have declined can be called vertical cities while the growing ones are best thought of as horizontal cities. These two prototypes differ radically with respect to infrastructure, amenities, and housing stock. The vertical city, which evolved during the industrial era, has highway, mass transportation, and rail systems designed to link the suburbs to city center. Its population density is high, typically more than 10,000 persons per square mile. Its amenities include large public parks. And it is known for downtown offices, manufacturing, and shopping and cultural activities. Typically, about half of its housing stock was built before 1939. It is comprised primarily of rowhouses, walk-up flats, and apartment buildings that were located to permit walking (or riding mass transit) to work and play.

In contrast, the horizontal city evolved after World War II and is designed for rapid car and truck movement, not merely from suburb to city but also from suburb to suburb. There is very little mass transit or rail infrastructure. Instead, massive transportation expenditures have focused almost exclusively on facilitating auto travel. The density is low (typically less than 3,000 persons per square mile), and urban amenities are more private than public. Equally important is the fact that the housing stock is much newer, typically offering single-family houses with large backyards (and large garages to "house" cars). The horizontal prototype is not simply a newer or updated version of the vertical prototype—it is a different kind of city.

Much of the current interest in the historic preservation of old buildings and efforts to recreate the "old time" urban fabric romanticize cities of the past. The stark reality is that, for the majority of working people, the vertical city offered cramped and noisy housing, little privacy, and relatively crude public amenities. One only need stroll through Chinatown in New York on a hot summer day to get a sense of what everyday life was like for the common New Yorker 50 years ago. The vertical city was built to house immigrants who had little money and who could not afford cars. The horizontal city has been built for a society with much greater disposable income (as a result of real income growth and two-earner families) and different quality-of-life expectations. It is a city that owns (indeed loves) cars. It is a crude generalization, and one that the proponents of traditional urbanism resist, but the horizontal city seems to have provided a kind of life that the overwhelming majority of Americans consciously chose—in spite of their romantic image of the old vertical city.

Is population loss always a bad thing for a city? We think not. Cities with more than a million inhabitants were rare before the twentieth century. There is no reason to assume that a smaller city is worse than a large one. In fact, an argument can be made that when a city is smaller it is also more human in scale, more livable, less anonymous, with a more manageable and responsive government. The problem with the decline of U.S. cities is not a question of size but, rather, a question of who is leaving and who is staying.

The people moving out of our cities are predominantly middle-income families of all races while those remaining—and entering—are predominantly poor minorities. If the 77 largest American cities are evaluated in terms of a diverse set of social barometers, such as poverty and unemployment rates, the number of families on public assistance, infant mortality rates, and average household incomes, a clear pattern emerges. Comparing the cumulative average rates for the 26 cities that have shrunk since 1950, with the cumulative average rates for the 51 cities that have grown, the shrinking cities as a group are currently worse with respect to all of these social welfare indicators. Only crime levels appear to be comparable—and appallingly high—for both groups of cities, although even they are slightly higher in shrinking cities.

Cities with high vacancy rates

A city that has lost much of its population has—to borrow a real-estate phrase—a high vacancy rate. When a shopping mall has a high vacancy rate, the owner suffers not only because of the lost revenue on the empty space but also because the overall vitality and attractiveness of the center's shopping experience is diminished. This, in turn, makes other tenants more likely to vacate, depressing rents on leased space. So, too, for a city with a high vacancy rate: It suffers not only a loss to its tax base but, unless it is successfully repositioned, it becomes a less attractive place to live and work.

The owner of the mall with high vacancy rates has a limited number of options. To be more competitive he can lower rents or offer special lease terms in an attempt to attract and retain tenants. He can also offer special services to prospective (and current) tenants in order to raise occupancy. He can refurbish the mall to attract new tenants or "shrink" the mall so that its (now smaller) space is fully occupied. If this doesn't work, the costs associated with the operation of the mall may not be covered by its income, and, in the short run, the owner will have to absorb the losses. If, in the end, he cannot cover his costs, the owner will close the mall and seek an alternative, more profitable use.

Of course, you cannot close a city. Some cities have privatized parts of their urban services (such as garbage collection and education) in an attempt to reduce their operating costs. Like a troubled mall owner, a city with a high vacancy rate can try to refurbish itself by redeveloping its downtown. Examples of urban redevelopment projects include stadiums, aquariums, world trade centers, river-boat gambling, and convention centers. Unfortunately, these strategies generally yield a poor return on public funds.

Cities need to mimic the strategies of the shopping-center landlord by lowering taxes, reducing onerous regulations, increasing the levels of public services, and improving the quality of local infrastructure. But this requires an admission that excessive taxes, burdensome regulations, and inadequate services have contributed to the city's decline. Such admissions do not come easily to a generation of politicians who have lived on the uphill slope of the Laffer Curve, raising taxes and regularly bemoaning the levels of support received from Washington and state governments. Unfortunately, as documented by Robert Inman of the Wharton School, cities that have "high vacancy rate" problems have already reached the point where further increases in local taxes produce declining tax revenues and an even greater decline in urban occupancy. Upon reflection, this is not surprising—imagine the fate of a troubled shopping center if the owner continuously raised rents as vacancy rose.

What happens when a city loses population? The fiscal difficulties associated with a reduced tax base are obvious. But, like a shopping mall that loses tenants, a city that loses population experiences additional problems. First, although people have left, the cost of maintaining the old infrastructure designed for the larger population—the roads, sewers, and transit systems—remains. In the case of the cities that expanded during the early 1900s, this infrastructure is in need of extensive repair and replacement. Just like the mall owners, cities must decide which services to curtail. Most city managers (like most shopping-center owners) invariably choose to defer infrastructure maintenance.

A second effect of population shrinkage is a reduction in population density. In theory, this should increase the quality of life. However, density is usually reduced by the creation of irregular gaps in the urban density pattern. Although the densities in vertical cities are still three or four times greater than in the horizontal cities, the vertical city was designed to function most efficiently with relatively continuous concentrations of people. As depopulation occurs, not only does the provision of normal municipal services become more expensive (unplanned vacant space is expensive to secure and maintain) but there may no longer be a sufficient population base to support neighborhood social and retail activities in many areas. This results in services being further reduced, inducing those who can to move away. Similarly, depopulation in vertical cities creates a lack of social energy and dynamism, as well as a reduced sense of safety. In short, shrinkage undermines the strategic operating engine of a vertical city.

Perhaps even more importantly, a vertical city with population gaps no longer possesses a continuous urban fabric. Instead, it becomes a series of disjointed areas separated by unplanned abandoned and vacant areas. Servicing a discontinuous city is very expensive. At the very time that vertical cities need to find more efficient servicing techniques to offset their declining tax bases, they are faced with an increasingly inefficient and expensive population pattern.

Finally, shrinkage lowers the quality of urban life. Buildings remain vacant, most in various stages of total decay. Lots become empty as buildings are burned and collapse. These lots become dumps, strewn with garbage of all types. While vacant space in the countryside can be aesthetically pleasing, and horizontal cities frequently include massive tracts of vacant space, population gaps are disastrous for vertical cities. Vacant buildings become vulnerable to further vandalism. They also become havens for illegal activities—a breeding ground for diseases and unsafe playgrounds for children. Streets lined with empty lots and deserted buildings become indefensible spaces, veritable "wild zones." That urban dereliction is a cancer is an apt cliché. Population gaps are not merely symptoms, they are primary causes of the continued disintegration of urban life in vertical cities.

The regional government solution

What is to be done? The most common political response has been to counteract the social costs associated with a shrinking (and increasingly poor) population by raising taxes. This is a self-destructive response that makes the city an even less attractive place to live and work. Mayors, planners, and city-government officials must learn to accept the fact that the older, shrunken vertical cities will never grow back to their earlier size and prosperity. The goal must be, instead, to make their cities more livable, more attractive, and, probably, even smaller. They must reconfigure their cities to be competitively viable in modern times.

An examination of the 1992 population figures for cities shows that, although a few cities like Oakland, Louisville, Akron, and Rochester, New York have managed to reverse their earlier decline and are growing (very modestly), most shrinking cities continue to shrink. True, the rates of population decline have generally slowed, perhaps suggesting that a sustainable city may be evolving. But Philadelphia, Boston, Washington, D.C., St. Louis, Detroit, and Baltimore, which shrank even more rapidly during the 1980s than during the previous decade, continue to lose population in the 1990s. Such cities must reinvent themselves, becoming better cities as they grow even smaller than they are today.

One solution commonly proposed for shrinking cities is regional government. Since metropolitan areas as a whole are expanding, linking (poor) shrinking cities to (relatively rich) growing suburbs appears to provide the former with access to the financial resources of the latter. This argument has been advanced recently by David Rusk in *Cities Without Suburbs*. He presents convincing evidence that new growing cities (e.g., Houston, Phoenix, and San Diego) that have annexed suburban counties have many advantages over older cities whose boundaries remained largely unchanged.

There are, however, practical difficulties with the regional government proposal. Regional government is constitutionally difficult in most states; only Portland, Oregon is part of a directly elected regional government. It is true that several cities, such as Houston, Miami, Jacksonville, Charlottesville, Indianapolis, Nashville, and Minneapolis, have a system of cost sharing. However, with the exception of Minneapolis and Indianapolis, these are all growing cities. Troubled shrinking cities have little to offer suburban counties. As a result, suburbanites—most of whom consciously fled the city to leave its problems behind—can be expected to oppose any attempts at regionalization. The central cities themselves will resist, especially those with large numbers of ethnic minorities, who would lose their hard won political clout if they were incorporated into a larger, wealthier regional electorate.

In any case, regional government has its drawbacks. While size may generate some modest economies of scale with respect to infrastructure and finance, it also greatly increases inefficiencies of scale for the delivery of many services. Regional government would be more remote from—hence less responsible to—the voters, resulting in more corruption and inefficiency. Regional government, while it may solve the problems of servicing poor areas, will not address issues like an old and noncompetitive housing stock and the population gaps already prevalent in vertical cities.

Smaller is better

The clock cannot be turned back. The industrial cities that grew rapidly during the first half of the twentieth century (and shrank almost as rapidly during the second half) will never recover their primacy. History teaches that cities grow and decline. The most dramatic example is probably ancient Rome, which shrank from about a million at its imperial zenith to less than 100,000 by the Middle Ages. The population of Venice peaked in the seventeenth century at 180,000, but, as its mercantile empire collapsed, the city shrank, reaching a low point of 132,000 in 1880. The population in Venice today is only about 137,000. The populations of the great industrial cities of northern Britain—Glasgow, Liverpool, and Manchester—peaked in 1900 and have been declining since.

The population of Vienna peaked in the decade before the First World War and, today, is about 20 percent smaller than at its zenith.

The critical lesson of Vienna, Venice, and even Glasgow (which has recently experienced a modest revival) is that a smaller city can be made a good place to live. Using these cities as role models, the question for shrinking cities is not, "How can we grow big again?" but rather, "How can we prosper and have a wonderful, smaller city?"

A fundamental change in mind set is required once we accept that smaller can be better. A city that has irretrievably lost large amounts of its population needs to examine ways to redesign itself to become more compact, perhaps even smaller in area. This will not be easy. City planners have traditionally favored growth and expansion. It is now time for planners to look for ways to shrink our cities. Just as physicians should allow gracious and healthy decline as people age, so too must our planners manage older cities. However, just as aging is not merely adolescence in reverse, urban planning for shrinkage is fundamentally different than planning for growth.

Historically, vertical cities expanded from the center by developing land at the periphery, by building on flood plains and near urban disamenities (e.g.; railroads), and by extending their urban infrastructure. But a shrinking city cannot merely retract its perimeter. Population losses have not been experienced equally across all parts of the city. Outlying parts of the city are generally quite strong, as are some city centers. Between these areas lies a complex web of decrepit housing stock and abandoned industry but also strong neighborhoods.

Are there alternative uses for the empty tracts? One could imagine formally planned versions of what has occurred in an unfunded and unplanned way in Detroit and East St. Louis, where vast empty lots are reverting to a sort of urban wilderness. In some cases, empty land might be turned into parks and recreation sites. This requires funds to undertake the expensive process of rehabilitation, soil replacement, and landscaping. The City of New York currently owns 20,000 vacant lots and has proposed asking private corporations to pay for converting empty land into parks and playgrounds. In return, the city would allow the companies to use the space for their own advertising. Corporate sponsorship is expected to provide on-going maintenance, which was lacking with earlier efforts, such as the Lindsay administration's "vest pocket parks." There are also commercial outdoor recreation possibilities. A developer has recently built a 30-acre golf course on vacant land in downtown Chicago, near the convention center. Large tracts could be consolidated and sold to the U.S. Department of the Interior for the creation of environmental zones, belated versions of the urban green belts that were a staple of Garden City planning in the early 1900s.

Another option would be to take advantage of the availability of empty land to begin to transform the vertical city into something that more closely resembles the horizontal postwar prototype. The three- and four-story rowhouses that characterize cities like Baltimore and Philadelphia were built at now commercially unacceptable densities of 30 to 40 dwellings per acre. Downzoning of residential areas would allow two-story, semidetached houses at lower densities of about 20 dwellings per acre, or detached cottages of 5 to 10 dwellings per acre. However, such densities are only affordable if cities greatly reduce their development costs and regulations. In reducing these burdens they need to strive to become competitive with the most competitive suburb. If old cities cannot annex surrounding suburbs, they can, at least, begin slowly to transform part of their housing stock and begin to provide the kind of housing that today's households desire—single-family homes with space for backyards and off-street parking—rather than continuing to offer them a housing stock designed for their grandparents. The combination of much lower density housing with easy access to high-density downtown amenities may be the starting point for a new, postindustrial, urban prototype.

A radical proposal

Cities should also consider even more drastic alternatives. For example, they could de-annex parts of their territory to private developers. If large tracts, in excess of 100 acres, say, were sold as de-annexed, unincorporated areas with associated suburban cost structures, it is possible that developers would find this an attractive opportunity to create new "suburban" municipalities in the central areas of the city. Prototypes include such communities as River Oaks in Houston and Highland Park and University Park in Dallas. These "suburban" communities have been developed within the fabric of the city boundaries. New municipalities would be legally independent of the city. They would control their own governments, schools, and regulations. Like most suburbs, we suspect they would preserve a high degree of autonomy and probably a degree of exclusiveness. In fact, these new municipalities would probably need to alter traffic flows through the surrounding city into the community in order to provide the type of housing sought by today's buyers. Given the pattern of new planned communities in the United States, some form of common interest housing development governed by homeowner associations is likely to result.

The sale by the city of such property would create a more viable smaller city. How? First, the sale of the land would generate much needed funds, which would be used to offset years of deferred maintenance of urban infrastructure. Given the differential cost of operation and development in an unincorporated suburban municipality versus the city, the value derived from selling such land could be substantial. The city would also no longer be responsible for the maintenance and security of the land once it becomes a legally independent community. Third, and perhaps most importantly, although the city itself would shrink, the city's urban fabric would be enhanced as the new municipality developed. Many of the population gaps in the urban fabric could be filled in. There can be little doubt that these vacant parcels would develop more rapidly and successfully as independent suburban communities rather than as part of the city. In short, the city would be smaller, richer, and less vacant. At the same time, the population cavities would start to disappear.

Critical impediments to altering the current state of vacant urban tracts include irrational environmental standards. Too often these regulatory standards and procedures ask the irrelevant question, "Is it perfectly clean?" rather than the more pragmatic question, "Is it cleaner than it would have otherwise been?" The imposition of 1990s environmental sensibilities on areas that provided the factory jobs for previous generations means that massive tracts in urban areas are forever doomed to be economically undeveloped. As a result, the soil remains contaminated, the chemicals continue to seep into the groundwater, children continue to play in these abandoned lots, and the urban fabric continues to deteriorate. Environmental regulators, like city politicians, must realize that these areas will not be developed (and hence no environmental improvement will occur) unless dramatic compromises are made. These compromises may involve using federal funds to clean up these properties. Alternatively, development could be allowed if it significantly improves the environmental quality of the property, even though such clean-up may fall considerably short of current standards.

Future city

In our view, consolidation and de-annexation are not a "desirable" option for a city; however, for many shrinking cities, we see no other viable alternative. When population loss has passed a certain point, urban revival is likely to require drastic measures. Rehabilitation has usually worked only in downtown areas. Enterprise zones and empowerment zones have proved to be only marginally effective—where they have succeeded at all. Besides, they depend on the infusion of federal or state funds, which are not always available.

In any case, the obstacles to dealing effectively with urban shrinkage are massive, even possibly insurmountable. But to solve a problem, reality must be faced. In this case, the reality is that many cities will continue to shrink. Municipal politicians whose electoral bases will be eroded by consolidation or de-annexation can be expected to resist the idea of downsizing. Since the inhabitants of many of these affected areas will be minorities, the politics of consolidation and shrinkage will be opposed by these groups. Neighborhood activists, whose careers have been spent trying to promote local economic development from within will view shrinkage policies as defeatist, not the least because they will lose their own political power bases. Moreover, if selected urban areas are allowed to become autonomous suburban municipalities, the city as a whole will have to be protected from complete disintegration.

Shrinkage will also be seen by many as weakening the mechanism that has traditionally been used to elicit federal urban aid. Historic preservationists will undoubtedly object to wholesale demolition, since even decrepit areas contain buildings of architectural merit, and some of the worst areas are the locations of so-called industrial landmarks. Obviously, much will depend on how successfully consolidation deals with issues of dislocation, new housing, and new community services. But the challenge is clear: Our cities must be radically redesigned to be both better and smaller.

WITOLD RYBCZYNSKI is Martin and Margy Meyerson Professor of Urbanism at the University of Pennsylvania. His *A Clearing in the Distance* is published by Simon & Schuster. PETER D. LINNEMAN is the Albert Sussman Professor of Real Estate, Finance and Public Policy at the University of Pennsylvania and serves as senior managing director of Equity International Properties.

The case for sprawl.

SUBURBAN MYTH

By Gregg Easterbrook

The ideal restaurant would have terrific food, moderate prices, and would be unpopular, so lines would never inconvenience diners. Legislatures could make restaurants less crowded by, say, mandating that some tables be kept vacant even when customers are queued. Those already seated would surely benefit. But others would stew over being denied service, while business and jobs would be lost.

It's worth remembering this as politicians begin to tackle the issue of suburban "sprawl," currently emerging as a primary topic in the run-up to Campaign 2000. Polling data and focus groups show that sprawl has hot political Q-scores; last fall, state and local voters approved nearly 200 ballot measures to limit development or preserve green space. Vice President Gore has unveiled a "livability agenda" to ease traffic and other frustrations of suburban commuters. As Gore notes, "Parents want to spend more time with their kids and less time stuck behind a steering wheel." And Gore is hardly alone. New Jersey Governor Christine Todd Whitman, a Republican, is leading the charge for a $1 billion program to set aside half the state's remaining wildland. Even Ralph Reed is touting sprawl politics.

Of course, everybody wishes there were fewer cars on the road, fewer strip malls, and less demand for living space or commercial square footage. But how do you discourage such things without denying a place at the table to those who have not yet been seated—especially in a country whose population is growing? If suburbs are where Americans choose to live—and that verdict is in, the suburban class now constituting the majority of Americans—then brainpower should be applied to making burbs as livable as possible. It's a good sign that policy organizations such as the Brookings Institution are turning their attention to such tasks as planning for "smart growth."

But, as an issue, sprawl can also sound awfully similar to exclusionary zoning and other pull-up-the-ladder ideas that comfortable communities have used in the past to keep out unwanted arrivistes—often minorities and immigrants. One person's greenspace preservation is another's denied housing permit. So here are a few qualms about the emerging national buzz on sprawl:

Sprawl is infuriating but not statistically significant. The footprint of the United States reflects an ever-bigger shoe size; the Chicago metropolitan area, for example, grew 46 percent from 1970 to 1990. The Sierra Club estimates that 400,000 acres per year are being converted to developed use. Yet are these figures really as worrisome as they seem? Four hundred thousand acres, for example, sounds like the circumference of the Crab Nebula but represents 0.02 percent of the U.S. land mass: 50 years of sprawl at the current rate would be required to consume a single percent of America's expanse.

Just 3.4 percent of the United States is urban, suburban, or otherwise "built up," according to federal figures. If roads are added to the calculation, the total concretized area of the country rises to 4.8 percent. The forested portion of the United States is, by contrast, 20.4 percent, meaning there are four acres of woodland for every acre of development. Even if the definition of "developed" is expanded in the most liberal way, to include all land used for crops or grazing, the United States is still two-thirds wild, one-third under the hand of man. Sprawl is a local problem, not an all-encompassing effect.

Recent concerns about agricultural land-use patterns, often spun in the media and by lobbyists as a crisis of "vanishing farms," also diminish on close examination. "Land in farms" fell 16 percent between 1964 and 1997, according to the Agriculture Department. But this much-cited category incorporates considerable acreage that owners were calling farms only for tax purposes. Since the 1960s, "total cropland" is down only about one percent, while "harvested cropland," or land under cultivation, is up eight percent. And production per acre—what matters most—is way, way up, thanks to high-yield crop strains.

Moreover, the trend line is toward the *decline* of sprawl, relative to people at least. David Rusk, a theorist of the smart-growth movement, estimates that U.S. metro development covered 208,000 square miles in 1950 and by 1990 had sprawled out to 345,000 square miles. But, through that period, the population of those areas rose from 84 million to 159 million. This translates to a 66 percent increase in physical area for a population increase of 89 percent. America isn't gobbling up more space per capita; it's gobbling less—mainly because developers are responding to market incentives to use land more efficiently. Sprawl theory assumes that builders despoil the land without restraint. Yet price is already an important restraint; land is an expensive resource.

People fled city centers because they wanted to. One motivator for suburban expansion was white desire to escape contact with blacks. As *Brookings Review* recently noted, "Race has been a major factor in the spatial configuration of our metropolitan areas." That aspect of sprawl does not reflect well on American society, but the rest of the phenomenon is mainly a voluntary choice. Blacks are now sprawling, too: mainly African American, middle-class burbs are expanding in Georgia, Maryland, and elsewhere. Detached homes, verdant lawns, lower crime rates—for many millions of Americans, including many millions of minority Americans, such things represent a lifelong dream. People of all races seek the sprawled areas because that's what they *like.*

People also sought the suburbs to escape the corruption and mismanagement of urban government–especially the disastrous inner-city school systems. Suburban government is usually clean and responsive, if ho-hum; if people like honest government supervising their driveways and lawns, why should public policy argue with that judgment? Intellectuals have long disdained the expansion of the burbs, despite works such as *The Levittowners* that demonstrate little urban-suburban distinction in sophistication. Of course, many suburbanites have trite values and nothing to say, but then the same goes for many who reside in Upper West Side walk-ups and hold subscription seats for the opera. And, for reasons never entirely clear, twentieth-century liberalism swooned for Le Corbusier's contention that human beings deserve to be packed into high-density tower housing that rises from the landscape like so many vertical penitentiaries. Maybe there was once a reason to believe that such structures were the only way to bring decent living standards to the masses, but now it's clearly possible to bring detached homes to the masses. That's an important social achievement, not a cause for angst.

We know from the choices of housing buyers, and from the unhappiness of housing-project residents, that most Americans despise living in cramped quarters. Despite this, some sprawl theorists assert that, since the average density of an American metro area is one-fourth the density of metro areas in nations such as Germany, public policy should strive to force a dramatic compression of American living space. But if Germany, or any of many other European or Asian countries, had more land area, its citizens would clamor for detached homes and lawns, too. The fact that other nations lack the expanse in which to offer the majority of their citizens homeownership hardly means that America, blessed with such space, should prevent citizens from occupying it.

Sprawl has economic utility. Some cities have spread out in a jumbled, ill-thought-through manner that causes awful traffic bottlenecks, wasted fuel, and an excessively asphaltized ambiance. But it is not the case that tract housing, overpasses, multilane roads, malls, and other aspects of suburbia happen solely because of rapacious developers or civic pandemonium. Most happen because they are economically efficient.

Subdivision development is nowhere near as tasteful as an elm-shaded, turn-of-the-century Cape Cod in the university district, but it has the virtue of being affordable to many more families. Malls may be stupefying, but they are a furiously efficient means of retailing. Two-car, two-earner families with husband and wife commuting in opposite directions may lead to daily stress but might also be one reason for the American economy's flexibility. The United States has experienced unprecedented economic growth, low unemployment, and improvement in living standards during the very period of burb explosion and traffic jams. Maybe these factors are positively correlated, not negatively.

Consider the assumption that road construction is odious. Roads are not only much cheaper to build than mass transit systems; they are also more flexible. The excellent subway system in Washington, D.C., which I ride to work, is fixed in its downtown-outward configuration: tens of billions of dollars would be required to rebuild the system to reflect the between-burb commuting that has been the main urban transportation trend of the past 20 years. Roads, on the other hand, can reflect changes in commuter patterns instantly—people just point their cars at different destinations.

Cars, in turn, are consumers of money and fossil fuel, and we belittle ourselves when we regard them as status symbols. But automobiles also promote economic efficiency and personal freedom; there are good reasons why even anti-sprawlers want to own one. As new cars approach negligible levels of pollution emissions, environmental objections to them decline. And an annoying little secret of suburban life is that, even with traffic congestion, it's almost always faster to get somewhere in a car than by riding public transit. Cars are ubiquitous partly because people make rational time-money trade-offs regarding their use, and those sorts of judgments, though sometimes wrong on the micro scale, are usually logical on the macro scale.

Thus, the fact that the federal government spends about $28 billion a year on road construction, compared with about $6 billion on mass transit, isn't necessarily the outrage that current sprawl politicking suggests. It surely can be argued that shifting some spending toward mass transit makes sense, though such purposes can be far more quickly and flexibly achieved by better bus service than by the rail lines that urban planners adore. But roads and car culture aren't a crazed anti-people conspiracy. The challenge is to make roads and cars serve us better while bugging us less.

The Michigan Land Use Institute, an impressive new smart-growth organization, recently proposed a sensible middle course along these lines for Traverse City, Michigan. Local officials currently plan to bracket the metro area with a high-speed highway bypass. The Michigan Land Use Institute offered a detailed alternative plan for improving existing major arteries and left-turn lanes, speeding up traffic within the city but preventing cars from being sucked away from established commercial zones. Compromises like this admit that the automobile is here to stay as America's primary means of transportation but seek to adjust car culture to avoid construction that isn't really needed.

Sprawl is caused by affluence and population growth, and which of these, exactly, do we propose to prohibit? The Census Bureau projects that the American population will expand to 394 million by the year 2050, half again the level of today, with almost all that growth attributable to (legal) immigration, which currently runs at about 900,000 arrivals per year. Do we want to halt or deeply restrict immigration? Unless we do, the country's stock of houses, roads, commercial space, and other construction must substantially enlarge in decades to come.

Meanwhile, the reason Americans keep buying more housing, more SUVs, more swimming pools, and other space-consuming items is that they can afford these things. And so . . . affluence is bad? The literature on sprawl is rife with sarcastic references to the square footage of the typical new home and to the spread of McMansions—"spacious" is a sneer word in this context—as if cramped quarters or adjoining walls are what human beings ought to prefer, damn it! There are many philosophical reasons why people might be more content with a modest lifestyle. But these are arguments about materialistic culture and the modern soul, not about appropriate housing-lot size. If prosperity puts the four-bedroom house within reach for the typical person, it's hard to see why public policy should look askance at that.

Sprawl complaints might justify exclusionary zoning. If political opposition to sprawl leads to smarter growth, or more parks and wildlife habitats, or better bus service, or better traffic regulation, then the public good is served. The trouble is, some sprawl concerns would not serve the public good.

Aspects of environmentalism have long been criticized as using ostensible concerns about nature to serve private purposes such as property values. Sprawl theory is now being hailed as an alternative to this. Since every person, rich or poor, is equally inconvenienced by being stuck in traffic, *The New York Times* recently opined, Gore's livability initiative will "take the lingering elitist tinge off environmentalism." Actually, it's the other way

around. Sprawl control has much greater potential to wander into have-and-have-not inequity than does, say, regulation of CFCs or dioxin.

In a passage of his 1992 book *Earth in the Balance*, Gore worries about a glade of trees removed to build a new housing subdivision near what was then his Virginia home. "As the woods fell to make way for more concrete," he writes, "more buildings, more parking lots, the wild things that lived there were forced to flee." When he wrote these words, Gore was himself living in a large suburban house built on cleared woodland and parking his car on concrete. Why are comfortable homes and long driveways all right for those who already possess them, but threatening when others ask for the same?

Adopting smart-growth policies and better transportation plans is something every community should do. But, if communities take the kind of steps that would really stop sprawl, they would confer a windfall on those already entrenched, while damaging the prospects of those who long to attain the detached-home lifestyle. It's not for nothing that the Supreme Court has long taken a dim view of regulations whose official purpose is to keep communities leafy and quiet but whose effective result is to lock in the favored at the expense of new arrivals.

Everybody wants symbolic action against sprawl, but real action would drive people crazy. Gore's "livability agenda" matches great p.r. ring with hardly any content. Its chief plank is federal support for about $9.5 billion in local land-preservation bonds. This is a fine idea, though a one-shot infusion that won't change the larger panorama of land-use politics. (For my own admittedly politically improbable proposal to require developers to preserve at least one acre of land for every new one they build on, thus making ever-greater increments of land preservation a permanent part of American public policy, see "Greener Pastures," TNR, March 2, 1998.) The rest of Gore's initiative are inoffensive, small-change items, such as $10 million to help schools become "community centered" or $17.2 million for safeguarding ex-urban agricultural land—an amount that will buy roughly two farms per state.

Announcing the livability initiative, Gore mused about "the Lakota storytellers who described the vast clearness of the Western sky as a metaphor for inner courage." It's easy to see why he would rather discuss the Lakota than the emphatic actions that would really cut down on sprawl. One would be exclusionary zoning. Another would be the denial of environmental or sewer permits, which brings business expansion to a halt. Another would be revoking the hugely popular mortgage-interest deduction. Another real-world restriction would be raising gasoline taxes.

If mortgage interest were not tax-deductible, and gasoline prices were quadrupled (putting them on a par with Europe's), demand for those sinister spacious homes would wane, enthusiasm for public transportation would rise, and the market could be relied on to take care of the rest. But do *you* want to be the politician who advocates a $3-per-gallon gasoline tax? Think of Bill Clinton's panicky 1996 retreat from a 4.3-cents-per-gallon gas-tax increase—not exactly a metaphor for inner courage. There is little chance any major candidate will advocate higher gasoline taxes during Campaign 2000. And, if the political world is afraid of this moderate reform—which would not imperil car culture, just trim some of the tonnage off our SUVs—where is the will for real change?

Other anti-sprawl proposals have similar implausibility quotients. Rusk and other theorists, for example, call for consolidating urban and suburban governments to prevent local entities from playing one off the other in development contests. It's an admirable idea, and a few cities and their suburbs have voluntarily combined, notably Indianapolis and Jacksonville. But, if you live in the ring burbs around Newark, Detroit, or Washington, D.C., you'd have to be dragged kicking and screaming into combination with their corrupt, incompetent governments. Some have proposed that combining the tax bases of suburban and urban jurisdictions would reduce sprawl contests and promote equity by improving schools in poorer neighborhoods. The latter goal is totally justified, but where is the political support for this idea? Tax-base sharing is currently foundering in Vermont, one of the most liberal states.

And, if you want decisive action against sprawl, don't you want land-use planning? Imagine how poll numbers will shoot up for the candidate who proposes that! Regional land-use planning has done well by the city of Portland, which has both controlled its boundaries and seen its economy prosper. But Portland is a special case; its geography imposes physical limits on growth. Portland's high land values and high quality of life tell us land-use planning and prosperity are not incompatible, which is an important lesson for local officials who traditionally have felt compelled to approve any and all construction. But the kind of land-use planning that's worked in Portland may not work nationally, especially since Portland has pretty much closed its doors to population growth, which is not an option for the country as a whole.

Hey, these movie-theater lines are too long! You bet the lines at the movie theater are too long. My proposed solution is to forbid you from going to the movies. Your proposed solution is to forbid me. We both claim a noble public purpose—the shorter movie line. But sometimes what seems like concern for the public square is really a declaration of "me first."

Thoughtful study of smart-growth alternatives is in everyone's interest and will lead to improvements in suburban livability. But many of the people who now grouse about sprawl themselves live in spacious houses, own an SUV, owe their good fortunes to the growth economy, and would be entirely outraged if there were not ample roads, stores, restaurants, and parking wherever they went. They wish everybody else would get off the highway so that they can have the road to themselves. In this way, the sprawl issue touches on the selfish downside of democracy. Smart growth is a smart idea, but those who pursue it must be wary of favoring the enfranchised and the organized, which our politics does too much of already.

Who pays for sprawl?

Hidden subsidies fuel the growth of the suburban fringe

BY PHILLIP J. LONGMAN

Time was when only nature lovers and urban sophisticates would get worked up about suburban sprawl, but no more. Growth moratoriums have sprung up around the country. Conservative think tanks and even institutions like the Bank of America (which has a huge stake in construction loans) sponsor reports attacking the economic costs of continuing to convert undeveloped land into low-density tract housing and strip malls. And according to recent market research, most ordinary Americans, though still favoring detached, single-family homes, are increasingly fed up with the congestion and sprawling commercial development that too often come as part of the package. Today's consumers say they are particularly annoyed by commercial strips and that in principle they would prefer neighborhoods clustered around a downtown or village center.

Yet sprawling development continues apace. In a report issued last year, the American Farmland Trust estimated that the United States is losing about 50 acres an hour to suburban and exurban development. At this rate, the United States will lose 13 percent of its prime farmland by the middle of the next century and, the report says, could conceivably become a net food importer.

What's behind this sprawl phenomenon? Some factors are obvious: Houses built in cornfields, for example, are often affordable, as a result of low land costs. But to an extent rarely acknowledged, suburban sprawl is also encouraged by government subsidies—both deliberate and unintended.

Residents of new suburbs rarely pay the full cost of their government services.

The subsidies start with transportation spending. The House of Representatives and the Senate are currently negotiating about spending between $214 billion and $217 billion on a new transportation bill. Whatever the final number, the lion's share of this money will go for highways. Many of these highways will open up new land for development, and if the patterns of the past continue, much of this development will take the form of sprawling tract homes and strip malls. In Atlanta, for example, regional planners predict that the new transportation bill will wind up funding new roads through the still-rural areas outside the city, thereby causing sprawl to expand out to another layer of counties.

The highway lobby (construction companies, unions) claims that motorists who move to these new developments will pay for the new roads they'll use. But according to the U.S. Department of Transportation, that's not true. Tolls, gasoline taxes, and other user fees cover about 70 percent of the direct cash costs of building and maintaining the nation's road system. The rest—amounting to tens of billions of dollars per year—is financed by general revenues.

And this subsidy is only a tiny fraction of what drivers actually receive. Driving imposes other external costs on the American economy, from damage caused by air pollution to the cost of mending people injured in traffic accidents to the need for strategic involvement in oil-producing regions of the world. It's impossible to do an exact accounting of these external costs, but even conservative estimates show them adding up to at least 22 cents for every mile Americans drive. As urban planner Reid Ewing notes, that number implies that a gas tax of $6.60 a gallon would be necessary to make drivers fully pay for the cost that car travel imposes on the economy.

Wealth transfer. Who pays and who benefits from this subsidy? Since the farther out one lives, the more miles one is likely to drive, the biggest net beneficiaries are people who move into the expanding sprawl zones, while the biggest net losers are people who live in denser communities. The transfer of wealth is indirect, but it involves a subsidy every bit as real as a government check.

In addition to the nationwide subsidy of roads and driving, the suburban-sprawl pattern shifts economic burdens within a region. In a low-density tract development, the cost of most government services goes up. Sewer lines must be longer, school buses must travel farther, and more fire stations and miles of road are needed to serve a given population. Sprawl also forces governments to spend money on new schools and other capital projects that would not be needed if residential patterns remained more compact. Between 1970 and 1995, the number of public-school students in Maine declined by 27,000, yet the state spent more than $338 million building new schools in fast-growing suburban towns.

Who pays for it? The residents of new low-density developments pay taxes, of course, but are rarely charged the full cost of the government services they consume. Instead those costs are usually averaged across a whole region or state, in effect charging the people in the older areas for the costs of sprawl.

Consider, for instance, the cost of providing new sewer hookups to various neighborhoods in Tallahassee, Fla. According to a study by James E. Frank, an urban-planning professor at Florida State University, the actual costs were about $4,447 for the mostly black, center-city neighborhoods nearest the sewage treatment plant but $11,443 for the upscale Lakeshore neighborhoods at the northern edge of town, where politicians and lobbyists tend to live.

Despite this nearly $7,000 difference in real cost, all households pay the same price, about $6,000, for sewer connections, regardless of where they are. That means that the poor families living near the sewer plant not only have to endure its odor but also pay considerably more for their sewer hookup than it actually costs the government to serve them. Meanwhile, affluent residents escape both the smell and the full bill for their waste treatment.

Clearly, such subsidies do not *cause* people to move to the suburbs. But they do artificially lower the costs, skewing the factors citizens weigh when making a move or stay decision.

As suburban sprawl expands, property values in the central city and close-in suburbs usually decline. To compensate, these areas have to raise property tax rates, passing still more costs on to their residents. This pushes still more middle-class families to move farther out, leaving center cities with their familiar mixture of very rich and very poor.

The cycle might go on forever, except that ultimately huge infrastructure problems build up, commute times become long, and "urban" problems such as crime and pollution reach even the outer suburbs.

What to do? So far, attempts to control sprawl through regulation have proved disappointing. In 1985, for example, Florida passed a comprehensive growth-management plan that was hailed around the country as a model of enlightened land-use regulation. But the top-down regulatory approach engendered huge frustration and backlash among landowners and developers, and the legislation was effectively gutted.

Regional planning and growth management may help contain sprawl— Portland, Ore.'s "growth boundary" has shown some success—but so long as low-density development remains heavily subsidized, the effect of regulation is like tapping on the brake with one foot while keeping the accelerator to the floor with the other. Ultimately, the best way to cope with sprawl is to stop subsidizing it, so that its full costs are built into public and private decisions about land development.

Levittown to Littleton

How the suburbs have changed.

CHRISTOPHER CALDWELL

The day after the shootings at Columbine High, many newspapers ran a 2″ x 2″ inset map of the school neighborhood in Littleton, Colorado. There was a grid of high-speed roads a mile to a block. There were residential cul-de-sacs squiggling into empty quadrants. And looming up in the corner like a 747 hangar was the monolithic high-school building.

Such brand-new landscapes, almost wholly unfamiliar to northeasterners, make up virtually all of the middle-class neighborhoods in any western metropolis—Phoenix, Albuquerque, Houston. What was odd was that the Littleton map generally ran amid columns of copy seeking out the root causes of the shooting, and seeking them most everywhere: guns, television, affluence, big schools, divorce, Hollywood, the Internet, Goth music. Looking for simple explanations for a tragedy like Littleton is probably a fool's errand. But if one is going to engage in the exercise, the suburban layout described in the little map belongs on the list.

In the weeks following the massacre, many Americans have begun to think so too. News articles and television specials have cast towns like Littleton as un-"nurturing" at best, an adolescent hell on earth at worst. People are once again deeply troubled by "suburbia." Fifty-five percent of Americans live in suburbs now—but only 25 percent of that number mention the suburbs as the place they'd most like to live.

Well, yeah, yeah, one might say. People have been beating up on suburbs since Bill Levitt developed his first neighborhood on Long Island in 1947. So what else is new?

As it turns out, *everything* is new.

The argument over the sterility of suburban developments like the various Levittowns was thrashed out decades ago, and largely settled in favor of suburbia. Witnesses for the prosecution began appearing in the 1950s: Allen Ginsberg's poetry, the Pete Seeger folk song (written by Malvina Reynolds) called "Little Boxes" (" . . . made of ticky-tacky / And they all look the same"), novels of corporate anomie like Sloan Wilson's *Man in the Gray Flannel Suit*. For the campus protestors of the 1960s, the suburbs were synonymous with conformity, repression, and racism. For the radicals' largely conservative opponents, they meant family, patriotism, and decency. In retrospect, we can view this as an early sign of the Left's conversion to elite snobbery: What really bothered the Left about Levittowns was that they were so *working class*. Happily, and unsurprisingly, conservatives won this battle.

But the Littleton problem is not the Levittown problem. And conservatives' victory in earlier battles has made them too quick to dismiss the complaints that

■

People have been beating up on the suburbs for years. So what else is new? As it turns out, everything.

■

have spawned dozens of panicky books in the past two years and have come to a boil in the wake of the shootings. Al Gore's attacks on suburban "sprawl" may retain much of the earlier anti-suburban liberal snobbery. The "livability agenda" that he plugs may lack intellectual seriousness. But Gore's very lack of seriousness should alert us that there's a real problem here. The vice president is a sufficiently unoriginal man that he would not be flailing about for a solu-

---

Mr. Caldwell is senior writer for *The Weekly Standard*.

From *National Review*, May 31, 1999, pp. 30, 32. © 1999 by National Review, Inc., 215 Lexington Avenue, New York, NY 10016. *www.nationalreview.com*. Reprinted by permission.

tion if he hadn't already found deep discontent in suburban focus groups.

The problem with Levittown was its physical monotony, a problem that diminishes over time, as trees grow and suburbanites modify their homes. What's more, since Tocqueville we've been told that a tendency to uniformity comes with the democratic territory. The problem in affluent "McMansion" suburbs like Littleton is that children grow up in almost hermetic seclusion—a newer and more soul-destroying condition, with dismal implications for democracy. Large lots, dead-end streets, and draconian zoning laws mean that there are vast distances to travel to reach any kind of public space. For parents, this means dependence on cars. For children unlucky enough to inhabit a dead-end that has no children on it, this means: No friends for you. Until adolescence, not even a child who is an ambitious walker can escape, since other neighborhoods are separated from his not by streets but by highways. (Town planners may christen them "avenues" or "boulevards," and real-estate agents may sell them as such, but they're highways.) No child in Levittown faced this problem.

This seclusion, in turn, creates an abject dependence on parents for automobile travel, and with it, a breakdown in any socialization of children that could be called normal. In the largely suburban eastern town where I grew up, a 5-year-old could walk about the neighborhood, and a 10-year-old could walk all over town. Twelve-year-olds could ride their bikes most places, and 14-year-olds could ride them to other towns. When you were 16, you could take the car if you really needed it. Entry into adult mobility was gradual and supervised. By contrast, a 15-year-old Littleton resident lives in a state of dependence considerably greater than that of my 5-year-old neighbors—or of 5-year-olds in any Levittown, for that matter. When a child of the western suburbs reaches driving age, his parents face a choice: either maintain the kid in his infantile seclusion until you send him off to college (where he can go nuts) or buy him a car and unleash him as a demigod of the highways.

There are, no doubt, cultural and historic factors at work along with questions of suburban landscape. For one, anonymity—which the locals describe as "privacy"—is a cherished cultural value in the western United States. (So is rootlessness: How many kids in Littleton High have parents from Littleton? How many were born in Littleton themselves?) For another, western suburbs were always doomed to be more sterile than their eastern counterparts, since the East was already too heavily settled for automobile-based suburbs to gain absolute dominion over the landscape: Drive out of a planned development in Massachusetts or New Jersey and you can easily wind up on a village green.

The upshot is that Levittown has as much in common with the Olde Village Greene as it does with Littleton—and is a much better place to live for that reason. The ghastly solitude of much of the American upper-middle class was well evoked by Edward Luttwak in his recent book *Turbo-Capitalism:* "There is a lot of lonely space not only between but inside the ideal dwellings of the American dream, the veritable mansions of the richest suburbs, which could house parents, grown children and their children in familial communion if only all were poor enough, but which mostly house only one ever-so-busy male and as busy a female, with surviving parents in their own retirement abodes, distant children pursuing their budding careers, and few friends, whose degree of loyal commitment might rate them as mere acquaintances in other climes."

Littleton is perhaps best described as Levittown plus affluence plus limitless buildable land—and the result is something qualitatively different, even unprecedented. If in Levittown the issue is conformity, in Littleton it's identity. In Levittown, you get kids banding together lamenting that their life is less heroic than that of their parents: It's *Rebel Without a Cause.* In Littleton, you get kids building the wildest fantasies in their interminable solitude, with the help of their computers, their televisions, and their stereos: It's a high-tech version of *The Wild Boy of Aveyron.* (As the architecture professor William Morrish told the *New York Times:* "They're basically an unseen population until they pierce their noses.")

Critics of the Fifties complained that Levittown's sameness could lead to conformity—although there was never much proof that it did. Today's critics warn that the loneliness of Littleton produces something very like the opposite of conformity. We can only hope that the evidence they're right doesn't continue to mount.

WHAT WORKS: IN 22 YEARS, MONTGOMERY COUNTY HAS ADDED 10,000 MODEST HOMES.

A Fair Share in Suburbia

JAY WALLJASPER

Devonshire East, in many people's minds, embodies the American Dream in full glory. A subdivision of new homes set among a stand of trees, Devonshire's winding streets and $275,000 property values seem to guarantee a haven of comfort and satisfaction. Even critics of soulless suburban architecture might find something to like in these brick town houses, whose handsome design recalls classic neighorhoods in nearby Washington, DC. Located in Montgomery County, Maryland, which is the sixth-wealthiest county in the nation and is full of blossoming high-tech businesses and federal agencies like the National Institutes of Health, Devonshire East is home to the managerial and professional class that has benefited so enormously from the nineties economic boom.

It's also home to Michelle Dove, a 37-year-old African-American single mother, and her three kids—two of whom are now attending college. How she affords to live in Devonshire East, on top of college costs, with the modest salary of an elementary school teacher is no miracle of financial planning. It's the result—a small miracle itself—of Montgomery County's housing policy. Every subdivision of more than fifty units built here over the past twenty-two years has been required to include a share of affordable housing (between 12.5 and 15 percent). Even more surprising, a third of these affordable units have been set aside for purchase by the county's public housing authority or nonprofit groups that rent to lower-income families.

Dove rents her three-bedroom apartment for $991, well below the market rate in this county (where the median price for a new town house is $189,000 and the average new single-family house exceeds $300,000), from Interfaith Housing Coalition, a group of congregations involved in social issues. Devonshire East's affordable units maintain the same look and architectural standards as the market-rate town houses across the street, but costs are kept down by tucking a second apartment atop each ground-floor unit.

Jay Walljasper is editor at large of Utne Reader. *This article is the seventh "What Works?"—a feature that examines projects making a positive difference in people's lives—and the first in a two-part series on strategies for regional revitalization.*

"I like living here," Dove says. "It's nice and quiet. I'm just a nine-minute drive from work and my daughter goes to a very nice middle school." She says she's felt no tension from her more upscale neighbors since moving here four years ago and notes, "There's a good sense of community among the people living right here on the street."

Dove's hope is someday to buy her own house in Montgomery County, the place where she grew up and now teaches in the local schools. This would be an impossible dream in many wealthy suburban enclaves, where sky-high home prices and restrictive zoning codes bar many folks—including young people who grew up in these towns as well as teachers, firefighters, nurses, office workers and other middle-income employees who play a vital role in the life of the community. Even current residents facing economic setbacks due to divorce, layoffs, death in the family or medical bills find themselves unable to continue living in their own hometown. But Montgomery County's "Fair Share" housing legislation, called the Moderately Priced Housing law and enacted in 1974, requires that all new developments include housing affordable for people making approximately 65 percent or less of the county's median income. The MPH law has fostered the creation of 10,000 moderately priced units in the past two decades. At least two-thirds of these homes are available for sale, offering people like Michelle Dove a chance they otherwise would not have.

Montgomery County's record in opening up suburban neighborhoods to people of lesser means is gaining national attention now that affordable housing is being recognized as not simply an inner-city problem. A recent report from the Department of Housing and Urban Development notes that one-third of families with "worst case" housing needs now live in the suburbs—almost 2 million households. This crisis has led to the adoption of Fair Share housing legislation (sometimes called "inclusionary zoning") in many places—other affluent counties ringing Washington, DC, as well as the states of Connecticut and New Jersey, plus Tallahassee, Florida; Burlington, Vermont; and several dozen communities in California. Although inspired by Montgomery County's efforts, none of these programs go so far as Montgomery County in reserving some of the units for public housing families. Also,

Reprinted with permission from the Janaury 25, 1999, issue of *The Nation*, pp. 15-21.

in most places the Fair Share laws rely on voluntary incentives rather than mandatory requirements.

The success of Montgomery County's housing policies is also being touted by a growing number of policy-makers and activists who identify the concentration of poverty as one of America's most damaging social problems. Fair Share housing has become a central element of innovative regional strategies aimed at reducing social inequities and insuring the vitality of America's metropolitan areas. David Rusk, a former mayor of Albuquerque who has become a prominent spokesperson for regional solutions to urban problems, says, "As a society we are now slowly lowering the barriers defined by race but raising the ones defined by income. Among American communities Montgomery County stands out for its integrated neighborhoods—integrated by both racial and ethnic group and, most uncommonly, by income class."

In researching his book on regional strategies for urban revitalization—*Inside Game/Outside Game: Winning Strategies for Saving Urban America*, published in March—Rusk compared Montgomery County to Oakland County, Michigan, near Detroit. In 1970 both counties were wealthy white enclaves bordering troubled central cities. On an index of economic segregation, with 100 representing absolute segregation by income, they each measured 27. By 1990, class segregation in Montgomery County had remained at a low and stable level, inching up six-tenths of a point on this scale, while Oakland County shot upward eleven points—a direct result of Montgomery County's Fair Share housing ordinance, according to Rusk.

Rusk points out that Montgomery County's housing policies are local rather than regional, covering just part of an area with 4.5 million people that includes two states as well as the District of Columbia. He admits that the county's Fair Share housing law has had limited impact in boosting the fortunes of poor people in inner-city Washington, but it has prevented the county from becoming a fortress for the privileged. Montgomery County's population is ethnically diverse (13.4 percent African-American, 7.6 percent Hispanic, 9.6 percent Asian-American), with 5 percent of residents living below the poverty level. Moreover, poor households are found throughout the county, not just in the hand-me-down older housing near the District of Columbia line: Two-thirds of the affordable units created in compliance with the Fair Share ordinance have been built in the newer, more affluent western portion of the county.

Oakland County, on the other hand, replicates the same pattern of clear-cut economic and racial segregation that devastated Detroit. Its poor and minority residents are clustered in certain portions of the county, notably the hard-hit city of Pontiac. The per capita income ratio between the wealthiest and poorest census tracts in Oakland County is 15 to 1, compared with 6 to 1 in Montgomery County.

One of Rusk's allies in this emerging regional movement is Myron Orfield, a Minnesota state legislator who describes how fast-growing areas such as the rich suburbs of Oakland County are able to capture most of the benefits of economic growth in a region while passing the social costs to poorer central cities and working-class suburbs. Affluent communities are able to do this, Orfield explains, through exclusionary zoning: ordinances that prohibit smaller houses, establish minimum lot sizes, require two-car garages or restrict multifamily dwellings. The overall effect is to outlaw affordable housing, forcing low- and many middle-income people to live elsewhere in the metropolitan region in spite of the fact that they contribute directly to the well-being of these upper-income suburbs. "These are the people who take care of wealthy suburbanites' kids, take care of their parents at the rest home, serve them coffee, answer the phone in their offices, yet they can't live in these communities," says Russ Adams, who works closely with Orfield as director of the Alliance for Metropolitan Stability, an activist group in the Minneapolis–St. Paul area.

Exclusionary zoning forces poor people—especially minorities—to cluster in certain neighborhoods, creating new stresses for social services and the social fabric in those communities. Even as the tax base shrinks, taxes often rise to meet low-income people's increased need for local government services, and problems more prevalent in poor communities intensify: crime, underachieving public schools and a culture of hopelessness. All of this, along with America's ongoing anxiety about race, fuels middle-class and business flight from these communities, usually in the direction of the newer suburbs that practice exclusionary zoning.

In a nutshell, this is the story of American cities since World War II. But it is not the way things must turn out. "If you want different outcomes," Rusk notes, "you need to change the rules. Fair Share housing is one of the key rules you need." The Portland, Oregon, metropolitan area recently incorporated Fair Share housing principles into its long-range regional plan, which will be implemented by local governments. "It's a huge victory," says local affordable-housing activist Tasha Harmon, who notes that a recent study shows a deficit of 35,000 low-income housing units in the region. "But there's a lot of work to do to see that it actually happens."

The Portland measure drew support not just from social justice activists, who believe that low- and middle-income people will be better able to fill the new jobs being created in upscale suburbs if they can live in the vicinity, but also from environmentalists, who see it as a chance to reduce auto traffic by allowing people who work in these booming communities to live closer to their jobs. Homebuilders, worried about how Fair Share housing would affect new-home sales, lobbied against the measure, and so did some suburban mayors who feared that their communities would be stuck with a disproportionate share of low-income housing. But because Portland's Fair Share principles are merely guidelines in a regional planning document, not concrete proposals being debated by a city council, there have been few objections from the public at large.

Measures designed to mix low-income housing into affluent suburbs usually spark substantial criticism wherever they are proposed. "Fair Share housing goes right to the heart of people's fear about race and class," Rusk notes. The fiercest opponents are people who think they've insulated themselves from the problems of modern urban life by settling in a suburb that practices exclusionary zoning. They often mount intense campaigns against Fair Share ordinances, framing their opposition as resistance to social engineering schemes rather than as unwillingness to live near poor or minority people.

Yet exclusionary zoning is social engineering in its purest form, Rusk points out. "You can see the social engineering right on the signs that say 'New Houses from $149,000.' " He adds that critics of Fair Share housing overlook the fact that mixing of incomes (although not races) was an ordinary feature of American life until the suburban boom of midcentury, when subdivisions began to be developed along strict economic lines and zoning codes became more exclusionary. Even silk-stocking neighborhoods in the years before World War II were sprinkled with inexpensive apartments above stores and the occasional boardinghouse.

Now, Myron Orfield explains, "people are afraid of affordable housing [because] they fear they will be the only ones to do it and they will get piled up on." In this sort of climate, how did Montgomery County enact such a far-reaching Fair Share housing policy? One answer is its form of government, in which the county board, rather than municipal government, is invested with most of the decision-making authority. This has made the Fair Share ordinance more effective and politically palatable: It covers the entire county with the exception of two older municipalities and six villages, so there is less fear about one community absorbing the social costs associated with low-income housing while others do not. Montgomery County's system represents a step toward the kind of regional government advocated by Rusk, Orfield and others proposing regional strategies for urban revitalization.

Another part of the answer is the particulars of the place. Montgomery County (population: 819,000)—probably better known to most people as the place where Bethesda, Silver Spring, Chevy Chase and Takoma Park are located—stood out in the sixties and seventies as a peculiar political anomaly: liberal suburbia. Many of the folks who came to Washington to work on New Frontier and Great Society social programs built houses in the suburban stretches of Maryland, bringing along their beliefs in can-do government. In 1965 it became one of the first places below the Mason-Dixon line to pass a fair housing law banning racial discrimination. By 1970, however, it became clear that racial integration would stall in this prosperous county if economic segregation was not addressed. The League of Woman Voters and local civil rights groups began pressing the county council for legislation to insure a supply of affordable housing in all neighborhoods. The result, after years of organizing and debate, was the Moderately Priced Housing law.

Developers immediately objected, claiming the ordinance violated their rights under the "takings" clause of the US Constitution, which has been interpreted to mean that citizens must be compensated when government action diminishes the value of their property. But the MPH law had been drafted with this objection in mind, and the county council decided that it did not violate the takings clause since developers were granted a density bonus: the opportunity to develop more units than zoning ordinances permitted in exchange for building the required affordable units. As they began constructing the affordable units (known as Moderately Priced Dwelling Units, or MPDUs) developers realized that the ordinance increased their profits, and they've been supportive of it ever since. Tom Doerr, a local developer, notes a distinct advantage of the program from the point of view of homebuilders: During periods when the housing market is slow they can continue constructing MPDUs, which are assured of immediate sales.

The MPDU program still encounters occasional resistance from local residents—especially as Montgomery County loses its distinction as a liberal bastion—who worry that lower-income households in their midst will drag down property values and spawn ghetto-style social problems. But a recently released study by the Innovative Housing Institute analyzed real estate transactions from 1992 to 1996 in eight Montgomery County subdivisions and found that the change in property values of homes located directly next to MPDUs was no different than that of other homes in the same subdivision or in the same ZIP code.

Deep-seated fears about poor and minority people are not easy to allay with statistics, but a twenty-year track record has convinced the vast majority of county residents that low-income people will not harm their neighborhoods. In researching his book, David Rusk door-knocked the streets of an upscale Montgomery County subdivision adjacent to MPDUs, asking people how they liked the neighborhood. In more than twenty interviews only two of the upscale homeowners even mentioned the MPDUs: a white retired Army colonel and an Asian-American realtor. The colonel, who was an officer of the homeowners association, admitted he was "a little apprehensive when I first moved into the neighborhood, but it's turned out OK." The realtor pointed out that although the units look the same at first glance, a closer look shows they were not constructed with the same overall quality, but added, "The county's housing laws are the best laws we have.... Montgomery County is a very good place."

This is the program's greatest achievement: proving that people can get along. "In 99 percent of the cases it works out fine," says Lillian Durham, assistant director of resident services for the Housing Opportunities Commission (HOC), Montgomery County's public housing authority. "People figure out how to get along. But when there are problems it's often about lifestyle. If there's a big family with a lot of people coming and going, the neighbors may think it's drug traffic."

Durham runs HOC's counseling services, which aim to head off cultural clashes between public housing families, 70 percent of whom are African-American, and others in a county that is 74 percent white. A counselor visits every public housing family soon after they move in, offering help with specific problems and general advice—such as, don't park cars on the lawn, don't go outside in pajamas or a bathrobe, don't yell at your kids out the window. To a large extent, poor and minority families are expected to conform to suburban middle-class standards, but in most cases they're willing to do it in exchange for what they see as the advantages of living in a well-off neighborhood.

"We don't want our units to stick out," notes Roy Appletree, assistant executive director of HOC, as he gets down on his knees to rearrange the position of a concrete drain basin so that it will better catch the flow of rainwater from a gutter spout. "And it's very important for our residents, too."

Appletree is giving me a tour of subdivisions with HOC properties, and to his satisfaction I can rarely guess the ones rented to public housing families. "The whole idea of this," Appletree says, "is that when you disperse low-income folks, institutions are better able to absorb problems—schools, recreation programs, hospitals. I hate correlating social needs with income, but there is a tipping point where a concentration of poor people overwhelms the local institutions. Like the hospital in a low-income neighborhood that gets all the hard emergency-room cases."

"Schools are the classic example," he adds, as we drive into another subdivision with a sign announcing "homes from the mid-$300,000s." We pass a school bus, with high school kids of all races and ethnicities jumping off and walking toward home in groups of twos and threes. "In these subdivisions you've got the rich, the middle class and the poor all going to school together. The kids socialize with each other. If there are kids with less support at home, at least here they are not so concentrated."

"Moving poor children and their families from an inner-city ghetto to a prosperous suburb is likely to increase their chances to do well in school," notes Rusk. "Even if the home environment is nurturing, a kid in an inner city is surrounded by poverty. He's surrounded by few examples of kids who have succeeded and done well in the world. There are no after-school jobs. Teachers and counselors at schools have lowered expectations. That's why I say housing policy is education policy."

Montgomery County's HOC rents about 1,000 MPDUs to low- and moderate-income families (out of a total of some 5,300 units of public housing in the county), while non-profit housing groups like the Interfaith Housing Coalition own a number of additional low-cost units. Even though the program is limited to people living or working in Montgomery County, it's still very competitive. Cutbacks in Department of Housing and Urban Development funding since the Republicans gained control of Congress in 1994 make matters worse because the housing authority now has very little money to purchase new MPDUs as they come up for sale.

The majority of Montgomery County's MPDUs are not rented to public housing families but sold to middle-income families as part of a program open to anyone living or working in Montgomery County who makes 65 percent or less of the county's $63,000 median household income. Again, it's a very competitive process. Eric Larsen, the county's MPDU coordinator, notes that 1,800 buyers are now on the waiting list for homes that are being built at the rate of 250 a year. However, because this program operates as an automatic part of the hous-

ing market—whenever new developments are built, new MPDUs are sold—it's not dependent on government funding beyond a few administrative costs.

Buyers of MPD homes in Montgomery County are 26 percent white, 46 percent Asian-American, 23 percent African-American and 5 percent Hispanic, with an average household income of $26,500. For people like Bonnie and Dave Ellsbury, a white couple who earn $10 an hour as a data entry worker and $12 an hour as an office furniture installer, it means they and their four children can afford to live in the county where they both grew up and now work. If they had not been able to buy their four-bedroom MPD house last year for $112,000 in a subdivision where most houses go for $200,000, they would have had to move out of the county to a cheaper area much farther from their jobs. Bonnie, 34, who lived in public housing for a number of years as a single mother, attended homebuying classes offered by HOC, one of many career and financial planning programs offered by the housing authority.

I love owning a house," she says. "The yard, it's not huge, but it's ours. The kids go to school with all the other kids in the neighborhood, and there's no problem. No one looks down on us."

"We have an awful lot of people who would not be living in this county if it were not for this program," notes Richard Ferrara, executive director of HOC. The Fair Share housing ordinance has made Montgomery County different from most suburban areas across the country, both in the idealistic goal of mixing households of different incomes and the perhaps more self-serving purpose of heading off urban decline in its own midst.

The complex set of economic, social and racial forces that have overwhelmed America's urban neighborhoods don't suddenly disappear at the city limits. Many suburbs, especially those adjacent to central cities, are now experiencing the same spiral of poverty, crime and decay as inner cities. They are losing middle-class residents and established businesses to newer developments springing up on the edges of metropolitan regions. These suburbs sometimes find themselves in worse shape than central cities. In metropolitan Los Angeles, for instance, eighty-six suburbs now have a lower tax base per household than the city.

The Fair Share housing ordinance protects Montgomery County from these trends by making sure that lower-income people are not concentrated in struggling communities. By limiting the scope of exclusionary zoning, Montgomery County has been able to stabilize its less wealthy communities and stem middle-class flight. The benefits of this are enjoyed not just by lower-income families who have access to a wider choice of places to live but by a large number of county residents who can be more secure that they won't one day feel forced to sell their homes out of fear of an encroaching ghetto.

"These policies represent a win-win solution all the way around," David Rusk explains. "You integrate lower-income families into middle-class communities and middle-class schools. And you don't add to the concentration of poverty in the older, more humble middle-class neighborhoods."

Are New England's Counties As Expendable As They Seem?

ALAN EHRENHALT

One by one, the counties of Massachusetts are becoming extinct. Middlesex, Hampden, Worcester and Franklin are already gone; two years from now, Essex, Hampsire and Berkshire will be gone as well.

Not in a geographical sense, of course. It will always be possible to look on a map and find where each one begins and ends. But as units of government—political entities that elect officers, raise money and do business— their career is over.

It has been a long career, if not always a distinguished one. County government was well established in Massachusetts in revolutionary times, when the word "Minuteman" was coined in the courthouse in Worcester, and Paul Revere rode through "every Middlesex village and farm" to warn about the British. It survived the early years of the Republic, when angry farmers stormed county seats all over the state and threatened violence if their debts were not canceled.

But it will not survive this century, at least not in most parts of Massachusetts. Two years from now, there won't be a functioning county courthouse west of Boston. Of the 14 counties that have existed largely intact since the 18th century, only half will retain any real governmental function at all.

You might expect this event to be the occasion for some tearful nostalgia, especially in a state that takes so much pride in its history. But you would be wrong. County government is disappearing in Massachusetts with scarcely a goodbye being uttered on anyone's part. Specialists in local affairs seem as happy as anyone to see it depart. Most of them appear to agree with Roberta Schaefer of the Worcester Municipal Research Bureau: "County government in Massachusetts is a disaster. It had to go."

Counties are different kinds of animals in different places. In much of America, especially rural America, it was the counties that came first, and the municipalities that followed later. County government became the primary unit of local public life, responsible for the crucial decisions on health, education, taxes and roads. The courthouse became the center of political power and intrigue.

It has never been that way in New England. There, the towns were first. Virtually every acre of colonial ground was incorporated as part of one town or another. There just wasn't much territory left that needed county government to look after it.

In fact, about the only indispensable function for counties in New England was to meet the requirements of the legal system. The states had to have courts, and the courts had to be divided into districts. Each district had judges, sheriffs and prosecutors, commissioners to levy property taxes for those operations, registrars to keep track of property, and clerks to run the elections.

That wasn't an enormous bureaucracy, even in the more populous areas, but it was enough to create a cozy nest of patronage positions and give New England counties a permanent role in state politics. By the 1950s, however, consensus was growing in the region that if this was all counties were going to do, they could just as easily be dispensed with. In 1958, Connecticut became the first to declare county government all but obsolete, turning the courts over to state control and eliminating all county offices and functions except one—an elected county sheriff to provide courthouse security, serve legal documents, transport prisoners, and stash away a few minor patronage jobs for hungry partisans. Rhode Island did virtually the same thing.

County government has hung on longer in Massachusetts. The counties have continued to elect not only sheriffs and registers of deeds but treasurers and boards of commissioners as well. All the municipalities in each

Reprinted with permission from *Governing* magazine, October 1998, pp. 7-8. © 1999 by Congressional Quarterly, Inc.

county pay a portion of their local property taxes for the upkeep of the county apparatus.

The problem is that most of the county governments no longer have the money to pay for even the modest roster of work that they are called upon to do. As a result of the statewide tax limitation amendment that became law in Massachusetts in the 1980s, no county can raise its taxes by more than 2½ percent in any one year. The inevitable result, for most of them, is either mounting debt or an emergency bailout by the state. Often, it is both.

In the western suburbs of Boston, Middlesex County—with nearly 1.5 million people, the largest jurisdiction in the state—had long been in hopeless financial shape when the state put it out of its misery in 1997. Before it could dispose of Middlesex, the legislature had to appropriate $24.6 million to pay off its debts and liquidate its assets. Even that wasn't enough; a bill appropriating $5.5 million more is under discussion right now.

Worcester County, second largest in Massachusetts after Middlesex, didn't get into quite as much trouble. Still, when it ceased operations on July 1, 1998, it faced unpaid bills of more than $10 million, most of them run up by a hospital. The state agreed to take care of those bills, but the residents of the now-defunct county will be paying off the state for the next 10 years, at about the same rate they were paying to keep the county government going. Any taxpayers counting on an immediate dividend from county extinction will be disappointed.

EVEN AN OLD COURTHOUSE nostalgia softie like me can't argue with much conviction that Massachusetts is making a big mistake. Given its history, its weaknesses and its financial condition, county government as constituted in the Bay State wasn't a very good investment.

But doing without it won't be painless, either. Massachusetts needs some layer of government between the state and its municipalities. Every state does. If you don't think so, think about what's happened in Connecticut in the past 40 years. Without any larger entity around them to deliver services, apportion tax money or plan for development, the cities of Hartford, New Haven and Bridgeport have fallen into depressing decline, plagued by a shrunken tax base and surrounded by affluent suburbs that show little interest in their problems.

The county government structure that Connecticut abolished in 1958, like the one Massachusetts is abolishing now, wasn't up to solving that problem. But suppose, instead of declaring its counties dead, Connecticut had launched an effort to re-create them as modern governments with serious regional responsibility. Would Bridgeport, Hartford and New Haven have become basket cases by the 1980s? I bet not.

Massachusetts thought about this, at least for a little while. Four years ago, a subcommittee of the legislature issued a white paper arguing that the proper course for the state was not to abolish its counties but to take advantage of the crisis to strengthen them. That course wasn't followed, in part because the money problems were so daunting and in part because the existing nests of courthouse cronyism seemed like poor material to build with.

But some of the localities around the state do seem to realize that they have created a vacuum, and that they need to fill it. Franklin County, whose citizens voted its government out of business, is trying to make its 26-town Council of Governments into a regional planning entity. The Worcester area has launched a Regionalism Education Project to try to figure out what to do now that the county functions there are gone. Most impressively, Barnstable County on Cape Cod has fought off extinction by taking steps to strengthen itself, taking on problems of sprawl, pollution, waste control and drug trafficking that its individual towns have found difficult to handle.

Not every part of the state has shown this much foresight. When Middlesex County disappeared last year, its individual communities chose to go their own separate ways, rejecting any idea of regional government altogether. That may happen in a majority of counties that go out of business in the next few years. Local rivalry and turf consciousness are hard to overcome.

They may be especially hard to overcome in Massachusetts, where some of the local entities have been quarreling with each other for the past 250 years. County government, at least in its first incarnation, didn't do much to bring them together. But that doesn't mean it isn't worth a second try.

Unit 6

Unit Selections

Key Points to Consider

❖ Approximately how much money do you (or your parents, if you are not a full-time wage earner) annually pay to local, state, and national governments, respectively? Is this an easy question to answer? Why or why not?

❖ Property tax, a tax on the value of real estate and buildings, is a primary source of revenue for local governments. Do you think people who live in rented apartments or houses avoid property taxes? Why or why not?

❖ Why do you think that the national government has assumed more and more of the burden for raising revenues for all three levels of government?

❖ What do you think is the best means for state and local governments to raise revenues: property taxes, income taxes, sales taxes, lotteries, user charges, or something else?

❖ Some people think that lotteries and casinos run by state governments are inappropriate or wrong because they contribute to the tendency of some citizens to gamble excessively. On the other hand, lotteries and casinos raise revenues for state and local governments. That, in turn, can reduce tax rates. All in all, do you support gambling operations as a way of financing state and local governments? Why or why not?

DUSHKIN ONLINE Links — www.dushkin.com/online/

24. **Assessor.com**
    http://www.assessor.com

25. **Council for Urban Economic Development (CUED)**
    http://www.cued.org

26. **Economic Development Administration**
    http://www.doc.gov/eda/

27. **Good Things Lotteries Do**
    http://www.gtech.com/good.htm

28. **National Association of Development Organizations (NADO)**
    http://www.nado.org/links/index.html

These sites are annotated on pages 4 and 5.

All governments need financial resources to carry out their activities. State and local governments rely on a variety of revenue sources, including sales taxes, income taxes, and property taxes; user charges (for example, motor vehicle registration fees and college tuition); lotteries; and grants of money from other levels of government. But despite this diversity of funding sources, the overall financial situation of state and local governments is often far from satisfactory.

Conspicuous attempts to curb spending at all levels of government have been made in recent decades. Most prominent among such measures was Proposition 13, passed by California voters in a 1978 referendum. Proposition 13 put ceilings on local government property taxes and, in turn, affected the programs that local governments in California could offer. The Proposition 13 tax revolt soon spread to other states. By now, measures designed to limit government spending have come into effect in states and localities across the country. At the national level, a constitutional amendment has been proposed and legislation has been passed in attempts to make it difficult for Congress to adopt an unbalanced budget.

Unlike the national government, state and local governments get a sizable portion of their revenues from intergovernmental grants. The national government gives money to state and local governments with various conditions attached. Money can be given with virtually no accompanying strings or with considerable limitations on how it can be spent. Similarly, states provide state aid to local governments under varying sets of conditions. Governments providing financial grants, of course, exercise control over the amount of funds available and the conditions attached to such funds. This, in turn, can cause considerable uncertainty for governments relying on grant money. As should be apparent, intergovernmental relations and state and local government finances are areas that overlap considerably.

The financial situation of state and local governments differs from that of the national government in other important respects. The national government has considerable ability to affect the national economy by controlling the money supply and by budgetary deficits or, at least in theory, budgetary surpluses. By contrast, most state and local governments are legally required to balance their budgets. For those not required to have balanced budgets, it is difficult to borrow money for large and persistent budget deficits. The fiscal crises of New York City and other local governments during the 1970s showed that lenders will go only so far in providing money for state and local governments whose expenditures are consistently greater than their revenues. The declaration of bankruptcy by Orange County, California, in late 1994 reveals how tempting it is for local governments to pursue risky, although potentially very profitable, investment strategies, especially in difficult financial times. In 1997, several dozen school districts in Pennsylvania learned a similar lesson. Risky investment decisions made on their behalf by a reputed "financial wizard" resulted in the loss of millions of dollars and jeopardized the school districts' financial futures.

The national government, state governments, and local governments all seek to promote economic development. New industries employ workers who pay taxes and, thus, increase government revenues. What is new on the state and local scene is the energy and persistence with which states and localities compete with one another to attract industries to their areas.

Finances are a complicated but critical aspect of state and local government. The first section of this unit treats taxes, lotteries, and related revenue-raising matters. The second section focuses on activities of state and local governments related to economic development.

FINANCE

Taxing the Weightless Economy

BY PENELOPE LEMOV

**Most state tax systems are geared toward an age
of heavy industry that ended a long time ago.
Sooner or later, they will have to change.**

WEST VIRGINIA IS taking on a job that many other
states have declared to be impossible: It is getting ready
to rewrite its tax code from top to bottom. It's not just
talking about broadening the base, or tinkering with the
rate structure. It's re-examining every assumption it has
about the way it collects revenue for public purposes.

When the state's legislators convened in January, they
found a 47-page executive report from the Governor's
Commission on Fair Taxation sitting on their desks. After
the regular session is over, they will most likely be called
back to Charleston for a special session that will take up
taxes and nothing else. When the meeting is over, tax reformers hope, the state will have a tax code suitable for
the future, rather than the past.

It certainly doesn't have one now. The current tax system is weighted down with dependency on the struggling
coal industry and on a whole array of heavy-duty goods,
many of which are manufactured elsewhere and bought
and sold within the state.

But if the commission gets its way, West Virginia will start the new century with a less regressive personal-income tax; a general excise levy on goods and services instead of the current exemption-riddled sales tax; elimination of many of the quirky personal-property-tax categories; and—most important—a single tax on business to replace a multitude of narrow-based taxes that bedevil some industries but don't apply to others.

The new business tax would hit every corporation, store and other commercial enterprise that does business in the state—but it wouldn't necessarily hit them hard. The tax, based on a value-added approach, would be pegged to a relatively low rate and would focus on such big-ticket items as payroll, rent, interest, profits and depreciation.

The momentum for all these changes began with the need to find a new funding mechanism for statewide education, but it's being driven by a recognition that, as Shawn Konchesky of the taxation commission puts it, "we have a patchwork of laws, many of them coming out of the Depression, that don't reflect the shifts going on in the economy. We want a system that will be stable for the 21st century."

Most other states don't have West Virginia's problem, but that's largely a question of degree. Virtually all of them are running tax systems geared to yesterday—to a "heavy" economy based on old-fashioned industrial production. If it isn't coal, it's steel, or textiles, or furniture. But as we all know, that isn't the economy they have anymore. The new economy is "light," or maybe "weightless" is the proper word. It's an economy based on the exchange of services and information, not the movement of bulky goods. It's an economy in which companies find it easy to leave the asphalt streets and large office buildings of a downtown location in one city and set up an office in a suburb or even a rural hamlet in another state or country—using the airiness of fax lines, computer connections and telecommunications to stay in touch.

Thirty years ago, goods accounted for roughly half of the gross domestic product in the United States, while services totaled about 40 percent. Today, goods are below 40 and services have zipped beyond the 60 percent mark. Moreover, as the weightless economy floats toward the 21st century, the goods that are produced in America are increasingly less dependent for distribution on the brick-and-mortar structures of stores. Books, clothing and even automobiles are moving from manufacturer to consumer over the evanescence of the Internet.

The list of heavy-duty taxes unsuited to a weightless economy is a long one. Manufacturing companies, for example, don't have to tolerate heavy taxation of capital equipment and inventory. They can pick up

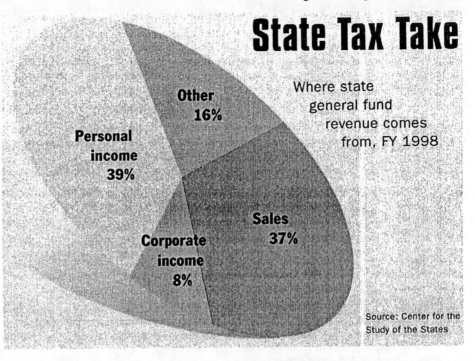

State Tax Take

Where state general fund revenue comes from, FY 1998

- Other 16%
- Personal income 39%
- Corporate income 8%
- Sales 37%

Source: Center for the Study of the States

warehoused stock and equipment-laden plants and move to more tax-hospitable environments. They do it every day.

Industry-specific taxes on telecommunications and electric utilities are increasingly impractical as these former monopolies compete to survive. Localities that rely heavily on the value of electricity plants for local

There's no good time to rewrite a tax code. But a time of surplus is better than most.

property taxes will be hit hard by deregulation and, under the current rules, will be all but forced to shift their property-tax burden to homeowners—the most politically perilous thing they can do.

And state taxes are no longer positioned to capture revenue from the areas of the economy that are growing fastest. The most dramatic example is the Internet: As more and more of the goods that are produced are sold by the likes of Amazon.com and eBay—nearly $8 billion in consumer goods

and $40 billion in business-to-business products were sold over the Internet last year—sales-tax collections dry up.

For the next three years, states and localities are precluded by federal law from taxing Internet transactions. If the ban is eventually lifted, states will be challenged to find a politically acceptable way of taxing this activity. And if it is not lifted, they face an even tougher task: maintaining an adequate overall fiscal base with a large chunk of their economies exempt.

There is no easy time to rewrite a tax code. But you might argue that the present moment, with most budgets in surplus, is about as good a time as states will ever get, and they should take advantage of the opportunity. A few of them, like West Virginia, have thought of that. But only a few.

Why? Beyond the obvious problem of short political time horizons, many states appear unmotivated to work on tax reform because of the good times themselves. "What is operating," says James Papke, a public-finance professor at Purdue University, "is a feeling of complacency, that this will go on forever."

Tax-revenue collection is startlingly robust in so many places, and revenue has been running so far ahead of forecasts, that institutional memories may be slipping. How many governors or legislators want to recall the big budget deficits or the cash shortfalls early in the decade that led some to delay paying vendors or defer pension contributions? Only half a dozen years ago, California's budget was such a deficit-ridden mess that the state treasurer ended up printing IOUs while legislators grappled with the dilemma. Now California, like most other states, is awash in money: Its 1998 haul from income taxes in the third quarter was up more than 12 percent over the same quarter in the previous year, and sales taxes inched up some 6 percent over 1997, itself a very healthy year. So perhaps it is no surprise that California is among the vast majority of states making no effort to push open what may be a small window of tax-reform opportunity.

Still, some are trying—if not massively, like West Virginia, then one step at a time. Here and there, tax rates are being adjusted to modern reality, and tax credits are being rewritten for the purpose of enhancing future economic growth. Following the lead that Virginia established last year, old-fashioned taxes on certain categories of personal property—automobiles in particular—are being eliminated in a number of states. Others are moving incrementally to modernize the base for consumption taxes, including in the base such services as dry cleaning and admission tickets to amusement parks and the movies. For the first time in several years, there is some talk of taxing professional services. It is a quiet effort at best and one that is likely to become louder only when the economy slows its pace—although, ironically, that will be a more difficult time to get the job done.

If there is a pattern among the states that seem willing to work on tax reform this year, it is that activity is more pronounced in those places where the current system is noticeably out of balance and creating political problems as a result.

New Jersey, for instance, has the highest per-capita property taxes in the country, a situation that some trace in part to the state income-tax cut engineered by Governor Christine Todd Whitman in 1994. Two years ago, the property-tax problem almost cost Whitman reelection. When the legislature convened this January, she proposed using state money to buy down individual property-tax burdens. Since Republicans are in the majority, the legislature is likely to deliver on Whitman's promise—to help a fellow Republican and to avoid association with the dangerous property-tax problem.

Other states are struggling with imbalance because they have never enacted one of the traditional elements of the standard tax repertoire, a sales or personal-income tax.

New Hampshire doesn't have either one. And as the legislature opened its session this winter, it was in political extremis: The state supreme court had ruled the system of funding education unconstitutional because of its heavy reliance on local property taxes. The governor and lawmakers were given until April 1 to institute a fairer system, which will cost somewhere between $600 million and $900 million, according to the current range of estimates. Legislators are trying to avoid creating an income tax or sales tax to raise the money—if they have to add something, a statewide property tax seems more palatable to most of them. But one thing is certain: A year from now, New Hampshire will have a substantially different tax code, not because of innovation but because of desperation.

Wyoming, which has also struggled with court-ordered school finance changes, does not have quite as eccentric a tax system as New Hampshire's. But it collects no income tax, and as a result is overly dependent on the mineral revenues that sustained its economy in a much different time. "Our tax policies are virtually on one industry," says state Representative John Hines, who chairs both the tax-reform and revenue committees. "When their prices are down, as coal and oil prices currently are, the state really hurts for finances."

> *Everybody wants to see some experiments. But they want the experiments to take place somewhere else.*

During the past decade, Wyoming has seen state spending increase by 29.7 percent, while revenues increased by only 13.5 percent. One study estimates that overall revenues will need to rise by 1 percent a year over the next eight years just to maintain existing services to its school system.

This year, Hines' tax-reform committee recommended adding a personal-income levy to the tax mix. It has also been looking at ways to boost the haul from sales taxes, which are crucial to state revenue and are threatened, as in other places, by catalog and Internet sales. The suggestions include broadening the sales-tax base to professional services, which would make the tax somewhat less regressive since those services tend to be used by wealthier individuals.

None of these have been popular suggestions. "They say a revenue committee is a good way to end your career," Hines jokes, noting that a personal-income tax in particular is not something constituents are wild about. "But whether it's popular or not," he says, "it should be discussed."

Neighboring Montana, also short on revenue, has the opposite problem: an income tax but no sales tax. Voters have repeatedly and unambiguously rejected the idea of adding a sales tax, even though local property taxes have grown particularly burdensome and the top income-tax brackets are among the highest in the country. Moreover, old-fashioned taxes on heavy equipment tend to make Montana an expensive place for manufacturers to do business. "The state's tax system," one of the state's leading newspapers editorialized recently, "is poorly balanced, full of inequities and downright unfriendly to new business and industry."

In other words, Montana's tax system is particularly unsuited to the modern weightless economy, a point not lost on Governor Marc Racicot, who has put his considerable popularity behind a drive for comprehensive tax revision that, among other things, would eliminate the levy on business equipment and replace it with a business-consumption tax. Every corporation in the state would pay a 4 percent value-added tax on the total of its labor costs, depreciation, interest and profit. Many businesses would no doubt pass the tax on to consumers.

Racicot would lessen the pain of the new system by spending some of the VAT-raised money on property-tax relief for homeowners and businesses, a reduction in motor-vehicle taxes and lower income-tax rates. Nonetheless, his ideas have drawn little support in the legislature, even among his own Republican majority. The legislature seems more interested in asking voters, who have already shown their disdain for a sales tax, to vote on it by referendum one more time.

Tennessee, which has never had a personal-income tax but which faces no particular fiscal crisis at the moment, seems a little further along on the road to significant change. Governor Don Sundquist is promoting a plan that combines a narrowing of the sales-tax base (grocery foods would be exempt) with a replacement of the state's franchise and excise tax by a 2.5 percent tax on business profits and payrolls.

The reason for this change is the proliferation of limited-liability companies, which pay minimal fees for the right to do business in the state. Since the LLC option was created in 1994, it has been possible for Tennessee businesses to generate profits and pass them along as personal wealth to individuals, who in turn face no personal tax on that money. The result has been a serious revenue drain.

Sundquist's tax program has drawn heated opposition from elements of the state's business community—particularly small businesses, which fear that they will be hurt by it most. Still, the governor has made tax revision the centerpiece of his second and final term, and seems destined to achieve at least a good portion of what he is asking for.

ut when it comes to sheer ambition and scope, the main event is the one in West Virginia, where tax reformers are not only calling for a complete overhaul of the system but are asking the legislature to approve it on an all-or-nothing basis. "If you take away one of the funding mechanisms, it will pull the system out of whack," Konchesky explains. "You can't take away a leg of the table. It won't stand."

In order to get the package enacted, the reformers will have to convince the state's most important legislator, Speaker Bob Kiss, who currently admits to having some doubts. Kiss doesn't deny that the tax code as it stands is poorly suited to the 21st century. But he is nervous about such drastic change.

"Stability is a big issue here," he says, noting that even under the current flawed tax code, West Virginia has erased a $300 million budget deficit and attracted considerable new business in the 1990s. A Toyota plant, which set up shop in Buffalo and started production a few months ago, is bringing in 800 new jobs to replace ones being lost in the coal industry. "If we start making changes, we may wind up with a two-, three- or four-fold increase in tax burdens," Kiss warns. "So that's worrisome. We don't want to rock the boat."

It's rational to be worried. The reform commission's proposed single business tax would take off the books hundreds of millions of dollars in existing revenue and replace it with the take from an entirely new levy with a very limited track record. Only Michigan, and to a lessor extent New Hampshire, have value-added taxes right now, and Michigan, with an economy still dominated largely by giant auto companies, has little in common with West Virginia. The VAT could end up shifting some of the fiscal burden to small businesses—and West Virginia is, more than most, a state of small businesses. "It may make even more sense to move slowly," Kiss says. "Maybe we don't want to be almost the only state with a VAT. We may not want to be the only state in the nation that applies a sales tax to professional services. Although we all will be forced to go there, we're not sure we want to be the first."

From a national perspective, a large part of the problem is that *nobody* really wants to take the risk—every state would like to watch somebody else experiment with a 21st-century tax system, and then take advantage of the lessons learned, the painful as well as the pleasant ones.

But as Kiss admits, somebody has to go first. At the moment, West Virginia is the closest thing we have to a volunteer.

It's Not a Miracle, It's a Mirage

As more and more states legalize gambling, its benefits as a revenue source become more and more dubious.

Steven D. Gold

Steven Gold is the director of the Center for the Study of the States, Nelson A. Rockefeller Institute of Government, State University of New York. A version of this article appeared in *State Fiscal Brief* published by the center.

Casino mania is sweeping the country. Until a few years ago, the only places where intrepid gamblers could legally try their luck at blackjack or slot machines were Nevada or New Jersey. Now at least 10 states (not counting Indian reservations) authorize casinos, and all signs points to a rapid proliferation of gambling palaces from coast to coast.

New forms of state-sponsored gambling—like video poker machines and keno—are popping up. And 37 states offer lotteries.

One of the main reasons for the popularity of legalizing new forms of gambling is the lure of easy money. With legislators struggling to balance state budgets and citizens resisting tax increases, gambling looks like a bonanza—a way to raise revenue painlessly and at the same time spur economic development.

Unfortunately, expectations about the benefits of gambling are wildly inflated because:
• It is unrealistic to expect gambling to generate enough revenue for states to significantly reduce reliance on taxes.
• As casinos open in ever more states, their potential for producing state revenue and stimulating economic development diminishes. Casinos are most beneficial when they attract many residents from outside states. As more states have casinos, more competition will exist among them, and fewer out-of-state residents will be attracted to any particular state.

People often are confused about the role of gambling in state finances for three reasons:
• Failure to distinguish between gross and net revenue: For example, in 1991 state lottery sales were $19.2 billion. But $10.4 billion was paid out in prizes and $1.2 billion went for administration, leaving $7.6 billion for state coffers. In other words, only 40 percent of lottery sales were available for state programs after paying out prizes and covering administrative costs.
• Not understanding relative magnitudes: $7.6 billion sounds like a lot of money, and it is from many perspectives. But total state tax revenue in 1991 was $311 billion. Lotteries pro-

duced less than 2.5 percent as much as taxes; excluding the states that did not have lotteries, the proportion rises to 3.2 percent. Lottery revenue looks like small change compared to the revenue from sales and income taxes.
• Counting revenue gains from newly initiated lotteries: State lottery revenue increased nearly sevenfold between 1980 and 1991. Some of this increase came from expansion of the 13 lotteries that existed at that time. But most of the growth is attributable to new lotteries, which sprang up in 19 additional states.

Composition of Gambling Revenue

The biggest contributor to gambling revenue in most states is the lottery. In 1991 lotteries generated $7.6 billion in net revenue. By 1993, this had risen to approximately $9.3 billion.

These figures include not only traditional lotteries (scratch cards, lotto games, etc.) but also so-called video lotteries, which are often nothing more than video poker games. Although these games are essentially a form of the slot machine, they are called video lotteries because the state lottery organization oversees them or the

From *State Legislatures*, February 1994, pp. 28–31. © 1994 by the National Conference of State Legislatures. Reprinted by permission.

euphemism apparently makes them more morally and politically acceptable.

Lotteries look enormous compared to the revenue states receive from pari-mutuel taxes (mostly from bets on horse races but also from dog tracks and jai alai). In 1991, revenue from that source was only $635 million. This was 3.5 percent less than the year before, which in turn was 1.2 percent less than revenue in 1989. In fact, pari-mutuel taxes are the slowest growing source of state tax revenue. In 1991, they produced less for states than they did in 1980 when they raised $731 million.

Pari-mutuel tax revenue has been hurt by competition from lotteries and by the waning popularity of horse racing. In response to the economic problems of racetracks, many states have reduced their taxes on the industry. Thus, although betting at tracks has grown slowly, revenue has actually decreased.

What about casinos? Nevada's gambling and casino entertainment taxes in 1991 produced $348 million, along with another $57 million from licenses for slot machines and other games. These taxes brought in about 24 percent of Nevada's tax revenue. When other business taxes and the tourism it produces are counted, the gaming industry accounts for about half of Nevada's state tax revenue. But Nevada is unique. It combines a population of less than 1.5 million with a huge gambling industry. Gambling could not have nearly as much impact on state finances in a more populous state.

Consider, for example, New Jersey, population nearly 8 million, where the state's take in 1991 was $246 million in casino gross revenue taxes, along with another $50 million from licenses for casinos and slot machines. New Jersey's total state tax revenue was $11.6 billion, so these taxes and license fees were only about 2.5 percent of that total. Even if the taxes paid indirectly through spending at hotels, restaurants and other establishments are included, gambling accounts for less than 4 percent of state taxes.

A Closer Look at Lottery Revenue

The table on this page shows lottery revenue available for state programs in 1991 in relation to population and total tax revenue. Massachusetts had the highest lottery revenue per capita, $78. The lottery produced more than $50 per capita in eight other states (Connecticut, Florida, Illinois, Maryland, New Jersey, New York, Ohio and Pennsylvania). In general, per capita

State Tax and Lottery Revenue Per $1000 of Personal Income, 1980 and 1991

Tax	1980	1991
Total	$6.79	$6.70
General sales	2.14	2.23
Personal income	1.84	2.14
Motor fuel	0.48	0.45
Corporate income	0.66	0.44
Motor vehicle licenses	0.24	0.22
Other licenses	0.12	0.13
Insurance	0.15	0.13
Public utilities	0.17	0.12
Tobacco	0.19	0.09
Property	0.14	0.07
Severance	0.21	0.07
Death and gift	0.10	0.04
Alcoholic Beverages	0.12	0.01
Corporation licenses	0.07	0.11
Document Transfer	0.04	0.04
Pari-mutuels	**0.04**	**0.01**
Other	0.08	0.11
Lotteries	**0.05**	**0.18**

Note: Personal income excludes District of Columbia.

Source: U.S. Census Bureau, *State Government Finances;* personal income provided by U.S. Bureau of Economic Analysis, estimates as of Sept. 2, 1992.

revenue tends to be considerably higher in urban than rural states.

Lottery revenue is a small factor in state revenue systems. Lotteries in 1991 raised only 3.2 percent as much as taxes (counting only the states where lotteries existed).

Compared to other states, lottery revenue is the highest proportion of total state tax revenue in Florida (6.1 percent) and in South Dakota (5.6 percent). Both of these states have relatively low tax revenue, in part because they are among the nine states that do not impose a personal income tax. Florida benefits from lottery purchases by tourists while South Dakota was the national pioneer in allowing widespread video lotteries.

South Dakota's video lottery revenue continued to shoot up after 1991, primarily due to higher tax rates. The state raised the tax rate from 20 percent to 25 percent in January 1991 and

then to 35 percent. Recently it went up to 36 percent. Per capita net revenue to the state from video lotteries was about $68 in FY 1993, far higher than any other state. Oregon, which has the second most successful video lottery operation, projects per capita revenue of $32 in FY 1994.

Lottery revenue has grown surprisingly slowly if one excludes expansion due to adoption by additional states. Between 1985 and 1991, lottery revenue rose more slowly than other tax revenue, falling from 3.7 percent to 3.2 percent of total revenue in states with lotteries. To some extent, this drop occurred because lotteries were not very productive in many of the states where they started after 1985. But the growth of lottery revenue also lagged behind that of tax revenue in several states with well established lotteries, including Maryland, New Jersey, Illinois, Pennsylvania, Michigan and Rhode Island.

Lotteries differ from other sources of revenue in several respects, one of which is that they need substantial marketing effort to produce increased money for the state. Much of the growth of revenue has been attributable to introduction of new games, and lotteries have to be advertised extensively to maintain interest.

By the late 1980s, many state lotteries had already adopted the features that have been successful in stimulating interest and increasing participation. Future growth probably depends heavily on nontraditional games like video lotteries and club keno.

Gambling Is No Panacea

- Lotteries, casinos and other forms of gambling cannot generally produce enough state tax revenue to significantly reduce reliance on other taxes or to solve a serious state fiscal problem.

- As ever more states allow casinos, the potential economic development and tax benefits diminish greatly.

- Lotteries produced $7.6 billion for state programs in 1991, which represented only 3.2 percent of tax revenue in the states that had lotteries.

- Pari-mutuel taxes were the slowest growing sources of state tax revenue between 1980 and 1991.

State Lottery Revenues

Fiscal Years 1985 and 1991

State	1991	Rank	Per Capita 1985	Rank	Percent of Tax Revenue 1991	1985
National Average	*$40.74*		*$34.99*		*3.16%*	*3.51%*
Massachusetts	78.46	1	40.51	4	4.86	3.60
Maryland	68.98	2	59.74	1	5.24	6.10
New Jersey	67.83	3	51.31	2	4.52	5.03
Florida	64.34	4			6.21	
Connecticut	60.10	5	39.99	5	3.97	3.66
Ohio	58.10	6			5.50	
New York	52.31	7	32.15	7	3.34	2.76
Illinois	50.59	8	45.11	3	4.39	5.57
Pennsylvania	50.30	9			4.62	
Michigan	45.81	10	39.57	6	3.87	4.14
South Dakota	41.80	11			5.56	
Virginia	41.18	12			3.78	
Delaware	37.15	13	22.48	8	2.17	1.70
New Hampshire	30.67	14	4.21	13	5.43	0.97
Maine	27.85	15	3.77	14	2.21	0.44
Indiana	26.95	16			2.45	
California	25.50	17			1.73	
Rhode Island	24.75	18	18.32	9	1.98	2.06
Wisconsin	24.42	19			1.72	
Arizona	22.92	20	7.15	12	1.82	0.77
Vermont	22.25	21	1.74	15	1.84	0.20
Washington	19.67	22	10.69	10	1.24	1.03
Colorado	16.67	23	9.02	11	1.75	1.27
Idaho	15.57	24			1.34	
Minnesota	14.88	25			0.94	
Kentucky	14.65	26			1.08	
West Virginia	13.76	27			1.06	
Iowa	13.69	28			1.11	
Missouri	12.68	29			1.31	
Oregon	12.41	30			1.20	
Kansas	8.87	31			0.79	
Montana	5.52	32			0.55	

Note: Revenue excludes prizes and administrative costs.

Source: U.S. Census Bureau, *State Governmental Finances.*

Cannibalism

The figures cited for state revenue produced by gambling do not consider negative effects on tax revenue. If people buy lottery tickets or lose money at a casino, they have less income available to spend on goods and services subject to the sales tax or excise taxes, like gasoline, alcoholic beverages and cigarettes.

Relatively little research is available on the extent of such cannibalism. According to Mary Borg and associates, who issued a report, *The Economic Consequences of State Lotteries,* the magnitude of the tax loss depends on whether a state relies heavily on sales and excise taxes or whether it imposes a substantial personal income tax. The impact is larger in states that rely more on consumption taxes. They generalize that the loss of tax revenue is usually less than 15 percent of lottery revenue, although it can go as high as 23 percent.

For casinos, the impact on tax revenue depends not only on the state tax system but also on the extent to which casinos attract gamblers from out of state. It is more positive if the casino is part of a destination resort rather than being patronized heavily by day-trippers.

Economic Development Benefits

In addition to the revenue that states receive directly from taxes on casinos and places like racetracks, they also benefit indirectly from the employment created there and at businesses like hotels and restaurants that serve their patrons.

Once again, the magnitude of this economic benefit depends on the extent to which patrons live in or out of state. If they are in-state residents, their spending on gambling takes away from their outlays on lotteries and products subject to the sales tax.

As casinos spread across the landscape, their economic development potential diminishes because it becomes increasingly difficult to attract a high proportion of out-of-staters. Except in Nevada, the gaming industry is not large enough to make a big difference in a state's economy.

Magnitude Not as Great as Thought

The point of this analysis is not that gambling fails to add to state revenue. It does. Because of gambling, states can increase their spending and provide more service. But the magnitude of this effect is not as great as people often think. The potential revenue from gambling is relatively limited when viewed in the overall context of a state budget.

The benefits of gambling need to be weighed against its regressivity and the social costs that are often associated with it:

• Easier access increases the prevalence of compulsive gambling. Few if any states have established effective programs to deal with that.

• Casinos require substantial investments in public infrastructure and increases in services like police protection. Their costs should be subtracted from gambling. (This point applies to any job-creating activity, not just casinos.)

• Gambling tends to undermine the work ethic. It is particularly questionable for a state government to spend heavily on advertising that encourages "get rich quick" dreams when the odds are heavy that playing a lottery will make one poorer, not richer.

We appear to be on the threshold of an unprecedented situation. In the past, casinos in the United States and Europe have usually been located in remote vacation settings. If in a large city, they usually catered to a limited, elite clientele. Now for the first time we are likely to have large casinos in big cities open to the masses. The social consequences could be more serious than we have seen in the past.

The momentum toward widespread availability of casinos and games of chance like video lotteries and keno appears irresistible. If it were just a matter of providing people with new forms of entertainment—that would be one thing. But as a painless way to solve the fiscal problems of state government, gambling is a mirage.

THE GAME OF
MYSTERY BUCKS

We all know where lotteries get their money. What's not so clear is where the money ends up.

BY ELLEN PERLMAN

When the Florida lottery was created 10 years ago, it was marketed as a way to support a good cause: education. Schools and colleges were to benefit from every ticket bought, adding a hefty boost to what the state was already spending on education. To make the point even more unmistakable, the fund set up to receive the lottery money was named the "Florida Educational Enhancement Trust Fund."

Not many people call it that anymore. The program's critics, of whom there are many, think that a more appropriate name might be something like "The Fund to Fill in Budget Holes After the Legislature Shifts Education Spending Somewhere Else." In their view, the state is merely playing a shell game, using lottery money to supplant general revenue funds for education, while the legislature reassigns those dollars to Medicaid, corrections and social services.

They have a point. When the lottery was introduced in 1988, the state was spending 60 percent of its budget on education. Once the lottery was in place, the percentage started dropping. By 1993, it was down to 51 percent. Nobody could say precisely how the lottery dollars were improving education—or which fiscal column they were ending up in.

The state does, in fact, place 100 percent of the lottery money in the Educational Enhancement Trust Fund. But the legislature, knowing those dollars are there, is perfectly free to take away other dollars it would have spent on schools if the lottery didn't exist. That is exactly what it does.

Indeed, that is what happens in many, if not most, of the states that earmark lottery funds. Of the 37 state lotteries now in existence, two-thirds promise that the proceeds will go toward helping particular departments or programs. Ten states direct money toward education, as Florida does. Fifteen others earmark money for tourism, parks and recreation, economic development, public buildings or other purposes. Sometimes they divvy up the pot among more than one of those. But while the state government bottom line may improve when lottery money comes in, it is nearly always misleading to say the money benefits a particular program or department.

Frequently, of course, a promise to earmark the proceeds is the tool used to gain the political support that got the lottery started in the first place. People might lose their money on a lottery ticket, it is claimed, but their dollars will shore up favored programs or departments. They are rarely told that an influx of lottery money simply generates a chain reaction, often making it a zero-sum game for the earmarked cause in the end. "It's a little subterfuge," says Robert Goodman, executive director of the United States Gambling Research Institute. "The public is led to believe that some goody-goody program is getting the benefit when it's actually the governmental structure."

Oregon earmarks lottery money for economic development, job creation and education. Most of the education money goes into a designated State Schools Fund, but not to any identifiable program. The legislature simply treats it as general revenue for education. "It pays for books, teachers' salaries, heating and everything else," says David Hooper, spokesman for the Oregon lottery. "It goes into the big melting pot of school finance." As in Florida, the lottery money is not a supplement to education spending; it is a replacement for part of it.

The same appears to be true for economic development. "It's obvious you can treat the lottery and the general fund as a single pot," says Bill Scott, Oregon's economic development director. "They give us as much money as they want. I don't think we're particularly benefiting from the lottery allocation."

Even where lottery money has been melting into the general treasury for years, state officials often can't resist portraying it as something it is not. In Virginia, for example, all of the money raised by the lottery has gone into the general fund since the program's creation in 1988. But the legislature nevertheless portrays it as earmarked education money, and the Virginia lottery has run advertisements announcing just how much it is turning over to the state in a given year to support public education.

This past year, the ad ran into a storm of ridicule from critics who called it deceptive, insisting that the lottery in no way increases the bottom-line amount the state spends on schools. The state's education budget is more than $8 billion, and the lottery contributes less than $350 million, so the effect of the "earmarking" is insignificant anyway.

"There's absolutely no point in earmarking except for fooling people into thinking we were doing something for education when we didn't do a thing," says House Minority Leader S. Vance Wilkins Jr. "It didn't change the budget one penny. It's a sham."

Penelope Kyle, the head of the Virginia lottery, ultimately issued an apology. "We absolutely did not intend for the announcement to imply that the lottery contributed $343 million on top of what the General Assembly had previously appropriated for educational purposes," she wrote. Future ads will tell Virginians that the lottery proceeds go to the general fund, which supports education as well as other programs and services.

The lottery shell game and its resulting confusion hurts the education cause in more ways than one. Polls have found that people will vote against referendums to spend more on schools if they figure the lottery is already paying for them. When the Florida lottery was created, says Brewser Brown of the Florida Education Department, "voters thought the order of magnitude of money would be tremendous. They thought they would never have to pass a tax or a bond issue because with the lottery you'd hit the jackpot." They balk when they're asked to tax themselves for schools. "People say, 'What the hell did you do with the lottery money?' "

Of course, there's an answer to that, but it's not a very satisfactory answer: The lottery money floated away into the general fund, and it's a pittance when it comes to solving the state's education needs anyway.

Is it possible for a state to create a lottery law that does guarantee extra money to a favored cause? Apparently, yes. Georgia seems to have done it.

All the funds from the Georgia lottery are earmarked not just for education but for specific education programs that didn't exist before the lottery started up. The proceeds pay for three things—college scholarships, pre-kindergarten classes and technology for classrooms. It is illegal to use it for anything else. "Not a dime of it goes to the general fund, so it doesn't get lost," says Steve Tompkins, spokesman for the Georgia Student Finance Commission.

In the three years since Georgia's lottery started up, state funding for education has increased from 52 percent to nearly 54 percent. "Georgia clearly has a different take on the lottery, in some ways a much better one," says Robert Goodman. "The budget for

> **Georgia ties its lottery to a scholarship fund, not to the overall education budget.**

scholarships is tied to it, not the education budget."

Some 62,000 children now are attending pre-kindergarten classes funded with lottery money. More than 275,000 students have attended college on the lottery-subsidized HOPE (Helping Outstanding Pupils Educationally) scholarship. The clear connection between gambling and the new programs may be one reason Georgia's lottery has been more successful than projected, increasing its sales each year. "People can actually see what the money goes to," Tompkins says. "People pumping gas will go in and buy a lottery ticket because they have kids on a HOPE scholarship or in pre-kindergarten."

Of course, good sales are not unusual for a new lottery. If Georgia is like most other states, those sales records are likely to falter at some point. Lotteries tend to experience a drop after a few years, when the novelty has worn off. If that happens, the pre-kindergarten and scholarship programs will be vulnerable, since they are not allowed to dip into the general fund money pot, as they would be in other states.

In any case, the early returns from Georgia have been so positive that other states seem likely to follow its lead. New Mexico

has already done that. When it created its lottery in 1995, it chose to guarantee 60 percent to public school construction and 40 percent to a tuition fund for students to go to state colleges and universities. None of it will disappear into the general fund.

What is not so clear is whether the Georgia solution will help states such as Florida, where lotteries are deeply entrenched under a different system and where legislatures are accustomed to using the money simply as a way of offsetting other costs.

Florida is actually seeking to reform its lottery financing rules in hopes of generating more public support. Last year it created the Bright Futures Scholarship Program, modeled after Georgia's HOPE scholarship. And this past November, when the legislature decided to issue bonds to ease school overcrowding and pay for school construction and repairs, it specifically assigned lottery funds to pay the $180 million-a-year debt.

Florida had to do something. Mounting market research data had shown that the public was catching on to the lottery shell game, realizing that the money being added to the Educational Enhancement Trust Fund really wasn't enhancing education, but merely covering costs somewhere else in the budget.

Brewser Brown, of the state education department, argues more of these sorts of changes are inevitable. "People are angry," Brown says. He believes the only way the lottery can restore its reputation is by designing airtight rules that really do require the money to go where it is supposed to go. "Otherwise," he warns, "the people of Florida are going to continue to be confused and disgusted."

Two Cheers for the Property Tax

Everyone hates it, but the property tax has some good

attributes that make it indispensable

BY STEVEN GINSBERG

TO MOST AMERICANS, THE PROPERTY TAX IS ABOUT as revered as communism and as popular as a pro-lifer at a NOW rally. The reasons are not hard to understand. At first glance, the property tax system seems arbitrary, unreasonable, and just plain unfair. Every year property owners are hit with a large tax bill, demanding a nearly immediate lump-sum payment. In many jurisdictions, including our nation's capital, the government isn't even required to do you the courtesy of mailing that bill; if you miss the deadline, you must pay late fees whether you received your notice or not. Furthermore, as far as many homeowners are concerned, the manner by which both tax rates and individual property values are determined could not be more random if they were plucked out of a hat. In some cases this is because on-site assessments are only done infrequently—like every five or 10 years. This forces assessors to rely on unreliable estimation methods in the intervening years, such as setting the value of a property based on what neighboring real estate sold for that year, regardless of how the condition of those properties compares with that of the building being assessed. Thus a shack and a renovated loft in the same area can be valued at the same amount. In other communities, like those in California, property values are reassessed only when a building is sold. So a young family of four buying a home in San Francisco's pricey real estate market is slapped with an exorbitant tax bill, while the filthy-rich investment banker down the street is still paying the same amount in taxes as when he first purchased his home in 1979.

Property tax rates are just as varied. In each community, homeowners, businesses, and non-homestead residences (like apartment buildings) vie to lighten their portion of the tax load. Often, regardless of actual property values, whichever group happens to have the most lobbying clout gets a break, while the losing parties are left to shoulder more than their fair share of the burden. In Minnesota, for instance, between 1977 and 1990 homeowners were able to cut their share of property taxes from 45 to 36 percent, even as their share of real estate values rose from 51 to 56 percent. All of this financial finagling, of course, only strengthens taxpayers' conviction that the system is inherently unjust and highly politicized.

It's not surprising then that the property tax has earned such a bad rep among voters—and even less surprising that politicians have latched onto the issue. If you're looking to win votes, opposing the property tax is a no-brainer: It's like declaring that you're anti-drugs. Already, states as politically diverse as Oregon and New York have moved to defang the property tax.

But before we pop open the champagne to toast these developments, we need to take a close look at the upside of the property tax. (And, yes, there is a considerable one.) For although the list of the system's failures is long, people who advocate lowering or abolishing the tax outright are in many cases not considering the big picture.

For starters, contrary to popular belief, the property tax serves as a vital complement to other types of taxes. For instance, our income tax system may be geared to collect more from the affluent, but it also includes numerous loopholes that allow the rich to slip out of paying

STEVEN GINSBERG *is an editorial aide at* The Washington Post.

Reprinted with permission from *The Washington Monthly,* October 1997, pp. 33–35. © 1997 by The Washington Monthly Co., 1611 Connecticut Avenue, NW, Washington, DC 20009. (202) 462–0128.

an amount of tax truly commensurate with their wealth. The property tax picks up where the income tax leaves off. Even if they manage to downplay their annual income, chances are, rich folks are going to buy property. They can't resist owning that summer home in Nantucket, that weekend home in the Hamptons, or that colonial mansion in Georgetown. After all, what's the point of having all that dough if you're not going to spend it? Thus the amount of property you own is as important an indicator of how well-off you are as the income you're officially pulling in each year.

Similarly, property taxes improve the accuracy with which the wealth of senior citizens—whose assets tend to dramatically outweigh their cash incomes—can be taxed. Without property taxes, many seniors would only be taxed on their fixed incomes—which often grossly underestimate how well-to-do they actually are. Now, we're not talking about the 70-year-old Brooklyn couple whose fixed income barely covers the taxes on the brownstone they bought 30 years ago. (An exemption can and should be made to ensure taxes don't force elderly people out of their homes.) But lots of seniors have invested in real estate other than their primary residences. Take the case of a retired speculator who bought property years ago and has watched gleefully as its value skyrocketed. He can enjoy the benefits of his good fortune long before he actually sells those investments. For instance, ownership of pricey real estate makes him eligible for large loans on which the interest is tax deductible. Furthermore, he can spend his fixed annual retirement income without a second thought—knowing that if he's ever low on funds, he can simply cash in his property. The property tax ensures that his tax bill reflects his good fortune. It's not surprising then, that the powerful AARP seniors lobby is pressuring states for an overhaul of the property tax system. And as baby boomers slide into their golden years, we can expect this branch of the anti-property tax lobby to grow even stronger.

Who Will Pick Up the Slack?

No doubt the rich and the elderly recognize that abolishing or lowering property taxes would deal a crushing blow to the schools in their communities—which is where the bulk of the tax's revenues go. But that's no skin off their noses: The rich can always send their kids to private school, and most old people's kids have already flown the nest. Of course, cash-strapped communities are unwilling to stand by as their schools are devastated and may raise other kinds of taxes—like sales taxes—to make up for lost revenue. But such taxes shift more of the burden onto the middle and lower classes, who must buy basic goods, even if they can't afford property.

If you have any doubts about the kind of fiscal havoc the elimination of the property tax can cause, you need only look at what's happened in the states that have "reformed" it. In Florida, the large and religiously anti-

property tax seniors population has pushed lawmakers into reducing the property tax rates for some, and completely exempting others. The result is a maze of slimmed-down services and hidden "non-tax" fees that end up unfairly shackling the middle class. Worst of all, these alternative methods simply can't raise the same amount of revenue as the property taxes did. Consequently, notes Kurt Wenner, an economist with Florida TaxWatch, "the schools don't have much of a chance." Small wonder that Florida kids consistently place near the bottom in national reading and math tests, alongside much poorer states such as Louisiana.

In Texas, voters overwhelmingly approved Proposition 1, a ballot measure providing $1 billion in property tax "relief." The law's supporters in the legislature said they had to act "before there was a taxpayer revolt." Of course, almost immediately after the bill passed, school districts across the state announced that they would have to raise other taxes to make ends meet.

Taxpayers in Maine are looking to reduce their property tax bills by expanding the homestead exemption by $20,000, a measure that would rob the state of $200 million in funds. To compensate for the reduction in real estate taxes, Maine will be forced to extend its 6 percent sales tax to a wide range of everyday sources that directly hit middle-class wallets, including movie theaters, bowling alleys, beauticians, and barbers.

The situation is no different in New York; Governor Pataki, along with a slew of legislators, has vowed to cut property taxes. But as property taxes go down, local taxes, user fees, and college education prices continue to surge to make up the difference. The New York proposals are so unbalanced they prompted Patricia Woodworth, director of the budget for the State of New York, to complain to *Newsday* last April, "the benefits are going to go to those who have the greater monetary and financial interest in property holdings, which is not the average person. This plan is not truly tax relief."

But it is Oregon that gives us the most vivid example of what happens when property taxes are slashed. The northwestern state passed Measure 5 in 1990, putting a cap on all property tax increases. This, in turn, forced a massive transfer of state funds to support schools, which left the state with no choice but to cut spending on child welfare, prisons, and state police.

The bottom line: When property taxes are cut, other taxes must be raised to make up for lost revenues. And, as Chris Herbert, an economist at the Harvard-MIT Joint Center for Housing Studies, points out, the property tax is far more progressive than the alternatives. "Cutbacks in property tax have got to be made up and they're not going to be done by a more progressive tax," he says. "Localities can't get states to pick up the tab, so there's a big shift to user charges. You start getting taxes on trash collection and recreation facilities. With user fees things are becoming less progressive because you're paying as much as the next guy"—regardless of whether he happens to be a millionaire.

Mend It, Don't End It

But if we want to get the property tax off the political hit list, we need to address the legitimate problems with the current system. A handful of governments around the country have already started the ball rolling, instituting models that correct some of the more egregious flaws.

Washington state has perhaps the best system, having tackled the issue of favoritism head-on and passed a constitutional amendment declaring that statewide property tax rates must be uniform. For example, all real estate property is currently taxed at approximately 1.2 percent. In addition, all property tax revenues are split between the state and localities. This allows states to tap a deep vein of revenue and distribute it equitably. Under such a system, localities ultimately get to administer their portion of the pot, but the disparity between rich and poor districts is not so wide. "The real key is that the system is administered fairly," says Kriss Sjoblon, an economist at the Washington Research Council. "We have a good system of assessment that eliminates inequities, and the uniformity is vital. People should be treated fairly and folks shouldn't get deals."

Even jurisdictions with special needs can establish systems that are less arbitrary and that make sense to the average taxpayer. Pittsburgh, for instance, has initiated a "split-rate" system in an attempt to foster urban renewal. Property tax is really two separate taxes, one on land and one on building values; Pittsburgh simply separated these two values. The city then lowered the tax on buildings, giving property owners an incentive to maintain, build, and improve their properties, while at the same time increasing the levy on land values, thus discouraging land speculation and stemming urban sprawl. In Pittsburgh and other Pennsylvania cities where the "split-rate" is employed, 85 percent of homeowners pay less than they would with a flat rate, according to analysis by the *American Journal of Economics and Sociology*. The analysis also found that those who do pay more tend to be wealthier homeowners.

Most importantly, the system achieves its goal of encouraging economic growth in urban centers. A study conducted by University of Maryland economists Wallace Oates and Robert Schwab, comparing Pittsburgh to 14 other eastern cities during the decade before and the decade after Pittsburgh expanded its two-rate system, found that: "Pittsburgh had a 70.4 percent increase in the value of building permits, while the 14-city average decreased by 14.4 percent. These findings are especially remarkable when it is recalled that the city's basic industry—steel—was undergoing a severe crisis throughout the latter decade."

Aside from these more comprehensive systems, there are a number of basic steps localities could take to alter the perception of unfairness and ease the burden of property taxes:

• Use the property tax to pay for more than just schools. If seniors and the wealthy feel that the taxes support services they need, they will have reason to pause before directing their lobbying muscle against it.

• Raise the level of exemptions for people over 65. Property taxes do blindside some senior citizens, and there's no reason why they should have to move out of their lifelong homes because the market value of the house has gone up. A moderate raise in the exemption level would prevent poorer seniors from losing their homes, while still raising revenue from the wealthy.

• Stagger payments. A major reason property tax is so unpopular is that it's administered in huge chunks and people aren't allowed much time before hefty late fees kick in. Distributing the burden over four or more payments a year, with more advanced notice, would take some of the sting out of the bill.

• Upgrade technology. Set it up so people can pay electronically. It's a small thing, but it will make a difference. Most cities allow offenders to pay parking tickets with credit cards, there's no reason they can't do the same with property tax.

Rooting out favoritism and slipshod assessment methods will help make the tax palatable to the majority of citizens. They will no longer see the property tax as a mindless ogre coming to swallow up their hard-earned money. Instead, they will see it as the soundest way to make sure that everyone, especially the wealthy, contributes his share to ensure a high level of public services. In short, they will see it for what it is.

Romancing the Smokestack

There's no end in sight to the competition for industry. But a few places are starting to think the game should have some rules.

Charles Mahtesian

If there's a politician these days who seems to understand the futility of smokestack chasing, it is Illinois Governor Jim Edgar. Since his election in 1990, he has lectured his colleagues on the folly of making extravagant offers to lure businesses or to keep them from leaving. He even convened a private Washington, D.C., summit between governors and corporate leaders to talk the matter over. In August 1993, Edgar was the architect of a truce adopted by the National Governors' Association that, among other things, urged states not to use public resources merely to influence the location of private investment.

But before Edgar left Springfield to announce the treaty, he took care of some of his own business—okaying the use of public resources to influence the location of a wavering in-state company. The deal gave Tootsie Roll Industries $20 million in loans, $1.4 million in state and local tax exemptions and $200,000 in job training funds. Then, when Edgar returned, he signed off on a tax incentive package amounting to nearly $30 million, plus $700,000 in job training funds, for a Nabisco plant producing Fig Newtons and Oreos.

Edgar's ambivalent approach to the prevailing economic development strategy is hardly unique among public officials. In 1991, three years after hammering his election opponent for lavishing incentives on a foreign carmaker, Indiana Governor Evan Bayh muscled out nine other finalists with a $291 million incentive offer for a United Airlines maintenance facility.

While virtually every governor, legislator and development official laments the zero-sum nature of the contest, the industrial recruitment wars continue with no end in sight.

As with the Cold War arms race, no state or city is willing to disengage unilaterally. And the bidding game is by no means played only by industrial giants such as Illinois and Indiana.

Since statehood in 1889, North Dakota governors have seen fit to call only nine special legislative sessions. Usually they have dealt with emergency or war-related measures. The 10th and latest special session, however, concerned a less lofty subject—luring a $245 million corn processing plant to the state. These days, the prospect of attracting a new industrial facility passes for both an emergency and a war.

In order to compete with rivals Minnesota and South Dakota, North Dakota Governor Ed Schafer felt the state's tax code needed some adjustment. So over three days this past summer, the legislature, almost without opposition, carved out various tax exemptions to make their state a more attractive place to process corn. They won't know just how attractive they've made it until sometime next year, when the Northern Corn Processors Cooperative makes its decision.

As economic development battles go, these governors got off lightly. None had to appear on the Phil Donahue show, as seven others did when General Motors' Saturn auto plant was up for grabs in the mid-1980s. The Tootsie Roll logo will not have to appear on top of the scoreboard at University of Illinois football contests, as the Mercedes-Benz insignia did at a Crimson Tide game last year when Alabama was seeking the company's new sports-utility vehicle plant.

And Nabisco never bargained with an "ideal incentive matrix," a 104-item wish list that the Intel Corp. issued in 1992 to those interested in landing two new computer chip factories. In addition to tax breaks, the company sought incentives such as immediate resident status for its employees and their dependents (so that they could receive lower, in-state college tuition), discounts on moving expenses and mortgage costs, and other assorted goodies.

While Intel's wish list might sound outrageous, in the current incentives war between the states, it is fast becoming the norm. The company actually found two Southwestern states—Arizona and New Mexico—that acquiesced to many of its demands.

But there is a positive side to nightmares like the incentive matrix: The more brazen and costly relocation demands become, the more state and local officials find themselves reexamining their industrial strategies. Ever so slowly, they are starting to distribute incentives more judiciously, implement accountability measures and demand remuneration if companies fail to deliver on their promises.

Smokestack chasing is not a new phenomenon, just more publicized—and more costly—than ever before. The most recent round dates back to the early 1980s, when Tennessee put together an incentives package that paid roughly the equivalent of $11,000 per job for a Nissan automobile manufacturing plant. Five years later, the Volunteer State also won the Saturn circus after a 30-state winnowing process. By then, the per-job costs had more than doubled to $26,000.

Not to be outdone, Kentucky offered an estimated $150 million in incentives in its successful 1985 effort to bring a Toyota plant to Georgetown. Broken down by the job, it comes out to about $50,000 each.

But it was Alabama's 1993 deal with Mercedes-Benz that heated up the smoldering debate over smokestack-chasing mania. When the dust settled after a 35-state, 100-site battle royal for the sports-utility vehicle plant, Alabama was left standing with an incentives package estimated at about $300 million—or somewhere in the neighborhood of $200,000 for each of the 1,500 expected jobs.

Early on, company executives told inquiring state officials they would not be moved by a bidding war. But once states began offering tax abatements, Mercedes willingly played auctioneer. Unsuccessful competitors for the plant groused that the company played states off each other to get the best possible deal. Judging from the final agreement, it is hard to conclude otherwise.

In the end, Alabama had committed to building a $5 million welcome center for visitors to the plant, purchasing a fleet of the new vehicles and paying workers' wages while they are in training. Almost $80 million in state money will go to infrastructure improvements and close to $100 million will pay for site development.

Governor Jim Folsom argued that, at least for his state, the Mercedes deal was a steal, if for nothing other than its symbolism—that is, to break through old stereotypes and announce to the corporate world that Alabama is open for business. There is certainly some precedent. Kentucky's mad scramble for industry has left little doubt in business circles as to its hospitality toward industry and commerce.

But critics of the Mercedes deal think it stands for something more ominous: The state's willingness to give huge tax breaks to healthy firms while, at the same time, it is under a judicial mandate to spend hundreds of millions of dollars to fix up its inadequate public school system.

"Many of the states are in the position they are in because they failed to invest in basic infrastructure over the years—the infrastructure of education, the road system, technology systems, financial systems," says Brian Dabson, president of the Corporation for Enterprise Development and co-author of a 1994 report, *Bidding for Business: Are Cities and States Selling Themselves Short?* "Those building blocks of economic development are simply not well enough developed for them to compete. We are talking about decades of neglect, so they can ill afford to chase companies."

The traditionally underdeveloped southeastern region has garnered much of the industrial recruitment notoriety, but it is clearly not a regional fad. On the West Coast, for example, California is weathering not only a crippling recession but an invasion of economic development pirates seeking to persuade businesses to relocate out of state.

More than 20 state and local offices are scattered across Southern California, staffed by individuals who make a living by trying

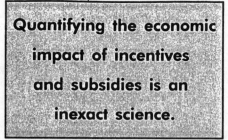

Quantifying the economic impact of incentives and subsidies is an inexact science.

to induce California business executives to move their operations out of state.

The height of ignominy may have come last year, when 65 state and local economic development organizations from across the country held a business relocation expo in Anaheim, designed to lure away Golden State businesses.

Even truces and treaties have been unable to stop the practice of interstate raiding. Anyone who doubts that needs only to look toward the East Coast, where poaching characterizes the relationships among New York, New Jersey and Connecticut.

In 1991, the last time the three states agreed to a non-aggression pact, New Jersey Governor James Florio broke it within months. Worse yet, he rubbed New York's face in it by creating a recruitment fund paid for out of revenues from the World Trade Center—jointly owned by both states.

Actually, it's not difficult to understand why Florio did what he did. If nothing else, the politics of smokestack chasing are simply too enticing. Any job-creation venture—even those with dubious claims—translates into great press. And if the deal turns out to be a bomb, the evidence likely will not filter out until long after an administration is out of power—if it surfaces at all.

"Industrial recruitment remains so tempting that a lot of states are going to continue, primarily for political reasons," says Peter Eisinger, director of the LaFollette School of Public Policy in Wisconsin and an authority on economic development strategy. "Unfortunately, governors have found it to be an easier strategy than saying, 'I put $15 million in a high-tech consortium that in 15 years will employ 5,000 people, but right now employs 15 people in little white lab coats.'"

Part of the problem is that there is generally very little pressure on officials to refuse to compete for such potentially lucrative prizes. Although a few existing firms occasionally squawk about the fairness of subsidizing newcomers, for the most part the business community has been an implicit co-conspirator in the incentives war. For example, local business leaders have been known to snipe at governors such as Edgar in Illinois or John Engler in Michigan for their failures to romance wayward industry.

In a recent report, the National Governors' Association pointedly asked business

leaders to stand by state officials when one company is seeking unreasonable incentives at the expense of other businesses or the state. "In some cases, we laid cover for governors who didn't want to get involved in bidding wars," says Jay Kayne, policy director for NGA. "It was tough for some governors to say, 'I'm not going to go after Mercedes-Benz or Toyota.'"

One reason state chambers of commerce have been reluctant to lead the charge against incentives is because their members are generally divided over the issue. After all, the reasoning goes, some may have the opportunity to cash in sometime down the road.

Oddly enough, small business has not been heard from either, despite the fact that most of the goodies are going to bigger firms. "In terms of lighting torches, taking up pitchforks and marching on the capitol, that's not what's happening," says Jim Wiedman of the National Federation of Independent Business. "It doesn't affect anyone directly."

Perhaps they should be taking up their pitchforks. In essence, incentives mean that existing business is subsidizing new business. The money for related development—such as schools, roads and other services—has to come from somewhere. Given the corporate tax, excise tax, inventory tax, raw materials tax, sales tax and other assorted tax exemptions freely distributed these days, that money is certainly not coming from the new businesses.

"If you are going to allow a new company to get away with not paying any taxes for 10 years, somebody else has to offset that," says Dabson. "Those costs are borne by existing companies. So basically what you're creating is an inequitable tax system where existing companies are paying taxes on behalf of new ones."

But rather than agree to halt the bidding game, many existing firms have simply upped the ante. This past summer, New York City officials found themselves forced to cough up millions in concessions to a company that publicly admitted it had no intention of moving away but thought it ought to get in on the action.

To understand what happened, it is necessary to go back to 1989, when the NBC television network threatened to bolt the city for New Jersey. In return for staying put, the city offered $100 million in tax breaks and other concessions. Four years later, rival network CBS received a $50 million payoff. So, naturally, ABC came knocking at city hall. It came away with $26 million in sales tax abatements and electricity cost concessions by promising to create 185 jobs.

Was it worth it? It's almost impossible to tell for sure. As with most other incentive packages, there's a pretty good chance that no one will ever know. "Nobody in the press does a cost-benefit analysis. Nobody ever looks to see if the jobs promised materialized. Nobody ever looks to see whether the new plant sparks associated growth," say Eisinger. "There are, however, banner headlines saying, 'South Carolina Beats Out Dozens of Other States for BMW Plant.' "

Economists themselves are divided over the effect incentives have on relocation decisions. Surveys of business executives and relocation consultants indicate incentives are merely one of many factors taken into consideration. But quantifying the incentives and subsidies is also an inexact science. And the economic impact of a new or upgraded facility is unclear because so much depends on the economic forecasting model or multipliers used.

"Even if costs and effects of incentives were known, it is hard to quantify how much the resulting development contributes to public revenues and public costs," notes Hal Hovey in *State Policy Reports,* "not to mention benefits and costs that don't find their way into state and local budgets."

But it doesn't always take an economist to figure out which of the most recent deals have disaster written all over them. And that may be the best news of all in the incentive wars. Because the more deals disappoint, the more closely both lawmakers and the public will scrutinize incentives. In fact, the recent shuffle steps toward holding companies accountable are based not necessarily on a desire for better public policy but on the fear of being burnt on a bad deal.

The debacle in Pennsylvania, where Volkswagen opened the first foreign auto plant in America in 1978, is among the most notorious. It took a $71 million incentives package to win the bidding battle with Ohio, but a giddy Governor Milton Shapp promised the plant could one day produce as many as 20,000 jobs. It never came close. Within five years, half of its 6,000 workers were laid off. Within a decade, it had closed down for good.

Plenty of other deals went sour in the 1980s—including a Playskool toy factory in Chicago and an Anchor Hocking glassmaking plant in West Virginia. In both cases, the companies took state or local incentives, then attempted to move away. After bitter court battles, Chicago and West Virginia were able to extract settlements.

More recently, Minnesota's arrangement with Northwest Airlines has attracted attention. In 1992, the state agreed on an $840 million loan, grant and tax-break package for the St. Paul-based company to site two repair facilities in the state's economically depressed Iron Range region. Within months, the airline was teetering near bankruptcy. Northwest still went ahead and accepted part of the deal—a $270 million loan—then announced that the facilities were "on hold." The state is reluctant to pursue any action which could push Northwest over the brink.

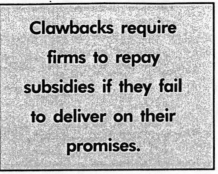

> Clawbacks require firms to repay subsidies if they fail to deliver on their promises.

Those ultimately unsatisfying results have underscored the need to make companies uphold their end of the bargain. Among the recent mechanisms: "right-to-know" laws that require estimates of jobs created or destroyed, sophisticated cost-benefit analyses and incentives targeted at specific industries. Most are manifestations of deals gone sour or unkept promises. "The laws are reactions to horror stories or are in lieu of litigation," says Greg LeRoy, a policy consultant to the Federation for Industrial Retention and Renewal, an advocacy group that calls for increased accountability measures. "It's a city or state's attempt to say, 'No one will do that to us again.' "

In response to a recent industrial recruitment uptick—and its accompanying tax breaks—the Arizona legislature tightened state statutes this year to dissuade in-state business poaching, to target key industrial "clusters," such as high technology, and to require a cost-benefit analysis for large-scale incentive packages.

Still, the legislation is loaded with potential loopholes, such as ways to get around the cost-benefit analysis, notes Mary Jo Waits, author of a 1993 economic incentives study for the University of Arizona's Morrison Institute for Public Policy. "It's not totally 100 percent wonderful," she says. "But it's a step in the right direction."

Yet none of the new measures can guarantee that the promised benefits of a new company will ever materialize. For that reason, a growing number of places—including Arizona—are exploring a mechanism widely used in Western Europe, known as the "clawback." Under a clawback provision, firms must repay all or part of subsidies if they fail to deliver, under-perform or over-promise.

The township of Ypsilanti, Michigan, could have used such a measure back in 1992 when it sued General Motors for closing its 4,500-worker Willow Run plant. Local officials insisted that 17 years of tax abatements—which they said totaled $1.3 billion—had included job-security pledges by GM. In a closely watched case, the township won an injunction at the circuit court level, but saw the decision overturned in 1993 by the state Court of Appeals.

The city that won the GM bidding war, Arlington, Texas, did not make the same mistake. If the GM agreement is breached, the city not only gets back taxes but penalties and interest as well.

There are limits, however, to the effectiveness of clawbacks. For starters, development officials are less than enamored of them, if only because relocating companies dislike them. Besides, enforcement is, and is likely to remain, uneven mostly because public officials are reluctant to penalize already financially troubled companies.

"Clawbacks certainly are increasing," says the University of Wisconsin's Eisinger. "But the jury is out on how effective they are going to be. There are a lot of loopholes for firms. They are imperfect devices."

That's what worries critics of Indianapolis' agreement with United Airlines. While the contract includes clawback provisions, its terms allow maximum wiggle room when it comes to the definition of jobs created. "It's starting to percolate out just how insane the United Airlines thing is," says Bill Styring, president of the Indiana Policy Review Foundation, a conservative think tank.

A federal role in smokestack chasing may also be brewing, much to the consternation of virtually everyone involved in the industrial recruitment battles. In one case, Wisconsin's congressional delegation drafted protective legislation in August after Milwaukee employer Briggs & Stratton announced it would shift local jobs to Missouri and Kentucky—a move partly subsidized by federal block grant funds.

The outcry for federal involvement, though, is mainly coming from advocacy groups that are on the outside looking in. There is about as much chance that governors and legislators will join the call for the feds as there is that the governor of Alabama will be seen driving a Yugo.

"It would be a disaster," warns Phil Burgess, president of the Center for the New West, a Denver-based think tank. "The last thing we need is the federal government ruling on whether a state could entice business. What authority does the federal government have to say anything about a state's industrial policy or lack of one?"

For the time being, the answer is none. Which means in all likelihood states and localities will continue their hot pursuit of industry and jobs. And in the end, it may take an economic development disaster, not regulation by the feds or any other body, for them to fully recognize the risks of indiscriminate smokestack chasing.

"The change will come not because we put a gun to their heads," says the NGA's Jay Kayne, "but because it represents good public policy."

Or because, in the long run, wooing businesses too extravagantly would be bad public relations.

THE NEW URBAN GAMBLE

BY DAVID BARRINGER

David Barringer, a freelance writer and lawyer, has written for *Playboy, Details,* and the *American Bar Association Journal.*

When it comes to abject poverty, few cities rival East St. Louis, Illinois. Of the approximately 40,000 residents there, 98 percent of whom are black, roughly half qualify for public assistance. Forty-four percent of the population lives below the poverty line, and per capita income is $6,400—the worst in the state.

East St. Louis has pinned its hopes for urban renewal on a casino riverboat.

Four years ago East St. Louis officials pinned their hopes for urban renewal on a casino riverboat, following the lead of several other cities along the Mississippi River. Today that establishment, the Casino Queen, is booming: The boat takes in some $250 million a year, of which the city claims $6 million in taxes. Every night, Metrolink commuter trains carry thousands of patrons from the wealthy, predominantly white communities across the river, depositing them—their pockets stuffed full of cash—at the casino's entrance. What could be better for a depressed inner city so starved for capital?

A lot, actually. The passengers on the commuter trains bypass East St. Louis itself, and it turns out that prosperity has bypassed the city as well. Both figuratively and literally, the casino is its own world. A tall security fence with two watchtowers separates the boat from the city. Guards patrol the perimeter. The official unemployment rate of 12 percent—also the worst in the state—hasn't budged since the casino arrived, even though the national rate has been steadily declining for several years. And many of the workers from East St. Louis who have managed to gain employment at the casino move to better neighborhoods when they earn enough money—which is good for those casino employees who can escape the inner city, but doesn't do much for the residents who remain in the area.

A similar fate may await Chattanooga and Detroit, Miami and Las Vegas, and several other cities that, like East St. Louis, have spent millions of dollars subsidizing privately operated entertainment attractions. The nature of the attractions varies from city to city—some places it's casinos, some places it's stadiums, some places it's both—but all are designed with the same basic goal in mind: turning cities into oversized carnivals that will lure visitors from the suburbs and beyond, thus recapturing the wealth that began seeping out years ago.

For sure, these glitzy projects can inspire the weary. Last year no less a symbol of urban despair than Detroit approved not just a dual stadium complex but three casinos as well—a sign, local leaders said, that Detroit was finally making a comeback. Yet cities like Detroit may be in for an unpleasant surprise when they discover that the carnival city model requires constant and expensive reinvention just to remain competitive and, thus, economically viable. Although local governments try to disguise public funding for these projects as taxes on tourists or special bond measures, inevitably money spent on these carnival attractions is money not spent on other, more worthy public investments. The economic stimulus of carnival city projects is ambiguous at best; when the construction is finished, inner-city residents could end up as impoverished as before—too poor to afford the price of admission to attractions, let alone the price of escape to the suburbs.

REINVENTING THE ROULETTE WHEEL

In the 1980s, U.S. cities spent about $750 million on sports arenas. Since 1992, the country has spent more than $1 billion on arenas, and more than $7 billion is earmarked for future construction. In Baltimore, $210 million of public funds built the Orioles a new Camden Yards stadium. In 1990, without a professional team, St. Petersburg, Florida, boldly built itself the $138-million ThunderDome, a dowry that for years failed to attract suitors. And when the White Sox threatened to flee Chicago for St. Petersburg, Chicago met the team owner's demand: a new $185-million Comiskey Park across from the old one.

The carnival city model requires constant and expensive reinvention to remain competitive.

Economists who have studied such programs say that subsidized stadiums are almost always profitable for team owners—and almost never for the cities [see "Skyboxed In."]. In response to the crescendo of criticism, stadium project boosters now pull the camera away from a close-up and move it back—way back—until it captures the pleasing panorama of consequences of each new arena: a burger joint here, a T-shirt shop there. Boosters justify stadiums in terms of their power to catalyze area business, which benefits the city with increased tax revenue. Without the arenas, boosters say, wealthy suburbanites might not return to the cities at all.

This sounds plausible, but the logic doesn't hold up. Private business also demands public subsidy. In the end, the increased tax revenue is unlikely to recoup the city's stadium investment and will most likely go to cover the costs of subsidies for future development

gambles that accompany the stadium. The Texas Rangers' Arlington Ballpark, for example, has a baseball museum, a Walk of Fame, and a private restaurant—and now a Six Flags water park is being built next door. Jacobs Field, in Cleveland, has a museum, a children's play area, and a restaurant overlooking the diamond. Coors Field, in Denver, has the Sand Lot Brewery next to its pedestrian plaza and children's play area.

Recently some cities have asked team owners to increase the ante, insisting that stadium projects be true public-private partnerships. In Detroit, for example, taxpayer money accounts for just 50 percent of the stadiums' construction cost, much less than the national average of 80 to 100 percent. To help fund the $505-million dual-stadium complex, voters approved a 1 percent tax on hotels and a 2 percent tax on car rentals, which should generate $5.5 million a year to support $80 million in bonds. The state is chipping in with $55 million of Indian-casino revenue, the city's Downtown Development Authority with $85 million, and the two team owners will raise the final $285 million.

Still, while the public investment is less, the threat of team defection remains, as Oakland, Los Angeles, Baltimore, and St. Louis know all too well. Since the Lions left Detroit once already, increased public subsidy—better leasing deals, for instance—may be needed in the future just to keep the team in the city. Now and then, sympathetic experts suggest reducing taxes on team owners to prevent rival cities from luring teams away with public subsidy. But giving team owners even more money becomes a never-ending game: A decade ago South Florida, known for its lax tax requirements, hurriedly built an arena to lure hockey and basketball teams. The teams came but found the otherwise plush arena wanting because it didn't have enough luxury skyboxes. Now each team is getting a new, publicly financed arena of its own, and local officials are debating whether to turn the "old" Miami Arena into a giant flea market—even as they pay off millions in leftover construction debt.

On the surface, casinos might seem like a better gamble. If nothing else, they seem to guarantee a boost in tax revenue: When Gary, Indiana, imposed a 5 percent tax on its two casino riverboats, it generated $5.9 million in state revenues in just the first four months—and 5 percent of all casino winnings go direct to the city of Gary. Revenue from the Casino Queen in East St. Louis helped pay for an improved police force in the area. Community gifts are another benefit. Don Barden, owner of the Majestic Star riverboat in Gary, gave cash donations to the city for police cars and to the schools for computers and scholarships. In Detroit, Barden donated $100,000 to the Museum of African-American History, in an apparent effort to rouse community support for his bid for a license.

But with gambling comes crime and corruption. Casino owners and government officials often have trouble avoiding the slip from the virtue of gift-giving to the vice of graft-grabbing. According to newspaper reports, when casinos came to New Orleans, city council members accepted Hawaiian trips from a casino contractor; other city officials hid gifts in a not-for-profit organization; a casino operator paid $250,000 to a law firm with ties to the mayor; and a construction manager, hired by the city to monitor its interests, was paid $580,000 a year for three years by the casino.

To its credit, Detroit, which will be the largest urban area with casinos, is opting for strong ethics rules to guard against corruption. To ensure that the casinos take the city seriously, Detroit is also insisting on several mandates on the casino licensees: They must attach a 1,000-room hotel, take a Vegas partner, and spend at least $800 million on the project.

Skyboxed In

BY AMY D. BURKE

In 1995, the NFL's Cleveland Browns abandoned Ohio for greener pastures in Maryland, illustrating a basic fact about professional sports today: Money talks and teams walk.

Browns owner Arthur Modell moved his team to Baltimore when the city offered him a stadium deal—complete with free rent, public financing, and revenues from concession sales—that he could not refuse. Thus the Browns are now the Baltimore Ravens while the city of Cleveland, bereft of a football team, has pledged to spend precious municipal dollars to construct an expensive new stadium in the hopes of being awarded a new Browns team when the NFL expands.

In the transformation of the Browns into the Ravens lies a basic question: Are wealthy team owners holding cities hostage by demanding—and often receiving—huge public subsidies for the construction of posh stadiums whose economic benefits accrue mainly to players and to the owners themselves? Or as the owners would have it, do the direct and indirect benefits to the surrounding community of subsidizing a professional sports stadium more than justify its costs?

"There are huge benefits both emotionally and economically" to building a stadium for the Ravens in Baltimore, explains John Moag, chairman of the Maryland Stadium Authority. Anyone who has lived in a city where a major sports team was competing for a championship can attest to the contribution to civic pride a stadium makes. More tangibly, new jobs and increased consumer spending provide real economic benefits to communities that build stadiums or arenas.

According to Rodney Fort, a professor of economics at Washington State University, "hundreds of thousands of people who never go to a game still get benefits," through job creation, tax revenues, and fan-driven commercial prosperity. Fort points out that the willingness of fans to pay voluntarily for major-league-sports tickets, along with the indirect economic benefits a local sports team can produce, do justify some city spending on stadiums.

But Andrew Zimbalist, an economist at Smith College, disagrees. The overall economic impact of a sports stadium or arena is "very close to zero," he says; publicly financed sports complexes are therefore decidedly not in the best interest of already financially strapped municipalities. For a stadium to have a positive effect on a local economy, it would have to increase the overall amount of spending on leisure activities. But because the amount of time and money that people have to spend on such activities is inherently limited, it is very difficult to prove that the addition of a professional sports team to a city community does anything more than shift leisure spending from one area to another. Stadium deals, in Zimbalist's view, often do more to drain communities' public resources than to spur new economic activity.

Moreover, many of the stadium's direct benefits, such as the high salaries paid to players and managers, flow out of the local economy. "Sports teams fundamentally employ the players and a few people in the front office. Everyone else who is employed is working part-time, low-wage jobs," says Zimbalist. Thus public financing for stadiums amounts to "doing an income transfer from people who pay sales taxes," mainly those in the middle- and lower-income brackets, to the owners and players, who then respend much

But all of this begs another question: How many more casinos can regional economies actually support? Casino owners are expected to continue their expansion through the year 2000, but with Americans' gambling losses quadrupling since 1986, many analysts doubt the industry can sustain its growth. Toward the end of last year, the stock of Trump Hotel and Casino Resorts fell two-thirds while the stocks of riverboat-gambling companies fell by half. The Stratosphere, a $550-million casino tower, failed miserably at a poor location in Vegas. Only the major gambling outfits are doing well; MGM Grand Incorporated tripled its profits in the first half of last year. The little guys, meanwhile, are sinking into debt, or cashing out.

Part of the problem is market saturation, which the carnival city model is likely to exacerbate. To manage the downsides of casinos—more crime, reduced spending power of residents, restaurants squeezed out by cheap or free casino eats—a city must be prepared to launch a public-relations campaign to bring in tourists. Casinos, if left to prey only on locals, will infect and cripple the host city. Thus, the casino riverboat in Council Bluffs, Iowa, targets tourists from Omaha, Nebraska. Las Vegas draws a large southern-California crowd. Not surprisingly, the competition has become fierce: When casinos in Gary, Indiana, opened, the revenues at casinos in nearby Joliet, Illinois, dropped 32 percent. Detroit's casinos are designed, in part, to recapture the

of their huge salaries in other states.

Supporters of municipal stadium financing observe that the total dollar value of each citizen's taxes that goes to stadium building is very small—smaller by far than the amount many fans willingly pay in the form of tickets and concessions. But James Quirk, a retired professor of economics at the California Institute of Technology, points out that much of the burden falls on people who have no interest in sports or who would not willingly spend money on a sports complex—or on the increased local taxes or hotel, rental car, and parking fees that localities levy to raise funds for the project. And it's not just locals who must foot the bill: A change made under the Tax Reform Act of 1986 inadvertently fueled the stadium-building trend by facilitating the use of federally tax-exempt bonds in arena construction. This means that the costs of building a stadium in Baltimore are diffused throughout the country.

Why is the demand for new stadiums so high? One reason, of course, is that owners want new stadiums with a greater number of hugely profitable corporate luxury skyboxes, and will

threaten to move their teams if cities do not build them. But the real problem is that professional sports leagues maintain almost exclusive control over expansion decisions. This means that the leagues can reject a city's application for a team if they believe a city's stadium or arena is not new or fancy enough—new or fancy enough, that is, to produce big revenues for league coffers. Thus if a city wants a team, it has to raise money to buy the team a spiffy, heavily skyboxed home. "Cities are forced to make decisions that really aren't financially prudent," says Robert Baade, an economist at Lake Forest College.

The solution may be to curtail the leagues' monopolistic control over which cities get awarded teams. For example, if any city that wanted a new team got one, leagues would lose their bargaining power. Baade suggests expanding both major and minor leagues to provide teams to all interested cities to prevent damaging bidding wars. Without more leverage for cities, however, teams will continue to demand outrageous subsidies. "There's an artificial scarcity of teams maintained [by the leagues] on purpose, for just these reasons," Fort explains. One way league mo-

nopolies might be rolled back is through federal legislation. In January, New York Senator Daniel Patrick Moynihan introduced legislation to end the use of federally tax-exempt bonds for stadium financing. "Using their monopoly power, owners threaten to move, forcing bidding wars among cities. End result: new, tax-subsidized stadiums with fancy amenities and sweetheart lease deals."

While passage of Moynihan's bill might be a step in the right direction, its prospects are dim because many team owners have close relationships with legislators. Public support for teams remains very high and vocal. When a team leaves a city, residents and fans tend to see this as an abdication of civic responsibility on the part of city and local government. Thus local officials remain focused on short-term remedies such as stadium building to keep their teams from migrating, and can't concentrate on fixing the system. But until changes are made or public support for teams dries up, the leagues will likely remain in the driver's seat, leaving cities little choice but to accept owners demands or wave good-bye to the home team.

money of its hometown gamblers who cross the Detroit River to drop millions at the casinos in Windsor, Ontario.

But when does the game end? In 1992, Chattanooga christened a $45-million aquarium. Attracting one million visitors a year, it spawned other entertainment and retail businesses, like the Creative Discovery Museum and an Imax Theatre, and its renovated riverfront has become a tourist destination. But now tourism has levelled off, and civic leaders are beginning to appreciate the burden of being a tourist town. Inherent in the carnival city model is the need for perpetual upgrading: To keep tourists coming back, the city must constantly reinvent itself. Not only does this cost money—it taxes the imagination.

Las Vegas has been doing just that. To the gamblers who knew Sin City a decade or two ago, the modern Las Vegas is surely unrecognizable. Setting the curve for the rest of the country's would-be carnival cities, Vegas has become a city of mega-complexes and super-casinos. In 1989, casino mogul Steve Wynn opened his Mirage resort and adorned it with a waterfall and volcano, an indoor lagoon, a tropical rain forest, caged white tigers in the Secret Garden of Siegfried & Roy, a dolphin tank, and a 20,000-gallon shark aquarium. Mirage's success inspired other casinos. The MGM Grand Hotel and Casino has a 5,000-room hotel and a 33-acre theme park. The recently opened New York New York Hotel and Casino features a roller coaster that weaves through a Manhattan skyline. One casino hotel under construction is housed in a giant glass pyramid guarded by a sphinx.

Despite the shocking glitz of the architecture of ostentation, the crisis for civic leaders is that when cities build more and more carnival attractions, they start to look alike. The high-speed trains being constructed to link cities like Detroit and Chicago will make travel easier, but the similar offerings will make travel less compelling. The pressure on a city to distinguish itself will drive future development toward Vegas extremes, and those too will be doomed to lose the interest of tourists increasingly inured to the outrageous.

THE CARNIVAL CON

Of course, to bring in tourists—which for many cities means whites not just from out of state but from their own middle-class suburbs—cities are finding that they must address tourist fears, which are partly justified by crime and partly exaggerated by race and class anxieties about minorities and the dangerous poor. Polling more than 600 voters from three counties, the *Detroit Free Press* found the number one need of potential casino-goers to be safety. Following the casino task force to Vegas, its reporters found some tourists who said they would come to Detroit only if there were attractions in addition to casinos—and others who admitted Detroit's crime-ridden image would keep them away completely.

Casinos won't spawn urban redevelopment unless they pump money into surrounding neighborhoods.

But this reveals the other basic tension in the carnival city model. Casinos won't spawn urban redevelopment unless they pump money into businesses in surrounding neighborhoods. Yet given the existing fear of crime in these areas, civic leaders and establishments alike will be tempted to appease the prevailing fears with the construction of security gates and watchtowers and the installation of surveillance cameras and armed guards—similar to the scene back in East St. Louis. This leaves us with disappointing images of an urban future: segregated, shameful, and potentially volatile. Opera houses, stadiums, casinos, theme parks—all appear to be commercial paeans to a white culture strategically gated within a black city. What is safe may come to be defined racially—that is, whites with pass cards, blacks without. That perception, too, will likely be strong among the urban community, such that black city residents will feel slighted and shut out from what was supposed to have been their saving grace, rejected by those who had promised to save them.

As cities race to build the next upscale attraction, the best assurances of civic leaders will not be enough to prevent many from being written out of the carnival city story. Initially, even the most fortunate city denizens will be left, at best, to operate a few rides and sweep up after the elephants. Job creation is a systemic problem, not easily solved: Even Detroit's empowerment zone, with $100 million at its disposal, has managed to create only 2,750 jobs for a zone population of more than 100,000, 30 percent of whom are unemployed.

Undaunted but cognizant of some of the obstacles, civic leaders are nevertheless trying to summon community involvement; this is something most city bureaucracies are very bad at, especially when they are busy courting pro sports teams and being wooed by casino operators. In addition to the two public-private coalitions making up its civic sector, Detroit recently created a committee for Community Reinvestment Strategies, intended to coordinate resources and enlist community input. The question is whether current residents will actually get a say in the use of resources. Are they saving themselves, or being saved?

Community participation has always been part of former HUD Secretary Henry Cis-neros's pitch for the continued viability of empowerment zones, and in many cities it's working. But citizen responsibility is often a euphemism for citizen obedience. To qualify for Detroit's renewed public housing, for instance, hopeful residents must participate in job training, education, and home-ownership programs. If they don't consent to the majority's imposition of the culture of customer service—that is, if they don't appreciate the courses in hospitality management, slot machine repair, and card dealing now being offered by several community colleges—then they are likely to lose out.

In those places where carnival cities are already a reality, the primary goals of civic leaders—including public, private, and community representatives—should be minimizing the costs of perpetual reinvention and avoiding the descent into economic colonialism. Otherwise the lucky, who have always been lucky, will carouse behind the guarded walls of their personal Disneylands. And the unlucky, for whom the rebirth of cities is ostensibly intended, will be accosted with a demand they cannot meet: "Tickets, please."

The Terrible Ten
Corporate candy store deals of 1998

BY GREG LEROY

Every year, cities and states around the country hand out government subsidies to corporations with few strings attached. It's the candy store school of economic development. Public outcry about the giveaways has prompted some change for the better in recent years. More states and cities are starting to attach conditions when they offer big companies tax incentives. Some are asking for guaranteed wages, money-back guarantees, and disclosure and monitoring safeguards.

But corporations are still getting a lot of sweet deals in American towns and cities. Consider my terrible ten deals for 1998. I found one city that admits it pays for jobs in other states. In five instances, taxpayers subsidize companies to the tune of more than $100,000 per job—and one at more than $1 million a job. Two states admit they let corporations avoid corporate income taxes altogether for fifteen to twenty years. Three deals involve companies in the midst of major labor disputes. And then there's a little-known but nefarious giveaway, tax-increment financing: A form of property tax diversion originally intended to help revitalize blighted urban areas, it now goes to pay for new corporate developments and suburban sprawl.

Greg LeRoy is the author of the 1994 book "No More Candy Store: States and Cities Making Job Subsidies Accountable," and the director of Good Jobs First, a project of the Institute on Taxation and Economic Policy in Washington, D.C. He is accepting nominations for the 1999 Terrible Ten at goodjobs@ctj.org.

No. 1
Economic Development's Black Hole

In a deal with paper giant Willamette Industries for the expansion of a paper and pulp mill in Hawesville, state officials in Kentucky give Willamette tax credits worth $132.3 million. Jobs the company must create in return? Fifteen. In other words, a tax credit entitlement of up to $8.8 million per job!

Willamette spokeswoman Catherine Dunn declined to verify my tax credit computations. But the Kentucky Cabinet for Economic Development, a state agency, did confirm them. Cabinet spokeswoman Pamela Trautner hastened to add that it's unlikely the project will generate enough profits to qualify for all the credits Kentucky is offering. In other words, it's unlikely Willamette Industries will pay any income tax to Kentucky on the Hawesville project for fifteen years. No one knows how much of the $132.3 million Willamette will actually claim because corporate income tax returns are not public.

Although the financing agreement requires the company to create only fifteen new jobs, Trautner said Willamette's application refers to eighty-two new jobs. But she declined to give me a copy, saying that the document is confidential. Willamette Resident Manager Mike Maloney in Hawesville says the company has actually hired 105 new full-time employees, with hourly workers averaging $17.50 an hour plus lots of weekend premiums.

We'll take his word for it. At 105 jobs, the tax credit entitlement clocks in at $1.26 million per job.

"When these corporations don't pay their fair share, the taxpayers pick it up in all sorts of subtle little ways," says Doug Doerrfield, a member of Kentuckians for the Commonwealth. Doerrfield's sewer and water rates, in Rowan County, just went up 37 percent because, his group says, a nearby (subsidized) auto parts plant has exhausted the systems' capacity.

No. 2
The Big Apple's Biggest Bite

No place in the United States has paid out more to companies that threaten to leave town than New York City. It's hard to assemble a comprehensive list, but some of the companies that have threatened to leave if they don't get a tax break are: the New York Mercantile Exchange; Travelers, Inc./Smith Barney; Capital Cities/ABC; Republic National Bank; Morgan Stanley; Prudential Securities; Credit Suisse First Boston; Coffee, Sugar, and Cocoa Exchange; the New York Cotton Exchange; Nasdaq/American Stock Exchange; McGraw-Hill; The New York Times (printing facility); the New York Post (printing facility); Viacom; Reuters; Condé

Nast; CBS-TV; ING Barings; and Paine-Webber.

Now comes the mother of all retention deals in U.S. history: a package worth at least $600 million (some say $900 million) for the New York Stock Exchange.

The Stock Exchange reports it has 1,482 direct employees. Its press release on the deal refers to "more than 3,000" other workers it helps sustain indirectly—traders, brokers, and specialists on the floor. Spokesman Rich Adamonis now claims 4,000. That means the stock exchange got between $109,449 and $133,869 per job—for retention, that is—no new economic activity, just maintaining the status quo.

"All of the city's spending for development goes to Wall Street, high tech, media, and retail—either very high-income or very low-wage jobs," says Brad Lander of the Ad Hoc Coalition for Real Jobs. "Basic family-wage industries like printing, publishing, baking, garment, and fashion are being neglected."

No. 3
'No Justice! No Bonds!'

That was the cry as the Campaign for Justice at Audubon Hospital picketed in Louisville, Kentucky, last year. Campaign members were protesting taxpayer-financed bonds that would save Norton Healthcare at least $2 million a year, perhaps twice that much, for buying out three hospitals owned by Columbia/HCA.

Why the protest? Nurses at Audubon had been trying to organize a union for more than five years. A judge from the National Labor Relations Board ruled in 1997 that Columbia/HCA had committed such "serious and substantial" violations of workers' rights that chances for "a fair election are, in my opinion, nonexistent." In a strong remedy, the judge issued a "bargaining order," recommending the company recognize the union and start bargaining in good faith.

But Columbia/HCA appealed instead, and that is where the matter stood when it chose to sell the three hospitals. Norton bought them, and refused community requests that it meet with the nurses.

Besides the unresolved labor dispute, the campaign warned about a decline in the quality of care at the hospital and said the buy-out could mean job cuts.

Despite the Campaign's mobilization, the Fiscal Court—the local bond-granting agency—approved the bonds by a 3-to-1 vote last October. Within five months, Norton announced it was closing Audubon's pediatric unit and its labor/delivery and mother/baby unit. It also announced it was outsourcing its housekeeping jobs at Audubon and four other hospitals, costing many workers wages and benefits.

Norton spokeswoman Kathy Bernson acknowledges the cuts, but counters that the chain has almost tripled the size of Audubon's

emergency room and is expanding emergency, outpatient, and mother/baby facilities at another of the bond-financed hospitals.

Kay Tillow, lead organizer for Nurses Professional Organization/AFSCME, believes that the Norton bond fight has changed the landscape in Louisville. "We feel like the union movement and the community are more aware of the dollars going to corporations and are going to be more watchful of community and worker interests in these deals," she says.

No. 4
The Great Land Grab

The fastest-growing yet least-understood form of development subsidy in America today is tax-increment financing (TIF). Chicago, for example, now has sixty-four TIF districts.

Tax-increment financing is a property-tax diversion device, originally intended to help revitalize blighted inner-city areas. In such districts, when new development causes incremental increases in property tax revenues, the money does not go for schools or other public services. Instead, it goes back into the neighborhood to subsidize more private development.

State rules vary, but eligible areas can float bonds, build infrastructure, or directly reimburse developers. The diversion typically lasts five to fifteen years, shifting the burden onto other property taxpayers.

But what was once a progressive development idea has turned into a boondoggle for corporate developers. In the Kansas City area, for example, TIF is tied to sprawl, with suburbs using the program to lure employers toward the metro fringe.

Good Jobs First, the labor-issues think tank I founded, recently released an analysis of 525 economic development deals in Minnesota.

Statewide, we found thirty-eight subsidy deals authorized with subsidies of $100,000 or more per job. Thirty-one involve tax-increment financing. Ten TIF projects were approved at $200,000 or more per job. (These sums are diverted from both local property taxpayers and all Minnesota citizens because the state reimburses school districts about $112 million a year for school revenues lost to tax-increment financing.)

In eight projects, companies got TIF subsidies to simply relocate from one Minnesota city to another. Since cities—not the state—grant these subsidies, companies can pit cities against each other for TIF deals. It's a classic zero-sum game.

Would you like to get the data on your state's subsidies? Chances are you can't. Only Minnesota and Maine (beginning May 1, 1999) have detailed disclosure laws.

No. 5
Conserving Industrial Parkland

Last November, the city of Hazelwood, Missouri, announced plans for a 322-acre industrial park in the Missouri Bottoms, a lush farming and wetlands flood plain northwest of St. Louis. The plan would be subsidized by $17.2 million in tax-increment financing.

Missouri law restricts tax-increment financing to "blighted" or "conservation" areas. Hazelwood declared the Bottoms a "conservation area" at risk of blight, based on criteria including the observation that most homes there are more than thirty-five years old.

Bottoms residents were furious. They feared that being declared at risk of blight would harm property values. And they saw the whole maneuver as a gimmick to justify the industrial park. Sparked by Bottoms resident Leon Steinbach, they launched a petition drive. Forty-nine volunteers, many of them past retirement age, braved winter drifts to go door to door. To signal their support, residents adorned their homes and mailboxes with yellow ribbons.

Despite a shrill mailing from the city (Do YOU WANT TO PROTECT HAZELWOOD'S FUTURE OR LET IT SLOWLY DECAY LIKE SOME OTHER OLDER ST. LOUIS COUNTY SUBURBS?), the Yellow Ribbon Committee raked in signatures. One petition, signed by 34.5 percent of the area's registered voters, seeks to make future TIF projects subject to referendum. Two other petitions aim to repeal the industrial park deal.

But at a February 17 city council meeting, the city clerk ruled that all three petitions had failed.

Hazelwood City Clerk Colleen Klos, explaining her ruling, said the charter petition contradicts Missouri law on municipal powers four different ways and had other procedural flaws. She said the petitions to overturn the industrial park deal contained "tons of duplicates" and thus fell short of the required number.

The Committee is scrambling to raise money for a lawyer, hoping a lawsuit will uphold the petitions and give local residents more say in future development deals.

No. 6
Impoverished Schools and Mercedes-Style Subsidies

Since 1993, under the so-called Mercedes law—a special tax credit passed for the car company, which, by law, had to be extended to other companies—Alabama granted a long list of corporations subsidies and tax breaks. Under the law, it was required to publish that list.

But the Alabama legislature gave the Mercedes law a haircut in 1995, after a statewide coalition, Alabama Arise, blew the whistle. Spiraling tax credits, the coalition warned, were threatening the state's ability to fund schools, a constitutional obligation. In a mysterious footnote to that reform, the legislature also deleted the disclosure requirement. Now, Alabama taxpayers get only one page a year, from the Department of Revenue, summarizing approved deals.

On March 8, the Revenue Department issued a four-sentence statement. It said 207 projects had been approved in 1998, to create "approximately 22,668 jobs with a total of $6,363,812,471 in total capital costs for the capital credit." Under the capital credit, a company gets to deduct 5 percent of its capital costs annually for twenty years from its state income-tax bills. In other words, the companies are entitled to as much as $6.4 billion in tax credits for creating 22,668 jobs—more than $280,000 per job.

"The practical effect is they don't pay any [corporate] income tax for twenty years in Alabama," says George Howell, director of economic development in the Alabama Department of Revenue. In actuality, Howell added, the credits will not reach $6.4 billion because companies will not achieve rates of return on their capital investments that would garner the full credit. But the state does not know what share of the $6.4 billion will be claimed, Howell admitted, because it has not estimated those rates of return.

In exchange for these credits, the companies have to pay either wages of $8 an hour or wages and benefits of $10 an hour. In other words, the tax credit the companies qualify for is equal to almost seventeen years of pay they're required to give workers.

Mike Odom, director of the Center for Public Trust in Montgomery, Alabama, recently tried to estimate the value of a deal for a Canadian steel company, Ipsco, to set up a mini-mill in Mobile. Dogged persistence by reporters at the *Mobile Register* finally priced the Ipsco deal between $166,000 and $187,500 per job. Corporate income taxes lost by the state were estimated between $30 and $45 million.

"More than 200 companies have gotten this income tax break since 1995," says Odom. "It's outrageous that the public is denied access to even the names of these companies. So long as the details of these revenue giveaways are kept secret, the legislature is in the dark during its worst budget crisis in years."

Meanwhile, Alabama ranks thirty-eighth in high school graduation rates, according to the U.S. Census.

No. 7
Is Peter Paying to Rob Paul?

When taxpayers find out they are paying for corporate relocations, they often get upset. Wisconsin citizens, for example, flooded Washington, D.C., with petitions in 1994 when they learned that U.S. Department of Housing and Urban Development funds were slated to subsidize job flight from the Milwaukee area to Missouri and Kentucky.

As a result of such disputes, the major federal programs have rules prohibiting their use for interstate job piracy. Besides HUD, major subsidies from the Departments of Labor, Commerce, and the Small Business Administration carry such safeguards.

But states still raid each other. They just make sure to use state and local money instead of federal funds in such deals.

Officials in Brownsville, Texas, now find themselves subsidizing a plant that may be receiving equipment from Iowa. And taxpayers are paying for companies that don't generate any new net economic activity in their area.

Titan Wheel International, headed by CEO Maurice Taylor, won a $30 million package from the Brownsville Economic Development Council in late 1996. The deal includes more than a dozen different subsidies for land, sewer/water hookup, highway construction, a test track, job creation, and training. The company also received property tax reductions, a state franchise tax cut, and a refund on sales taxes.

As the Brownsville plant was being built, Titan's labor relations collapsed with the Steelworkers Union in Des Moines. The 670 Iowa workers went on strike in May 1998.

A few weeks into the strike, Titan announced it was moving equipment from the Des Moines plant to Brownsville. The Associated Press reported on June 5: "Titan Tire made good on its threat to striking workers, announcing Thursday it will move tire-making equipment and hundreds of jobs to Texas because union leaders have not reached an agreement with the company." But in a recent interview, CEO Taylor claims he was misquoted. If Des Moines lost jobs, he says, it was only because two of his company's customers took their work back in-house.

However, a February 11 ruling by a Labor Board judge contradicted the CEO, finding "the transfer and diversion of significant amounts of equipment from Des Moines to Brownsville from May to August 1998." A May 14 press conference transcript quotes Taylor as saying, "We will start moving equipment out of the Des Moines facility to the Brownsville location, and it will be irreversible. . . . It's gonna be a lot of truckloads." Taylor suggests Iowa employment will decline from 650 to 300. The judge recently directed Titan to restore the Des Moines operations to their previous condition. But the standoff continues.

The labor dispute is of little concern to the Brownsville Economic Development Council. Communications director Rick Luna, asked about the controversy, emphasized his town's 12.5 percent unemployment rate and said: "We don't get into internal company issues." The Council's policy on subsidizing footloose companies? "We have done incentive deals for companies coming from other parts of the country," he said. "It's the nature of business these days." How about a company relocating from elsewhere in Texas? "That does make a difference. We'd frown on something like that."

No. 8
High Tech, Low Taxes

Microchip plants are considered a great catch in the economic development profession. At a recent national conference, state and local officials showed deference to two Silicon Valley executives as the speakers barked their site location demands.

So it's not surprising that in 1995, Eugene, Oregon, warmly embraced Hyundai's plans for a chip plant by granting it a 100 percent property tax abatement.

The estimated cost to the community: $27 million in lost revenues for local services. That was for only the first of three phases. The taxpayer cost later grew to an estimated $43 million.

The company thought it had a 100 percent abatement deal covering all three phases. But in 1996, voters in Eugene and several other cities approved Measure 50, curbing cities' ability to raise property tax revenues.

In response, Eugene and Lane County reduced Hyundai's tax abatements on phases two and three to 85 percent. Instead of avoiding $129 million in property taxes, the company would save an estimated $110 million.

Hyundai responded in August 1997 by suing the city and the county in Oregon tax court. The city contends that it never committed beyond phase one. Company spokesman John Lively argues that "the rules were changed" after Hyundai started the project. The court's decision is pending.

No. 9
Subsidies and Environmental Justice

Louisiana's system of industrial property tax exemptions has long favored capital-intensive industries such as chemical, petroleum, and paper, which are also the biggest emitters of toxic waste.

Environmentalists celebrated last September when Shintech, Inc., a U.S. subsidiary of a Japanese chemical company, withdrew plans for a $700 million polyvinyl chloride (PVC) plant in Convent, St. James Parish. (PVC is a known carcinogen and a source of dioxins. St. James Parish is part of Louisiana's notorious "cancer alley," a corridor of polluting factories and high cancer rates from New Orleans to Baton Rouge.)

Shintech's pullout enabled the company to avoid a potentially adverse precedent. Half the population of St. James Parish is nonwhite. Three-fourths of the residents around the plant are African-American. In

1997, six environmental groups filed suit with the EPA, seeking to block federal funding to the state Department of Environmental Quality for its alleged discriminatory handling of the Shintech permitting process. The dispute thus became a test case under the U.S. Environmental Protection Agency's new "environmental racism" rules.

The plant would also have been heavily subsidized. The Louisiana Coalition for Tax Justice estimated total tax breaks at about $119.6 million.

For a projected 165 Shintech jobs and 90 contract jobs, that would have been $469,000 per job.

Shintech controller Dick Mason said the coalition's estimates are "reasonable," but added: "These are all off-the-shelf incentives." In other words, $469,000 per job is not a special deal just for Shintech. "We just fill out the forms," he said. Texas, Mississippi, Alabama, and Canada all offered comparable incentives.

The Shintech dispute was a two-year melodrama. When Tulane University's legal aid clinic came to the aid of Parish residents, Governor Mike Foster called the clinic a haven for "vigilantes" and threatened to encourage donors to the University to withhold money [see "Motion Denied," by Frank Wu, March issue]. A subsequent court decision severely narrowed the clinic's eligible clientele. The state's economic development director ordered an investigation of the Tax Justice Coalition after it questioned Shintech's tax breaks.

The Shintech campaign was spearheaded by St. James Citizens for Jobs and the Environment and by the Louisiana Environmental Action Network. Shintech is now seeking permits for a smaller plant upriver in Plaquemine. "Shintech has been a turning point for the environmental movement and for the people of Louisiana," said Louisiana Environmental Action Network executive director Marylee Orr. "We are not willing to trade our health for a few highly subsidized jobs."

No. 10
Subsidies and Labor Law

In 1993, the 5,000 workers at Avondale Industries voted to join a union—the New Orleans Metal Trades Council. The workers mostly build ships for the U.S. Navy. The union says they are the lowest-paid workers among major U.S. shipyards, with average pay half to two-thirds the rates at other big yards. Since the union vote, the Navy has awarded Avondale $2.7 billion in contracts, the AFL-CIO reports.

But despite the 1993 vote, Avondale workers don't have a union contract. In a highly litigious campaign, the company has resisted a first contract, appealing the vote instead. In February 1998, an administrative

law judge of the National Labor Relations Board found that the company had committed seventy-three unfair labor practices and recommended reinstatement and back pay for twenty-eight wrongfully fired workers.

Besides pay issues, the workers had another big reason for voting union: safety. Union leaders say Avondale's fatality rate is worse than that of any other major Navy yard. Twelve Avondale workers were killed on the job between 1982 and 1994. The Occupational Safety and Health Administration (OSHA) recently completed an inspection at Avondale and is conducting a separate examination of medical records, according to an OSHA spokesman. Outcomes are not yet known.

In addition to its dependence on Navy contracts, Avondale is a heavily subsidized corporation. In testimony before the Louisiana senate, Metal Trades researcher Will Collette catalogued Avondale's many subsidies: sixty-four property tax abatements worth $22.8 million; $9.7 million in enterprise zone benefits; an estimated $45 million saved through tax-exempt bonds; $40 million for a design center; and $1.5 million for another facility—$119 million altogether. Despite those subsidies, the union testified, the plant's estimated average wage of $9.45 is so low it would qualify a family of four for food stamps and the Earned Income Tax Credit.

Avondale spokesman Ed Winter disputed the union's data on wages and bond savings. As Louisiana's largest private employer, he said, the company's annual impact on the state is estimated by a University of New Orleans economist at $1 billion. He declined to comment on whether subsidies entitle the public to hold the company to a higher standard on its labor relations.

Honorable Mention

For sheer chutzpah, hats off to *Time* magazine for raiding the *Philadelphia Inquirer* of Pulitzer winners Donald Barlett and James Steele. *Time* gave them a year and a half to assemble a stunning four-part November series on corporate welfare. *Time* included in the first installment a box that conceded that it was part of the problem, under the headline: TIME WARNER: WE PLAY THE GAME TOO.

After listing its goodies in Florida, Tennessee, and California, the media giant announced that it expects to ask New York City "for a large incentives package for building its new headquarters" in Manhattan. Time Warner hastened to add that its president "emphasized that the project was not contingent upon receiving [the incentives]," but then cited nine other media companies that have been paid to stay in the Big Apple.

Suggested *Post* headline: TIME WARNER TO RUDY: IT'S A GIMME AND WE EXPECT OURS.

Unit Selections

Key Points to Consider

❖ List all the occasions in a typical day in which you come into contact with state and local government services, programs, regulations, and the like. Compare your list with a similar list of daily encounters with the national government.

❖ Identify some policies pursued by your state government or one of your local governments that you consider undesirable. Identify some desirable policies, too.

❖ What do you think about the pros and cons of state and local governments contracting with others to produce goods and render services such as garbage collection, fire protection, school maintenance, prisons, and so forth? Do you think that the private sector can generally do a better job in producing goods and services than can the public sector? Why or why not?

❖ Do you think it is fair that parents who send their children to private or parochial schools still have to pay property taxes to support public schools in their school district? What about people without any children? Should they have to pay taxes to support public education? Why or why not?

❖ Do you think that your state's system of higher education is satisfactory? Why or why not? Do you think that students attending state colleges should have to pay tuition? Why or why not?

❖ What do you think is the single most important service that state governments are primarily responsible for providing? Local governments? The national government?

❖ If you were an elected state government official, on what policy areas would you concentrate your efforts? If you were an elected local government official?

DUSHKIN ONLINE Links   www.dushkin.com/online/

These sites are annotated on pages 4 and 5.

One only has to look through a daily newspaper to realize the multiple and diverse activities in which state and local governments engage. Indeed, it would be an unusual American who, in a typical day, does not have numerous encounters with state and local government programs, services, and regulations.

State and local governments are involved in providing roads, sidewalks, streetlights, fire and police protection, schools, colleges, day-care centers, health clinics, job training programs, public transportation, consumer protection agencies, museums, libraries, parks, sewerage systems, and water. They regulate telephone services, gambling, sanitation in restaurants and supermarkets, land use, building standards, automobile emissions, noise levels, air pollution, hunting and fishing, and consumption of alcohol. They are involved in licensing or certifying undertakers, teachers, electricians, social workers, child-care agencies, nurses, doctors, lawyers, pharmacists, and others. As these listings should make clear, state and local governments affect many, many aspects of everyday life.

Among the most prominent state and local government functions is schooling. For the most part, public elementary and secondary schools operate under the immediate authority of local school districts. Typically headed by elected school boards, these districts are collectively responsible for spending more than $200 billion a year and have no direct counterparts in any other country in the world. State governments regulate and supervise numerous aspects of elementary and secondary schooling, and school districts must operate within the constraints imposed by their state government. In addition, most states have fairly extensive systems of higher education. Tuition charges are higher at private colleges than at state institutions, and taxpayers make up the difference between what students pay and actual costs of operating state colleges. While the national government provides some aid to elementary, secondary, and higher education and involves itself in some areas of education policies, state and local governments remain the dominant policymakers in the field of public education.

Crime control and order maintenance make up another primary state and local government function. Criminal statutes, police forces, prisons, traffic laws (including drunk driving laws and penalties), juvenile detention centers, and courts are all part and parcel of state and local government activities in the area of public safety. Presidential candidates sometimes talk about crime in the streets and what to do about it, but the reality is that state and local governments have far more direct involvement with this policy area than does the national government.

Singling out education and public safety in the preceding two paragraphs is not meant to slight the many other important policy areas in which state and local governments are involved: planning and zoning, roads and public transport, fire protection, provision of health care facilities, licensing and job training programs, and environmental protection, to mention just a few. Selections in this unit should provide greater familiarity with various activities of state and local governments.

The first section of this unit focuses on the issue of service delivery. It is important to distinguish between *provision* and *production* of goods and services by state and local governments. For example, a local government may be responsible for *providing* garbage collection for residents and might meet that responsibility by paying a private firm or a neighboring unit of local government to *produce* the service. Similarly, a state government may be responsible for *providing* penal institutions to house certain kinds of criminal offenders, but might meet that responsibiity by paying a private concern or another state government to *produce* (plan, build, organize, and operate) a prison where offenders will be confined. In recent years, the concept of privatization has figured prominently in discussions and decisions about the best ways for state and local governments to deliver services.

The second section of this unit treats issues facing state and local governments in various policy areas. Interactions among national, state, and local governments frequently play important roles in shaping such policy issues.

Topics in this unit of the book can be viewed as the consequences of topics treated in earlier units. Intergovernmental relations and finances, elections, parties, interest groups, and governmental institutions all shape the responses of state and local governments to policy issues. In turn, policies that are adopted interact with other components of state and local politics and modify them accordingly. Thus, the subject matter of unit 7 is an appropriate way to conclude this book.

Service Delivery and Policy Issues

Making Cents: Better City Services for Less

John C. Weicher

Better municipal services, for less money, are being geared up in many American and Third World cities, as some old ideas are finding new applications.

The ideas are competition and privatization, and they are as old as Adam Smith. Under the leadership of a new generation of reform-oriented mayors, cities are turning to the private sector to provide many public services. City governments are selling facilities to private owners and putting services up for bid between private providers and municipal agencies.

• In Indianapolis, Mayor Stephen Goldsmith has privatized the management of a large wastewater treatment plant (after the federal government would not let him sell it), and has contracted for maintenance services on the city's fleet of trucks and heavy equipment.

• In Chicago, Mayor Richard Daley has hired private firms to provide janitors and parking lot attendants at O'Hare Airport, and privatized the management of city-owned golf courses.

• In Jersey City, Mayor Bret Schundler has hired private firms instead of using municipal employees to remove graffiti, with an added twist: The firms are picked by neighborhood residents.

• These cities are following in the footsteps of Phoenix, which began competitively contracting many services nearly twenty years ago.

Indianapolis Leads in Privatization

The acknowledged leader in the movement is Indianapolis. Since Goldsmith was first elected in 1991, the city has moved more than forty services into the marketplace, sometimes by selling facilities but more often by competition. Contracts have been awarded for trash collection, pothole repair, transit service for the disabled, golf course maintenance and more. In each case, the awards are made after competitive bidding.

Some contracts have been won by the municipal departments that already provided the service. But in the process of competing they became more efficient and eliminated unnecessary jobs—using, for example, four workers and one truck on each pothole crew, instead of eight workers and two trucks.

Goldsmith argues that monopoly is the fundamental barrier to effective local government. Because government agencies have no competition, they have no incentive to provide decent service at reasonable cost. The mayor believes that public employees are often good people working in bad systems. Successful agency bids to provide pothole repair, fleet maintenance, and trash collection seem to bear him out.

Goldsmith's accomplishments have brought municipal officials from across the U.S. to Indianapolis including the mayors of New York and Los Angeles. He has also met with mayors from Israel.

When Should City Government Provide a Service?

Goldsmith and other mayors are taking a hard look at the conventional wisdom of local governance. The traditional reason for government to provide a service is the economic concept of a "natural monopoly." In most industries, there are several firms that can compete effectively, and their competition holds down the prices that consumers pay. But for some services, technology only leaves room for one efficient firm. Public utilities are typical examples: electricity, gas, water, telephone, cable television.

Running a second power or gas line through the same neighborhood is needlessly expensive, but a monopolist could charge a prohibitive price for necessities such as water or electricity. Local governments have therefore usually chosen either to operate a public utility themselves or let a single firm operate it, while regulating charges and conditions of service.

Competition is now being recognized as an efficient option for many of these services. Trash collection is an example. E.S. Savas, professor of public management at

Baruch College, part of the City University of New York, is probably the leading expert on privatization in America. He has found that private firms provide the same quality service for about one-third less, on average. The savings range from 15 to 50 percent.

Savas also concludes that the efficient scale of operations is small. He recommends dividing a city into trash collection districts and conducting competition in each district. Different firms can serve adjacent neighborhoods.

In Indianapolis, Goldsmith split the city into 11 districts. The Department of Public Works won the contract in four, while the others went to four different private companies. All the winners must provide effective service or risk losing the contract when it comes up for renewal in three to five years. Savings of 20 percent are estimated.

Other services are less easily contracted out, but still offer possibilities for privatization and competition. It may be efficient to have the government provide water or run a subway system, but the government does not need to bill water customers or clean the subway stations. Many private firms do exactly the same work, and they can bid for contracts with government agencies just as they bid for contracts to handle accounts receivable or clean office buildings for private firms.

Urban Transit: A Case Study

A century ago, urban transit was also—briefly—a natural monopoly. Until the invention of the electric street railway in 1883, public transit was largely provided by horse-drawn cars, and most American cities had several competing companies. Streetcars were much more efficient, and they did not pollute the environment. They operated on a very different scale than the horsecars. An entire municipal system of streetcars could be powered from a single generating plant. There was no economic reason to have two streetcar systems in the same city.

The streetcar quickly became the dominant mode of urban transit, but its dominance was short-lived. Usage peaked in the U.S. in 1916. It lost out to the internal combustion engine and the bus. Buses, which were used as early as 1905 in New York, did not change the way transit systems were organized. In many cities, they were owned by the same municipal agencies or private firms that ran the streetcars. They were part of the local monopoly.

But buses differ from streetcars. Each bus has its own source of power, and they can be much smaller than streetcars—as small, in fact, as automobiles, which were used as common carriers as early as 1914. These "jitneys," as they were called, did not serve fixed schedules or even fixed fares, but they became very popular. UCLA economist George Hilton has calculated that 62,000 were operating by 1915, a year after the first one

took its first passenger. Indeed, they were so popular they were outlawed, because they threatened the solvency of the established streetcar and bus companies, which had become important constituencies and opposed to competition.

It was not until the 1980s, in the course of a wave of deregulation in the transportation industry, that jitneys were again allowed to operate in some cities, including San Diego; Portland, Oregon; and Seattle. Indianapolis legalized them in 1994. Other small-scale private transportation services have developed in recent years, such as vanpools and commuter buses. Gradually, competition and privatization have crept back into the American urban transit system.

Is this experience relevant to cities in developing nations? Proof that it is comes from similar efforts underway in many Third World countries.

Privatization in Third World Countries

Privatization has been advocated and fostered by the World Bank for about a decade. The impetus came from A.W. Clausen, who became president after being chairman and CEO of the Bank of America and thus was familiar with both the public and the private sectors. In recent years, the World Bank has been making loans in a number of countries for private production of infrastructure, such as electric power plants in the Ivory Coast and Guatemala, and water and sewer facilities in Buenos Aires.

But privatization is not limited to activities sponsored by the World Bank, and its use in the Third World did not originate with the bank. Gabriel Roth, a longtime World Bank staff analyst who is now a private consultant in Washington, has documented the private sector's "pervasive" role in developing countries.

Urban transit provides the most extensive and most noticeable examples of privatization, so it is not surprising that Roth, whose specialty is transportation, became interested in the concept. In this area, developing countries have followed the lead of the industrialized nations.

The dominant urban transit mode in most of the world is the bus, operated as a government or private monopoly. But in many cities there are alternatives. Much smaller vehicles—minibuses, vans or even station wagons—are operated as public transportation by private individuals or businesses. They are somewhere between a bus and a taxi, both in size and type of service. Their operating policies vary from one city to the next. They may serve routes that the big buses do not, or the same routes. They may have fixed schedules, or they may follow a policy of waiting for a full load.

A wide variety of vehicles is used around the world. For example:

• In Nairobi, people ride *matatu*, which are either minibuses or pickup trucks.

- In Istanbul, there are *dolmus*, which are five-seat taxis or seven-seat station wagons.
- In Manila, the "jeepneys" prevail. Originally built on the chassis of U.S. Army jeeps after World War II, they are now manufactured locally.

These vehicles are typically owned by individuals, often by their operators. They are cheaper than the municipal buses, or they provide better service, or both. Like the original American jitney, they often serve poor people who cannot afford the officially sanctioned bus or who do not live near a bus route.

They are also usually much smaller, with a capacity of five to twenty-five, compared to a hundred or more for conventional buses. Partly for that reason, they are able to operate with higher load factors. But size is not a crucial difference. For example, full-size private buses are operated profitably in Calcutta and Colombo.

Unfortunately, these private services often confront the same obstacles as the American jitney did. In most cases, they operate in the face of official opposition. Some are technically illegal.

Government-sponsored bus companies have been able to force them out of business, as in Abidjan and Buenos Aires—at least for a time. The companies claim that the jitneys are taking away their business and causing them to lose money, and they have enlisted the power of the government to protect their franchises. Even so, where these alternatives are legal or at least tolerated, they are essential to the local economy.

- **Privatization Becoming an International Trend**

The international popularity of privatization and competition is surprising, because American and Third World cities have very different economies and face different problems in providing public services. In many U.S. cities, there has been a long period of decline in the tax base, as many middle-class and well-to-do residents move to the suburbs. The cities are left with public service systems that were intended to serve a larger population. They do provide some services to suburban commuters and shoppers, but many suburbanites avoid visiting the city.

In Asia, Africa and Latin America, on the other hand, many cities are growing rapidly as they lead their national economies into modern industrial society. They are repeating the experience of European and American cities during the Industrial Revolution, as they strain to serve a burgeoning population.

Yet despite these differences, privatization has spread in the Third World as well as the First. The great advantage of competition and privatization is the lower cost associated with them. Private firms in a competitive situation have a profit motive. They need to provide a service as efficiently as possible, or they will lose money and go out of business. Government agencies have less incentive to do a good job. Their managers are rarely held responsible for losses.

For the same reason, privately provided services are often better as well as cheaper. Because they have to satisfy their customers or lose the contract, private firms have to pay attention to what their customers want. Competition and privatization are not panaceas. They will not solve all the problems of cities in either the First World or the Third. Yet they can help to revitalize cities. By relieving the financial pressures on beleaguered governments, they leave room for more spending on important services that cannot be privatized.

Indianapolis, for example, has been able to devote up to $15 million more each year to police and fire protection, while cutting total municipal employment by 30 percent. In addition, more efficient local public services may be an economic stimulus. Major businesses weigh the quality of life in deciding where to locate, and high-quality public services are part of what they look for.

Competition and privatization, then, are proving that they can make cities better places to work and live. The upshot is that the private sector is showing that it *can* perform a public service.

John C. Weicher is a Senior Fellow with the Hudson Institute. He served as Assistant Secretary for Policy Development and Research at the U.S. Department of Housing and Urban Development from 1989 to 1993. He is the author most recently of Privatizing Subsidized Housing *and a forthcoming book,* Federal Housing Policy. *Reprinted with permission from* The World & I, *February 1997.*

GUIDE TO PRIVATIZATION

Counting on Competition

As governments everywhere contract out services to the private sector they're looking for ways to measure what they are getting for their money.

BY DIANE KITTOWER

PROPOSALS TO PRIVATIZE A GOVERNMENT AGENCY or service are often accompanied by grand promises of efficiency and cost savings. As state and local governments continue to explore the complicated and risky world of privatization, many have come to realize that the only way to determine whether the process works is to develop methods for measuring the outcomes.

So how do you gauge how well a contractor is doing with such undertakings as a child support enforcement agency, a water treatment plant or a golf course? The answers vary as much as the projects do.

Virginia has taken something of a scientific approach to the question: In May 1994, officials set up an experiment to compare how well the private and public sectors could manage child support enforcement. Two offices that would remain state-operated would serve as a control while two comparable offices were to be run by Lockheed Martin

> When considering a government operation for privatization, figuring out the current full cost is a crucial step. Virginia relies on a computer program.

IMS. The state Division of Child Support Enforcement regularly analyzes the collection numbers from the privatized offices in Chesapeake and Hampton, as well as those from the two publicly run offices in Fredericksburg and Portsmouth.

The most recent full-year figures, for fiscal 1997, show that the privatized offices collected more money overall and more money for families that receive no aid from the state, but that the publicly run offices were collecting more effectively for families that do receive benefits under the Temporary Aid to Needy Families program. The distinction is important, because the state takes a percentage of the money collected from a spouse of a family that receives aid.

In the first quarter of this year, the total amounts collected also show a mixed picture: The privatized Chesapeake office had secured a total of $2.8 million in both child support categories, and the privatized Hamp-

Employees as Owners

Virginia soon may be trying an entirely different brand of privatization. The state's Commonwealth Competition Council is following up on a suggestion from some state employees who wanted to restructure their agency as an employee-owned company.

The council studied the history and benefits of employee stock ownership plans, in which employees own at least some of the company's stock. It was impressed enough with their track record that it now is evaluating state government agencies with an eye toward which ones might succeed as ESOPs.

This month, the council expects to recommend that several agencies try becoming ESOPs. Managers and employees at the agencies would decide whether to go for it. Those that did would get a contract for up to five years, to give them time "to grow the business" while they have a guaranteed income, says Phil Bomersheim, the council's executive director. Then the employee-owned operations would have to bid for the business on the same basis as other companies.

ton office had collected $3.8 million. The figures for the state-operated Fredericksburg and Portsmouth offices were $3.3 million and $2.4 million, respectively.

Other responsibilities of the offices include locating absent parents and establishing child support orders, and the state also tracked those figures. In fiscal 1997, the number of parents found by the Chesapeake, Hampton and Portsmouth offices decreased, while Fredericksburg's increased. In terms of child support orders established, the publicly run offices out-performed the privatized offices: Portsmouth increased the number of orders it established by 8.5 percent, while Fredericksburg pushed its total up by a full 52 percent. The privatized Chesapeake office established 5.9 percent fewer child support orders, while Hampton established 2.6 percent more.

The child support division also tracked the child support offices' operational efficiency, and found that the privatized offices cost $16,185 less to run in fiscal 1997 than the state-operated ones. In addition, the agency concluded that the cost-benefit difference between the two approaches has been on the decline for the past two fiscal years. The experiment is no longer merely a pilot project; the General Assembly now permits privatization as one way the state can operate these agencies.

The year after legislators set up this experiment, they went even further in exploring privatization by creating the Commonwealth Competition Council. It was mandated to encourage innovation and competition in state government, evaluate opportunities to privatize, and help with the privatization process. The council's 10 members come from the General Assembly, the executive branch and the private sector. Of the five steps it follows as it does

its mandated job, two involve measuring performance.

Once a state operation is being considered for privatization, figuring out the current full cost is a crucial step, says Phil Bomersheim, the council's executive director. For that purpose, the council developed a computer program called COMPETE, which is designed to run on a PC and come up with the fully allocated cost of any function or activity. Costs such as direct and indirect operating expenses, capital asset depreciation, and overhead all go into the calculation. The spreadsheet has been made as simple as possible, Bomersheim says, to allow agencies to essentially plug in numbers to get answers. (The Air Force uses a similar, but more complex, program.)

In addition, the council creates an ongoing quality-assurance program to monitor each privatized project and does a post-performance review at the end of each contract. It reported $13.9 million in net savings for

---

In Martin County, Florida, a performance auditor was hired and given the responsibility of writing a monthly report on the city's water and sewer service.

---

last year from 20 projects. Perhaps one measure of the state's success is that Kansas, North Carolina, Texas and Utah are considering legislation modeled on Virginia's.

AUDITING POWER

Quality assurance in Martin County, Florida, takes the form of a performance auditor, whose job is to make sure that water and sewer services are up to the standards promised by the people providing them. Those providers are public employees, who won out over more than 20 other bidders in 1996. The memorandum of understanding between the employees, who became a "contractual division," and the county projected $10.5 million in savings over five years. The employees remain public workers but are obligated to meet the terms of the five-year pact.

To achieve the savings, employees agreed to reduce the number of positions from 62 to 40 by the beginning of the second year. That was an effective way to cut costs, since a county analysis had determined that personnel accounted for 64 percent of operating expenses; in fiscal year 1998, after the reduction in employees, personnel costs were accounting for 46 percent of operating expenses. Employees' plans also included fewer supervisors, centralized plant and field maintenance, and more use of technology, such as for plant monitoring.

All the ideas sounded good, but the county commissioners wanted objective documentation of how things actually were going. Productivity can be great at the beginning of a privatization contract but then slack off, says Deputy County Administrator Randall Reed, and there is always the possibility of falsified reports. Performance indicators had not been sufficiently spelled out when the services were publicly run, so a new set was written to make evaluations easier, including specifics of such things as how pumps were to be maintained.

More important, a performance auditor was hired and given the responsibility of writing a monthly performance report. He checks items such as the amount of water produced and how much wastewater has been treated, and reviews maintenance logs for the pumps. The likeliest way to undermine the memorandum of understanding would be through change orders, a classic problem in contracting out, Reed says, so the auditor also reviews all change orders. His salary is paid by the contractual division. During the first year, he visited every month; now he visits every two months.

Developing a checklist is the hard part, says Malt Dominy, the performance auditor and director of managed competition services at HNTB, a company that specializes in privatization services. He based his on the request for proposals, the employees' proposal and the memorandum of understanding. The checklist had to be written on a pass-fail basis rather than being subjective, Dominy says: "Have they done it? Is it reported?" For example, the employees said one key way of achieving economies was by moving from reactive maintenance to preventive maintenance, something Dominy therefore monitors. The contractual division sends him a monthly report—a three-inch thick binder, he notes—to review.

At the end of the first year, the division came in $362,000 below its $4.1 million bid price for that period. Reed gives a lot of credit to performance auditing: "It is essential to make sure what is said to take place occurs." In fact, he believes that more government officials should learn how to monitor contracts.

FOCUS ON THE CONTRACT

A performance auditor comes in after a contract is signed; Cranston, Rhode Island, officials put their emphasis on preparing the contract itself. They made the deal simple: Either the private contractor provides proper, uninterrupted wastewater treatment, or Cranston owes it nothing. But the city went into great detail about how that should happen, negotiating a 300-page contract that was signed in September of last year.

To make sure that the plant is returned in at least as good condition when the contract ends in 25 years, the city had it surveyed before turning it over. Other standards, such as odor level, are harder to pin down. Still, Cranston had a panel that determined the acceptable level of odors at and around the plant so that it has a baseline for future comparisons. The condition of the plant, odor and wastewater quality are among the topics that are discussed at required monthly status meetings. The contractor also must provide regular progress reports.

Another contract requirement that the city is monitoring is capital improvements. If they go over bid or are not done on time—things the city can evaluate easily—it will demand either a specified amount of damages or, if the overage or delay is severe enough, possibly deem the contractor in default.

Naturally, the city expects the company to comply with all regulations that relate to water-quality permits. Again, penalties consist of fines and default.

THE DEALS ON THE BUS

Las Vegas took precisely the opposite tack from Cranston's detailed approach to contracting when it created a bus system and privatized its operations.

In 1990, the city's voters, frustrated with traffic congestion, approved a ¼-cent sales tax dedicated to mass transit. To get the system up and running as quickly as possible, and believing that it also would save money, city officials decided to contract out bus operations. However, policy-setting and long-term oversight were reserved for the public Regional Transportation Commission. In its contract with Citizens Area Transit, the private contractor that provides bus service, the allocation of responsibilities was clearly spelled out.

The thinking is that the public sector is better at dealing with policy issues, but the private sector is more flexible, says Lee Gib-son, the authority's planning manager, so having the two work together creates a well-balanced partnership. Gibson's staff does the scheduling, for example, and the contractor gets 30 days to comment on the schedules in writing before implementing them.

To keep the partnership running smoothly, the RTC chose not to lay out specific numbers of transgressions that would result in punishment. Instead, the approach was to make sure everyone agreed on the procedures to collect the data—such as on-time performance—and then create a working group representing the RTC and CAT that would meet regularly to unsnarl any problems and reach consensus. There is no "finger-pointing," Gibson says.

So the RTC monitors missed trips, failure of buses to be on time, compliance with the Americans with Disabilities Act, maintenance, the number of complaints from riders, and whether drivers collect fares properly. The results are discussed at the working group. Although the city agency has the right to demand financial penalties, it never has.

Of course, being late is the one thing bus riders will always complain about, and Gibson cites an average on-time rate of 95 percent. When buses are behind schedule, he says, it's usually because of some factor beyond the contractor's control.

Another measure of how well a transit system is operating is whether an increasing number of people are using it. Las Vegas's 215 buses carried 41 million riders in 1997, a 175 percent increase over 1993. The growth in ridership has averaged 34 percent every year since 1992, Gibson says, while annual vehicle miles have doubled since the first year. Enough people use, and see, the buses that the RTC was able to sell its vehicles' visibility: This year it will receive

The Privatization Comparison

After Virginia privatized two of its child support enforcement offices, it found that in fiscal year 1997 the privatized offices collected more money for families that do not receive Temporary Aid to Needy Families. Two comparable offices that remained state-operated collected more money for families that do receive TANF benefits. The figures below are for dollars collected per case for FY 1997; in the first quarter of FY 1998, the privatized offices collected more child support overall.

| | Privatized | | State-Operated | |
	Chesapeake	Hampton	Fredericksburg	Portsmouth
TANF cases	$390.20	$375.08	$458.64	$365.89
Non-TANF cases	$1,039.81	$1,067.97	$1,179.51	$897.81

Source: Virginia Division of Child Support Enforcement.

Las Vegas is earning more than a million dollars this year from advertising on its privatized bus system.

Photograph courtesy of the Clark County Regional Transportation Commission

Privatization: More on the Way

If a jurisdiction does choose to privatize, officials say, monitoring performance is critical. A U.S. General Accounting Office report on privatization by states and localities noted that several jurisdictions with successful projects called this step the weakest link in the process.

More officials will have to pay attention to performance measurement, however, because there are clear indications that privatization's popularity is increasing. For example, the National League of Cities asked members last year about their plans for use of privatization: 41 percent said they planned to use it at the same level, 25 percent said they wanted to do more, 29 percent said they didn't use it and 5 percent said they wanted to cut back.

A recent Council of State Governments survey asked members to report whether the number of privatizations had increased over the past five years and to predict future use: 32.8 percent said use had remained the same, 58.6 said use had increased and 3.4 percent said they did not use privatization. For the future, 55.2 percent said they wanted to increase the number of privatizations, 34.5 percent said they would probably maintain the current level, 3.4 percent planned no privatization and 6.9 percent did not reply.

more than a million dollars for permitting buses to be "wrapped" in advertising.

Las Vegas officials think the bus system works well enough, Gibson adds, that they are considering creating a privatized light rail system following the same model.

PARTNERS IN RECYCLING

The city of Newport News, Virginia, liked the idea of treating its contractor as a partner, too, so it tried that approach on its recycling contract. The city had gotten a lot of complaints about the first contractor it had hired, and it was eager for the second one to succeed because it wasn't interested in getting into the recycling business itself. In addition to negotiating the privatization deal, city officials worked with Tidewater Fibre Corp. to create a mission statement that listed six goals, including timely collection and public education.

Rating sheets provide the basis for discussion at frequent meetings between line-level employees of both sectors. In this way, the contractor is evaluated by the city and some of the company's employees on how well the job is being done in nine areas, such as timely collection, customer service, public education and communications. If any area receives a low rating by most participants, it becomes a meeting topic. Problems such as lack of spare drivers

New Haven's municipal golf course is making money since it was privatized last year, and the course is better maintained.

Photograph countesy of the city of New Haven

Newport News, Virginia's recycling contractor is rated by the city and by the company's own employees in nine areas of performance.

and responsibility for bin replacement have been brought up and resolved.

These days, the complaint rate about the contractor is about the same as for the city-run trash collection operation, says Sue Hogue, a spokeswoman for the public works department, and the city figures that's pretty good.

GREEN ON THE GREENS

New Haven, Connecticut, officials also wanted to give the private sector a shot at a service. They city's 18-hole golf course was losing money: $23,000 in 1994, $131,000 in 1995 and $98,000 in 1996. On top of that, it was not well maintained.

That made it easy to set performance standards when the city privatized the course's management. The fairways were to be kept cut, green and fertilized, the broken sprinkler system was to be repaired, and sand in the sand traps was to be replaced.

New England Golf, which runs municipal and private golf clubs throughout the region, took over the course last June. By December, it reported an operating income net profit of $85,000. More important than the money, says the city's budget director, Frank A. Altieri, is that the quality of the course has been brought up to par. Greens are now groomed and cross-cut, and required repairs have been completed. As a result, he says, membership has boomed to the point that applications from out of town are on hold until resident demand is sated.

New ways of education

CHESTER E. FINN, JR. & REBECCA L. GAU

CHESTER E. FINN, JR., is John M. Olin Fellow at the Hudson Institute and president of the Thomas B. Fordham Foundation.

REBECCA L. GAU is a graduate student at the Terry Sanford Institute of Public Policy at Duke University.

EDUCATION in America is in a state of rapid and unprecedented change: unfamiliar schools, hybrid policy arrangements, mutating school-choice strategies, and other startling novelties are appearing throughout the country. Today's education atlas, in fact, needs to be updated as often as maps of the former Soviet Union. Such was not always the case.

Yesterday's education map held just two continents. The first, of course, was public education where all schools were run by government bureaucracies and staffed by public employees; each community had just one school "system"; every school (with rare exceptions such as the Bronx High School of Science) was essentially identical to every other; and the bureaucracy assigned you to a school district and then to a particular school building. All funding came from taxpayers via complex formulae and regulations devised by at least three levels of government.

The second, far smaller, continent was "private schools." These had little to do with government; they were privately financed; and you could send your children to whichever one you liked—provided that you could afford it and it was willing to accept them. Private schools could hire whom they wished and, for the most part, teach what they wanted. The evidence indicated that they produced somewhat stronger student achievement than public schools while conferring such added benefits as safety, character development, and, often, religious education. Yet, for all that, most private schools followed the same fundamental design as public: the same 180-day year, six-hour day, and low-tech, grade-by-grade, textbook-by-textbook, one-teacher-per-classroom notion of what a school should be.

That was then. Today, three momentous developments have sparked reform: First, awareness is growing that the current U.S. education system at the primary and secondary levels is producing woeful results and that incrementalist strategies for reforming it (smaller classes, added graduation requirements, etc.) haven't made much difference. Bolder alternatives—including some that overturn yesterday's axioms and power relationships—are now thinkable. Second, there is a widening recognition that "one-size-fits-all" education does not work very well in our pluralistic democracy. As people have demanded additional options, new types of schools have come into existence along with new ways of enabling families to choose among them. Not only do some of those novel schools better suit America's varied educational needs but the marketplace of parental choice also helps to hold them accountable for student achievement and client satisfaction.

Third, shifts can be seen in the organizational arrangements of public and private enterprises of all kinds, shifts designed to make them more productive and efficient. On the public side, this is sometimes called "reinventing government." It includes outsourcing, decentralizing, new incentives, and accountability arrangements. In the private sector, it takes the form of corporate restructuring and downsizing, eliminating middle-men, shrinking bureaucracies, debulking rulebooks, and installing "total quality management" strategies. In both sectors, the goal is to achieve better outcomes (satisfied customers, greater output, higher achievement, etc.) with fewer wasted resources. Such language is no longer alien to our schools.

New forms of schooling

By our count, today's education map contains—in addition to traditional public and private institutions—a dozen other forms of schools and schooling.

Reprinted with permission of the authors and *The Public Interest*, Winter 1998, pp. 79-92. © 1998 by National Affairs, Inc.

1. Magnet schools. Between 1984 and 1994, student participation in magnet schools tripled. Usually district-based, these are purposefully created specialty schools with particular themes or emphases: music and art, science and technology, Hispanic cultures, etc. The first magnets were mainly intended to integrate schools by attracting youngsters to distant classrooms without compulsory busing. But magnets now serve multiple purposes. Indeed, a few communities have turned all their schools into magnet schools, thus backing into comprehensive public-school choice programs. Montclair, New Jersey provides a good example of both achievement gains and racial integration via magnets. Each of the town's public schools now has a distinctive focus and more than half of Montclair's children now choose schools outside their neighborhoods, producing greater racial balance as well as rising test scores.

2. Alternative schools. Developed primarily for hard-to-educate and misbehaving youngsters, these are not so much schools that parents select as schools that are chosen for children with problems. Most often they are secondary schools with low pupil-teacher ratios, modified curricula, and flexible schedules. For example, Southwest Open High School in Cortez, Colorado serves 16- to 21-year-olds and offers infant-care classes for teen parents, high-school-equivalency preparation, and employment training. Eight states now mandate alternative education. And many districts are now moving in this direction, partly in response to teachers who find they cannot handle certain youngsters in "regular" classrooms, partly in response to political, legal, and community pressure not to just "suspend" or "expel" such youngsters.

3. Charter schools. Ranging from back-to-basics to Montessori methods to schools for disabled kids, with a hundred other models in between, charter schools are a fascinating hybrid: public schools with some features of private schools. As public institutions, they're open to all who wish to attend, paid for with tax dollars, and accountable to public authorities for their performance (especially student achievement) and certain operating rules (e.g., non-discrimination). But they also enjoy features heretofore associated primarily with private schools: self-governance, freedom from most regulations, the ability to hire whom they like (usually without a union contract), control of their own (secular) curricula, and attendance only by youngsters whose parents elect them. Besides accountability to state or local authorities, they must satisfy their customers—or they won't have students.

The charter movement has grown in just a few years to about 750 schools enrolling some 170,000 youngsters, equivalent to the student population of New Hampshire. Almost 30 states have passed enabling legislation (though in some it's weak and pallid). Today, charters are moving from being a marginal option for a relative handful of disgruntled families to a major source of educational alternatives for a great many kids.

4. Home schooling. It appears that between 1 percent and 4 percent of U.S. children are now being taught at home by their parents. This practice is legal in every state. Sixteen states don't even regulate curricula, testing, or parent qualifications. Historically, home schoolers were religious families dissatisfied with the public-school curriculum and not comfortable with (or unable to afford) private schools. Lately, more parents cite reasons such as mediocrity in the public-school system.

An intriguing variant involves youngsters who attend school part time and are taught at home part time. In Idaho, public schools must allow home-schooled (and private-schooled) children to participate in any school activity, including sports as well as academics. A Massachusetts family sends its son to school only for chemistry and printmaking, handling the rest at home. His older brother, before going to Brown University, played in the school orchestra but learned his academics at home. Several charter schools now specialize in this kind of arrangement, making it easier to obtain the best of both worlds.

5. Schools-within-schools. There is no reason why a single school building must contain only one education program. This insight inspired the well-known public-school choice program of East Harlem's District 4, but it is also a strategy well-suited to rural areas where there aren't many schools. Fitting more than one program into the same building makes it easier to offer instructional alternatives without worrying about bricks and mortar. It also cuts the risk—and drama—of starting a new program. If one doesn't work out, or students don't want it, makeovers are fairly simple and pupils can select different offerings by going up or down the stairs.

6. Mini-schools. New York City, with help from philanthropist Walter Annenberg and inspiration from Deborah Meier, a veteran education entrepreneur in District 4, has started several dozen high schools with just 100 to 200 pupils each, schools with some of the freedoms of charter schools but also with distinctive curricular themes and the intimate scale so acutely absent from the city's regular public high schools. Some, like the Manhattan Village Academy, stick to rather traditional curricula. Another—the School for the Physical City—collaborates with Outward Bound to provide a curriculum centered on New York's infrastructure. Regardless of their emphases, city officials say that these schools are safer and that their attendance is high (though those good results do not keep the Chancellor's office from threatening to re-regulate the schools themselves).

7. Tech-prep schools. One hundred and sixteen community colleges in 33 states have joined forces with local high schools to blend the last two years of high school with the first two years of college, often leading to an associate's degree as well as a high-school diploma. Also called "11–14 schools" after the grade levels involved, the concept is especially well-suited to young people more interested in jobs than academics.

8. After-school schools. Partly because of changing family patterns and work schedules, and partly because of dissatisfaction with regular schools, more and more families, churches, and community organizations are supplementing children's schooling with a wide array of programs and offerings. Some resemble the "juku"—cram schools—of Japan. Many are nonprofit, but some of the fastest-growing ones are owned by commercial firms. Sylvan Learning Centers offer personal instruction programs from pre-school to college. Sylvan has also joined with the National Geographic Society to provide "hands-on experiments and exploration activities" in school facilities, run—after school hours—by Sylvan employees. (Parents pay for the program.) Voyager Expanded Learning also offers after-school programs on school premises, engaging teachers from the school to work the additional hours and follow its thematic curriculum. With over 100 locations in Texas, the Dallas-based company is expanding into other states and working with school districts on a "discovery learning hour" during the school day. It also served 17,000 youngsters in 17 states with "hands-on learning" programs last summer.

Other after-hours programs concentrate on the moral and character issues that are frequently slighted in the regular school program. Civil-rights hero Rosa Parks runs one in Detroit that teaches children "quiet strength" to resolve problems and also offers self-paced study. The Rosa Parks Institute for Self Development has now become the seedbed for a future charter school, showing how one educational innovation can lead to another.

9. Chains of "proprietary" schools. Private schools always included a handful of profit-seeking schools as well as the more familiar nonprofit variety. But they were mostly single-campus, mom-and-pop operations that afforded a living for the family that owned them. Today, whole chains of for-profit schools are emerging, complete with shareholders and corporate managers. Nobel Education Dynamics, for example, operates 123 schools in 14 states and is building more. The firm prefers to open several schools in the same area in order to provide a seamless preschool-through-eighth-grade education.

10. Design-based schools. The corporate (and Annenberg) financed, non-profit, New American Schools Development Corporation (NASDC) sponsors seven design teams that have created, and are now marketing, distinctive designs for innovative schools. Several are openly "progressive" in their educational concepts—full of "developmentally appropriate" curricula and "cooperative learning"—while another bears the curricular fingerprints of former Education Secretary William J. Bennett.

Several different designs may co-exist in the same community. Memphis, Tennessee has schools featuring all but one NASDC design. Six Memphis schools use CoNECT (Cooperative Networking Educational Community for Tomorrow) curricula designed by BBN Systems and Technologies—the firm credited with building the Internet. Four other schools employ the Bennett-inspired Modern Red Schoolhouse curriculum, which has a back-to-basics core with a technological twist. Not far away in Nashville, the entire school system is installing the "Core Knowledge" curriculum pioneered by E. D. Hirsch, which is also popular in many charter schools.

11. Virtual schools. Need students come to school at all? Using the Internet and e-mail, they can interact with their teachers (and with lesson plans and homework assignments) without leaving home. In the old days, families living in the mountains or posted to distant lands could obtain mail-order curricula for their children. Today, technology makes possible "classrooms" that are open 24 hours a day. California's Choice 2000 program "enrolls" approximately 130 middle- and high-school students. Combining a computerized bulletin board and downloaded curriculum software, students can work at their own speed. For those who need help, chat rooms and on-line communication allow teachers to guide them.

12. Privately managed public schools. Close to a dozen firms are in the "school-management" business in the United States. They attempt—via charter or management contracts with the district—to run public schools and to make a profit along the way. The best known among them are Educational Alternatives, Inc., which embarked on large, but ill-fated, ventures in Baltimore and Hartford, and the Edison Project. Though it remains to be seen whether investor profits will follow, it's apparent that public education in the United States is becoming amenable to "outsourcing."

The Edison Project (with which one of the authors was previously affiliated) has contracts (or charters) to run schools in Michigan, Kansas, Massachusetts, Florida, Colorado, Texas, California, and Minnesota. Today, Edison operates 25 schools enrolling 13,000 students. Though the oldest of these schools are only in their third year—and Edison insists that five years are necessary to demonstrate results—early studies show encouraging test-score gains in the earliest grades. Enrollments in schools run by Edison are growing, and most communities with Edison contracts want to expand the relationship.

Not every innovation succeeds, of course. Families change their minds. Boards and principals fight. Teachers quit. Charter schools close. Private contractors may not make a profit and stick with the business. Some appealing school designs do little for student achievement. That's the price of change. Yet new kinds of schools keep popping up. Many of them embody not only curricular and instructional breakthroughs but also changes in the ancient organizational and structural assumptions of American education. They are effectively rewriting our hoary definition of a "public" school: Instead of "a school run by the government," today's public school can be run by a committee of parents, a team of teachers, a local Girls and Boys Club or community college, even a for-profit company. What makes it "public" is who can attend it, how it's financed, and how it's held accountable for results, not whom it employs or how many assistant superintendents order it around.

End of the neighborhood school

Another development is the demise of the assigned school. Twenty-four states (as well as Puerto Rico and the Northern Mariana Islands) have some form of open enrollment within their public-education systems. Minnesota and Delaware have perhaps gone the farthest down this path. Their basic policy is that you may attend any public school in the state. Last year, 19,000 young Minnesotans attended school in a district other than the one they live in. In Delaware, 6 percent of all students applied for the state's new choice program.

Other jurisdictions loosen the traditional arrangement in special circumstances. In Oregon, a student who earns low test scores for two years is allowed to opt out of his assigned school. In California, students must be allowed to attend a school close to their parents' work or child-care facility, even if it's not in the same district as their residence.

Twenty states now allow some form of inter-district open enrollment, though participation is sometimes optional for districts and commonly constricted by availability of classroom space and by court-ordered desegregation schemes. Besides Minnesota and Delaware, Iowa and Utah have mandatory open enrollment laws. In Ohio, districts may participate in the program if they wish. (Today, that means primarily rural districts; most urban and suburban districts have declined.) In Michigan, 7,700 youngsters crossed district borders last year to attend school.

Minnesota also launched the "post-secondary options" program, whereby high-school students may take courses at local universities, thus obtaining a wider (and presumably more challenging) array of educational opportunities while completing their formal schooling. Virginia and Oregon have similar programs, as does Washington State, where private and home-school pupils also participate.

Vouchers and virtual vouchers

For all the noise around vouchers, public dollars already underwrite private-school attendance in a variety of ways. Many such arrangements are beyond political controversy because they result from the state or district deciding for itself that it cannot serve certain children in its public schools—but must ensure that they obtain an education.

This practice is well-established in the world of "special education," where youngsters with severe or esoteric disabilities (or litigious parents) can invoke federal and state laws and district policies to gain access to private schools at public expense. But disability is no longer the only grounds for such arrangements. Minnesota's High School Graduation Incentive Program allows families of students who are lagging behind to select one of several state-contracted private schools. Districts themselves often contract with privately run "alternative" schools for disruptive youngsters. Both New Mexico and Texas have communities with such arrangements. Even simple overcrowding may trigger a private-school contract: The Houston Independent School district currently farms out several hundred pupils (of its choosing) to private schools with excess capacity.

Districts also engage private providers for specialized educational services, such as the supplementary instruction for disadvantaged youngsters provided under the federal Title I program. In addition to its tuition-based after-school instruction, Sylvan Learning Systems now delivers Title I services in 32 public-school districts. Although many districts have long outsourced bus transportation, building maintenance, and cafeteria operations (and buy everything from chalk to computers from private vendors), what's new is allowing private firms to provide actual instruction—and to operate entire schools.

The political heat and noise levels begin to rise as we turn from state-selected private schooling to the parent-chosen kind. Yet a number of jurisdictions routinely subsidize the peripheral costs of private schooling. Louisiana is spending some $34 million this year on its private schools, mostly for technology, transportation, and instructional materials. Connecticut, Indiana, Maine, and Iowa reimburse parents for transportation or textbooks. Ohio does that and also has several programs of more direct assistance to "chartered" non-public schools. The state underwrites auxiliary services, such as math and science equipment, guidance counselors and nurses, and any supplies and administrative costs related to state tests. It also reimburses private schools for costs that they incur by complying with state regulations. (For example, the school may receive as much as $250 per pupil for taking daily attendance and reporting it to the state.) It's not uncommon for an Ohio private school to obtain 10 percent to 20 percent of its revenues from state sources—but, in return, it must obey more regulations than are applied to private schools in other jurisdictions, including a controversial state testing program.

Rather than funding private schools directly, some jurisdictions deploy their tax codes to help parents with tuition, fees, and other out-of-pocket expenses. Minnesota recently enacted a major program of tax credits and deductions for families with children in public or private schools. The credits let parents reduce their taxes in proportion to sums they expend for school supplies, transportation, and tutoring—but not for tuition. Families making less than $33,500 a year can get up to $2,000 in tax refunds with this program. In addition, all manner of educational expenses (including private-school tuition and public-school fees, textbooks, etc.) are deductible, within certain limits, for Minnesota taxpayers in all brackets. That provision has already passed constitutional muster with the Supreme Court.

To encourage people to support privately funded vouchers, Arizona offers a new tax credit (up to $500) for donations to such programs. But similar programs are spreading without special tax incentives. In more than 30 communities, donors are helping low-income youngsters to shift from unsatisfactory public schools to more appealing private alternatives. Some 14,000 youngsters currently benefit from these programs, in which student demand nearly always exceeds the scholarship supply.

In several celebrated—and controversial—instances, the state or district actually pays private-school tuition. That wall has been breached. The issue is no longer whether America will ever have vouchers but, rather, where will they turn up next. (A definitive Supreme Court ruling on their constitutionality—likely within the next year or two—will naturally color these prospects.) Vermont and Maine have long allowed local governments to pay (secular) private-school tuition for children who live in rural areas without suitable public schools. (In practice, this usually means that a village or small town with its own public elementary school "tuitions out" its high-school students to private schools.)

The New England arrangement could be deemed more a convenience for the community than the family. In Milwaukee and Cleveland, however, low-income children may obtain state-financed vouchers to enroll in private schools simply because their parents believe they will get a better education. The numbers are limited, and complicated court challenges still beset both programs, particularly with respect to attendance at church-affiliated schools. Nonetheless, legislators in several other states—and in the U.S. Congress—are eyeing similar programs. Were it not for a presidential veto threat, the District of Columbia would have a publicly funded voucher program today. Several bills are currently pending on Capitol Hill, some for Washington alone, some for nationwide voucher "demonstration" programs. Although more voucher activity at the state level still seems likelier than Congress's ability to override a veto, it is entirely imaginable that federally funded vouchers of some sort will become available within the next several years.

Barriers to change

Many interests are deeply vested in the status quo: teacher unions, textbook publishers, school-board associations, colleges of education and administrator groups, plus dozens more. This is the public-school "establishment." Though yielding slowly to some contemporary reforms (e.g., statewide academic standards), that establishment attacks every change that might under-

mine its control of public education. The fierceness of its tactics is proportionate to how threatening a proposed change appears. Thus it has greater tolerance for (and ability to co-opt) magnet schools and other forms of "open enrollment" among institutions it still controls than for truly independent charter schools or vouchers. That is why, for example, virtually every state charter law includes a tight "cap" on the number of such schools and why any proposal to loosen the cap meets forceful opposition at the statehouse.

Less noted, but also significant, is the change-averse and self-interested private-school establishment. It enjoys a cozy niche, enrolling about 11 percent of the student population, and has reason to be apprehensive about new forms of competition. A 1996–97 Hudson Institute survey indicates that 12 percent of charter pupils were previously enrolled in private schools; that means about 20,000 youngsters in the current year—enough to fill 40 typical elementary schools—may have forsaken private schools for these new, independent public schools. (The figure may be exaggerated since several states permit private schools to convert to charter status and those that do presumably hold onto their students.) If the charter movement should spread—President Clinton has called for 3,000 such schools by decade's end—it could prove as unsettling to private schools as to traditional public education.

A number of private-school leaders are also wary of publicly funded vouchers, fearing the government regulation and loss of independence that such a funding mechanism is apt to bring. And a handful of vocal libertarians and "school-state" separationists would have all levels of government withdraw from elementary and secondary education, leaving it to parents to purchase out-of-pocket if they want it for their children.

But if the public-school establishment is no longer the only source of resistance to novel policy strategies for widening school choice at taxpayer expense, it remains the greatest and most potent source of opposition. Two favorite weapons in establishment hands are the still-uncertain constitutional foundations of choice schemes that involve parochial schools and the patchy research evidence on student achievement in schools of choice. A definitive Supreme Court ruling would, of course, resolve the first of those, at least with respect to the U.S. Constitution. Some state constitutions, however, have "Blaine amendments" and other provisions that are more restrictive than the First Amendment's religion clauses. As for research, it continues with much vigor, including an important study of New York City's new private voucher program. But with the nation's oldest charter and privately managed public schools in just their third or fourth year of operation, it's still too early to be certain of their results. What's indisputable today is that their current clients are pleased with them and more people would like to attend them.

Tomorrow's education map

Despite the uncertainties and opposition, movement is palpable. Education ventures that five years ago were the stuff of academic disputation are actually happening today. The question about vouchers is simply where they'll turn up next. The uncertainty about charter schools is whether three years hence we'll have 1,500 or 3,000 of them—and how far efforts will get to "re-regulate" them. The issue for privately managed schools is not whether school boards will agree to this arrangement, whether people will attend them, or whether such schools will provide high-quality education but, rather, whether investors will enjoy an agreeable rate of return.

Survey data, moreover, show steadily growing public support for such innovations. As recently as 1993, just 24 percent of those polled by Gallup favored "allowing students and parents to choose a private school to attend at public expense. In 1997, supporters numbered 44 percent. When the question is phrased differently (such as, "be able to choose any school, public, private or parochial"), approval levels rise higher still, particularly among minorities and city dwellers, whose children are least well-served by their current schools. Nor is the public waiting for more research results. According to Gallup, 65 percent of Americans (including almost three-fifths of parents of public-school pupils) believe that achievement would rise among students who shift to private schools. Even home-schooling, arguably the farthest-out of choice strategies, enjoys rising approbation: from 16 percent on Gallup's 1985 poll to 36 percent this year.

Politically, too, tantalizing changes are visible. Teacher-union heads now claim to favor charter schools—and shutting down, or "reconstituting," unsuccessful public schools. Union-sensitive Democratic politicians, including President Clinton, now claim to favor practically every form of school choice short of public funding of wholly private schools. A few have even broken ranks on that issue, including Connecticut Senator Joe Lieberman and (retiring) New York Congressman Floyd Flake. Martin Luther King, Jr.'s niece has become a crusader for school choice. National Urban League head Hugh Price has made clear that, as much as his organization loves public education, it loves children more, and, if big-city public schools cannot do right by them, the Urban League will welcome alternatives. School choice—and choices—could well turn into a bona fide civil-rights issue.

It's no flood, but it's more than a trickle. Besides, the eventual point of the new choices may not be that they replace the old system. The point may simply be that once it's clear that people can no longer be confined against their will to old-style public (and private) schools that do not work for them, system-wide reform will be unavoidable. For that to happen, however, the alternatives must be genuinely viable and accessible in the short run for lots of children and families. Which, of course, is precisely what the defenders of the old arrangements are doing their utmost to prevent.

Charter Schools
Learn a Few Lessons

**There are many ways to set up a charter school system.
Some work, and some don't.**

BY CHARLES MAHTESIAN

Four years ago, Arizona and Kansas sprinted to the forefront of the school reform movement by introducing a new form of choice into public schools.

They were among the first states to take a chance on charter schools–the independent, experimental schools designed to add a competitive element into public education. The idea is to seize upon the creativity of parents, teachers and community leaders–rather than the local school district–and leave the creators free to design their product in virtually any way they wish.

In Arizona, it is working. Today, nearly 50,000 students–6 percent of the total pupil population–are enrolled in 400 charter schools all across the state. There are Montessori schools, schools for the hearing-impaired, schools for agribusiness and the performing arts. One high school focuses on pregnant and parenting teens. Another targets juvenile ex-offenders. Twelve school charters alone have been awarded to Education Alternatives, a for-profit education management company.

Kansas, on the other hand, has done virtually nothing. It is home to one lone charter school, servicing about 70 students in the rural southeastern part of the state. The reason isn't difficult to figure out.

One solitary charter school may not have been what Kansas legislators intended, but given the bill they passed, it was about as much as they could expect. There is a distinct difference between a law that encourages charter schools and a law that merely permits them. Kansas merely permits them.

In fact, it permits only 15 charter schools in the entire state. There is a single chartering authority, and no appeals process for applicants who are rejected. Existing public schools are eligible for charter conversion, but private schools are not. Neither are for-profit schools. There is no automatic waiver from teacher certification regulations. If a charter school wants freedom to hire teachers with an unconventional background, it needs special permission from the state.

In short, the Kansas system represents the opposite of the approach that has led to a flowering of charter school experiments in Arizona.

There, nearly anyone is eligible to submit a charter school application. Nearly any school can qualify. There is no limit on the total number of charter schools in the state.

And there are several different ways to get approval. If one of the three panels with chartering authority–the local school board, the state education department or the state charter board–rejects an application, the decision can be appealed to one of the other chartering bodies. Most state and local education regulations, including the rule that teachers must be certi-

Reprinted with permission from *Governing* magazine, January 1998, pp. 24–27. © 1998 by Congressional Quarterly, Inc.

fied, do not apply. The only requirements are that the schools comply with federal and state health, safety and non-discrimination laws. Charter school detractors and supporters alike refer to Arizona as the "Wild West."

But if there is something wild about Arizona's free-wheeling experiment with charter schools, there is something exciting about it as well. In just a couple of years of operation, it has begun to make the state's traditional public schools look lifeless and hidebound by comparison. Indeed, the Mesa school district, home to 22 charter schools, is losing so many students from its regular schools that it is advertising in newspapers to attract new ones.

"This is gradually changing the shape of the education system in Arizona," says state School Superintendent Lisa Graham Keegan. "It leaves the traditional district wondering what happened."

There are a few other states currently celebrating the giddy experience of charter school creation fever. But there are also quite a few like Kansas, states that enacted a charter school law but have yet to see many experiments flowing from it.

New Mexico, which passed its law a year before Arizona did, has just five charter schools. Rhode Island has just one. Arkansas, where only public school personnel can apply for charters, and Wyoming, where 10 percent of a district's teachers must support creation of a school, are still awaiting their first.

As of the beginning of this school year, reports the Washington, D.C.-based Center for Education Reform, close to 800 charter schools were in operation across the country. But they are overwhelmingly located in the states that, like Arizona, passed relatively free-wheeling laws. Where the legislative process brought forth tightly restrictive rules and regulations, very little has taken place. "By and large," says Ted Kolderie, a charter school advocate at the Center for Policy Studies in Minnesota, "either nothing is happening in those states or, if it is, it is just an enlargement of

alternative school programs. The point of having a law like that is to avoid having a stronger law."

Nothing in the strong law/weak law debate, of course, answers the question of whether competition will ultimately change the public schools. It does, however, raise the possibility that many states will never find out.

The basic charter design, first devised by Minnesota in 1991, is a publicly funded school under contract or charter to a public agency such as a school district. The new institution is exempt from most regulations governing other public schools, although it must comply with health, safety and non-discrimination laws. It cannot charge tuition and, space permitting, it must take all comers.

Each school is free to devise its own testing and curriculum. After a certain time period, if it fails to attain the expected outcomes specified in the proposal, the sponsoring authority can choose not to renew the charter.

It is simple, but in many states, it became a recipe for instant controversy. Teachers' unions and school boards responded with reactions ranging from outright hostility to cool indifference, viewing the charter schools as, in the words of National Education Association president Robert Chase, "a halfway house en route to privatization."

In Michigan, the teachers' union filed suit soon after passage of an expansive charter law in 1993, claiming that charter schools should not receive state funding because they were not public schools. A state appellate court agreed in 1994, but by then it was irrelevant. Lawmakers had already amended the law to bar home schools, one of the most objected-to provisions. Then, universities involved in chartering schools—under Michigan law, universities qualify as sponsoring authorities—found themselves threatened by public school teachers and school district officials who refused to accept student teachers from charter-granting institutions.

In other states, the debate has centered on teacher certification and collective bargaining questions. The most contentious charter school issue, however, concerns provisions that allow for-profit companies to run schools. "What I am afraid of is that these bills are in the best interests of a private organization like the Edison Project," says Bob Cribbs, government relations specialist for the Georgia Association of Educators. "That's where our skepticism comes in."

Skepticism is a good way to characterize the uneasy relationship that currently prevails in many states between teachers' unions and charter schools. Nowhere have organized teachers become outright charter school enthusiasts. But they rarely launch full-scale assaults on the idea anymore. Instead, they are zealous in beating back attempts to broaden individual charter school laws and subtle in attempting to add restrictions.

Part of the reason for this approach is the undeniable allure of charter schools to many rank-and-file teachers. The formerly antagonistic National Education Association for example, actually plans to open six charter schools of its own—including one in Arizona.

The NEA and its state affiliates are politically astute enough to recognize a losing fight when they see one. When a charter proposal is bundled together with vouchers or other private-school assistance in a school choice package, the package can usually be defeated. But once the two issues are decoupled, as they have been in many states, it is more difficult to make the case against charter schools without appearing to be obstructionist.

In any case, say charter school advocates, it is not the teachers' unions that currently pose the most serious threat to their success—it is local school districts. In many states, as the sole chartering body, school districts are uniquely positioned to transfer their quarrel with charter schools from the state capitol to the local level. Often, they take full advantage of the inherent conflict of interest in a mechanism that grants local school boards life-or-death approval authority over their would-be competitors.

Charter schools are, after all, adversaries. Every student lost by a local district to a charter school represents the loss of thousands of dollars in per-pupil funding from the state, and the erosion of a small measure of control. "The local school board has no interest in encouraging competition against its own schools," says Kansas state Representative Kay O'Connor, a leading national proponent of school choice. "They don't want another school in town taking its students away and, in other words, its money."

"It's tough to go before your local board and ask for divorce," agrees Lisa Graham Keegan in Arizona. She stresses the importance of establishing multiple chartering authorities. They offer an alternative for applicants who find a local school board unwilling to consider their ideas.

But even in states that provide for different sponsoring authorities, there are frequently built-in obstacles to getting a charter program off the ground. In California, for example, one district requires that a charter school kick in a 10 percent fee for administrative purposes. It also charges the school to lease space. During a recent fiscal squeeze, the district requested an additional 10 percent charge. Palm Beach County, Florida, the only sizable school district in that state to require charter applicants to secure financial bonds and a wide-ranging insurance policy, is also, not coincidentally, the only one in the state without a charter school.

These obstacles exacerbate the already burdensome task of school startup and operation. Few states, for example, guarantee charter schools the same per-pupil level of funding provided to local school districts. Some, such as Minnesota, only allocate the state portion—not the district portion—of the funding formula. Others simply allow sponsoring school

The bad news is that a few charter schools are failing. The good news is that, unlike regular public schools, they can be shut down.

districts to negotiate funding with charter schools. Many school districts would like to keep it that way.

Of course, the ultimate question about charter schools is not how to create more of them. It is whether they deliver, as promised, an improved education. So far, many appear to be thriving, but most are too new to gauge how well they measure up with traditional schools or whether they produce higher student achievement. Since charters vary so much from state to state, and even within a single state, it is difficult to make broad generalizations. Education policy makers are often forced to distinguish between battling studies.

But some of the initial criticisms were muted by one of the most definitive reports to date, a recently published federal study as of January 1996. Racial composition of charter schools, according to the U.S. Department of Education study, roughly mirrors statewide averages. Charters serve slightly lower proportions of students with disabilities and limited English proficiency, but there is no evidence that they "cream" the best students. About one-third of charter students are eligible for free or reduced price school meals—roughly the same as public schools.

What the report did not address is the growing number of charter school failures. More than a dozen schools across the country have closed down for reasons ranging from internal

power struggles to financial mismanagement.

Perhaps the most damaging blow to charter school credibility came from a *60 Minutes* television report about a Washington, D.C., charter school where a reporter was attacked by school administrators and students. The school's principal later scuffled with police officers who arrived at the scene, leading to her conviction last year on assault charges.

In Los Angeles, within 18 months of opening in 1993, Edutrain Charter School became the first to have its charter revoked after audits revealed evidence of fraud and questionable expenses. The school's president, it turns out, used school funds to lease a $39,000 sports car and to hire a bodyguard. Another $30,000 went toward furnishings for administrative offices.

In Arizona, Citizen 2000 shut its doors after just over a year under a cloud of fiscal mismanagement charges. In addition to violating state accounting procedures, the school was found to have exaggerated its enrollment figures to receive more public funding.

"If you are going to create a charter school system, the state is going to have to take a more active responsibility in monitoring them," says Tom Pickrell, legal counsel for the Arizona School Boards Association. "Citizen 2000 was an example of a monitoring system that was nonexistent at the time it went under."

But many charter proponents argue that critics are missing a larger point about these errant schools. At least they could be shut down—something that cannot be said of failing traditional schools.

"It is unsettling," says Sean Duffy, a charter school analyst with the Pennsylvania-based Commonwealth Foundation, "but the good news is that they are more accountable than conventional public schools. You can't close *them*."

News of the recent revocations does not appear to have dampened legislative enthusiasm for charters during the past year, either in the states where the scandals occurred or elsewhere. Indeed, a new wave of charter legislation is rolling through, this time aimed at strengthening charter school laws.

The irony is that most of it is taking place in states with pre-existing strong statutes. California and Minnesota, two charter pioneers, have lifted caps on the total number of charter schools permitted statewide. Texas has upgraded its law to boost the cap from 20 schools to 100, and does not count against the cap any school in which 75 percent of the students are previous dropouts. Arizona has approved capital facilities aid for charters and, in a bow to criticism, now requires an annual independent financial audit.

But where the laws are weak, as in Kansas and Georgia, efforts to strengthen them have met with less success, largely for the reasons that placed restrictions on the program to begin with.

In a few places, charter school proponents have maneuvered around statewide opposition by targeting new measures to specific localities. Chicago is now granting wider latitude in creating charters than communities elsewhere in the state. An Ohio pilot project allows charter schools in the Toledo area.

The reasoning behind these new efforts is unlikely to re-create Arizona's experience, but then again, it is likely to avoid the problems Kansas has encountered. "By concentrating charter strategy on the areas of greatest need, it becomes easier to do," says Kolderie. "You don't have to agitate all the school boards in the state, many of whom may be doing, or think they may be doing, an adequate job."

RICHARD ROTHSTEIN

When States Spend More

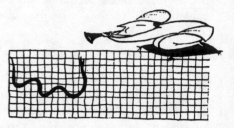

Liberals and progressives have generally believed that shifting federal authority for social programs to the states will typically lead to a "race to the bottom" as states try to attract business and keep taxes down by cutting expenditures and regulations. But a common trend of the last quarter century has also been a race to the top in which state policies can become more generous over time and even rival those of the federal government.

Education is the social enterprise for which state and local governments have always had almost exclusive responsibility. Public education has never won much federal support (only 6 percent of spending comes from the federal government, and at the height of federal involvement in 1979, it was still less than 10 percent), so if there was an inevitable trend in our federal system for competitive inadequacy, we might expect to see it in the public schools. And we did see it in the South, until about 1970 when dual school systems were finally abolished. But since then, the race has been to the top, not the bottom, in public education. With California being the stark and sole exception, all states have spent more money on their schools. What is even more surprising is that historically low-spending states have played catch-up, increasing their expenditures on schools even more than the average.

It might be supposed that a downward competitive spiral does not apply to schools because public education benefits the middle class—compared, for example, to welfare, which helps only the poor. Perhaps state governments are willing to spend more money on the education of middle-class constituents' children, but still race to the bottom where the interests of politically less powerful groups are concerned.

Yet much of the new state investment in public education has been for special education for the handicapped and for compensatory education for minorities and the poor. While some (although disproportionately few) of the beneficiaries of special education programs may come from middle-class families, these are still not majority-benefiting programs. And while there have been federal mandates and dollars for both special and compensatory education, most states have increased spending beyond what the federal government required or would reimburse. Nearly two-thirds of the states, for example, now supplement federal funds (Title I) for low-achieving students from poor families, even without a mandated federal match.

Part of the explanation for the growth in state education spending lies in coalition politics: the effective organization of parents, teachers, and interest groups (in special education, for example) to demand that state government invest in education. Yet much of the stimulus for the growth in education spending has come from state court decisions—often by conservative judges not necessarily swayed by electoral considerations—and some of these decisions, requiring higher taxes and more spending in poor districts, have not been uniformly popular.

States also have invested in education because business and government believe improved education promotes economic development by providing necessary skills with which to attract investment. But this explanation is also incomplete. The biggest destination of new funds, special education, has little relationship to economic growth. In Texas, the legislature now provides school districts with additional funds, beyond a standard supplement for children in poverty, for each pregnant teenager they enroll. This group, while deserving, is hardly central to business's workforce upgrade strategy.

In short, while economic self-interest has certainly played a role, popular concerns about equity and justice have also influenced state education policies. And if states have been engaged in a race to the top in education, it may suggest further examination of whether this instinct has been and can be mobilized at the state level in other social policy areas.

Kentucky, a poor state, presents an emblematic illustration of how coalition politics managed to tap both equity and economic development concerns. There, recent education-spending growth and equalization of spending have both been well above average. Kentucky benefited from broad-based demand for education reform, and a set of happy circumstances. In the latter category was the appointment, in 1980, of Edward Prichard, an "elder statesman" who had been a New Deal whiz kid and clerk to Felix Frankfurter, to head a committee to examine the state's higher education. The committee was initially comprised of 30 community activists, many from the League of Women voters, along with small-businessmen, African-American community leaders, a few lawyer-politicians, and a couple of corporate representatives. When the committee had written its report (recommending, for example, more research capacity at the state university), it decided, on its own, to reconstitute itself to evaluate elementary and secondary schools. The committee met once a year in the early 1980s, but in 1984 it convened a series of town meetings across the state that drew 20,000 citizens concerned about what was wrong with public schools. Following this, the committee's director, Bob Sexton, embarked on a speaking tour across the state—illustrated with posters charting problems like the state's high rates of school dropouts and teen pregnancy. In 1984, a Louisville Chamber of Commerce luncheon

speaker, an MIT professor, called the state a "Third World country," unable to compete economically with the rest of the nation because of its inadequate school system. The speech was widely publicized, and education became the, state's major obsession for the next decade. In 1985, the state's business leadership council publicly offered to support a corporate tax increase if the money were earmarked for education.

Meanwhile, a group of 66 property-poor school districts, represented by former Governor (and Prichard Committee member) Bert Combs, filed an equalization suit in 1985. The case worked its way through the courts and a state supreme court's decision in 1989 went far beyond expectations; it not only ruled against unequal property tax financing, but found the entire system of education constitutionally inadequate. Both massive new funds and curricular reform would be required to fix it. By the time the decision was handed down, however, the Prichard Committee, the Chamber of Commerce, and all the education interest organizations (representing teachers, school boards, administrators, and parent activists) had reached a consensus on the reforms that would be needed. A bipartisan coalition in the legislature eventually enacted them.

HOW AND WHERE SPENDING GREW

It's difficult to know how state education spending has grown, because precise measurement tools do not exist. In 1970, for example, state and local governments spent an average of $883 per pupil on public elementary and secondary education, ranging from $485 in Missis-

sippi to $1,395 in New York. (These figures, and those that follow, do not include any funds the states or school districts received from the federal government.) And there was a regional pattern to this variation. Even without including Mississippi or New York, other southeastern states spent an average of $629 per pupil, while other states in the mid-Atlantic spent $1,025.

These data are of limited use, however, because there is significant variation in costs between states. Providing education is less expensive in Mississippi than in New York. Because living costs are lower and there is less competition from

> The last quarter century has seen a race to the top, in which state education policies became more generous and came to rival the federal government's.

other employers of college-educated professionals, it probably cost less in 1970 for school districts to hire comparably qualified teachers in the Southeast than in the mid-Atlantic.

Yet government statistical agencies collect and analyze no "cross-sectional" data on costs of living, comparable to data they collect on inflation (changes in the cost of living not from place to place, but from year to year). Partly this failure results from daunting conceptual problems. An inflation index can price a relatively fixed "market basket" of goods (although the frequency and methods of updating it is a subject of some dispute), but a cross-sectional index would need different market baskets in each state. (Consider, for example, whether heating costs should have the same weight for Mississippi as for Maine.)

To estimate relative costs of education in different states, the following narrative utilizes academic analyses of data initially collected for corporate personnel departments. There are several such collections, used to determine how firms should adjust salaries (to purchase a comparable lifestyle) when executives are transferred from place to place. Using these data to compare education costs is imperfect, because purchasing patterns of corporate executives differ from those of schools: Simply because it costs more to rent a three-bedroom house in one state than in another does not mean it costs more to hire a high-quality teacher. Nonetheless, the two are probably related; this appears to be the best available surrogate for a cross-sectional school price index.

Using these corporate cost-of-living data, we can convert school spending in each state to "purchasing power parity" equivalents. If we know what each dollar of a state's per pupil spending can buy in quality and quantity of teachers, pencils, and school buildings, compared to what an education dollar buys in Kansas, we can estimate how many "Kansas dollars" another state would have had to spend to purchase the teachers, supplies, and facilities that its nominal spending level actually purchased. In these terms, there was a narrower range of variation. In "Kansas dollars," southeastern states spent, on average, $663 in 1970, compared to $1,092 in the mid-Atlantic states.

To understand how this spending grew in the next 25 years, we must adjust these spending levels for inflation, estimating how many "1995 dollars" it would have taken in 1970 to purchase the same education inputs as southeastern states purchased for $663 and mid-Atlantic states purchased for $1,092 in that year. If we compare these estimates to actual spending in 1995, we can get a sense of spending growth.

Racing to the Top in Education

Again, however, there are data limitations. The Bureau of Labor Statistics (BLS) produces a consumer price index, based on the purchases of a typical urban family, but does not produce an index for school input inflation. And there is no reason to believe that in any state the price of teachers, facilities, and supplies went up at the same rate as the prices paid by consumers for apples, used cars, and dresses. Here, the best we can do is a BLS index for all "services," probably more appropriate for schools than the consumer price index because services, like schools, are more professional-labor intensive and rely less on technology than the products purchased by consumers. The BLS services index is reported for four broad regional areas. Applying these indices, we find that southeastern states spent, on average in 1970, $3,037 in "real" 1995 purchasing power parity terms, while mid-Atlantic states spent $5,184.

One additional adjustment to these 1970 spending figures is appropriate. Schools with children from more disadvantaged home environments have to spend more to provide the same quality of education that they provide to other children. Education policymakers generally estimate that it costs from 20 to 30 percent more to educate poor children. While this is almost certainly too low an estimate, it is a place to start, especially because we are here concerned only with state and local funds, and schools receive additional federal money for disadvantaged children. (More than half of all federal education spending is for this purpose.) Using the 30 percent estimate, we can adjust downward the 1970 "real" spending figures, based on the incidence of poverty in each state, because to the extent poverty is present, it takes more money to provide a comparable quality of education in that state. The 1970 census found a poverty rate of 22 percent in the Southeast, and 10 percent in the mid-Atlantic region. "Where States Spent More" [figure at right] shows the results of these adjustments: "need-adjusted real-purchasing-power parity" per pupil 1970 spending in the Southeast was $2,836, and $5,023 in the mid-Atlantic.

The same figure also displays similar calculations for 1995 spending (similarly adjusted for poverty and geographic cost differences), so we can see what happened in the intervening years. Spending in the Southeast grew 71 percent in this period, while in the mid-Atlantic it increased by 48 percent. While all states increased their real per pupil spending, spending growth was highest in the lowest spending states, so the gap narrowed. Poverty in the Southeast declined in this period (from 22 to 16 percent, as reported in the 1990 census), while it remained unchanged in the mid-Atlantic states. Thus, some of this narrowing gap is attributable to the fact that southeastern states had less relative requirement for spending in 1995 than in 1970. But even if we remove the poverty adjustment, the data show a similar, though less dramatic pattern: Per pupil spending grew by 60 percent in the Southeast, compared to 44 percent in the mid-Atlantic.

For the nation as a whole, real need-adjusted per pupil spending grew by 41 percent during the last quarter century. To be sure, this increase did not signify that education has received a growing proportion of national income: The share of gross domestic product going to education remains unchanged.

And it is also true that the physical facilities of schools show the signs of inadequate capital investment over the last few decades. The growth of education spending has been in other areas—average teacher-pupil ratios, for example, have declined from 22.3 to 17.4 during these 25 years. It would, of course, have been easier for the lowest spending states to "catch up" if the highest spending states had stood still. But the highest spending quartile of states saw spending grow by 44 per-

cent. The fact that the gap narrowed at all reflects considerable effort in the lowest spending states. In 1970, median per pupil expenditures in the lowest spending quartile of states was 60 percent of median expenditures in the highest spending quartile, compared to 66 percent in 1995.

Over the last 25 years, the regions became more equal in their education spending. The lowest spending regions, the Southeast and Southwest, are much closer now to the (much higher) national average than they were. The mid-Atlantic states are more unequal to the rest of the nation, but only because spending in these states has jumped even more than elsewhere. The Rocky Mountain states are farther below the national average now than then, but not as far below as the Southeast and Southwest were in 1970. Again, California is a unique exception to all of these generally positive trends.

THE ROLE OF THE COURTS

One early impetus for this burst in school spending, predating a more recent nationwide obsession with economic competitiveness and workforce skills, was a raft of state court litigation about the inequality of school spending between districts within a state. In most states, school districts had relied heavily for funds on local property taxes, so the level of per pupil funds raised by any district was dependent on the property wealth lying within its boundaries. A district could make greater effort (a higher tax rate per dollar of assessed value) than its neighbor, and still have more poorly funded schools. Schools with the greatest needs (children in poverty) were also often those with fewer resources—although contrary to conclusions many drew from Jonathan Kozol's book *Savage Inequalities*, the pattern has not been consistent. Urban metropolises, for example, are likely in many states to have both more per pupil property wealth and more poverty.

This system began to change with a 1971 California Supreme Court decision *(Serrano v. Priest)*, which found that property-tax-based school finance violated the federal and state constitutions. In 1973, however, the U.S. Supreme Court ruled that the equal protection clause of the Constitution did not require states to equalize school spending, if they deemed local control more impor-

WHERE STATES SPENT MORE

	1970 Spending (in current $)	1970 Spending (in 1995$)*	1995 Spending (in current $)**	Real Spending Growth 1970 to 1995
Far West	$1,004	$4,432	$4,263	–4%
Far West (except Cal.)	944	4,512	5,683	26%
Great Lakes	918	3,967	6,174	56%
Mid-Atlantic	1,178	5,023	7,458	48%
New England	944	4,056	6,019	48%
Plains	888	3,825	5,607	47%
Rocky Mountain	776	3,842	4,835	26%
Southeast	621	2,836	4,864	71%
Southwest	666	3,095	4,898	58%
United States	883	3,879	5,468	41%

*Current dollars, adjusted for 1970 regional cost differences, 1970 state poverty, and 1970–1995 regional services inflation
**Current dollars, adjusted for 1995 regional cost differences and 1990 state poverty

Source: Author's calculations.

tant. The California court then reaffirmed its decision, relying solely on the state constitution. Similar decisions followed in 14 other states.

Greater equality within states would not necessarily result in greater equality between states. The early suits did not require states to increase their school spending, only to equalize, which can be accomplished by capping or reducing expenditures in rich districts while increasing expenditures in poor ones. In such states as New Jersey and Texas, some reformers attempted to enact "Robin Hood" laws to take funds from the rich and give them to the poor school districts, but these have met with

Tighter state regulation has been accompanied by much more funding and curricular experimentation and reform.

strong political resistance. After such a scheme was enacted by the legislature in Texas, it was reversed in a 1993 statewide referendum by the overwhelming margin of 63 percent to 27 percent. Kansas, on the other hand, disguised its redistribution plan by simply assuming control of the local property tax system, collecting all property taxes directly, and making state per pupil grants to districts. In general, however, state legislatures have avoided conspicuous redistribution and have reacted to equalization pressures by leveling up, approaching equality by adding money to poor districts while keeping rich districts whole, or by placing strict limits on the right of rich districts to further increase spending while poorer districts were catching up.

Some state courts have gone considerably beyond *Serrano*. Beginning with a New Jersey decision in 1973,

state constitutions have been interpreted to require not only equal resources, but minimally sufficient resources—it is not enough to be equal if every district spends too little for an "adequate" education. And the *Serrano* court had said that the state *could*, if it wished, violate the requirement for nominal equality, spending more in districts where students had special needs because of poverty or other characteristics. But in other states courts have increasingly ruled that constitutional equality *requires* a state to spend more on low-income students than it spends on the average student. Some courts have gone further and ruled that a state must compensate districts to equalize any higher cost they may face—by giving more money to urban districts with higher costs of living, for example.

The bar is being set very high, perhaps unrealistically so. The Kentucky Supreme Court described the development of seven "capacities" (sufficient oral and written communication skills, understanding of governmental processes, grounding in the arts, and so on) to which all Kentucky children have a constitutional right. The Wyoming Supreme Court ordered the legislature to define the "best" educational system and cost it out; it went on to interpret the state's constitution as requiring that "all other financial considerations must yield until education is funded" under this standard. The Ohio State Board of Education suggests that its state courts should judge the adequacy of education by whether sophisticated parents would "be willing to have [their] children educated in any of the 612 school districts" in the state. Meeting this standard would end the well-established American middle-class tradition of moving to the suburbs to find better schools. But though it is difficult to imagine that this goal will ever be reached,

it has increasingly become the focus of state policies.

Many states have raised school spending (in most cases, with equalization at higher levels as well) either without court orders or after court decisions upheld the existing inequalities. Several states that were subject to court-ordered reform raised spending in advance of court orders, perhaps in anticipation of them, while other states equalized funding sufficiently to permit courts to reject challenges. Thus it is difficult to say whether a litigation strategy on the part of teachers, public-interest groups, and minority activists played the critical role, or whether a progressive state political climate was more important. In recent years, business-dominated coalitions have stimulated many states' education reform efforts, but much of the increased spending took place prior to this more recent trend.

In the 1990s, most states have pulled back, reducing per pupil spending, mostly because enrollment has been increasing very rapidly and total spending has not kept up. The only states to increase funds thus far in the present decade by more than 40 percent of their 1970 per pupil amount are Indiana, Kentucky, and West Virginia. Yet these states had a unique advantage: West Virginia has been one of the only states with declining enrollment in this decade, while enrollments in Indiana and Kentucky have been virtually unchanged.

Of the three states that boosted school funds the most from 1970 to 1995, Arkansas and West Virginia acted after state court decisions found their property tax finance system unconstitutional (although in each case, the state's progressive governors, Bill Clinton and Gaston Caperton, would undoubtedly have led an education investment campaign in any event). Only Indiana acted without an adverse court decision. A big increase came in Nebraska, where the courts upheld the school finance system after the legislature boosted state funding for schools; here, legislators were motivated mainly by a desire to head off a taxpayers' revolt over rising local property taxes. Other states that nearly doubled their real school spending over this quarter century include Connecticut and Kentucky, where courts overturned property-tax-based systems, as well as Michigan, Maine, Georgia, and North and South Carolina, where court decisions to uphold the existing schemes did not dissuade leaders from reforming them. Alabama and Mississippi also enacted big increases in school spending without being ordered to do so. Thus, the trend toward higher school spending cannot be attributed solely to judicial intervention, although the possibility exists in some states that spending was increased to avoid potential lawsuits.

In California, the *Serrano* decision was followed by a tax revolt. Voters may have decided that if they were going to be forced to spend money on other people's children, they would rather spend no money at all. But elsewhere, equalization decisions were followed by higher overall taxes and more per pupil spending. Taxpayer revolts in these states focused on property taxes, and permitted state governments to assume responsibility for school funding with sales, income, or business taxes. One recent academic study calculated that, in the aftermath of court-ordered reform, states increased spending in the poorest districts by 12 percent, in the median district by 8 percent, and left spending unchanged in the wealthiest districts.

Michigan's recent experience illustrates the complexities of school finance reform. Twice, in 1973 and 1984, the state's supreme court upheld a school finance system that was among the nation's most dependent on property taxes (which provided two-thirds of all school funds). Voters in 1989 had rejected a proposal for the state to take over

the school finance system by raising sales taxes. By 1993, rich districts like Bloomfield Hills were spending nearly $11,000 per pupil, while poor rural districts spent barely $3,000. Then, a small, rural, low-property-wealth district in the northern tip of the state voted to close its public schools rather than further raise its tax rate. Embarrassed, Republican Governor John Engler, supported by both Democratic and Republican legislative leaders, agreed to substantially replace the local property tax system with state funds, to be raised by a tripling of the state cigarette tax and an increase in the state sales tax rate from 4 to 6 percent. The tax hike was submitted to a referendum, with the threat that if the proposal was defeated, the legislature would instead raise the state income tax. (With food and heating fuel exempt, the sales tax was not fully regressive but liberal groups like the teachers' union, allied with the tobacco industry, opposed the sales tax hike in favor of the income tax proposal. The field coordinator for the referendum campaign, however, was a teachers' union lobbyist, on loan.) The referendum passed with 69 percent of the vote, and Michigan suddenly had one of the most state-dependent school finance systems in the nation, with nearly 80 percent of school funds coming from the state.

Michigan's new system immediately raised per pupil spending in the poorest districts by one-third. To reduce intrastate inequality further, it also prohibited such rich districts as Bloomfield Hills from raising their local property taxes more than 1.5 percent a year; yet Bloomfield Hills voters also voted for the new proposal by an 88 percent margin. This year the legislature added funds to reduce class sizes in inner-city schools and to pay for all-day kindergartens for children "at risk."

Concerns about equity and justice have influenced state education policy. Might the race to the top in education be replicated in other policy areas?

There has been no uniform pattern to the political motivation and economic conditions of these changes. As noted, California has been an exception, perhaps because of conservative control of the statehouse during much of the period when the number of immigrants and poor people was soaring rapidly. Yet the Republican establishments in New York and Texas have reacted with much less stinginess to the new immigration wave. And perhaps California exceptionalism will be only temporary. This year, after California finally emerged from a recession that ended much earlier elsewhere, the state began a big new investment program in education (a program that would not be reflected in the 1995 data used in the foregoing analysis). Utilizing an unexpected budget surplus from revived state economic growth, the Republican governor and the bipartisan legislative leadership agreed to fund the reduction of class sizes to 20 in grades K-3.

Think Locally Too

Since the New Deal, American liberal intellectuals have focused their policy energy almost entirely on the federal government. In the mid-1970s, believing that this focus was incomplete, a small group of state and local liberal political activists organized the National Conference on Alternative State and Local Public Policy to develop and apply progressive policy ideas. Its leaders were Colorado state treasurer Sam Brown, who had made the first efforts to use criteria of social responsibility in the investment of state funds; North Dakota tax commissioner Byron Dorgan; Boston city councilman Barney Frank; and New York local school board member Ruth Messinger, among others. For a half dozen years or so, the conference flourished, organizing meetings, developing policy, and recruiting progressive-minded local and state officials. Its emphasis was on public investment, economic development, and state budget policy, but there was some interest in education and welfare policy as well. (Some of the early attempts to subsidize employment for welfare recipients were developed by conference activists for the first gubernatorial administration of Michael Dukakis in Massachusetts.) But when Jimmy Carter was elected

President, the attention of the conference leaders again turned to Washington. Brown became director of the volunteer program ACTION, and Dorgan and Frank went to Congress. Many of the conference activists took federal appointments. A successor organization, the Center for Policy Alternatives, endures, but much of the earlier grassroots orientation has faded away.

Conservatives had similar ideas, as Newt Gingrich's careful nurturing of local leaders into congressional candidates attests. But conservatives, too, had their eyes on Washington, so state and local policy has developed over the last 25 years with little ideological coherence, but great creativity.

This long period of neglect by the national political media has left many liberals ill prepared to understand the consequences of devolution. Yet during this time, a massive state takeover of public education

took place virtually unnoticed (except by those involved), as local districts have ceded fiscal (and much policy) control to state government. In recent years, as state governments have contended with other priorities, there has been a shift back to localities as a source of revenues in education, but under much tighter state regulation than ever before. This change in control has been accompanied by much higher levels of funding and ongoing curricular experimentation and reform. Nothing resembling a "race to the bottom" has been evident. Perhaps there is a lesson here.

Richard Rothstein is a research associate of the Economic Policy Institute and an adjunct professor of public policy at Occidental College in Los Angeles, California.

When Welfare Ends

How do we know how welfare reforms are working? The rolls are shrinking, but lawmakers want to know how the families are doing.

By Jack Tweedie

Where have all the welfare recipients gone?

After a state labor official bragged that almost 4,000 former welfare clients were working, New Mexico Representative Edward Sandoval had to ask, "But our caseloads have dropped by more than 14,000 families. What happened to the other 10,000 families?"

No one had an answer.

Almost every state faces similar questions as it oversees welfare reforms. Across the country, state efforts have contributed to a stunning drop in cases. Nationwide, caseloads dropped by 40 percent from January 1994 to June 1998. That means that more than

Jack Tweedie is NCSL's expert on state welfare issues.

2 million families have left welfare. Many left just as work requirements and time limits were taking effect, raising questions about why. For all those leaving welfare, we don't know how many former recipients are working, how many have moved in with their own parents, how many have married, how many have moved out-of-state or how many don't have enough money to buy food or pay rent.

Reducing caseloads was one goal of welfare reform. Legislators emphasized ending dependence. But no one ex-

Representative
Edward Sandoval
New Mexico

pected the numbers to drop so quickly. And legislators' concerns do not end when a family leaves the rolls. Indeed, their vision of success focuses on what happens afterward. To judge how reform is working and how they can make it work better, legislators need to know what is happening to those families.

LEGISLATORS WANT TO KNOW MORE

"We're trying something new," says Senator Jay Bradford of Arkansas. "It's important to get recipients into jobs so they can support their families, but we don't know exactly how to do that. We legislators need to keep track of what's going on, what is working and what is not."

Senator
Jay Bradford
Arkansas

States are now starting to track families who leave welfare, with more than 35 initiating studies. They give us our first look at how welfare reform is work- ing. In Arkansas, Colorado and New York, legislators requested studies. In other states, legislators have encouraged efforts by the state welfare agency or governor's office. Some welfare departments are doing the studies themselves, while others have contracted with public health agencies, researchers in local universities or consulting firms.

Early attention has focused on the number of families working and those who suffer extreme hardship such as homelessness and abuse. Later assessments will examine job retention, advancement and whether families are moving out of poverty.

STATE STUDIES TRACKING FAMILIES WHO LEAVE WELFARE

- States that have released studies
- States that have commissioned studies
- States without studies

Source: NCSL, 1998

WHAT DO WE KNOW SO FAR?

States have taken a variety of approaches in these studies, including surveys, matching welfare records with administrative data such as unemployment insurance, and home visits to check on the well-being of the family. This is giving us a better idea of what happens when people leave welfare. Just because a family leaves welfare, doesn't mean a parent got a job. We know that under the old AFDC/JOBS program half the adult recipients left welfare for work. And between one-fifth and one-third returned to welfare within the next two years. So what kind of results can be expected under the new welfare programs, especially since families are leaving welfare so much faster now than they did then?

It is difficult to answer that question directly, but a look at what is happening in other states provides an idea of where states rank and shows what is possible:

◆ How many former recipients get jobs?

Surveys found that 64 percent in Indiana, 65 percent in South Carolina and 68 percent in Washington had jobs. Matching their welfare records with unemployment insurance data, Maryland found that 55 percent of its former recipients had earnings.

Several states focused on families who were removed from welfare because they failed to comply with new requirements or did not complete an individual responsibility contract. These are the parents less likely to be working. In Iowa, 53 percent of these people had found jobs, in Tennessee, 39 percent, and in New Jersey, 30 percent.

◆ How much do they earn?

In Indiana, 41 percent of former recipients earned between $6 and $7 an hour. The average wage in South Carolina was about $6 an hour. Washington's survey reported a remarkable median wage of $7.40 an hour.

◆ What kinds of jobs do they get?

No surprises here. In South Carolina, 73 percent of the jobs were in service, clerical or sales occupations. Kentucky had mostly service and retail jobs. Maryland reported the most jobs in the wholesale and retail trade, including "eating and drinking establishments."

◆ How do recipients without jobs support their families?

New Jersey's survey of families who had been removed from the rolls included a question about how the respondent expected to support her family

SEVEN KEYS TO GOOD FOLLOW-UP STUDIES

◆ Surveys and administrative data

Two basic methods are used to determine what has happened to families who leave welfare—surveys of former recipients and matching lists of families who left welfare with administrative data such as unemployment insurance. Unemployment data provide reliable information at regular intervals. Surveys allow researchers to address more questions, such as whether families experience hardships or what barriers they face in keeping jobs, but they cost more.

◆ Sampling

Looking at only a proportion of those who leave can be a good way to obtain information while limiting cost. There are two keys to good sampling. The sample size must be sufficient—200 to 400 for a simple analysis, up to 1,500 for an analysis that compares several regions in the state or different kinds of families.

Those who are analyzed should be selected at random. It is not valid to take the first families who respond.

◆ Persistence

Substantial efforts should be made to get responses from every member of the sample. A good response rate—the percentage of people who complete the survey after efforts to contact them—is 70 percent to 80 percent. Mail surveys cannot obtain that level. A good survey is one that attempts to contact respondents by phone more than once (at different times in the day) and if that fails, sends someone to their last address to try to locate them. It is not valid to start with a large sample and then stop when you get a set number of responses. (People who get jobs are more likely to return surveys than those who are unemployed, so results would overstate the percentage with jobs.)

◆ Independence

The analysis should be carried out by a fair and independent organization. In some cases, agency employees may be appropriate, but some external or legislative involvement should be included because of the stake of the agency and the governor's office in positive findings. Legislative audit and evaluation offices are well placed to manage these kinds of studies. Several states have passed legislation mandating a valid study with sufficient appropriations and requiring a prompt report to the legislature.

◆ Timing

Legislators need to know quickly how well reforms are working and what changes may be needed to improve the program. Many researchers are not used to providing information for policymaking, so it is important to set timelines that fit legislative schedules.

◆ Studies over time

Moving welfare recipients into jobs and helping them become self-sufficient is not a one-time event. Good studies need to track former recipients and the well-being of families over a long period of time to see if they stay in jobs and advance in employment. Surveys or administrative data should be collected periodically for several years.

◆ Investing in information

Good follow-up studies can require substantial investment. Careful design and thorough planning pays off with accurate information about how reforms are working. States can use federal block grant or state maintenance of effort dollars to fund studies.

without welfare. They then asked how she actually supported her family. More than half (53 percent) planned to get a job, but only 30 percent reported being able to do so. The burden of supporting them fell on relatives. Only 23 percent planned to depend primarily on their own families, but 47 percent reported having to do so. And child support played a very small role. Only 3 percent of the families relied primarily on child

CHECKING ON CHILDREN

Some states use follow-up studies to identify families who might be hurt because they lost cash assistance.

Iowa, Arkansas, Tennessee and South Carolina try to contact all families who lose welfare because they did not comply with new requirements or for reasons other than getting a job.

Senator Elaine Szymoniak co-sponsored Iowa's innovative program that sends public health nurses to check on children in families who were removed from the rolls.

"When we started this, there was a lot of concern about what was going to happen to the families who lost benefits," she says. "We had to make sure that those children were OK." These home visits enable agencies to provide additional services to families when they are needed and to remove children from the home if it is necessary.

Senator
Elaine Szymoniak
Iowa

support; 6 percent relied on boyfriends or girlfriends.

◆ **Do families experience hardships after losing cash assistance?**

South Carolina's survey asked families who had left welfare if they had suffered hardships while on welfare and then after they left. Asked if they had ever "had no way to buy food," 14 percent answered yes for the time after they left welfare compared with 6 percent while they were on welfare. Asked if they had "gotten behind in rent or other payment for housing," 18 percent said yes after losing welfare and 12 percent while on welfare. Questions about not being able to pay for child care showed little difference between the time when they received welfare and afterwards.

Home visit programs have found a few families in trouble. Of 971 families contacted in Arkansas, nine were classified as needing immediate services or help with food or rent. Home visits in Iowa and Tennessee also found a few families where children were at risk of neglect or abuse.

◆ **How many families come back to welfare?**

Maryland reports that 19 percent of those who left welfare had come back within three months. In Michigan, 24 percent of the families who left or were kicked off the rolls returned in three months. And in New Jersey, 38 percent of the sanctioned families applied to be reinstated.

POLICIES FROM INFORMATION

Tracking studies allow policymakers to adjust welfare reforms. South Carolina asked former recipients who were still unemployed about the barriers they face in finding jobs. Difficulties with child care and transportation topped the list, so the agency expanded these services and strengthened efforts to inform former recipients about them. Several state surveys found that most recipients get jobs near the minimum wage and that keeping jobs is still a critical concern. In response, those states are developing additional job training, mentoring and education for recipients already in jobs so they

WHAT ABOUT FAMILIES DIVERTED FROM WELFARE?

Several states have developed diversion programs designed to help applicants without enrolling them in welfare. Case-workers offer help with finding jobs, child care or car repairs so applicants can get or keep jobs. These programs have resulted in substantial declines in the proportion of applicants who complete the process and become eligible for assistance. Yet we know little about how these families fare after leaving the welfare office. Few states track families diverted from welfare, and no state has released any data on these families. Diversion policies are a key component of many states' reforms and more information is needed about how they work.

can stay employed and improve their wages.

MORE QUESTIONS

Even with the valuable information from these studies, critical questions remain.

First, what about the families that cannot be located? Have they moved out of state? Are they staying with relatives? Are they homeless?

Second, what about the families where the parents are not working? How are they supporting themselves without a job? Are these other forms of support stable or will these families come back on welfare?

Third, for those recipients with jobs, will they be able to stay employed? How will they cope when transitional child care and Medicaid end? Will they be able to improve their wages and move their families out of poverty?

These questions illustrate the challenges welfare reform presents to policymakers. Continuing efforts to find out how families fare off welfare and then using that knowledge to help them overcome remaining difficulties are essential to state efforts to realize the promise of welfare reform.

HELP FOR STATES

Legislators and staff may be interested in the report "Tracking Welfare Reform: Designing Follow-up Studies of Families Who Leave Welfare," written by staff from NCSL, the National Governors' Association and the American Public Welfare Association. It is a summary of a conference organized last winter by the three groups and sponsored by the Office of the Assistant Secretary for Planning and Evaluation, U.S. Department of Health and Human Services.

Call Jack Tweedie at (303) 830-2200, or look for it on the NCSL Web site: www.ncsl.org/statefed/welfare/trackbrf.htm.

I'LL STAND BAYOU

Louisiana couples choose a more muscular marriage contract

By Joe Loconte

The pipe organ at the First Baptist Church in Robert, Louisiana, erupts into "The Wedding March." The bride, Erlene Thompson, is a little nervous. She need not be: She has known the gray-haired groom for most of her life. More precisely, she has been married to John Thompson for the last 37 years. Together they have raised four children, who have given them eight grandchildren and one great-grandchild—an infant boy whom Erlene cradles in her arms as she steps down the aisle. "The vows this time were a lot more meaningful to both of us," she says later. "It just runs much, much deeper."

The Thompsons, however, didn't just renew their vows. They rewrote them, based on the state's new, tough-minded marriage law. Following a brief ceremony, they and more than two dozen other couples from their church signed a legally binding agreement, witnessed by a state notary, pledging "to take all reasonable efforts" to preserve their marriage unto death. "We wanted to be an example for our children and their children," she says afterward, "that no matter what kind of troubles and trials you have, you can weather them."

The Louisiana Covenant Marriage Act, passed into law last August, remains controversial, and with good reason: It is the first experiment in raising both the entrance and exit requirements for marriage since the no-fault divorce revolution began in the 1970s. On the front end, it requires premarital counseling. On the back end, it limits the legal grounds for divorce to adultery, felony conviction, abandon

From *Policy Review*, May/June 1998, pp. 30–34. © 1998 by The Heritage Foundation. Reprinted by permission.

ment, physical or sexual abuse, or separation of at least two years. It also requires that struggling couples get counseling before they may call it quits.

Here's the part that puts choice-loving liberals in a quandary: The covenant contract is purely optional. By leaving the existing no-fault regime untouched, Louisiana has created the nation's first two-tier marriage system. The message to couples contemplating the strength of their marital commitment: you choose—decaf or double espresso.

Barbs have come from all sides, from conservatives worried about "intrusive" government to feminists fearful of women being "trapped" in bad marriages. Skeptics point out that so far only a small number of newlyweds have chosen the covenant option. Others complain that it still offers couples a generous escape clause.

All of this misses the most remarkable aspect of the Louisiana effort: In a culture that disposes of commitments as easily as paper cups, the very existence of a more muscular marital contract can help redefine attitudes toward marriage.

"Law is a wonderfully powerful symbol of what we hold as important," says Steven Nock, a University of Virginia sociologist studying the impact of the Louisiana law. "The public discussion that covenant marriage already has provoked is a very healthy sign." Private discussions are important as well. Says Louisiana state representative Tony Perkins, who sponsored the legislation, "some couples may have their first and last argument over which type of marriage to choose."

Hundreds of congregations throughout the state have called Perkins's office to request information on the law. Leaders of entire denominations, from the Catholic Church to the Assemblies of God, are considering whether to endorse the idea. Many married couples already have: Over the last six months, thousands have converted to covenant arrangements. Thousands more are expected to follow suit in June in ceremonies across the state. Meanwhile, legislatures in nearly two dozen states are considering covenant-style reforms.

With little practical support, covenant advocates are persuading much of the state's religious community—and many outside it—to rethink their entire approach to shoring up marriage in America. "Law can change incentives, and incentives can shape behavior," writes William Galston, a former domestic policy adviser to President Clinton. "It is amazing how many people who believe (rightly) that civil rights laws helped change racial attitudes deny that any such consequences can flow from changes in the laws of marriage and divorce." Though less than a year

old, the Louisiana statute already offers both liberals and conservatives an object lesson that law can be used to instigate, but not compel, traditional virtue.

Last, Best Hope for Marriage

Religious leaders will be vital to this effort. Eighty percent of all marriages still take place in churches and synagogues. That makes the religious community, as one pastor puts it, "the last, best hope" for the recovery of marriage in America. No other institution has the moral authority to challenge men and women to make the commitments necessary for sustaining marriage. "Too many people want to use the church as a nice, pretty building to get married in," says Louis Husser, the pastor of the First Baptist Church of Robert. "That's not the way to help people over the long term."

As with every other issue in the nation's culture war, the covenant concept inspires handwringing as well as hallelujahs among religious leaders. Bishop Charles Jenkins, the leader of the Episcopal Church in Louisiana, reversed his predecessor's endorsement of the plan, warning that "it goes back to the bad old days" of fault-based divorce. Bishop Dan Solomon, the highest-ranking official of the United Methodist Church in Louisiana, has dismissed the law as "a denigration of marriage vows long held and faithfully honored."

The Catholic Church, the spiritual home of a third of churchgoing Louisianans, is still mulling over its position. The state's Catholic bishops praised the legislature's "commendable concern" for strengthening marriage. But they have stopped short of endorsing covenant marriage over the state's easy-exit licenses.

Catholic officials are unhappy with the law's requirement that engaged couples receive premarital counseling about the new conditions for divorce. Any discussion of divorce before marriage is anathema to Catholic doctrine and would "confuse or obscure" church teaching, the bishops

More clergy are declaring their congregations "no-fault-free" zones, refusing to marry any couples who don't choose the covenant contract.

Breaking the Covenant

Louisiana's covenant marriage law raises the requirements for ending a marriage. The grounds for legal separation and divorce follow:

Legal Separation in a Covenant Marriage

In order to obtain a legal separation (which is not a divorce and therefore does not end the marriage), a spouse to a covenant marriage must first obtain counseling and then must prove:

• Adultery by the other spouse;

• commission of a felony by the other spouse and a sentence of imprisonment at hard labor or death;

• abandonment by the other spouse for one year;

• physical or sexual abuse of the spouse or of a child of either spouse;

• the spouses have lived separate and apart for two years; or

• habitual intemperance (for example, alcohol or drug abuse), cruel treatment, or severe ill treatment by the other spouse.

Divorce in a Covenant Marriage

A marriage that is not a covenant marriage my be ended by divorce more easily than a covenant marriage. In a marriage that is not a covenant marriage, a spouse may get a divorce for adultery by the other spouse, conviction of a felony by the other spouse and his imprisonment at hard labor or death, or by proof that the spouses have lived separate and apart for six months before or after filing for divorce. In a covenant marriage, a spouse may get a divorce *only* after receiving counseling and may *only* get a divorce for the following reasons:

• Adultery by the other spouse;

• commission of a felony by the other spouse and sentence of imprisonment at hard labor or death;

• abandonment by the other spouse for one year;

• physical or sexual abuse of the spouse or of a child of either spouse;

• the spouses have lived separate and apart for two years; or

• the spouses are judicially or legally separated and have lived separate and apart since the legal separation for one year and six months, if there is a minor child or children of the marriage; one year, if the separation was granted for abuse of a child or of either spouse; or one year in all other cases.

covenant marriages. About 300 evangelical churches invited couples in their congregations to do the same on Valentine's Day.

Meanwhile, the Christian Coalition is instructing its state chairmen to make passage of similar measures one of their top legislative priorities. Evangelical Protestant leader James Dobson, whose Colorado-based Focus on the Family radio program reaches at least 3 million listeners a day, is also on board. "This is an idea whose time has come," Dobson said in a recent broadcast. "We're going to do everything we can to support convenant marriage."

Taking a Stand

After a slow start, Louisiana couples are steadily warming to the concept. Though only a few hundred newlyweds have chosen covenant marriage, state officials say that perhaps 3,000 married couples have upgraded their nuptials. At the First Presbyterian Church in Baton Rouge, about 60 couples signed covenant agreements in a single weekend. At Glad Tidings, an Assembly of God church in Lake Charles, 240 did so. And at a ceremony held by a large evangelical church outside Baton Rouge, 500 couples recently underwent a covenant conversion.

These just may be the stirrings of a sleeping giant. Church leaders are increasingly ready to declare their congregations "no-fault-free" zones: Many are refusing to marry couples who fail to choose the covenant contract.

The Bethany World Prayer Center in Baker, with an average weekend attendance of nearly 6,000, is one of the largest congregations in Louisiana. Pastor Ted Long and his staff quickly decided to require covenant marriage contracts; none of his 22-member pastoral staff will marry couples without one. Robyn Rodgers, Long's daughter, was the first to be married at Bethany under the new regime. "It really gives an added sense of security," Rodgers says. "We know that if we have problems, we can't just say 'I'm leaving.' "

The district board of the Assemblies of God, representing 238 churches across the state, is expected to recommend that all its pastors say "no" to no-fault unions. Congregations would be free to follow their own course, but the Reverend John Bosman, a denominational leader, calls the board's decision "a very strong statement." As this issue went to press, denominational officials were planning an April ceremony in which about 300 church delegates will convert their marriages to convenant agreements.

Pastors and parishioners alike stress the importance of setting an example of strong marriages for other couples and their families. At numerous

say. The state's seven dioceses are now reviewing proposed amendments to the law that attempt to address the counseling question.

Despite these setbacks, covenant marriage is being embraced by a growing number of conservative Protestant groups. It has gained the tacit endorsement of the Southern Baptists, the state's second-largest religious body after the Catholic Church. In a resolution that received unanimous approval, the Louisiana Baptist Convention praised the new policy as an attempt "to move the legal standards for marriage and divorce closer to the standards of the Word of God." Earlier this year, 150 Protestant pastors and their wives met in Baton Rouge to convert their own unions to ceremonies around the state, couples converting to covenant unions celebrate amid throngs of children. "Example is extremely important," says Stuart Lankford, an associate pastor at Glad Tidings. "It will cause couples to think more seriously about what they're getting ready to do."

Sociologists tend to agree. They say people rarely change their behaviors simply in response to a law or public pronouncement. "People typically take their cues from those they know and trust," says Nock of the University of Virginia. "With more role models and public examples, the law's standard is likely to gradually seep into the public consciousness."

Why Counseling Is Not Optional

Making a lifelong commitment is one thing, of course. Keeping it often requires help. Supporters say one of the law's most important dictates is that struggling couples must agree to counseling before they can take steps toward dissolving their union.

That makes perfect sense to the leaders at First Presbyterian in Baton Rouge, which now marries only covenant couples. The 1,600-member church has long offered a meaty premarital counseling regimen. Couples are required to give 90 days' notice before their wedding day, meet several times with a pastor, attend a day-long engagement seminar, fill out a compatibility questionnaire, and discuss the results with a church counselor.

The law's requirement that couples considering divorce must first seek help gives pastors even more leverage. "We can do the front-end stuff, but not the back-end stuff," Stevenson says. "When a couple really is having problems, you can't make them get counseling. But the law influences them." Bethany's Ted Long agrees: "Men are notoriously resistant to counseling. But the force of law means they are going to have to sit down and get some help."

People can choose either religious or secular mediators, but either way they'll be read the riot act. The law obligates them to talk frankly about their marital responsibilities as spelled out in their marriage license and in the Marriage Covenant Act, a pamphlet prepared by the state's attorney general.

Some newlyweds are, in fact, banking on tough medicine to help get them through the hard times. Ben and Jennifer Ramagos-Young had both been married and divorced before they met. When Jennifer told her attorney she was getting married again, this time under the covenant contract, the attorney tried to talk her out of it. But Jennifer insisted. "Slowing things down," she says, "will allow us to get the counseling we both may need before we make a rash decision." Buying time is

often exactly what marriages in crisis need: better for couples to be talking, even through clenched teeth, than consulting with divorce lawyers.

Under the new law, an abused spouse can still escape the relationship with relative ease. But for couples simply drifting apart, the law's two-year waiting period—rather than six months under no-fault—gives them a chance to work things out. "We're not erecting a barricade," Perkins says. "We're just putting in some speed bumps."

Studies show that couples who undergo counseling are likely to navigate the storms of conflict and stay afloat. Psychology professor Howard Markman has summarized 17 studies of the impact of counseling on marital satisfaction. He found that nearly three out of four distressed couples who got help reported significant improvement in their relationships. Markman, a professor at the University of Denver, says that "for couples who want to work on their relationship, there is no reason why the marriage can't be saved."

If Markman is right, then divorce may be avoidable far more often than we think. For one thing, most breakups are not driven by extreme abuse: About two-thirds result from "low-level conflict" in which couples slowly drift apart. Second, in most cases the decision to separate is not mutual. According to family scholars Frank Furstenberg and Andrew Cherlin, four out of five divorces occur despite the objections of one partner. Herma Hill Kay, a principal backer of California's no-fault divorce legislation in 1969, later offered a mournful observation on marital meltdowns: "Divorce by unilateral fiat is closer to desertion than to mutual separation."

All of this suggests that the key to rescuing failing marriages is to address issues of commitment and character, a process best tackled with extended, roll-up-your-sleeves counseling. No-fault divorce short-circuits this process. "The present divorce law is something we as pastors fight, because there isn't enough time to help people," Stevenson says. "It drains away the motivation of counseling, because the back door is wide open and people are ready to rush out."

Covenant marriage uses both law and civil society to confront couples with the nature of their commitment.

Finding Fault

The most controversial part of the Louisiana experiment is its return to a fault-based system for divorce—the same system discarded by the no-fault revolution. Critics claim that reintroducing fault would only fuel hostilities in failing marriages. But others point out that fault has not really disappeared from divorce proceedings, it just insinuates itself into battles over alimony payments, division of property, and child custody.

More importantly, they say, divorce laws ought to contain notions of objective fault to signal society's disapproval of certain kinds of behavior. "Collective condemnation of reprehensible acts is powerful and should occur," says Katherine Spaht, a law professor at Louisiana State University who helped craft the legislation. "Guilt 'and shame, if our society can restore it, often controls human behavior."

Maggie Gallagher, the author of *The Abolition of Marriage,* suggests that no-fault laws may even increase the likelihood of domestic violence by failing to identify and punish men financially for their marital crimes. Domestic violence is a clear ground for divorce under covenant marriage—a first for Louisiana law. "There is plenty of abuse and adultery out there," says Stevenson, a pastor for 36 years. "Couples deal much more realistically with their lives when they face the issue of fault where it can be identified."

The Law as Tutor

Feminists and other no-fault defenders argue it is a mistake to blame divorce laws for failed marriages. But pastors in the trenches of marital counseling say the message and mechanism of no-fault make it much harder to hold couples together. "They should crawl out from under their rocks and get in the real world where people are struggling," says Louis Husser, a Baptist pastor for 23 years. "No-fault has created a test-drive mentality."

Lawmakers nationwide want more couples to close the deal—and keep it closed. At least 24 states are considering covenant marriage legislation. "When you make a commitment of this na-

ture, you need to back it up with something," says Arizona state senator David Petersen, who is pushing a covenant bill. In Alabama, the house of delegates has approved a similar measure. "The state's role is to establish legal protections for an institution that God created," says Stan Watson, the director of research at the Alabama Family Council, which helped draft the legislation. Oklahoma state representative Jim Reese secured 52 co-authors for his bill, which passed the house 90 to 6. Reese says it is his "top priority" to publicly raise the bar for marriage through covenant-style reform.

The law as moral tutor—the very concept tends to make both liberals and libertarians shudder. Yet it is the premise underlying the covenant experiment. Says Spaht, "We're not all going to make it, but not having any ideal in the law lowers the standard." Or to cite an old Chinese proverb: He who aims at nothing hits it.

"The story about marriage contained in the law—of marriage as a temporary bond sustained by mutual emotion alone—is becoming the dominant story we tell about marriage in America," writes Gallagher in the religious journal *First Things.* The problem with this story is that it usually contains an unhappy ending: More than half of all new marriages in the United States will end in divorce or permanent separation, and most will involve minor children.

Must we settle for such failure and all the social consequences that go along with it? Must it be no-fualt or nothing?

Covenant marriage uses both law and civil society to confront couples with the nature of their marriage commitment. Such confrontation could help rewrite our nation's most troubling cultural tale. "Everybody now, as a result of the law, will be forced to make a decision," Nock says. "How they resolve that is going to be very interesting."

Joe Loconte is the deputy editor of Policy Review: The Journal of American Citizenship *and the author of Seducing the Samaritan: How Government Contracts Are Reshaping Social Services (Boston: Pioneer Institute, 1997).*

THE ANSWER TO DRUNK DRIVING?

LOWER THE BLOOD ALCOHOL LIMIT?

Fifteen states have lowered their legal limit for intoxication as a means of reducing drunk driving, adopting a .08 blood alcohol content (BAC) standard, rather than .10. But does the lower limit work? There are only a handful of studies available on the issue, and they conclude that .08 BAC is effective in reducing drunk driving. But the results of the studies are subject to interpretation and have come under attack for bias and selective comparison in the states that were used. Most of the .08 BAC laws have been in place a very short time, providing little data to measure long-term effectiveness. And as with any analysis of drunk driving countermeasures, the problem is sorting out the effect of one law over another. Does the lower limit target the right people? Those drinking and driving in the range of .08 to .09 BAC are often considered social drinkers. Are they the real problem? What about repeat offenders, who drink and drive, often on suspended licenses? And what about those with BAC levels more than twice the legal limit, who have caused terrible accidents and still continue to drink and drive? Should lawmakers adopt the .08 BAC limit or should they consider other options in reducing drunk driving? Following are two quite differing points of view on .08 BAC.

From *State Legislatures,* October/November 1997, pp. 33-35. © 1997 by the National Conference of State Legislatures. Reprinted by permission.

We at the National Highway Traffic Safety Administration are convinced that if a state lowers the illegal per se BAC limit to .08, it will save lives, reduce injuries and save billions in health care costs.

It is NHTSA's business to research and evaluate programs and see what works. We know that legislation, highly publicized and visible enforcement and public information and education can all reduce impaired driving. Some of the most effective legislation to date has been state laws that lower the illegal blood alcohol concentration (BAC) limit from .10 to .08.

Twice NHTSA has produced congressional reports regarding BAC limits for drivers. Both times we recommended that all states and the District of Columbia establish .08 BAC as the illegal per se limit for drivers, 21 and older.

There are good reasons for this position:

1) *Virtually all drivers are substantially impaired at .08 BAC.* Laboratory and test track research shows that the vast majority of drivers, even those who are experienced drinkers, are impaired at .08 in critical driving tasks. Performance in braking, steering, lane changing, judgment and divided attention is significantly decreased, sometimes as much as 70 percent.

2) *The risk of being involved in a crash increases substantially by .08 BAC.* The risk of being in a crash gradually increases at each BAC level, but rises very rapidly after a driver reaches or exceeds .08 BAC, compared to drivers with no alcohol in their system. Research by the Insurance Institute for Highway Safety indicates that the risk of being killed in a single-vehicle crash at BACs between .05 and .09 is 11 times higher than for a person who has not been drinking at all.

3) *Lowering the blood alcohol limit is an effective countermeasure that will reduce alcohol-related traffic fatalities.* In California, a 12 percent reduction in alcohol-related fatalities occurred in 1990, when .08 and an administrative license revocation law went into effect. In a recent study by Boston University, five states that lowered their BAC limit to .08 were compared with five states that maintained their .10 limit. There was a 16 percent reduction in proportion of crashes involving fatally injured drivers whose BACs were .08 or higher, and an 18 percent reduction in the proportion of fatal crashes involving fatally injured drivers at very high BACs (.15 or higher). A .08 law serves as a general deterrent to all drinking drivers, not just social drinkers or moderate drinkers.

YES: LESS ALCOHOL MEANS FEWER CRASHES.

By James C. Fell

4) *It is reasonable to set the limit at .08.* A .08 BAC is not reached with a couple of beers after work or a glass or two of wine with dinner.

5) *The public supports levels below .10 BAC.* NHTSA surveys show that most people would not drive after consuming two or three drinks in an hour and would support a lower limit.

6) *Most other industrialized nations have set the BAC at .08 or lower.* Canada and Great Britain are at .08 and so are Austria and Switzerland. The states in Australia range from .05 to .08.

NO DROP IN SOCIAL DRINKING

Some in the alcohol industry oppose .08 BAC laws. Perhaps they think people will drink less or stop drinking altogether if those laws are passed. There is no evidence of that in California. Per capita alcohol consumption did not drop in 1990, the year .08 went into effect, compared with the year before. There was also no evidence of that happening in three other states (Utah, Oregon, Maine) where data were available.

Opponents say that .08 won't affect the real problem—heavy drinkers who drive. But two studies show that .08 does affect these drivers. Some say staggered penalties, with more severe sanctions for very high BAC levels, are a better idea, but NHTSA has no evidence that such penalties are effective in reducing recidivism or alcohol-related crashes. This is not to say those ideas should not be tried, but they should not replace .08 legislation, which is a proven deterrent. Florida and Idaho have both .08 and staggered penalties.

Is a .08 law cost-effective? A .08 law involves minimal additional costs, with only a small increase in arrests. Yet, it sends a message to the public that the state is getting tougher on impaired driving. The potential benefit of .08 far outweighs any costs.

In summary, 15 states already have .08 per se laws, and the time is now for other states to adopt .08. It is a level at which critical driving tasks are impaired. It is a level at which the risk of a crash increases substantially. It is a level that most of the public agrees with and that most industrialized nations have adopted. It is a law that has proved to be effective in reducing injuries. We urge state lawmakers to consider the merits of this legislation and lower the illegal BAC to .08.

James C. Fell is chief of research and evaluation, Traffic Safety Programs, National Highway Traffic Safety Administration (NHTSA), U.S. Department of Transportation.

(Continued)

You and your neighbors are fed up with a few speeders who continue to race through your neighborhood. Although most drivers obey the posted 25 mph limit, a couple of reckless fools consistently drive 50 mph or more, especially on weekend nights. Two solutions are proposed at the next neighborhood meeting: 1. Demand better police enforcement of the posted limit, or 2. drop the limit from 25 mph to 20 mph. Which would you choose?

That is the essence of the traffic safety debate now being played out in Congress over the drunk driving problem. In an effort to reduce drunk driving deaths, New York Congresswoman Nita Lowey and New Jersey Senator Frank Lautenberg proposed redefining the problem to include responsible social drinking, the legislative equivalent of dropping the speed limit to catch people who ignore *current* limits.

If they succeed in lowering the BAC (blood alcohol concentration) to .08 percent, a person who has just two drinks in a social setting could be considered legally drunk and if apprehended, could face arrest, fines, jail, higher insurance rates and license revocation for behavior that is not part of the drunk driving problem.

Meanwhile, the real problem of alcohol abusers who drive goes unabated. According to the U.S. Department of Transportation (DOT), nearly two-thirds of all alcohol-related fatalities involve drivers with BACs of .14 percent or more, almost twice the level targeted by the legislation Congress is considering. Even the national president of Mothers Against Drunk Driving lamented recently that the problem is "down to a hard core of alcoholics who do not respond to public appeals." So why target currently legal drinkers?

Ironically, proposals to redefine "drunk" will actually hurt the fight against drunk driving. By diluting the definition of "drunk driver" to include social drinkers, lawmakers will automatically increase the pool of "drunks" by more than 50 percent without increasing the resources to fight it. This will have a debilitating effect on the already underfunded law enforcement efforts to stop truly drunk drivers.

But the worst part about the proposal to lower the arrest threshold is that it won't work. In the 14 years since the first states lowered their arrest thresholds to .08 percent, not one government study has been able to show that lower BAC levels save lives. In fact, the only study to make such a bold claim is a highly disputed four-page report written by anti-alcohol researcher Ralph Hingson (who, incidentally, sits on MADD's board of directors).

NO: DON'T PENALIZE THE SOCIAL DRINKER

By Richard Berman

The study—which compares five .08 percent BAC states with five "nearby" .10 percent BAC states—concludes that 500 to 600 lives could be saved each year if all 50 states adopted a .08 percent BAC arrest threshold.

Independent analysis of the Hingson research by Data Nexus Inc. found that "the conclusion of that study is not supported by the evidence." Hingson's results, the analysis found, "depend upon which states you choose to compare with the .08 percent law states." In other words, if you change the comparison states, the study falls apart. And DOT did its own, much larger, study of the same five .08 percent states and couldn't verify Hingson's conclusion.

THERE IS A SOLUTION

Training and experience make those of us in the restaurant and bar industry acute observers of American drinking habits. Our servers and bartenders are workaday social scientists whose data fields come with names, faces and highly visible types of alcohol-related behavior—both normal and abusive.

We see the mainly responsible customers who enjoy a few drinks over conversation or food and drive safely home. We see the few problem drinkers who—if we permitted—would tie on a hellbender, then stagger out to their cars to menace the same highways traveled by our friends, families and loyal customers.

Most important, we recognize the difference between these two types of drinkers. So should the law.

Is the restaurant and bar industry resisting a lower arrest threshold for its own selfish reasons, to "sell one more drink to obviously impaired patrons" as MADD has said?

Hardly. Ringing up a few extra highballs isn't worth the risk that drunk drivers pose to our shared communities, and it's bad business to boot. In fact, the downside costs of overserving (litigation, obnoxious drunks, police scrutiny) far outweigh the profit on humoring the occasional drunk with more drinks.

Our industry would like to pick up the torch that MADD once carried—and hold it to the feet of the drunk driver, at one time their prime target. The organization did heroic work in yanking him from the driver's seat.

Brian O'Neill, president of the Insurance Institute for Highway Safety and no apologist for drunks, says of the .08 crusade, "What [politicians] ought to be doing is to provide more resources to vigorously enforce the laws on the books, and they'll save many more lives."

Precisely. That's the goal of the restaurant industry. It should be the goal of MADD and the goal of state legislators, with whom we would gladly work to enforce—indeed, stiffen—laws against truly drunk drivers.

Richard Berman is general counsel to the American Beverage Institute.

THE COMEBACK OF THE COPS

Can the policing reforms that brought crime to its knees in New York City work elsewhere? New Orleans is finding out.

BY ROB GURWITT

Five times since early September, the same well-dressed man has pulled up next to a schoolgirl in New Orleans, told her he's a substitute teacher at her school and asked for directions. After persuading her to get in his car, he has driven to a quiet neighborhood, forced her to perform oral sex, then let her go.

It is now mid-October, and Donald Davis, the officer who works the schools in the city's First Police District, is going over the details—the man's appearance, his obvious familiarity with school uniforms, the teachers' handbooks with a number stamped on them that one victim saw in the back seat. Davis speaks with the faint awkwardness of a man who is not particularly comfortable standing up in front of a roomful of people, yet the others in the room—his district's command staff, platoon leaders and members of the "task force," the elite patrol unit that focuses on the district's high-crime areas at night—are engrossed. For the past hour, as other officers have gone over the week's assaults, robberies, burglaries and murders, the mood has been subdued. Now, no one is fidgeting or lost in his own thoughts.

"What time has this been happening?" someone asks. Between 7:30 and 8 in the morning, Davis says. "Are there any recently released sex offenders who fit the description?" someone else calls out. Not that Davis is aware of. Have all the victims seen the composite picture the police department has just put together? Does the school board keep pictures of employees? Has Davis checked on what the stamped number means? The questions come from all around the room, and Davis answers them carefully: He's taken care of the first two—the school board, he reports regretfully, does not photograph its employees—but not the stamped number. He'll get on that quickly, he assures his audience, and

then sits down. Captain Eddie Compass, the young, high-octane First District commander, wraps up the meeting by complimenting the squad leaders for their quick work on a quadruple murder the week before, but then notes that burglaries and robberies in the district were up over the past week. "We didn't have a great week this week," he says. "Let's go out and hit those hot zones hard."

Three years ago, it's fair to say, most of the New Orleans police department's district commanders wouldn't have known whether they were having a fine week or a lousy one, let alone which crimes were the biggest problems and where they were occurring. In the year since the department started tracking crimes and holding its commanders responsible for what they are doing about them, however, commanders such as Eddie Compass have become walking encyclopedias of crime on their turf; in meetings such as today's, they have made quite sure that their subordinates are becoming as well-versed as they are. Compass' squad leaders now know which crimes have been occurring where, whether there are any patterns to them, whether there are any suspects and what they look like, what burglars have been stealing—telephones and caller ID boxes have suddenly become popular—and how and where to concentrate their forces this week. Tomorrow morning and evening, a videotape of the meeting will be shown to patrol officers at roll call, so that they, too, will be up to date.

It seems like a simple thing, this weekly Wednesday afternoon gathering in the First. So do its counterparts in the other districts, and so does the big one, the citywide meeting every Friday morning at 8 at police headquarters. You get together, look at the week's statistics, share information and ideas, get grilled about particular

cases—there's no magic here. Yet something quite out of the ordinary has flowed from this process: The NOPD has been rejuvenated. Just a few years ago, it ranked among the most brutal, corrupt and inept police departments in the country. Crime was skyrocketing, murder was out of control, and the department was drawing international attention for its problems. Now, New Orleans is seeing double-digit drops in its crime rate, and police brass are arriving from as far away as Russia to study what the city is doing.

A lot has gone into building this glistening new reputation. Police Superintendent Richard Pennington has worked hard to drive out the corruption that plagued the department when he took over in 1994. Mayor Marc Morial has done some heavy political lifting to get the department additional resources, from new patrol cars to new technology to a substantial pay increase. The New Orleans Police Foundation, a group of business leaders who came to see a revitalized department as key to the city's economic survival, has done everything from running recruiting campaigns for new officers to persuading local car dealers to turn over titles for used cars that might be suitable for undercover work. But at its heart, the NOPD's revival has been crafted out of the process, known as "Comstat," that lies behind these meetings. "What it's brought," says Captain Michael Ellington, commander of the Sixth District, "is a different outlook: Policemen want to be policemen. Before, we were never really addressing crime-fighting issues. Now, we're a crime-fighting machine."

All over the country, police departments are looking for a bit of that unabashed self-confidence, and they're looking to the same source that New Orleans did: the New York City police department shaped by former Commissioner William Bratton. For two years, from 1994 until he was ousted by Mayor Rudolph Giuliani in 1996 for allegedly pursuing his celebrity status too enthusiastically, Bratton presided over a top-to-bottom reconditioning of the NYPD that coincided with an astounding drop in the crime rate—from close to 2,000 murders in 1993 to 983 in 1996, and similar declines in other categories. In 1996, the drop in New York City alone, in crimes ranging from murder to auto theft, accounted for 16 percent of the national drop in crime. Not surprisingly, cities everywhere have begun paying attention to, and copying, New York's tactics.

Of course, they haven't all been paying attention to the same thing. As Bratton himself says, "It's like community policing: Everyone says they're doing it, but everyone is doing it somewhat differently." In the public mind, the NYPD is most closely associated with so-called "quality of life" policing, in which the police aggressively go after the small things—public drinking, unruliness, graffiti, aggressive panhandling—on the theory that controlling crime at that level creates an atmosphere of public order and may keep more serious crimes from being committed. Cities such as Milwaukee and Los Angeles are emphasizing this approach. But there is another piece to New York's strategy that its architects consider even more crucial: Comstat. Although it draws its name from the computerized statistics that help police keep track of what's happening, Comstat is actually the process that flows from that data: the responsibility placed on the shoulders of district or precinct commanders for fighting crime in their territory; the tactics they use in doing so; the weekly meetings that track how and what they're doing and that keep the pressure on.

"I guarantee you this: You put this process in any city, in any jurisdiction in the world, and the crime will come down," insists Jack Maple, Bratton's former deputy commissioner, who invented Comstat and was brought in by New Orleans to establish it here. "Because whatever your problem is, it will focus you on it."

Ever since New York began getting the numbers it has over the last few years, a national debate has been developing over whether words such as Maple's are simple bravado or the simple truth. Police departments aren't waiting to find out. Boston has its own version of Comstat; Minneapolis is putting one in place department-wide this month; Hartford, Connecticut, has embraced it wholeheartedly; and a slew of other cities are considering it. Of them all, though, New Orleans is the ultimate test case. If it can work in New Orleans, goes the thinking in national policing circles, it really can work anywhere.

To understand why New Orleans merits this distinction, it might help to remember the start of Pennington's tenure. The day he was sworn in, a renegade cop named Len Davis had a hit man murder a mother of three children who had filed a brutality complaint against him. Davis also ran a drug ring made up of NOPD officers, a fact that Pennington learned the following day, when the FBI's special agent in charge informed him that the feds were getting ready to indict nine of his men. Not long after, another patrol officer, Antoinette Frank, held up a Vietnamese restaurant and, along with an accomplice, killed the two owners and an off-duty police officer named Ronnie Williams who was guarding it. Both she and Davis are now on death row.

Even in a city that had become inured to crime and cynical about police corruption, these events were stunning. "We'd gotten about as low as we could," says Lieutenant Robert Gostl, who heads up the First District's detectives. "I couldn't think of anything worse than Antoinette Frank and Ronnie Williams." The events helped etch New Orleans in the national mind as a city slipping beyond redemption.

But as shocking as the Davis and Frank cases might have been, they were simply the most dramatic manifestations of a department that had become, in Morial's words, "a completely dysfunctional agency." Deputy chiefs divided the department into personal fiefdoms, with officers loyal to one refusing to cooperate with those loyal to another. Pay was low—$17,000 a year for a rookie officer—and morale lower. Supervision and accountability were foreign concepts; the FBI agents working the Len Davis case found that a patrol officer could go for a year or two without ever seeing a supervisor. The so-called "detail" system, in which off-duty officers provided protection for private businesses, was subverting the command structure, since lower-ranking officers often wound up hiring the lieutenants and captains they answered to while on duty. Administratively, the department was geared toward answering 911 calls: officers were not expected to know anything about crime trends or even descriptions of perpetrators; warrants went ignored; districts paid scant attention to gathering information that might help them anticipate and fight future crimes. "It used to be, if you made captain, it was a fabulously easy job," says one veteran sergeant. "True accountability for crime in a district was never part of it."

All of this bred a police culture that could most charitably be called unhealthy. "Bitterness and cynicism are widespread," read an October 1996 report prepared for Pennington. "Long removed from its once proud reputation and achievements, the NOPD now has an operating culture whose instrumental values are individual survival, clan loyalty and stoicism in the face of disappointment." And that was just the good cops. Others felt free to work for drug dealers, beat up civilians, rob, rape and—as the Davis and Frank cases suggest—murder. For a long time, the city led the country in so-called "justifiable homicides" by police in the course of their work. "In the 1970s and '80s, when New Orleans was number one in the nation for civil rights violations, you were 14 times more likely to be shot by a cop here than in New York City," says Mary Howell, a civil rights lawyer who has made a career of handling charges against the police department.

Through all this, crime rose, from 2,000 crimes per 100,000 residents in 1960 to 13,000 in 1990. Murders peaked in 1994 at over 400, and although they dropped to 350 in 1996, the homicide rate was still about eight times the national average; only a bit more than a third were solved. New Orleans had achieved the rare distinction of topping the country on all the things that you don't want your city to be known for. "We had the three towers of dysfunction: crime and corruption and brutality," says Mayor Morial. "Other cities, like New York, maybe had a crime problem, or they had a brutality problem, or they had a corruption problem. They didn't have all three at the same time."

By late 1994, though, a number of things were beginning to change. Morial had been elected on a platform that highlighted both reforming the NOPD and driving down crime. The business community, which had fought its way out of the 1980s oil bust on the back of the tourist industry, had come to realize that tourists weren't just staying away because of the crime but also because of the police. And finally, after much controversy, Morial had brought in Pennington.

Pennington had made a name for himself first as a crime-fighting commander in one of Washington, D.C.'s most violent police districts and then as an accessible, community-oriented assistant chief, but nothing had prepared him for what he found. "I just came to be the chief," he says. "I didn't come to be known as a change agent." He quickly discovered that if he wanted to be the former, he also had to be the latter.

He spent his first two years wringing out the department. Dozens of officers were arrested, dozens more resigned under investigation and close to 300 were disciplined for various infractions. He disbanded the internal affairs division, which he considered impotent, and created a new Public Integrity Division with the authority to run "integrity checks"—essentially, stings—on officers and to monitor them for early signs of trouble. He banned details in bars and nightclubs and declared that the chain of command had to be maintained off-duty as well as on. He bulled his way through the intense isolation of coming from elsewhere in a city that torments outsiders for casual sport, gradually learning who was on his side and who wasn't, changing his command staff twice. "Being

manders. On the wall in front of them a projector displays a map of the district in question, with small icons for each crime that has been committed during the week.

"That's an awful lot of icons. What's going on?" asks Ronald Serpas, the deputy chief for operations who presides over Comstat. Sitting opposite him is the commander of the Eighth District, the French Quarter, who explains that a particular robbery suspect is still at large and apparently

deal is being made of analyzing patterns and studying problems, which seem to be simple common sense. As civil rights lawyer Mary Howell says, "I mean, good morning! What were they doing before?" But what becomes clear is that the Comstat process is not just about keeping track of crime and of the department's response. It is also a tool for instilling a particular set of values—in this case, fighting crime actively and creatively.

Getting intelligence, for instance, means not only pushing the department to gather data on crimes as they're reported and then being able to analyze them, it also means pushing detectives and patrol officers to make it second nature thoroughly to question everyone they stop or arrest, in order to learn as much as possible about what's happening on the street. By the same token, coordinating a response to a problem doesn't just mean figuring out how to attack it, it means making sure that every resource that might be needed is available, whether it's the warrant squad or mounted police or two different districts' burglary detectives. This, in turn, means breaking down the walls—between detectives and patrol officers, between narcotics specialists and homicide specialists, between one district and another—that develop in most police departments. "Policing tends to be a very secretive business, in which the common operating philosophy is the exclusion of people from sharing information," says Bratton. "Comstat requires a complete reversal, in which you have to argue why you should exclude someone."

Where all of this truly seems to be making a difference is in the districts. In New York, as Bratton puts it, decentralization created "76 little police departments" in the precincts, and the same thing is happening in New Orleans. The eight district commanders are able to deploy investigators, patrol officers, task forces and the resources of headquarters as they see fit; in return, they are answerable not for crime itself, but for how they're addressing it. So, in the districts, each commander has set expectations high.

In the First District, for instance, Compass has demanded hard work in part by working ungodly hours himself—"I'll get calls from him when I get off duty at 3 in the morning," says Sergeant Michael Glasser, who commands the district's task force—and in part by expecting his officers to work closely and nonstop when a particular problem emerges. When the First District had 22 burglaries in two weeks not long ago, Compass, working on the theory that the burglar couldn't live too far away—since he wouldn't want to lug his nightly haul all over town—got his entire district involved in identifying possible suspects and possible fences in the neighborhoods that had been hit. In short order, they'd

NEW ORLEANS ACHIEVED THE RARE DISTINCTION OF TOPPING THE COUNTRY ON ALL THE THINGS YOU DON'T WANT YOUR CITY TO BE KNOWN FOR.

an outsider, you'll have people that will be circumventing everything you want to put in place," he explains, "and there were some that I thought would be team players that later I found out they weren't." Perhaps most important, working with Morial and the president of the Police Foundation, title company executive John Casbon, he persuaded the city council to raise his officers' pay. "What we said was, 'You can't treat them like this and expect them to show up at your house and save your life, not really,'" says Casbon. "How much esteem are they going to have at $17,000 a year?"

At Pennington's behest, the Police Foundation in mid-1996 brought in John Linder, who had helped Bratton put together his blueprint for change in New York, and Maple, whose stocky presence, hard-boiled manner and tactician's mind made him ideal for the job of helping Pennington wrench the department out of its well-worn routines. With their help, Pennington put together a plan to bulk up the department and redesign its support functions, training and internal communications. Most important, he also instituted Comstat and pushed authority and resources—especially the 250 detectives who had been clustered at police headquarters—into the hands of the eight district commanders. By changing how it operated, he insisted, the department could drive crime down.

Probably the best way to get a sense of how this might happen is to sit in on a citywide Comstat meeting, which takes place in a specially arranged conference room down the hall from Pennington's office. The department's brass sit facing a rotating ensemble of district com-

at work. "What about this string of business burglaries here? What's happening?" Serpas asks. The patterns, he's told, fit the profile of a second-story man who was recently released from jail. Serpas turns to auto burglaries, most of which occurred in open-air lots during a New Orleans Saints football game. "I thought you and the First and the Sixth were going to put something together for Saints games," he says. "The Sixth is down, but you and the First have a little problem. What are you going to do differently?"

Serpas is somewhat controversial within the department, and watching him at work it's easy to see why: His expectations are high, and not much slips past him. "If you act a little bit unreasonable," Maple likes to say, "you get reasonable results."

The meetings are designed to do a lot of things, but perhaps the most important is to make sure the department is on top of itself. This morning, for instance, the commander of the Seventh District reveals that over the past few nights there has been a string of 15 armed robberies. "Hasn't the tactical unit been in the Seventh this week?" Serpas asks. It turns out that, indeed, the tactical unit, which roams from district to district to attack particular problems, has been there, but only during the day. It also turns out that the crime analysis unit is unaware of this sudden burst in robberies, and has been spending its time looking at previous weeks' cases; the sergeant in charge promises to get on the Seventh's problems as soon as the meeting is over. "In other departments, that stuff would never have been picked up on," Maple says later. "The longest something can go here is about a week before we know that something is screwed up."

Watching all this unfold, it is hard for an outsider not to wonder why such a big come up with 13 suspects, which they quickly narrowed down to one, who was eventually convicted.

All of this filters down. The commanders' high expectations, says Sixth District Sergeant Jim Keen, mean that "good cops are marketable now. It used to be that for guys with 20 years on the job, the topic of conversation was, 'How many years do you have left?' Now, I've seen guys who didn't like the district they were put in, they've

you have to change it. It's not like you can say, 'We'll do this but we don't have to have the Fourth Amendment any more.'" Howell suggests that one way to get at the issue would be to make complaint statistics one of the sets of numbers for which district commanders are held accountable through Comstat, a proposal that Maple has said he could support.

For a lot of people in New Orleans, though, it's hard to argue with success. For

neighborhoods. They point to cities such as Los Angeles, which has had a drop in crime without any particular change in police tactics, or San Diego, where the police declared themselves baffled by a sharp drop in burglaries. "I can't attribute drops in crime to the police," says Tony Bouza, a former chief in Minneapolis. "I believe in their mission, but I know they come in after the fact, after the criminal's been shaped and the crime has occurred."

THE COMSTAT PROCESS IS NOT JUST ABOUT KEEPING TRACK OF CRIME. IT'S A TOOL FOR INSTILLING A PARTICULAR SET OF CRIME-FIGHTING VALUES.

got six captains competing for them and they're walking a foot off the ground."

Not everything is perfect, of course. There are plenty of officers who complain that Pennington is too distant or that he hasn't done enough to ground promotions in merit. Everybody acknowledges that small-scale corruption is still a problem. And for onlookers, there is a flip side to a more enthusiastic, newly aggressive police force: Twice last year, overly aggressive patrol officers nearly caused riots with their in-your-face behavior at public housing projects. Overall, even though civilian complaints dropped in 1996, they are on the rise again, and Mary Howell believes that—especially in those instances where officers are enforcing quality-of-life laws—the department may be headed for trouble, just as the NYPD has been set back by the brutal mistreatment of Haitian immigrant Abner Louima. "My question is, Can you do this program without there being an increase in civil rights violations?" she says. "Because if you can't,

the first three quarters of 1997, violent crimes were down 22 percent over the same period the year before. Arrests were up 25 percent. The clearance rate on homicides was 61 percent, compared with 54 percent the year before. In some once-menacing housing projects where district commanders have placed community policing forces on-site, weeks go by without a single reported incident. Small wonder that, in public opinion polls, Pennington has been outscoring most of the city's other public officials.

The question, of course, is to what extent New Orleans' dropping crime rate is due to the changes Pennington and Maple have put in place—a question that gets asked with even more force when applied to New York. Criminologists have argued that everything from a drop in the number of at-risk young men to changes in the cocaine trade to, most recently, the decline in crack use, have had an impact on the murder rate. In New Orleans and elsewhere, they point to the growth of groups of black men dedicated to stopping violence as a sign of a growing weariness with the devastating toll crime has taken on black

But for police departments that have started to put some of New York's concepts into practice, there is no question that they are having an impact. In Minneapolis, a rise in gangs led to a sharp jump in the murder rate in 1995 and 1996; between June and August alone, in 1996, there were 40. Last year, after the police spent months analyzing what was going on and then began weekly meetings to coordinate a response, there were eight during the same period. "Police strategies and tactics can clearly make a difference in a neighborhood," says U.S. Attorney Dave Lillehaug, who was a regular participant at the meetings. "It's not just my observation; it's feedback I get from neighborhood meetings. People know very well whether or not police are dealing with the gangsters who moved in next door."

For his part, Maple doesn't have much patience for the question. "Look," he says, "this is not the end-all answer. Education and training could probably knock down crime more than this. However, I can't wait. And I do know that the police can do a much better job. You got to understand something: These criminologists—you think they want to be shown that they were wrong their whole life? Their whole world is being turned around. I would be happy to take half of any city in the world, and anybody else can take the other half. I'll put Comstat in one half. They can do whatever they want in the other half with the commanders they want. I'll put up $100,000 of my own money, winner take all. Let's see who wants to put up the hundred thousand with Fatso. Let's get ready to rumble here."

Making the case for graduated driver licensing

The nation's largest auto club argues for laws designed to reduce car crashes and deaths among teen-agers.

BY SUSAN PIKRALLIDAS

One day last October, a Greeley, Colo., teen-ager obtained his driver's license; every teen's dream—independence, mobility and adulthood. After school that day, with three of his best friends in the car, he ran through a stop sign and crashed into a tractor-trailer. The teen-ager and his three friends died—the dream just a few hours old. Crashes like this happen frequently across the nation, taking with them the dreams and aspirations of the young people killed or permanently injured.

Could this tragedy have been averted?

Obtaining an unrestricted driver's license at age 16 long has been con-

Susan Pikrallidas is managing director of Government Relations for AAA. Her office is in Washington, D.C.

sidered an automatic right. This "right" is being debated across the nation as states change their teen driving laws in reaction to crashes like this one and the alarming and disproportionate statistics surrounding teen drivers.

What's the problem?

Car crashes are the leading cause of death for teen-agers, totaling nearly one-third of all deaths in this age group. While teen drivers represent only 7 percent of the driving population, they are involved in 14 percent of fatal vehicle crashes and 20 percent of total crashes. More than 60,000 teens died in motor vehicle crashes in the last decade, more than the number of Americans killed during the Vietnam War. Within the 15–20 age group, 16-year-old drivers have the highest crash involvement

rate—more than three times that of 17-year-olds and five times that of 18-year-olds.

Is there a solution?

To combat these alarming numbers, AAA has launched a campaign that targets the high rate of crashes among new drivers. The campaign, "Licensed to Learn: A Safety Program for New Drivers," is being coordinated in all 50 states by local AAA clubs.

Foremost in this campaign is a drive to implement a process known as Graduated Driver Licensing in each state. Graduated Driver Licensing, or GDL, is a systematic approach to licensing that helps to ensure that new drivers are prepared prior to hitting the road on their own.

"Mistakes are a part of any learning process, including driving," said Mark Edwards, AAA managing director of Traffic Safety. "The issue is how to minimize the likelihood that crashes will occur while young people are learning to drive and how best to protect them from injury. GDL helps answer this problem."

Twenty-six states already have adopted a full or partial form of GDL, and all remaining states will consider similar legislation.

"The crash rate among inexperienced drivers is really astounding," said Terry Branstad, former governor of Iowa and chief proponent of Iowa's GDL legislation. "The graduated driver's license is an effective way for young people to gradually work their way into full driving privileges."

Iowa's legislation was adopted in 1998 and took effect Jan. 1, 1999.

"We expect Iowa's new law will save many lives and substantially reduce injuries," Branstad said. "It has been well received by young drivers as well as the general population of Iowa."

Massachusetts also has adopted GDL.

"We recognize that we need to provide an opportunity for new drivers to gain experience in the safest possible on-road environment," said Massachusetts Rep. Peter Larkin. "GDL will accomplish this."

Massachusetts Rep. Paul Casey agrees.

"It is imperative that young, inexperienced drivers focus on the skills of driving and the rules of the road before carpooling their peers. The legislation imposes a minimal burden on teens to demonstrate that they are capable, responsible drivers," Casey said.

How does GDL work?

GDL systems manage the driving experience of teen drivers by gradually introducing them into the traffic system and requiring them to progress through three stages:

The learner's permit stage, where the teen driver practices basic driving skills and safe-driving practices under totally supervised conditions;

A restricted or intermediate license stage that allows unsupervised driving during lower-risk times of the day; and

A full, unrestricted license at age 18 after successful completion of stage two with no traffic violations and the passage of a final road test.

In most cases, the learner's permit and restricted or intermediate license phases include conditions such as driving curfews, limits on the number and age of passengers and adult-supervised behind-the-wheel experience.

Pennsylvania Gov. Tom Ridge has introduced a young-driver reform plan aimed at better preparing young Pennsylvanians to drive safely, and reducing automobile-related deaths and injuries among teens. His legislative plan, which has bipartisan support, will make it more difficult for 16- or 17-year-olds to get

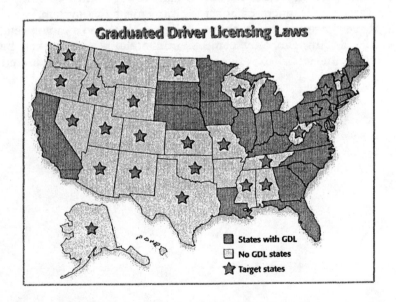

Graduated Driver Licensing Laws

■ States with GDL
□ No GDL states
★ Target states

licenses and will stiffen sanctions against junior drivers who incur high-speed or multiple traffic convictions.

"The overconfidence and risk-taking behavior that often comes with youth can lead young drivers into situations they just don't have the

skills to handle," Ridge said. "But statistics also show that with maturity, crash rates go down. We need to keep young drivers alive so they can grow out of risky behavior and learn the skills that only experience, practice and maturity can teach."

Is GDL effective?

"Since we implemented new novice driver standards, our fatality rate among teen drivers has decreased by 9 percent," said Rep. Rick Minton of Florida, where GDL was implemented in 1996. "The only regret we have is that we didn't implement the program sooner."

Despite the success in Florida, there are new plans to strengthen the existing law by limiting the number of teens who can travel in one car and moving the driving curfew to 9 p.m. from 11 p.m.

"While our success has been great, we recognize that the evening hours are the most dangerous for teen drivers, especially those driving

with a carload of fellow teen-agers," Minton said.

Who supports and opposes GDL?

In a 1997 survey conducted for AAA, 58 percent of those surveyed felt that public officials pay too little attention to safety issues involving teen drivers. Nine in 10 favored a new system of training and licensing for new drivers.

GDL coalitions in states around the country include local parent /teacher organizations, nurses and emergency medical workers, insurance companies, police officers and other state safety groups and parents. Support also comes from [an] unlikely source—teen-agers.

"If you ask teen-agers off-the-record, they say they really aren't comfortable with their driving skills," said Andy Zerzan, a Kansas teen who has testified for GDL in Kansas and Vermont, and participated in a national GDL press conference in Washington, D.C. "Teens know they need more experience."

Additional driving experience is central to the GDL process. AAA's proposal calls for 50 hours of adult supervised driving during the first stage of the licensing process. AAA's Edwards said, "Additional experience is a critically important part of this process, since much of what novice drivers need to learn about responsible driving can only come from behind the wheel experience.

Fifty hours is really the minimum. This experience should come over time, in different traffic, at different times of the day and in different weather conditions."

There has been opposition to [the] GDL proposal in some states. While parents generally don't oppose these laws, those who do are misinformed about GDL and think they'll have to drive their teens around until they are 18. Once they understand that in most cases teens can drive alone after six months of supervision, they are not opposed.

Some rural groups also have opposed GDL, citing the need for children to drive in support of family farm operations.

"Rural states can easily modified GDL legislation to ensure the law won't create an economic hardship for family farms," Edwards said.

Some state legislators and motor vehicle administrators have cited concern about the possible costs of operating a GDL system.

"We do not anticipate any significant increases in operating costs to implement this system," said Anne Ferro, Maryland's motor vehicle administrator. "What's even better is the drop in fatalities suffered when

a novice driver is behind the wheel. This spells an enormous savings not only in lives, but livelihoods."

Is this intruding on parents' rights?

Some have argued that these decisions are the right of a parent, but AAA disagrees.

"Parents do have the right to make decisions on behalf of their kids, but the consequences of motor vehicle crashes go far beyond the family."

"These crashes kill innocent people," Edwards said. "For that reason states have the right, and indeed the responsibility, to manage driving rights on behalf of their residents," Edwards said.

Resources

AAA has 41 million members in North America. The organization has played a prominent role in protecting the rights and safety of the traveler and motorist since its founding in 1902. For more information, contact AAA's Washington, D.C. office at (202) 942-2050.

Rescuing the Fire Department

As the number of fires declines, fire departments must find new ways to justify their funding and staffing levels, as well as maintain public support.

BY KAREN ANN COBURN

Back in 1968, when John B. Corso was a rookie firefighter, he and his colleagues in Louisville, Kentucky, responded to more than 5,000 blazes throughout the city. Now, Corso is Louisville's fire chief. And last year, the number of fire-related incidents fell to a historic low of 1,983.

But the reduction in fires doesn't mean that Corso and his crew have a lot of extra time on their hands. They definitely keep busy—just not necessarily in ways that you might expect. Indeed, Corso sounds more like a social worker than a firefighter when explaining the tenets of Louisville's Community Service Project. Convinced that fires, drugs and gangs "are symptoms of other problems, such as poverty, despair, lack of role models, lack of jobs," Corso asked each of his company chiefs in 1995 to identify a need in their neighborhood and help address it. The department now sponsors 28 programs serving residents from childhood through old age.

What has happened in Louisville is hardly unique. During the past 20 years, the total number of fires has dropped by nearly 40 percent nationwide, according to the National Fire Protection Association. But while citizens can take comfort in knowing that they are much less likely to be harmed in a fire than ever before, the situation creates something of a dilemma for fire departments: "The fire service is becoming less of a need," says Garry Briese, executive director of the International Association of Fire Chiefs.

As a result, fire departments are faced with the challenge of reinventing themselves to protect their bottom line. In the 1980s, that meant providing emergency medical services, now a mainstay—and revenue source—for many fire departments. But in the 1990s, even that is in jeopardy, as private corporations aggressively compete for city contracts to operate ambulances.

Most recently, wide-ranging community service programs have become a staple of neighborhood fire stations. The decision to offer everything from health clinics to home checks for vacationers is based on more than just the desire to perform good deeds, however. Fire chiefs clearly know what side their bread is buttered on. And the hope is that by re-establishing themselves in the everyday fabric of the communities they serve, fire departments can fortify a strong local constituency that could ultimately help drive away unwanted competition and ensure a prosperous future—even with fewer fires.

How is it that only about 12 percent of calls to fire departments today are actually for fires? At least partial credit is given to public education programs, which date as far back as 1925, when National Fire Prevention Week was launched. More recently, firefighters have presented fire safety curricula to schoolage children, who eagerly relay information about smoke detectors, fire drills, escape routes and rendezvous points to their parents.

But the greatest progress can be attributed to less visible efforts. Improved building codes and expanded local fire ordinances have played significant roles in reducing fires in commercial buildings. Smoke detectors, which became popular in the 1970s and are now found in 93 percent of homes, often alert occupants early enough for them to squelch a fire without ever having to call the fire department. Product changes in mattresses, bedding and upholstered furniture have dramatically cut the number of fatal fires. A wave of residential sprinkler ordinances is expected to further reduce the number of reported fires.

At the same time, there has been a dramatic increase in the number of calls for emergency medical services. EMS emerged after the armed forces in Korea and Vietnam demonstrated that the use of cardiopulmonary resuscitation and triage during transportation significantly reduced mortality rates. By the early 1970s, fire departments in Seattle, Miami and Los Angeles were already running successful EMS pilot programs.

By 1996, the NFPA reports, firefighters were responding to roughly 5 million medical emergencies for every 1 million fires. The rise in medical calls largely reflects the success of the 911 system and the nature of the health care system: The uninsured or underinsured have learned that it is easier to dial 911 and have the fire department arrive within minutes than to wait weeks or months for an appointment at a health clinic.

For years, private ambulance companies and fire departments worked together to respond to the growing numbers of EMS calls. Typically, firefighters would arrive at the scene first and, after treating the patient, pass him or her on to private ambulances for transport. Most of the time, however, fire departments were not getting paid for their services; ambulance companies were. Interestingly, out of all the EMS functions—dispatch, treatment, transport and follow-up—transport is the only one that is

To some firefighters, performing tasks that are arguably unrelated to fire suppression or health care can be a real headache.

reimbursed by Medicaid, Medicare and many private insurers.

In the course of the past decade, the consolidation among ambulance companies and the increased belt-tightening by fire departments has undermined the public-private coordination of EMS. Large national ambulance companies and local fire departments looking at the bottom line now see one another as rivals over limited transport dollars. To ensure that they receive third-party payments for transport, the two are now going head to head for the whole EMS pie.

That has clearly been the case in Seminole County, Florida. After working in tandem with private ambulances since the department's inception in 1974, Fire Chief Terry Schenk realized his department was already committing its resources—both apparatus and trained personnel—to EMS and could easily provide transport as well. The resulting revenue stream would pay operating expenses and, Schenk hoped, help the department operate more like a business. He submitted a bid to the county on the EMS contract when it came up for renewal in 1995.

The fire department found itself pitted against the nation's two largest ambulance companies. While the private firms brought in analysts Deloitte & Touche and Arthur Andersen, the fire department had to complete its own extensive internal audit to prepare its bid. After a fair amount of political mudslinging and a review process lasting nearly two years, an independent committee awarded the contract to the Seminole County fire department.

There are a number of reasons why firefighters might be the best candidates for the EMS job. The first, and perhaps most compelling, is that because fire departments have lots of equipment spread throughout a geographical area, they can respond to emergencies more quickly than most ambulance services. Even before they began providing medical services, fire departments planned their response times to prevent "flashover," the four to six minutes it takes a structure to burn beyond suppression. Four minutes is also the recognized limit to prevent brain damage when resuscitating a patient. The standards of the Commission on Accreditation of Ambulance Services, by which most private ambulance companies abide, require

ambulances to respond in 8 minutes and 45 seconds, 90 percent of the time.

Second, since most fire departments will be the first ones on the scene of an emergency, whether or not they are providing transport, they are in a position to provide continuity of care that will reduce anxiety in some patients. Finally, since the public is already paying for fire department equipment to arrive at the scene, it is not cost-effective to cut them out of the transport component. Indeed, the fire department is one of the few government agencies that must maintain its infrastructure—including equipment, fire stations and personnel—in order to respond instantly to intermittent crises.

While competition over EMS is likely to intensify, fire departments everywhere are diversifying their services in an effort to increase community support. For the most part, the new activities adhere to the fire service mission to protect lives and property. Immunization programs in Phoenix and other cities, for instance, have been instigated by firefighters troubled by the number of emergency medical calls to sick children. After years of responding to calls when trick-or-treaters were hit by cars, St. Louis' fire department trained more than 4,000 children in trick-or-treating safety. Last Halloween, no children were hit.

Several years ago, after a stranded motorist was found murdered on a highway outside of Charolottesville, Virginia, the fire department there instituted a new policy: Firefighters—unless they are responding to an emergency—are instructed not only to stop and call for assistance when they come across a stranded motorist but also, at the motorist's request, to stay at the scene until help arrives.

Fire departments have also been involved in licensing bicycles and conducting school physicals, as well as programs to address the escalating problem of juvenile fire-setters. There are fire chiefs who envision a future in which the fire department becomes an access point for many city services—or at least is trained to provide referrals to appropriate government agencies.

To some firefighters, however, performing tasks that are arguably unrelated to either fire suppression or health care can be a headache, as well as a drain on efficiency. Alfred

K. Whitehead, general president of the International Association of Firefighters, the labor union representing 225,000 members in the U.S. and Canada, says a fire chief has crossed the line when firefighters find themselves "bogged down and out of service." Firefighters licensing bicycles at a school, even if they have a radio, are not as prepared to respond to an emergency, he maintains. And real problems can arise when local governments enlist firefighters to perform tasks simply to save money.

Firefighters who share these sentiments have filed labor grievances when asked to do work that they—and their union—believed was not within the fire service mission. In addition to bicycle-licensing, Whitehead ticks off examples of firefighters painting libraries and curbs, doing custodial work and repairing fire engines—all in the name of community service. Most often, grievances come about when firefighters are not consulted about what type of service they will provide. Breise of the fire chiefs' association acknowledges that a surprising number of firefighters are resistant to community service programs. But they are "usually the ones that were hired a while ago, who say, 'That wasn't what I signed up to do.'"

Louisville's Corso recalls hearing the same not-in-my-job-description lament when EMS was first introduced. But it didn't last long, he notes. And now that the concept of community service is well established there, it has widespread backing among firefighters. The programs, designed by the firefighters themselves, include winterizing homes for the elderly, providing meals to shut-ins, mentoring children, sponsoring Boy Scout troops, hosting birthday parties and providing home safety inspections. Although the work is done on the clock, many firefighters have become so involved that they continue volunteering in their free time.

Corso is attempting to quantify the results of their efforts. A new system infuses information from the neighborhood-based programs into the department's Incident Reporting Database. He wants to be able to show city officials and citizens that, in addition to dealing with, say, $8 million in fire loss, the department conducted 2,500 blood-pressure checks and saw a reduction in calls for heart attacks.

Schenk in Seminole County also touts the wisdom of collecting as much data as possible—long before fire departments find themselves forced to defend their turf. Indeed, being able to highlight their strong suits—fire and rescue, EMS, community service—shows good business sense, which now seems as important to the profession as state-of-the-art equipment.

AE Article Review Form

We encourage you to photocopy and use this page as a tool to assess how the articles in **Annual Editions** expand on the information in your textbook. By reflecting on the articles you will gain enhanced text information. You can also access this useful form on a product's book support Web site at **http://www.dushkin.com/online/**.

NAME: _____ DATE: _____

TITLE AND NUMBER OF ARTICLE: _____

BRIEFLY STATE THE MAIN IDEA OF THIS ARTICLE: _____

LIST THREE IMPORTANT FACTS THAT THE AUTHOR USES TO SUPPORT THE MAIN IDEA:

WHAT INFORMATION OR IDEAS DISCUSSED IN THIS ARTICLE ARE ALSO DISCUSSED IN YOUR TEXTBOOK OR OTHER READINGS THAT YOU HAVE DONE? LIST THE TEXTBOOK CHAPTERS AND PAGE NUMBERS:

LIST ANY EXAMPLES OF BIAS OR FAULTY REASONING THAT YOU FOUND IN THE ARTICLE:

LIST ANY NEW TERMS/CONCEPTS THAT WERE DISCUSSED IN THE ARTICLE, AND WRITE A SHORT DEFINITION:

ANNUAL EDITIONS revisions depend on two major opinion sources: one is our Advisory Board, listed in the front of this volume, which works with us in scanning the thousands of articles published in the public press each year; the other is you—the person actually using the book. Please help us and the users of the next edition by completing the prepaid article rating form on this page and returning it to us. Thank you for your help!

ANNUAL EDITIONS: State and Local Government 00/01

ARTICLE RATING FORM

Here is an opportunity for you to have direct input into the next revision of this volume. We would like you to rate each of the 54 articles listed below, using the following scale:

1. Excellent: should definitely be retained
2. Above average: should probably be retained
3. Below average: should probably be deleted
4. Poor: should definitely be deleted

Your ratings will play a vital part in the next revision.
So please mail this prepaid form to us just as soon as you complete it.
Thanks for your help!

RATING

ARTICLE

1. The Federalist, No. 17
2. The Federalist, No. 45
3. Nature of the American State
4. Judicial Federalism: The Resurgence of the Supreme Court's Role in the Protection of State Sovereignty
5. The Devil in Devolution
6. Powerless Pipsqueaks and the Myth of Local Control
7. Flunking Local Districts
8. Reform Gets Rolling: Campaign Finance at the Grass Roots
9. How to Get Rid of Excellent Public Officials
10. My Life as a School Board Candidate: Lessons Learned in Local Politics
11. Who's Got Clout? Interest Group Power in the States
12. The Clamor of the Brave New World
13. More News, Less Coverage?
14. California, Here We Come
15. Direct Democracy Works
16. Grassroots Charade
17. Living within the Limits
18. Women in the Legislature: Numbers Inch Up Nationwide
19. Women as Leaders: Vive La Difference
20. Legislative Party Caucuses: Open or Closed?
21. Town Meeting Time
22. The Gulf of Government
23. It Pays to Know Where the Bodies Are Buried
24. Roaring Forward
25. Conservative Governors and the Joy of Spending
26. Nobody in Charge

RATING

ARTICLE

27. Justice by Numbers
28. Bench Press
29. When the Verdict Is Just a Fantasy
30. Can Cities Escape Political Isolation?
31. How to Save Our Shrinking Cities
32. Suburban Myth
33. Who Pays for Sprawl?
34. Levittown to Littleton: How the Suburbs Have Changed
35. A Fair Share in Suburbia
36. Are New England's Counties as Expendable as They Seem?
37. Taxing the Weightless Economy
38. It's Not a Miracle, It's a Mirage
39. The Game of Mystery Bucks
40. Two Cheers for the Property Tax
41. Romancing the Smokestack
42. The New Urban Gamble
43. The Terrible Ten: Corporate Candy Store Deals of 1998
44. Making Cents: Better City Services for Less
45. Counting on Competition
46. New Ways of Education
47. Charter Schools Learn a Few Lessons
48. When States Spend More
49. When Welfare Ends
50. I'll Stand Bayou
51. The Answer to Drunk Driving?: Lower the Blood Alcohol Limit?
52. The Comeback of the Cops
53. Making the Case for Graduated Driver Licensing
54. Rescuing the Fire Department

(Continued on next page)

We Want Your Advice

BUSINESS REPLY MAIL
FIRST-CLASS MAIL PERMIT NO. 84 GUILFORD CT

POSTAGE WILL BE PAID BY ADDRESSEE

Dushkin/McGraw-Hill
Sluice Dock
Guilford, CT 06437-9989

ABOUT YOU

Name _____   Date _____

Are you a teacher? ☐ A student? ☐
Your school's name _____

Department _____

Address _____ City _____ State ___ Zip ___

School telephone # _____

YOUR COMMENTS ARE IMPORTANT TO US !

Please fill in the following information:
For which course did you use this book?
_____

Did you use a text with this *ANNUAL EDITION*? ☐ yes ☐ no
What was the title of the text?
_____

What are your general reactions to the *Annual Editions* concept?
_____

Have you read any particular articles recently that you think should be included in the next edition?
_____

Are there any articles you feel should be replaced in the next edition? Why?
_____

Are there any World Wide Web sites you feel should be included in the next edition? Please annotate.
_____

May we contact you for editorial input? ☐ yes ☐ no
May we quote your comments? ☐ yes ☐ no